Each volume in this series of companions to major philosophers contains specially commissioned essays by an international team of scholars, together with a substantial bibliography, and will serve as a reference work for students and
nonspecialists. One aim of the series is to dispel the intimi-
dation such readers often feel when faced with the work of a
difficult and challenging thinker.

Charles Sanders Peirce (1839–1914) is generally considered the most significant American philosopher. He was the
founder of pragmatism – the view, popularized by William
James and John Dewey, that our philosophical theories must
be linked to experience and practice. The essays in this volume reveal how Peirce worked through this idea to make
important contributions to most branches of philosphy. The
topics covered include Peirce's influence; the famous pragmatic maxim and the view of truth and reality arising from
it; the question as to whether mathematical, moral, and religious hypotheses might aspire to truth; his theories of inquiry and perception; and his contribution to semiotics, statistical inference, and deductive logic.

New readers will find this the most convenient and accessible guide to Peirce currently available. Advanced students
and specialists will find a conspectus of recent developments
in the interpretation of Peirce.

Cheryl Misak is Professor of Philosophy at the University of
Toronto.

OTHER VOLUMES IN THE SERIES OF CAMBRIDGE COMPANIONS:

ABELARD *Edited by* JEFFREY E. BROWER *and* KEVIN GUILFOY
ADORNO *Edited by* THOMAS HUHN
AQUINAS *Edited by* NORMAN KRETZMANN *and* ELEONORE
STUMP
HANNAH ARENDT *Edited by* DANA VILLA
ARISTOTLE *Edited by* JONATHAN BARNES
AUGUSTINE *Edited by* ELEONORE STUMP *and* NORMAN
KRETZMANN
BACON *Edited by* MARKKU PELTONEN
SIMONE DE BEAUVOIR *Edited by* CLAUDIA CARD
DARWIN *Edited by* JONATHAN HODGE *and* GREGORY RADICK
DESCARTES *Edited by* JOHN COTTINGHAM
DUNS SCOTUS *Edited by* THOMAS WILLIAMS
EARLY GREEK PHILOSOPHY *Edited by* A. A. LONG
FEMINISM IN PHILOSOPHY *Edited by* MIRANDA FRICKER *and*
JENNIFER HORNSBY
FOUCAULT *Edited by* GARY GUTTING
FREUD *Edited by* JEROME NEU
GADAMER *Edited by* ROBERT J. DOSTAL
GALILEO *Edited by* PETER MACHAMER
GERMAN IDEALISM *Edited by* KARL AMERIKS
GREEK AND ROMAN PHILOSOPHY *Edited by* DAVID SEDLEY
HABERMAS *Edited by* STEPHEN K. WHITE
HEGEL *Edited by* FREDERICK BEISER
HEIDEGGER *Edited by* CHARLES GUIGNON
HOBBES *Edited by* TOM SORELL
HUME *Edited by* DAVID FATE NORTON
HUSSERL *Edited by* BARRY SMITH *and* DAVID WOODRUFF SMITH
WILLIAM JAMES *Edited by* RUTH ANNA PUTNAM
KANT *Edited by* PAUL GUYER
KIERKEGAARD *Edited by* ALASTAIR HANNAY *and* GORDON
MARINO
LEIBNIZ *Edited by* NICHOLAS JOLLEY
LEVINAS *Edited by* SIMON CRITCHLEY *and* ROBERT BERNASCONI
LOCKE *Edited by* VERE CHAPPELL
MALEBRANCHE *Edited by* STEVEN NADLER
MARX *Edited by* TERRELL CARVER
MEDIEVAL PHILOSOPHY *Edited by* A. S. MC GRADE
MEDIEVAL JEWISH PHILOSOPHY *Edited by* DANIEL H. FRANK
and OLIVER LEAMAN
MILL *Edited by* JOHN SKORUPSKI
NEWTON *Edited by* I. BERNARD COHEN *and* GEORGE E. SMITH
NIETZSCHE *Edited by* BERND MAGNUS *and* KATHLEEN HIGGINS
OCKHAM *Edited by* PAUL VINCENT SPADE
PASCAL *Edited by* NICHOLAS HAMMOND
PLATO *Edited by* RICHARD KRAUT
PLOTINUS *Edited by* LLOYD P. GERSON
QUINE *Edited by* ROGER F. GIBSON
RAWLS *Edited by* SAMUEL FREEMAN

THOMAS REID   *Edited by* TERENCE CUNEO *and* RENÉ
   VAN WOUDENBERG
ROUSSEAU   *Edited by* PATRICK RILEY
BERTRAND RUSSELL   *Edited by* NICHOLAS GRIFFIN
SARTRE   *Edited by* CHRISTINA HOWELLS
SCHOPENHAUER   *Edited by* CHRISTOPHER JANAWAY
THE SCOTTISH ENLIGHTENMENT   *Edited by* ALEXANDER
   BROADIE
SPINOZA   *Edited by* DON GARRETT
THE STOICS   *Edited by* BRAD INWOOD
WITTGENSTEIN   *Edited by* HANS SLUGA *and* DAVID STERN

The Cambridge Companion to
PEIRCE

Edited by

Cheryl Misak
University of Toronto

CAMBRIDGE
UNIVERSITY PRESS

PUBLISHED BY THE PRESS SYNDICATE OF THE UNIVERSITY OF
CAMBRIDGE
The Pitt Building, Trumpington Street, Cambridge, United Kingdom

CAMBRIDGE UNIVERSITY PRESS
The Edinburgh Building, Cambridge CB2 2RU, UK
40 West 20th Street, New York, NY 10011-4211, USA
477 Williamstown Road, Port Melbourne, VIC 3207, Australia
Ruiz de Alarcón 13, 28014 Madrid, Spain
Dock House, The Waterfront, Cape Town 8001, South Africa

http://www.cambridge.org

First published 2004

Printed in the United States of America

Typeface Trump Medieval 10/13 pt.   *System* LaTeX 2_ε [TB]

A catalog record for this book is available from the British Library.

Library of Congress Cataloging in Publication Data
The Cambridge companion to Peirce / edited by Cheryl Misak
    p.   cm. – (Cambridge companions to philosophy)
    Includes bibliographical references and index.
    ISBN 0-521-57006-9 – ISBN 0-521-57910-4 (pbk)
    1. Peirce, Charles S. (Charles Sanders), 1839–1914.   I. Misak, C. J.
(Cheryl J.)   II. Series.
    B945.P44C36   2004
    191 – dc22   2003061744

ISBN 0 521 57006 9 hardback
ISBN 0 521 57910 4 paperback

CONTENTS

List of Contributors   *page* ix

1   Charles Sanders Peirce (1839–1914)   I
    CHERYL MISAK

2   Peirce's Place in the Pragmatist Tradition   27
    SAMI PIHLSTRÖM

3   Peirce and Medieval Thought   58
    JOHN BOLER

4   Reflections on Inquiry and Truth Arising from
    Peirce's Method for the Fixation of Belief   87
    DAVID WIGGINS

5   Truth, Reality, and Convergence   127
    CHRISTOPHER HOOKWAY

6   C. S. Peirce on Vital Matters   150
    CHERYL MISAK

7   Peirce's Common Sense Marriage of Religion
    and Science   175
    DOUGLAS ANDERSON

8   Peirce's Pragmatic Account of Perception: Issues
    and Implications   193
    SANDRA ROSENTHAL

9   The Development of Peirce's Theory of Signs   214
    T. L. SHORT

vii

viii   Contents

10   Peirce's Semeiotic Model of the Mind   241
      PETER SKAGESTED

11   Beware of Syllogism: Statistical Reasoning and
      Conjecturing According to Peirce   257
      ISAAC LEVI

12   Peirce's Deductive Logic: Its Development,
      Influence, and Philosophical Significance   287
      RANDALL DIPERT

      Note on References   325
      Bibliography   327
      Index   343

CONTRIBUTORS

DOUGLAS ANDERSON is an Associate Professor of Philosophy at Penn State University. He is the author of *Strands of System: The Philosophy of Charles S. Peirce* and coeditor of *The Contemporary Vitality of Pragmatism.*

JOHN BOLER is Professor Emeritus of Philosophy at the University of Washington in Seattle. He is the author of *Charles Peirce and Scholastic Realism,* as well as numerous articles on Peirce and on medieval philosophy.

RANDALL DIPERT is C.S. Peirce Professor of American Philosophy at SUNY Buffalo. He has written extensively on the history and philosophy of logic, especially on Peirce and the nineteenth century. In aesthetics, he has published articles on music theory, performance practice, and authenticity and is the author *Artifacts, Art Works, and Agency* (Temple University Press: 1993).

CHRISTOPHER HOOKWAY is Professor of Philosophy at Sheffield University. His publications include *Peirce* (Routledge 1985) and *Truth, Rationality, and Pragmatism: Themes from Peirce* (Oxford University Press 2000).

ISAAC LEVI is currently John Dewey Professor at Columbia University. He is author of *Covenant of Reason, For the Sake of the Argument, Fixation of Belief and Its Undoing, Hard Choices, Enterprise of Knowledge, Decisions and Revisions,* and *Gambling with Truth* and is an editor of the *Journal of Philosophy.* He is a past president of the Charles Peirce Society.

CHERYL MISAK is Professor of Philosophy at the University of Toronto. She is the author of *Truth and the End of Inquiry: A Peircean Account of Truth* (the second edition of which is coming out from Oxford University Press in 2004) *Verificationism: Its History and Prospects* (Routledge 1995), and *Truth, Politics, Morality: Pragmatism and Deliberation* (Routledge 2000).

SAMI PIHLSTRÖM received his Ph.D. in philosophy from the University of Helsinki in 1996. He is Docent and University Lecturer of Theoretical Philosophy at the University of Helsinki. His publications include three books in English: *Structuring the World: The Issue of Realism and the Nature of Ontological Problems in Classical and Contemporary Pragmatism* (dissertation, 1996); *Pragmatism and Philosophical Anthropology: Understanding Our Human Life in a Human World* (Peter Lang, New York, 1998); and *Naturalizing the Transcendental: A Pragmatic View* (Prometheus/Humanity Books, Amherst, NY, 2003).

SANDRA B. ROSENTHAL, Provost Distinguished Professor of Philosophy at Loyola University of New Orleans, has published 11 books and approximately 200 articles on pragmatism and its relation to various issues and movements. She is on the editorial boards of several journals and book series and has served as president of various professional organizations, including the Charles S. Peirce Society, the Society for the Advancement of American Philosophy, and the Metaphysical Society of America.

T.L. SHORT is Chairman of the Board of Advisors to the Peirce Edition Project and author of many articles on Peirce.

PETER SKAGESTAD has taught philosophy at Williams College and at Trinity College, Hartford and currently teaches at the University of Massachusetts, Lowell. He is the author of *The Road of Inquiry: Charles Peirce's Pragmatic Realism* (1981), *Making Sense of History: The Philosophies of Popper and Collingwood* (1975), and numerous articles on philosophy, communication, and technology. He is an Associate Editor of *The Journal of Social and Evolutionary Systems*.

DAVID WIGGINS is Emeritus Wykeham Professor of Logic at Oxford University. He previously taught at Birkbeck College and is a Fellow of the British Academy as well as an Honorary Foreign Member of the American Academy of Arts and Sciences. His publications include *Sameness and Substance* (1986) and *Needs, Values and Truth* (a new edition of which was published in 1998), as well as numerous articles on ethics and metaphysics.

THE CAMBRIDGE COMPANION TO
PEIRCE

1   Charles Sanders Peirce (1839–1914)

I. INTRODUCTION

Charles Sanders Peirce was the founder of pragmatism – the view that our theories must be linked to experience or practice. His work is staggering in its breadth and much of it lies in a huge bulk of manuscripts and scraps. His few published papers include those of the 1870s series in *Popular Science Monthly* called "Illustrations of the Logic of Science," most notably "How to Make Our Ideas Clear" and "The Fixation of Belief." His Lowell Lectures in 1898 and 1903 and his Harvard Pragmatism Lectures in 1903 also contain essential material. But much of what is important is only now being published in the definitive chronological edition: *The Writings of Charles Sanders Peirce.*

Peirce was a difficult man and this was no doubt partly responsible for his being frozen out of what he most desired: a permanent academic position.[1] He worked instead for the U.S. Coast Survey – his scientific and mathematical endeavors there had a significant influence on his logic, on his work in statistical inference, and on his epistemology and metaphysics. He is perhaps best known today for his theory of truth and his semeiotics, as well as for his influence on William James and John Dewey. But because of the scattered nature of his work and because he was always out of the academic mainstream, many of his contributions are just now coming to light.

As Philstrom's essay in this volume makes clear, one of the most important influences on Peirce was Kant. There is also a strong gust of medieval philosophy blowing throughout his writing. It is from here that Peirce gets his Scholastic realism, which is

I

set against the nominalism of the British empiricists. (See Boler's contribution to this volume.) But there are also clear affinities between Peirce and the British empiricists. For instance, Peirce credits Berkeley's arguments that all meaningful language should be matched with sensory experience as the precursor of pragmatism:

Berkeley on the whole has more right to be considered the introducer of pragmatism into philosophy than any other one man, though I was more explicit in enunciating it.[2]

It has seemed to many that, despite Peirce's claims to be putting together a grand 'architectonic' system, there are substantial tensions in his work. Goudge (1950) declared that there were two incompatible Peirces. One is a hard-headed epistemologist/philosopher of science and the other is a soft-headed religious thinker prone to metaphysical speculation. Misak and Anderson argue in this volume that the two Peirces can and ought to be brought together.

Whether or not Peirce's work can be brought into a harmonious whole, the reader of this collection will be struck by the enormous range of debates to which Peirce was a serious contributor. In this introductory essay, a whirlwind tour of those contributions will be conducted.[3]

2. THE PRAGMATIC MAXIM

Peirce took the 'spirit' of pragmatism to be captured in the following maxim: "we must look to the upshot of our concepts in order rightly to apprehend them" (CP 5.4). There is a connection between understanding a concept and knowing what to expect if sentences containing the concept were true or false. If a concept has no such consequences, then it lacks an important dimension which we would have had to get right were we to fully understand it.

This criterion of legitimacy lies at the heart of Peirce's work. Not only does he criticise certain philosophical positions as pragmatically spurious, but he arrives at many of his own views by focussing on the consequences of, say, "P is true" or "x is real." The pragmatic maxim, that is, serves both as a standard for determining which expressions are empty and as a methodological principle for formulating philosophical theories of truth, reality, etc.

In "How to Make Our Ideas Clear," Peirce publically unveils pragmatism and sets out the maxim as follows:

Consider what effects, which might conceivably have practical bearings, we conceive the object of our conception to have. Then, our conception of these is the whole of our conception of the object. (W 3, 266)

Peirce suggests in this paper that knowing the meaning of an expression is exhausted by knowing its "practical" effects, which he characterizes as "effects, direct or indirect, upon our senses" (W 3, 266). These effects can be described by conditionals of the sort: if you were to do A, you would observe B. He says:

We come down to what is tangible and practical, as the root of every real distinction of thought, no matter how subtle it may be; and there is no distinction of meaning so fine as to consist in anything but a possible difference of practice. (W 3, 265)

As an example of how the pragmatic maxim operates, Peirce examines the meaning of "this diamond is hard." He says that it means that if you try to scratch it, you will find that "it will not be scratched by many other substances" (W 3, 266).

Notice that the practical effect here is formulated as an indicative conditional, as a matter of what *will* happen. Peirce sees that if he formulates practical effects in this manner, it makes little sense to describe a diamond which is in fact never scratched as being hard. He seems to be content with this conclusion in "How to Make Our Ideas Clear." But when he considers the matter later, he insists on a subjunctive formulation. He chides himself for making the nominalist suggestion that habits, dispositions, or "would-bes" are not real. A Scholastic realism about dispositions and subjunctive conditionals must be adopted: a disposition is more than the total of its realizations and a subjunctive conditional can be correct or incorrect, whether or not the antecedent is fulfilled. The practical effects which concern pragmatism are those which would occur under certain conditions, not those which will actually occur. His considered view about the unscratched diamond is that "it is a real fact that it *would* resist pressure" (CP 8.208).

This was not Peirce's only amendment to the pragmatic maxim. In his struggle to arrive at a suitable account of understanding, we sometimes find him suggesting something very similar to what we find later in logical positivism. The positivists' criterion effectively restricted meaning to statements about physical objects – to statements about that which is directly observable or verifiable. Statements about anything else – metaphysics or ethics for example – were literally meaningless. But, in further improvements to the pragmatic maxim, Peirce makes it clear that he is concerned to give a much more generous account of what is involved in understanding.

First, Peirce himself inclined toward metaphysics and he did not want to do away with it altogether. In metaphysics "one finds those questions that at first seem to offer no handle for reason's clutch, but which readily yield to logical analysis" (CP 6.463). Metaphysics, "in its present condition," is "a puny, rickety, and scrofulous science" (CP 6.6). But it need not be so, for many of its hypotheses are meaningful and important. It is the job of the pragmatic maxim to sweep "all metaphysical rubbish out of one's house. Each abstraction is either pronounced to be gibberish or is provided with a plain, practical definition" (CP 8.191).

Second, Peirce frequently claims that the pragmatic maxim captures only *a part* of what it is to know the meaning of an expression. In order to grasp a term, he argues, a threefold competence is required. The interpreter must be able to

(1) pick out what objects the term refers to or know the term's denotation,
(2) give a definition of the term or know the term's connotation, and
(3) know what to expect if hypotheses containing the term are true.

He takes these three aspects of understanding to spell out completely what someone must be able to do if she grasps a concept or knows the meaning of an expression.

A much-neglected implication of this view is that definition is not the most important project for philosophers: "Definition can no longer be regarded as the supreme mode of clear Apprehension" (MS 647, p. 2). That is, we must be alert to the fact that what Peirce arrives at when he applies the pragmatic maxim to a concept is not a definition of the concept, but rather, a pragmatic elucidation. He examines a concept through its relations with practical endeavors. That is one route to understanding a concept, the route Peirce takes as his own contribution to debates about what it is to understand something.

Third, Peirce tries to divert the philosopher from thinking that sensory experience is all-important. A perceptual belief, he argues, is merely a belief that is compelling, surprising, impinging, unchosen, involuntary, or forceful. Such beliefs need not arise from the senses. Peirce, unlike his verificationist successors, wants all hypotheses to be exposed to the pragmatic maxim; he does not exempt formal (or "analytic") sentences. Logical and mathematical hypotheses can meet the criterion because there is a kind of experience relevant to them – you can make manipulations in proofs or diagrams and observe unexpected results. And some metaphysical hypotheses meet the criterion as well. They must have consequences, Peirce argues, for ordinary, everyday experience. See the contributions here from Wiggins and Misak for a discussion of how mathematics and morals fit in this picture.

3. TRUTH AND REALITY

Peirce applies the pragmatic maxim to the debate on the nature of truth and reality. The philosopher must look to our practices and see what account of truth would be best suited for them: "We must not begin by talking of pure ideas, – vagabond thoughts that tramp the public roads without any human habitation, – but must begin with men and their conversation" (CP 8.112). As Wiggins's essay in this volume makes so clear, the upshot is a subtle and compelling view. Peirce's route to the concept of truth is through belief, inquiry, and deliberation: the practices linked to truth and to the seeking of truth. Peirce suggests that we concern ourselves with propositions we have arrived at, expressed, affirmed, or believed and those we shall arrive at, express, affirm, or believe.[4] By making this our focus, we will discover something about what it is at which we aim: truth. This does not mean that truth is an epistemological notion. Rather, this exemplifies one route to finding out something about truth: the route through our epistemological practices of believing, inquiring, and deliberating.

The correspondence theory, Peirce argues, can have no consequences for our practices. It holds that a true hypothesis is one which is in agreement with an unknowable "thing-in-itself." But:

You only puzzle yourself by talking of this metaphysical "truth" and metaphysical "falsity" that you know nothing about. All you have any dealings with are your doubts and beliefs.... If your terms "truth" and "falsity" are taken in such senses as to be definable in terms of doubt and belief and the course of experience ... well and good: in that case, you are only talking about doubt and belief. But if by truth and falsity you mean something not definable in terms of doubt and belief in any way, then you are talking of entities of whose existence you can know nothing, and which Ockham's razor would clean shave off. Your problems would be greatly simplified, if, instead of saying that you want to know the "Truth," you were simply to say that you want to attain a state of belief unassailable by doubt. (CP 5.416)

Peirce's thought here is that if one offered an account of "*P* is true" in terms of its consequences for doubt, belief, and perceptual disappointment, one would be offering a pragmatic elucidation of truth. That, if it were a correct specification of the consequences, would tell us something about truth. But a definition of truth which makes no reference to belief, doubt, and experience is empty. It is a mere definition – useful only to those who have never encountered the notion of truth.

Peirce sometimes states this objection to the correspondence theory by labeling it a "transcendental" account of truth (CP 5.572). Such accounts regard truth "as the subject of metaphysics exclusively" – spurious metaphysics, not pragmatically legitimate metaphysics. On the correspondence definition, truth transcends (and thus has no consequences for) belief, experience, and inquiry. He says:

The *Ding an sich* ... can neither be indicated nor found. Consequently, no proposition can refer to it, and nothing true or false can be predicated of it. Therefore, all references to it must be thrown out as meaningless surplusage. (CP 5.525)

The correspondence theory has it that there is an unbridgeable gap between a belief which is supported by experience and a belief that corresponds to reality. We could have the best possible evidence for a hypothesis and yet that hypothesis might fail to be true. The correspondence theory does not tell us what we can expect of a true hypothesis and so it is not capable of guiding us in our actions and inquiries. If truth is the aim of inquiry, then the correspondence theory leaves inquirers completely in the dark as to how they should conduct their investigations. The aim is not, Peirce says, "readily comprehensible" (CP 1.578). How could anyone aim for a sort of truth that transcends experience? How could an inquirer come up with a means for achieving that aim?

In anticipation of certain kinds of minimalist accounts of truth, Peirce focuses on what he thinks the transcendentalist has lost sight of – the unseverable link between truth on the one hand and assertion (and belief) on the other. To assert P is to assert that P is true and to assert that P is true is to assert P. (Alternatively, to believe P is to believe that P is true and to believe that P is true is to believe P.) The notion of truth is bound up with the notions of assertion and belief. But Peirce takes a step further than the minimalist. Once we see the internal connection between truth and assertion/belief, we must look to the practice of assertion/belief and to the commitments incurred in it, so that we can say something more. What we know about truth is that it is what we aim at when we assert, believe, or deliberate. Were we to forever achieve all of our local aims in assertion, belief, and deliberation (prediction, explanatory power, and so on), then the belief in question would be true. There is nothing over and above the fulfillment of those local aims, nothing metaphysical, to which we aspire. Were we to get a belief which would be as good as it could be, that would be a true belief.

Peirce sums up the matter thus: "A true proposition is a proposition belief in which would never lead to . . . disappointment" (CP 5.569). This is an account of what we can expect of a true belief: if we were to inquire into P, we would find that P would encounter no recalcitrant experience. We can predict that if we were diligently to inquire, it would not, in the end, be overturned by experience or argument. An alternative way of making the point is to say that we would expect the following: if inquiry with respect to P were to be pursued as far as it could fruitfully go (i.e., far enough so that the hypothesis would no longer be improved upon), P would be believed. A true belief is a permanently settled or indefeasible belief.

Peirce's view of reality is connected to his view of truth in that he often says that reality is the "object" of true beliefs – it is what true beliefs are about. Chris Hookway has recently improved our understanding of how Peirce saw this connection and the reader is advised to turn to his contribution to this volume for a summary of that new understanding.

4. SEMEIOTICS

Peirce was a pioneer in semeiotics. Not only is he responsible for the distinction between type ('human' as a general term) and token ('human' as applied to various individuals), but he developed a complex map of sixty-six kinds of signs, from which sprout 59,049 varieties. The details of this map are still of great interest to semeioticians, but they will not concern me here. Short's and Skagested's papers in this volume convey many of the important points. Short shows how Peirce eventually abandoned his early theory of signs and substituted for it a much less paradoxical one and Skagested shows how Peirce's theory of signs connects to issues about intentionality and the philosophy of mind.

It is important to notice for this broad overview of Peirce's work that his theory of signs has interpretation at its center. Peirce holds that the sign–referent relation is not able, on its own, to sustain a complete account of representation. Representation is triadic: it involves a sign, an object, and an interpreter. Each aspect of this representation relation corresponds to one of the elements in Peirce's division of signs into icons, indices, and symbols. And in each of these, one or another aspect of the linguistic competence alluded to in Section 2 is most prominent.

Icons are signs that exhibit their objects by virtue of similarity or resemblance. A portrait is an icon of the person it portrays and a map is an icon of a certain geographical area. Peirce argues that the meaning of iconic signs lies mostly in their connotation: what makes a painting or a map an icon is that its qualities or attributes resemble the qualities or attributes of its object.

Indices are signs that indicate their objects in a causal manner: an index "signifies its object solely by virtue of being really connected with it" (CP 3.360). A symptom is an index of a disease and smoke is an index of fire. The essential quality of an index is its ability to compel attention. A pointing finger, a knock on the door, or a demonstrative pronoun, such as 'there' or 'that,' draws attention to its object by getting the interpreter to focus on the object. So an index, by being object-directed, has its denotation or extension as its "most prominent feature" (CP 8.119). An index picks out or indicates its object; it points to 'that, that, and that' as its extension.

A symbol is a word, hypothesis, or argument which depends on a conventional or habitual rule: a symbol is a sign "because it is used and understood as such" (CP 2.307). Symbols have "principle" or pragmatic meaning; they have "intellectual purport."

Peirce contrasts pragmatic meaning with "internal" meaning (which he relates to icons and connotation) and with "external" meaning (which he relates to indices and denotation). He suggests that the pragmatic meaning of symbols has to do with a "purpose" (CP 8.119). A symbol has pragmatic meaning because if the utterer knows how interpreters habitually interpret a sign, she can use the sign to cause a specific effect in the interpreter. And Peirce calls this effect the "interpretant" of the sign. If, for instance, I write 'dog,' I intend the sign to cause a certain effect in the interpreter (perhaps I want the interpreter to think of a dog), whereas if I write 'odg,' I do not, as 'odg' is not a conventional sign. Or if I assert 'That bridge has a loose plank,' I might want the interpreter to be careful when crossing the bridge. Peirce characterizes an assertion as the attempt to produce a disposition in an interpreter; it is "the deliberate exercise, in uttering the proposition, of a force tending to determine a belief in it in the mind of an interpreter" (NE 4, 249).

Notice that if pragmatic meaning is about this sort of effect (having an effect on the beliefs of the interpreter), it is no longer about "effects, direct or indirect, upon our senses." Pragmatic meaning, rather, involves consequences for action or thought. In 1905 we find Peirce offering this version of the pragmatic maxim:

The entire intellectual purport of any symbol consists in the total of all general modes of rational conduct which, conditionally upon all the possible different circumstances and desires, would ensue upon the acceptance of the symbol. (CP 5.438)

Peirce thinks that "rational conduct" will eventually manifest itself in a modification of the interpreter's disposition to behave. And "rational conduct" includes the conduct of one's thought.

This twist in the pragmatic maxim – that the acceptance of a hypothesis must have effects on an interpreter's train of thought – coincides with a development in the early 1900s in Peirce's theory of signs. Here Peirce arrived at a complex theory of interpretants and he locates pragmatic meaning within this theory.

He distinguishes three types of interpretants. The "immediate" interpretant is the fitness of a sign to be understood in a certain way; the "dynamical" interpretant is the actual effect a sign has on an interpreter; and the "final" interpretant is the effect which eventually would be decided to be the correct interpretation. Pragmatic meaning, Peirce says, lies in a kind of dynamical interpretant: the "ultimate logical interpretant". A sign, Peirce argues, sparks a subsequent sign (an interpretant) in the mind of the interpreter, and since an interpretant is itself a sign, an infinite chain of interpretation, development, or thought is begun. Peirce stops the regress by introducing the notion of an "ultimate logical interpretant" or a "habit-change". He follows Alexander Bain in taking a belief to be a habit or a disposition to behave. And so this new habit is a belief or a modification of the interpreter's tendencies towards action. The pragmatic meaning of an expression, according to Peirce's theory of signs, is the action (which includes the action of subsequent thought, and which ends in a disposition to behave) that arises after an interpreter accepts it.

5. THEORY OF INQUIRY

The notion of inquiry occupies a central place in Peirce's thought. Philosophy, he insisted, must get along with other branches of inquiry. Indeed, the following motto "deserves to be inscribed upon every wall of the city of philosophy: Do not block the path of inquiry" (CP 1.135).

In "The Fixation of Belief," Peirce characterizes inquiry as the struggle to rid ourselves of doubt and achieve a state of belief. An inquirer has a body of settled beliefs – beliefs which are, in fact, not doubted. These beliefs, however, are susceptible to doubt, if it is prompted by some "positive reason," such as a surprising experience (CP 5.51). We have seen that Peirce takes experience to be that which impinges upon us – experience, he says, teaches us "by practical jokes, mostly cruel" (CP 5.51). When experience conflicts with an inquirer's belief, doubt is immediately sparked. And doubt "essentially involves a struggle to escape" (CP 5.372n2). Inquiry is that struggle to regain belief. The path of inquiry is as follows: belief – surprise – doubt – inquiry – belief.

Peirce does not take these points to be mere observations about human psychology; he thinks that psychology should be kept out of logic and the theory of inquiry. Doubt and belief, although they do have psychological aspects, such as making the inquirer feel comfortable or uncomfortable, are best thought of in terms of habits. A "belief–habit" manifests itself in an expectation: if we believe P, then we habitually expect the consequences or the predictions we derive from P to come about when the appropriate occasion arises. Inquirers are thrown into doubt when a recalcitrant experience upsets or disrupts a belief or expectation.

There are three stances an inquirer may have with respect to a hypothesis: believe it, believe its negation, or consider the matter open to inquiry. Only in the third stance are we left without a habit of expectation and thus it is agnosticism, which is the undesirable state. That is, doubting whether a hypothesis is true is not equivalent to believing that it is false – rather, doubting is not knowing what to believe. What is wrong with this state is that it leads to paralysis of action. An inquirer has some end in view, and two different and inconsistent lines of action present themselves, bringing the inquirer to a halt: "he waits at the fork for an indication, and kicks his heels ... A true doubt is accordingly a doubt which really interferes with the smooth working of the belief-habit" (CP 5.510). Doubt is not knowing how to act. And action, for Peirce, includes action in diagrammatic and thought experiments.

Peirce's theory of inquiry has a certain kind of empiricism at its core. Inquirers aim for beliefs that fit with experience, in Peirce's broad sense of that word. When we replace a belief which has come into doubt, that new belief stands up to experience better than the old one. So we accept it, act on it, and think for the time being that it is true. But we know very well that it eventually might be overthrown and shown by experience to be false. Peirce adds the more contentious claim that what we aim for is permanently settled belief. When we have a belief that would forever withstand the tests of experience and argument, he argues that there is no point of refusing to confer upon it the title "true." Only a spurious desire for transcendental metaphysics will make one want to distinguish perfectly good beliefs from true beliefs.

But in "The Fixation of Belief" Peirce says that a permanently fixed belief, *no matter how it is fixed*, is true. A problem of course looms large here. If beliefs could be settled by a religious authority, or by a charismatic guru, or by astrology, so that they were permanently resistant to doubt, his account would give us no reason for criticising them. Peirce trys to solve this problem by considering various methods of fixing belief and arguing that it is hard *really* to end the irritation of doubt.

The method of tenacity, or holding on to your beliefs come what may, will not work, he says, because doubt will be sparked when one notices that the opinions of others differ from one's own. Beliefs produced by the method of authority (fixing beliefs according to the dictates of a state or religion) will similarly be subject to doubt when one notices that those in other states or religions believe different things. Beliefs produced by the a priori method (adopting beliefs which are agreeable to reason) will eventually be doubted when it is seen that what we take as being agreeable to reason shifts like a pendulum and is really a matter of intellectual taste. None of these methods will produce permanently settled belief because they have a self-destructive design: the beliefs settled by them eventually would be assailed by doubt.

The agent of destruction which Peirce sees in each of the specious methods seems to be a purported fact about our psychological makeup: if an inquirer believes a hypothesis, and notices that other inquirers do not believe it, that first inquirer will be thrown into doubt. This impulse, Peirce says, is "too strong in man to be suppressed, without danger of destroying the human species" (W 3, 250). If this psychological hypothesis expresses a universal fact about us, then the unsatisfactory methods will indeed prove unreliable in the long run. They will not produce permanently settled belief and we should refrain from using them.

The psychological hypothesis, however, seems to be false. I have suggested (Misak 1991) that the way to resolve this difficulty is to focus on Peirce's thought that being responsive to or answerable to something is one of the "essentials of belief, without which it would not *be* belief" (MS 673, p. 11). The aim of inquiry is to get beliefs which are not merely fixed, but fixed in such a way that they fit with and respond to the evidence. They must be, in Peirce's words, "caused by circumstances not extraneous to the facts." Wiggins offers us here a ground-breaking analysis of this thought of Peirce's and of how it need not lead to a uniformly causal picture.[5] The requirement can be met by all sorts of belief.

There are two other cornerstones to Peirce's theory of inquiry: critical commonsensism and fallibilism. Critical commonsensism is a position about how we ought to regard those beliefs which are settled. It holds that there are many things which inquirers do not doubt and that inquiry must start with a background of beliefs which are not doubted. A body of settled belief is presupposed for the operation of inquiry in that there has to be something settled for surprise to stir up.

This doctrine arose as Peirce's response to his conception of Descartes' project – a systematic attempt to bring into doubt all hypotheses about which error is conceivable. Peirce argued that such doubts would be "paper" doubts. They are not genuine and they cannot motivate inquiry. The mere possibility of being mistaken with respect to what one believes is never a reason to revise those beliefs. Any of our beliefs might be false, but it would be absurd to doubt them all because of this. If we did, we would not possess a body of stable belief by which to judge new evidence and hypotheses, and hence, we would block the path of inquiry. We can doubt one belief and inquire, but we cannot doubt all of our beliefs and inquire. Peirce's point against Descartes is that if we were to set the requirements on knowledge as high as Descartes does, we would have nothing left to go on:

... there is but one state of mind from which you can "set out," namely, the very state of mind in which you actually find yourself at the time you do "set out" – a state in which you are laden with an immense mass of cognition already formed, of which you cannot divest yourself if you would ... Do you call it doubting to write down on a piece of paper that you doubt? If so, doubt has nothing to do with any serious business. (CP 5.416)

So Peirce is not concerned with sceptical questions about foundations for certainty and his arguments are not addressed to those who are.

But he is also a "contrite fallibilist," holding that all our beliefs can be doubted; that is, that none of them are certain. There is a tension here: how can it be that all our beliefs are fallible, or subject to doubt, but nevertheless, some of our beliefs must not be doubted if inquiry is to be possible?

Peirce's reconciliation of fallibilism with critical commonsensism is made in terms of his notion of truth. He thinks that many of our beliefs are indeed those which would survive inquiry, but since we cannot know for any given belief whether or not *it* would be indefeasible, we cannot know that it is true. That is, we do not know if the antecedent of this subjunctive conditional is fulfilled: "if inquiry were pursued as far as it could fruitfully go, then *P* would be believed." Inquiry may or may not have been pursued far enough with respect to *P*, and so we cannot have certainty with respect to any belief.

But the uncertainty or fallibility that in principle accompanies every one of our beliefs does not mean that we should doubt our settled beliefs. "Practically speaking," he says, many things are "substantially certain" (CP 1.152); we do not doubt them. While "it is possible that twice two is not four ... it would be difficult to imagine a greater folly than to attach any serious importance to such a doubt" (CP 7.108).

"Substantial certainty," however, is different from the "absolute certainty" which would result from knowing that we have permanently settled belief. We may have this settled opinion about many questions, but we must not infer that we "perfectly know when we know." Again, we cannot know that any given hypothesis is permanently settled upon or true – we cannot have absolute certainty. Nevertheless, in every state of intellectual development and information, there are things that seem to us sure "so that even though we tell ourselves that we are not sure, we cannot clearly see how we fail of being so" (CP 4.64). Practically, we must treat some hypotheses as certain. Settled beliefs must be regarded as infallible, in the sense that the inquirer does not doubt them for the purposes of inquiry; science has "established truths" to be used as premisses in further deliberation (CP 1.635). In this sense, we do not doubt what we believe, but in another sense, each of our beliefs can, or could, be doubted.

Peirce's theory of inquiry provides the key to understanding his view of the growth of knowledge and the progress of science. His position anticipates Neurath's metaphor of building a boat at sea, replacing defective planks one by one. Science, Peirce says,

is not standing upon the bedrock of fact. It is walking upon a bog, and can only say, this ground seems to hold for the present. Here I will stay till it begins to give way. (CP 5.589)

Accepted hypotheses and theories are stable until they are upset by experience. They are as good as they can be, given the state of evidence, technology, argument, etc. Knowledge is rebuilt bit by bit when experience forces inquirers to revise their beliefs. We have some reason to believe that we are advancing or getting closer to the truth, for the new beliefs will get along with experience better than the old ones. True beliefs are those which would, in the end, get along with experience and one explanation of our beliefs achieving more and more fit with experience is that a good number of them are true. A good number of them would be permanently doubt-resistant.

But Peirce's picture is not one of placing indubitable building blocks upon each other as we progress toward the truth. Rather, the picture is one of doubt (recalcitrant experience) forcing us to inquire until we reach another tentative doubt-resistant belief. The ground upon which inquiry walks is tenuous and it is only the danger of losing our footing that makes us go forward. Doubt and uncertainty provide the motive for inquiry. All our beliefs are fallible and when someone accepts a belief, she does so with the knowledge that it might very well succumb to the surprise of further experience. But if she knows that the belief is the result of a method which takes experience seriously, then she is warranted in accepting it, asserting it, and acting upon it.

In addition, Peirce's theory of inquiry invokes two regulative hopes: assumptions, such that, without making them, the participants in a practice could make no sense of that practice. We must, Peirce says, hope or assume that the community will continue indefinitely and we must hope that there would be, if inquiry were pursued far enough, a final settled answer to "the particular questions with which our inquiries are busied" (CP 6.610). We must hope, that is, that bivalence holds for the question at hand; we must hope that P or $-P$. He says,

A reasonable disputant disputes because he hopes, or at least, goes upon the assumption that the dispute will come to something; that is to say, that both parties will at length find themselves forced to a common belief which will be definitive and final. For otherwise, why dispute? (CP 2.29)

Inquiry is the asking of questions, and a presupposition of inquiry is that the questioner hopes for an answer. We have, Peirce says, some ground for this hope because all sorts of questions that seemed at one time to be completely resistant to resolution have been resolved.

6. LOGIC: DEDUCTION, INDUCTION, ABDUCTION

Peirce described himself as first and foremost a logician. He despaired of the state of philosophy in America at the turn of the last century; philosophers, he said, found formal logic too difficult. He classified inference into three types, deduction, induction, and abduction (which he also called retroduction or hypothesis) and made significant contributions to the study of each. Indeed, the very idea of abduction, what is today known as "inference to the best explanation," is due to Peirce.

As is made clear in Dipert's essay in this volume, Peirce's contributions to deductive logic are most impressive, although today it is Frege, not Peirce, who is regarded as bringing modern logic into the world. Peirce developed a logic of relations and quantifiers independent of and at roughly the same time as Frege, discovered the Sheffer Stroke twenty years before Sheffer, and invented a notation (utilizing normal forms) very similar to the one still in use. In mathematics, he anticipated Dedekind on the difference between finite and infinite sets and independently developed arguments about infinity similar to Cantor's.[6]

Peirce is also known for his work on induction. Some see in his writing an anticipation of Reichenbach's probabilistic response to Hume's scepticism about induction, while others see an anticipation of the Neyman–Pearson confidence interval approach to testing statistical hypotheses.[7]

What we usually think of as inductive inference (that which concludes that all As are Bs because there are no known instances to the contrary) is what Peirce called "crude induction." It assumes that future experience will not be "utterly at variance" with past experience (CP 7.756). This, Peirce says, is the only kind of induction in which we are able to infer the truth of a universal generalization. Its flaw is that "it is liable at any moment to be utterly shattered by a single experience" (CP 7.157).

The problem of induction, as Hume characterizes it, is about crude induction; it is about the legitimacy of concluding that all As are Bs or that the next A will be a B from the fact that all observed As have been Bs. Peirce assumes that Hume's problem is straightforwardly settled by fallibilism and critical commonsensism. We are right to believe that the sun will rise tomorrow, yet it is by no means certain that it will. To show that induction is valid, we need not show that we can be certain about the correctness of the conclusion of a crude inductive inference. Fallibilism holds that this is a pipe dream. What we have to show, rather, is that induction is a reliable method in inquiry.

Peirce holds that it is a mistake, anyway, to think that all inductive reasoning is aimed at conclusions which are universal generalizations. The strongest sort of induction is "quantitative induction" and it deals with statistical ratios. For instance:

> *Case*: These beans have been randomly taken from this bag.
> *Result*: 2/3 of these beans are white.
> *Rule*: Therefore 2/3 of the beans in the bag are white.

That is, one can argue that if, in a random sampling of some group of Ss, a certain proportion r/n have the character P, the same proportion r/n of the Ss have P. One concludes from an observed relative frequency in a randomly drawn sample a hypothesis about the relative frequency in the population. See Levi's contribution to this volume for a careful analysis of Peirce and quantitative induction.

Peirce is concerned with how inductive inference forms a part of the scientific method: how inductive inferences can fulfill their role as the testing ground for hypotheses. Quantitative induction can be seen as a kind of experiment. We ask what the probability is that a member of the experimental class of the Ss will have the character P. The experimenter then obtains a fair sample of Ss and draws from it at random. The value of the proportion of Ss sampled that are P approximates the value of the probability in question. When we test, we infer that if a sample passes the test, the entire population would pass the test. Or we infer that if 10% of the sample has a certain feature, then 10% of the population has that feature.

Peirce took the three types of inference to form the scientific method. The role played by induction is to test hypotheses. The job of abductive inference is to provide hypotheses for testing. In abductive inference "we find some very curious circumstance, which would be explained by the supposition that it was a case of a certain general rule, and thereupon adopt that supposition" (W 3, 326). The form it takes is:

> The surprising fact, C, is observed;
> But if A were true, C would be a matter of course,
> Hence, there is reason to suspect that A is true. (CP 5.189)

Peirce argued with Paul Carus about when an explanation is called for. Carus claimed that irregularity demands an explanation and Peirce disagreed. Nobody, he says, is "surprised that the trees in a forest do not form a regular pattern, or asks for any explanation of such a fact" (CP 7.189). Peirce suggests that irregularity is "the overwhelmingly preponderant rule of experience, and regularity only the strange exception." A mere irregularity, where no definite regularity is expected, he says, creates no surprise; it excites no curiosity. And it is surprise or anomaly which throws us into doubt – which demands an inquiry to explain the surprising phenomenon. An *unexpected* regularity or the breach of an existing regularity makes a demand for explanation. The interruption of a habit of expectation (a belief) calls for an explanation.

Abduction is "the process of forming an explanatory hypothesis" (CP 5.171) for such unexpected regularities or breaches of regularities. These hypotheses, however, are merely conjectures; we must "hold ourselves ready to throw them overboard at a moment's notice from experience" (CP 1.634). For an abductive inference "commits us to nothing. It merely causes a hypothesis to be set down upon our docket of cases to be tried" (CP 5.602).

So the first stage of inquiry is arriving at a conjecture or an explanatory hypothesis. Peirce argued that abduction and induction are "ampliative" and deduction is "explicative." In explicative inference, the conclusion follows from the premises necessarily; in ampliative inference, the conclusion amplifies rather than explicates what is stated in the premisses. He argues that ampliative inference is the only kind that can introduce new ideas into our body of belief. Being a form of ampliative inference, abduction allows us to infer, or at least conjecture, from the known to the unknown. We can infer a hypothesis to explain why we observed what we did.

The second stage is to deduce consequences or predictions from the hypothesis. The "purpose" of deduction is "that of collecting consequents of the hypothesis." The third stage is that of "ascertaining how far those consequents accord with Experience" (MS 841, p. 44). By induction we test the hypothesis: if it passes, it is added to our body of belief.

Peirce sees that the validity of abductive inference is a tricky matter. Its conclusion is not even asserted to be true:

> The hypothesis which it problematically concludes is frequently utterly wrong in itself, and even the method need not ever lead to the truth; for it may be that the features of the phenomena which it aims to explain have no rational explanation at all. Its only justification is that its method is the only way in which there can be any hope of attaining a rational explanation. (CP 2.777)

The reason we are justified in making abductive inferences is that, if we are to have any knowledge at all, we must make them. A logician, Peirce says, should have two goals – he should "bring out the amount and kind of *security* . . . of each kind of reasoning" and he should bring out the "uberty, or value in productiveness, of each kind" (CP 8.384). Abduction is such that "though its *security* is low, its *uberty* is high" (CP 8.388). It is the other two kinds of inference to which the notions of security and validity more aptly apply.

7. THE CATEGORIES

Peirce expended a great deal of intellectual energy engaging in a project which absorbed Aristotle and Kant – the categories. Peirce's ubiquitous classificatory scheme – the categories of Firstness, Secondness, and Thirdness – is designed to cover any object of thought. It is a classificatory scheme that takes each category to be an "independent and distinct element of the triune Reality" (CP 5.431). The doctrine, which permeates Peirce's work, is extremely complex and difficult.

Peirce had three methods for arriving at his list of categories. The first and earliest one is found in the 1867 "On a New List of Categories." The project is a Kantian one – to find out what "is" or "has being" by "reducing the manifold of sense impressions to unity" via an analysis of the proposition. The second method is an argument from phenomenology, which "ascertains and studies the kinds of elements universally present in the phenomenon" or "whatever is present at any time to the mind in any way" (CP 1.186). Both of these methods aim to show that everything that we experience or identify, that is, anything that "is," has an element of each of the three categories in it, and that we do not experience anything that goes beyond the three categories.

Both the Kantian and the phenomenological derivations of the categories rest on the Aristotelian/Scholastic method of prescission. This method separates or distinguishes different elements of a concept so that, although we cannot imagine a situation in which one of them is actually isolated, we can tell that the elements are distinct. We can 'suppose' one without the other, for we can, by attending to one feature and neglecting others, isolate features of phenomena which are not in fact separable. We can, for instance, suppose space without colour even though colourless space is not imaginable. Prescission, however, is not reciprocal, as it is a matter of discerning a logical priority of notions. Hence, we cannot prescind colour from space – we cannot suppose colour without spatial extension.

With respect to the categories, Peirce argues that we can abstract or prescind certain notions from experience and classify them as belonging to one or another of the categories. We can prescind Firstness from Secondness and we can prescind both from Thirdness, but we cannot prescind in the other direction.

So the categories are designed to describe the general features of each of the classes of elements that come before the mind or are experienced. Each class is distinct, but its members cannot stand in isolation. Each of the categories is present in everything we experience, but there are many cases in which one or the other of the categories is emphasised or predominant: "although they are so inextricably mixed together that no one can be isolated, yet it is manifest that their characters are quite disparate" (CP 1.284). And the list of three is all that is needed.

Perhaps the easiest way to set out Peirce's doctrine of categories is to concentrate on his third derivation, that which rests on the logic of relations. (This method, however, is discussed by Peirce as being part of phenomenology.) Here the categories are represented by n-place relations. Peirce argued that all relations fall into one of three fundamental classes: monadic, dyadic, and triadic. Each is irreducible to the others, and all predicates with more than three places are reducible to triadic ones. For instance, "a is red" is monadic, "a hit b" is dyadic, and "a gives b to c" is triadic. A four-place predicate such as "a put b between c and d" is reducible to two three-place ones: "a put b in spot e"; "spot e is between c and d." A three-place relation such as "gives," on the other hand, is not reducible to "a put b down" and "c picked b up," as these fail to express the intention of a that c have b.

The results of the three ways of inquiring into the ultimate categories are similar. Here is a brief description of those results, one which does not undertake the intimidating task of sorting out the relationships between all of the things that supposedly manifest each category.

The third category involves a medium or connecting link between two things; irreducibly triadic action is such that an event A produces an event B as a means to the production of an event C. Thirdness is often manifested in psychological concepts. We cannot grasp what it is for a to give b to c without the notion of intention mediating between a putting b down and c picking up b. Similarly, Peirce argues that representation is such that an interpreting thought mediates between sign and object. (One route to Peirce's claim that all experience is a matter of Thirdness is via his argument that everything we experience is of the nature of a sign or representation. There is no experience independent of our representation of it.) Peirce also says that law and necessity manifest thirdness. A law, or a necessary connection, mediates between the action of one thing upon another, making it more than an accident that they behaved in the way in which they did. Continuity and generality are other examples Peirce gives of thirdness.

We can cognitively isolate Secondness as the duality of action and reaction without any mediating force. It is brute existence and hence is the modality of actuality. It is found (by prescission) most clearly in the notions of struggle, action/reaction, cause/effect, and brute force. The second category is one "which the rough and tumble of life renders most familiarly prominent. We are continually bumping up against hard fact" (CP 1.324):

We can make no effort where we experience no resistance, no reaction. The sense of effort is a two-sided sense, revealing at once a something within and another something without. There is binarity in the idea of brute force; it is its principal ingredient. (CP 2.84)

A First is a simple monadic element. Peirce says that it suggests spontaneity, and it is real "regardless of anything else." In virtue of its very nature, it is indescribable; it can only be grasped by prescission:

It cannot be articulately thought: assert it, and it has already lost its characteristic innocence; for assertion always implies a denial of something else. Stop to think of it, and it has flown! ... that is first, present, immediate, fresh, new, initiative, original, spontaneous, free, vivid, conscious, and evanescent. Only, remember that every description of it must be false to it. (CP 1.357)

These "qualities of feeling" are mere possibilities:

I do not mean the sense of actually experiencing these feelings ... that is something that involves these qualities as an element of it. But I mean the qualities themselves which, in themselves, are mere may-bes, not necessarily realized. (CP 1.287)

So the first category is that of possibility.

One upshot of Peirce's doctrine of categories is that he thinks that reality comes in three grades. He is a "realist" with respect to all of the categories – possibility, actuality, and generality are real. He insists that "the *will be's*, the actually *is's*, and the *have beens* are not the sum of the reals. They only cover actuality. There are besides *would be's* and *can be's* that are real" (CP 8.216). And his Scholastic realism has it that laws or thirds are real; they are not mere mental constructions.

Peirce takes nominalism – the doctrine that "*laws* and general *types* are figments of the mind" (CP 1.16) – to be pernicious. He says:

... the property, the character, the predicate, *hardness*, is not invented by men, as the word is, but is really and truly in the hard things and is one in them all, as a description of habit, disposition, or behavior. ... (CP 1.27n1)

Peirce thinks that the fact that we can predict things ought to convince us of realism about generals. Scholastic realism explains prediction by holding that laws and dispositions have causal efficacy: "if there is any *would be* at all, there is more or less causation; for that is all that I mean by causation" (CP 8.225 n10). If a prediction has a tendency to be fulfilled, it must be the case that future events have a tendency to conform to a general rule. Peirce concludes that some laws or generals are real. Laws and dispositions mediate between possibility (Firstness) and actuality (Secondness) – it is the law that makes the possible actual, for laws or general patterns cause their instances.

But Peirce does not think that possibilities and generals actually exist; universals or generals are not "things." The realm of existence is the second category, and so possibilities and generals are real but not existent.

8. METAPHYSICS

The doctrine of categories is not Peirce's only metaphysical venture. He is set against determinism, which he takes to be the position that "every single fact in the universe is precisely determined by law" (CP 6.36). His "Tychism" has it that there is absolute chance in the universe – there is spontaneous deviation from the laws of nature. Peirce takes a corollory of Tychism to be that physical laws are statistical, something which physics now takes for granted.

Tychism is tied to Peirce's view of evolutionary cosmology, for Tychism has it that there is a tendency toward diversification in the universe. Laws, Peirce thinks, evolved from "pure possibility." The starting point "was not a state of pure abstract being. On the contrary it was a state of just nothing at all, not even a state of emptiness, for even emptiness is something" (CP 6.215). He usually says that it was pure Firstness – recall that spontaneity is paradigmatic of Firstness. It is a state which has no existing things (Secondness), compulsion (Secondness), or law (Thirdness): it is a state of pure chance or possibility.

From this state of possibility came accidental "flashes" (CP 1.412) which, again accidentally, reacted with one another. That is, Secondness emerged. And from these reactions arose a habit-taking tendency or Thirdness. Peirce says that it is the nature of habit to ever strenghten itself and thus, laws came into being. Evolution is the process of growth; the world becomes more and more rational and law-bound.

Another of Peirce's metaphysical doctrines is "Synechism," which has it that the notion of continuity is the key to philosophy. Sometimes he says that "Synechism is not an ultimate and absolute metaphysical doctrine; it is a regulative principle of logic prescribing what sort of hypothesis is fit to be entertained and examined" (CP 6.173). But at other times he presents it as highly metaphysical.

Like Aristotle, Peirce holds that a continuous series is not a collection of discrete points. A continuous series is rather a possibility of endless further determination. A continuum has no existing parts, but only a potential for being divided into parts. The infinite number of points on a continuous line are really places at which a point could be located; they are merely possibles or Firsts rather than actuals or Seconds. Continuity itself is an instance of Thirdness; it is a kind of ultimate mediation. For a continuous series is a path where we can always find one thing between two others. Peirce characteristically tries to link up this example of Thirdness with others, most particularly, with laws and generality.

Another metaphysical debate which Peirce joined is the debate about reality. Sometimes he writes of reality not in the way described in Section 3, where reality is the object of perfectly stable beliefs. But sometimes he places his view of reality within the idealism–materialism debate and sides for a kind of idealism. Reality, he says, is nothing but "effete mind" – "what we call matter is not completely dead, but is merely mind hidebound with habits" (CP 6.158). It is unclear whether this idealism can be reconciled with the view of reality elucidated within Peirce's account of truth. And it is unclear whether idealism, along with the other metaphysical doctrines touched upon here, can pass the pragmatic test, which requires metaphysical theories to have consequences for practice.[8]

9. INFLUENCE

The pragmatic theory of truth is still a going concern. Some of the current brands are not the one Peirce himself offered, but closer to those of William James and John Dewey, both of whom acknowledged their debt to Peirce. (See Pihlstrom's essay for an account of these relationships.)

Richard Rorty's pragmatism, for instance, has it that the very notion of truth is metaphysical and ought to be abandoned. Peirce, on the other hand, thinks that truth not only is a sensible notion, but, given that it is what inquirers aim at, it is a notion which is essential for inquiry. W. V. O. Quine (in some moods) and Hilary Putnam are more clearly the inheritors of Peircean pragmatism.

Another area where Peirce's influence is still felt is in the field of semeiotics, where many of his distinctions, classifications, and terminology still reign. His influence in the field of logic was impeded by his isolation and by the fact that the Boolean school was eventually edged out of the mainstream by the Fregean. Schröder adopted Peirce's notation, and some well-known results are written in it.[9] And Whitehead seems to have learnt quantification from Peirce. But despite the quantity and quality of his work in formal logic and statistical inference, he is probably best remembered in logic for introducing abductive inference, something which by its very nature cannot be formalized.

Unfortunately, Peirce's lack of success in securing an academic position, his perhaps abrasive personality, and his penchant for cumbersome terminology combined to render his views pretty much inaccessible during his own lifetime. He died penniless and unappreciated. It has only been recently that his work has found the interest it deserves and the excavation it requires.

NOTES

1. See Brent (1993) for an account of Peirce's woes in the academy. Menand (2001) is, I believe, an unreliable account: it is highly speculative about Peirce's character and bizarre in its analysis of the rise and fall of pragmatism's popularity in the United States.

2. Letter to William James in 1903, quoted in Perry 1936: vol. II, 425. See Misak (1995) for an account of Peirce's place in the empiricist tradition.

3. Much of the material that follows rests on Misak (1991) and (1995).

4. See also Hookway (2000).

5. See also Misak in this volume and (1991: 59ff).

6. See Dauben (1982), Dipert (1981a), and Putnam (1982) for details.

7. For the latter, see Levi (1980), Levi's contribution to this volume, and Hacking (1980). See Wiggins in this volume for a better Peircean

  response to Hume than the Reichenbachian one sometimes attributed
  to him.

8. Peirce did argue against some kinds of idealism on pragmatic grounds:
  "Very well; an idealist ... is lounging down Regent Street ... when some
  drunken fellow unexpectedly ... lets fly his fist and knocks him in the
  eye. What has become of his philosophical reflections now?" (CP 5.539).

9. For instance, Lowenheim's theorem and Zermelo's axioms: see Putnam
  (1982).

2 Peirce's Place in the Pragmatist Tradition

Your intensely mathematical mind keeps my
non-mathematical one at a distance. But so many of our
categories are the same that your existence and
philosophizing give me the greatest comfort.

> Perry 1935/1936: I, 224; James's letter to Peirce, March
> 27, 1897

Your mind and mine are as little adapted to understanding
one another as two minds could be, and therefore I always
feel that I have more to learn from you than from anybody.

> CP 8.296; Perry 1935/1936: II, 431; Peirce's letter to
> James, October 3, 1904

I. INTRODUCTION

"Who originated the term *pragmatism*, I or you? Where did it first appear in print? What do you understand by it?" Charles Peirce asked his friend William James in a letter on November 10, 1900 (CP 8.253; Perry 1935/1936: II, 407 n5). On November 26, 1900, James replied: "You invented 'pragmatism' for which I gave you full credit in a lecture entitled 'Philosophical conceptions and practical results.'"[1] The published version of that lecture (1898) is very likely to have been the first place where the term "pragmatism" was used in print, and James was the first philosopher known as a pragmatist. The pragmatist movement was largely developed by James, although Dewey, Royce, and even Schiller may have had an original and independent role to play in its formation. Nonetheless, James referred to Peirce's earlier unpublished usage of the term and acknowledged Peirce as the first to formulate a pragmatistic doctrine in the discussions of the Cambridge "Metaphysical Club" in the early 1870s.

The purpose of this essay is not to determine the origin of pragmatism.[2] It is, rather, my aim to situate Peirce's version(s) of pragmatism[3] in their context; that is, to investigate Peirce's place in the tradition of pragmatist thought that extends from the 1870s to the recent neopragmatisms of the 1980s and 1990s. We should remember that Peirce influenced twentieth century philosophers mainly posthumously. The collection *Chance, Love, and Logic* was published in 1923, nine years after his death, and the *Collected Papers* were published in eight volumes in 1931–1958. In any case, Peirce's works did eventually have an influence in the philosophical community, an enormous influence without which there would be nothing like pragmatism as we know it.

Peirce began to call his view "pragmaticism" after having perceived how the notion of pragmatism had been used after his original coinage of the term. The key passage from his 1905 *Monist* paper, "What Pragmatism Is," is worth quoting:

[James] first took [the word "pragmatism"] up, seeing that his "radical empiricism" substantially answered to the writer's definition of pragmatism.... Next, the admirably clear and brilliant thinker, Mr. Ferdinand C. S. Schiller... lit ... upon the same designation "pragmatism," which in its original sense was in generic agreement with his own doctrine.... So far all went happily. But at present, the word begins to be met with occasionally in the literary journals, where it gets abused in the merciless way that words have to expect when they fall into literary clutches.... So then, the writer, finding his bantling "pragmatism" so promoted, feels that it is time to kiss his child good-by and relinquish it to its higher destiny; while to serve the precise purpose of expressing the original definition, he begs to announce the birth of the word "pragmaticism," which is ugly enough to be safe from kidnappers. (CP 5.414/EP 2:334–35)[4]

Peirce did *not* claim James or Schiller to have "kidnapped" his "pragmatism." It is the use of the notion "in the literary journals" that was the cause of his anger; he did not want to replace "pragmatism" as such with "pragmaticism," but apparently intended his new coinage to refer to a subdivision of pragmatism. (See Haack 1998: 55; Kilpinen 2000: 35.) This is not to say that Peirce would have agreed with James and Schiller, but it perhaps shows that there *is* such a thing as the pragmatist tradition, originated by Peirce and continued by James, Dewey, Schiller, Mead, and their followers. There is no need to insist, as some scholars do, that the broader movement known as pragmatism is something essentially different from Peirce's own pragmaticism. Aggressively orthodox Peirceans who think only Peirce's views deserve philosophical attention tend to overlook the remarkable integrity we find among the pragmatists, despite their occasional profound disagreements. There are both unity and differences-in-unity in the pragmatist tradition. We should be skeptical about all attempts to find just two forms of pragmatism (e.g., Peirce's and all others') opposed to each other.[5]

Both the integrity and the disagreements among pragmatists are worth discussing. Since it is impossible to make any detailed comparisons between Peirce and other pragmatists in a single article, I shall focus on James (Sections 2–4), offering only general remarks on Peirce's relations to Dewey and Schiller (Sections 5–6), while Royce, Mead, and other classical thinkers can hardly be more than mentioned.[6] Finally, I shall compare Peirce to neopragmatists such as Putnam and Rorty (Section 7), before concluding with reflections on Peirce's and other pragmatists' relation to the realism vs. idealism dispute (Section 8). These comparisons, brief as they must remain, are intended to place Peirce in his position in the extremely rich tradition he founded.

2. PEIRCE AND JAMES: REALISM AND TRUTH

It has been suggested, plausibly, that the basic difference between Peirce and James in their partly conflicting characterizations of pragmatism was that the former developed a strictly logical method that would help us understand the meaning of scientific concepts, whereas the latter was interested in a wider application of the practice-oriented method of pragmatism in human concerns (Hookway 1997). This difference in their "philosophical temperaments" – to use James's term – and in their overall philosophical projects is reflected in a number of more detailed differences,[7] which, however, should not conceal their similarities. It is a mistake to interpret James's pragmatism as a mere misunderstanding or misapplication of Peirce's. James was an independent thinker. He did not simply misunderstand Peirce but employed pragmatism more broadly, partly because he had a different conception of science and the practical uses of inquiry (cf. Hookway 2000).

The opposition between *realism* and *nominalism* has been recognized as one of the issues dividing Peirce and James. Peirce always resisted nominalism, thinking that it committed the worst of philosophical sins, viz., blocking the road of inquiry (cf. CP 1.170, c. 1897). Peirce even came to resist some of his own early formulations of pragmatism as too nominalistic, and described himself as "a scholastic realist of a somewhat extreme stripe" (CP 5.470, c. 1906). Scholastic realism is essentially the doctrine that there are "real generals" (universals, dispositions, laws, habits). This view, Peirce thought, is required in any adequate formulation of scientific philosophy and metaphysics, including pragmatism itself. If universality and generality were "dependent upon what we happened to be thinking," science "would not relate to anything real" (CP 8.18, 1871).[8] James's pragmatism is more nominalistically inclined. Although it would be an exaggeration to call James a "nominalist," it is true that he focused on particular experiences and practical consequences of actions, whereas the consequences Peirce was interested in were general patterns and habits (Hookway 1997: 152). Another difference, related to scholastic realism, is this: while in some sense James went (or wanted to go) "round Kant" whereas Peirce's views were developed "through Kant" (Fisch 1986: 288), it turns out that James, contrary to his own self-image, was the more thoroughgoing Kantian. James's constructivistic pragmatism can be interpreted as a form of transcendental idealism, whereas in Peirce's case such a Kantian (re)interpretation is more difficult, because of his extreme realism (cf. Pihlström 1998a).

One of the points where James has been taken to have distorted Peirce's pragmatism is the *theory of truth*. But rather than interpreting James's pragmatist theory of truth as a misunderstanding of Peirce, we may see it as a "substantial extension" of Peirce's view, according to which truth is something that is satisfactory, useful, expedient, or good for us to believe, something that is "safe from overthrow by subsequent experience" (Haack 1976: 233-4). Because of his more nominalist bias, James focused on individual, concrete truths that were to be practically used in the course of experience, rather than on anything like the "Truth," or the final opinion of the scientific community (Haack 1976: 234). Peirce mentions James's doctrine of the "mutability of truth" as one of the "seeds of death" with which his original pragmatism became infected in the hands of later pragmatists (CP 6.485, 1908). Yet the pragmatist theory of truth is, according to Haack (1976: 236, 247), a "cosmopolitan" theory, containing both correspondence and coherence elements and receiving different emphases in different authors. It need not be a rival of the correspondence theory, but it is meaningful to say that there is one single pragmatist theory, differently developed by Peirce, James, Dewey, and others. Hookway (2000: 82, 89) also notes that James's theory of truth, instead of competing with the correspondence theory, was designed to elucidate what agreement with reality means – and so, though differently, was Peirce's.[9]

James, as well as Dewey, endorsed rather than rejected or misunderstood Peirce's formulation that truth is to be equated with the eventual outcome of inquiry, or with the convergence of belief. As Hookway (2000: 44) puts it, James accepted the connection between convergence of opinion and truth "as an account of 'absolute truth,'" whereas Dewey "agreed with it as an analysis of *truth* before concluding that logic and epistemology would do well to abandon this notion in favour of 'warranted assertibility.'" James (1907 [1975]: 107) treats "absolute truth" as a regulative notion, and Dewey (1938: 345) refers to Peirce's definition as "the best definition of truth," from the logical point of view.[10] It is Dewey's conclusion that the notion of truth has no significant role to play in logic or inquiry that Peirce did not draw.

The problems of (Scholastic) realism and truth only give us preliminary answers to the question of what distinguishes James's pragmatism from Peirce's. We have noticed differences of emphasis rather than of principle – but important differences nevertheless. Further elucidation is needed.

3. THEORY AND PRACTICE

Turning more closely to the opinions Peirce expressed about James's views, we can easily see that Peirce was critical of James's ways of developing the pragmatist ideas he had himself presented, while also admitting that his early formulations were relatively close to the pragmatism James developed.[11] Peirce also explored James's views in contexts not directly related to pragmatism. For example, he reviewed James's *The Principles of Psychology* (1890) in *The Nation* in 1891 (CP 8.55ff.).

Peirce respected James as a thinker. He admitted that James was a "perfect lover of truth" (CP 6.183, c. 1911; Perry 1935/1936: I, 540) and a great pragmatist: "You are of all my friends the one who illustrates *pragmatism* in its most needful forms. You are a jewel of pragmatism" (Perry 1935/1936: II, 427; Peirce's letter to James, March 16, 1903). There were, however, significant temperamental differences between the two, which Peirce recognized: "His comprehension of men to the very core was most wonderful. Who, for example, could be of a nature so different from his as I? He so concrete, so living; I a mere table of contents, so abstract, a very snarl of twine. Yet in all my life I found scarce any soul that seemed to comprehend, naturally, [not] my concepts, but the mainspring of my life better than he did. He was even greater [in the] practice than in the theory of psychology" (CP 6.184, c. 1911).

These differences can be highlighted by taking a look at what Peirce says about James's (1897 [1979]) doctrine of the "will to believe." In Peirce's view, this doctrine, assuming that "the end of man is action," pushes the pragmatic method "to such extremes as must tend to give us pause" (CP 5.3, 1902). James's pragmatism is "extreme," implying that "Doing is the ultimate purpose of life" (CP 8.115, c. 1900). Earlier, Peirce had remarked that "faith," though "highly necessary in affairs," is "ruinous in practice," if it means that "you are not going to be alert for indications that the moment has come to change your tactics" (CP 8.251, 1897; Perry 1935/1936: II, 222; see also CP 6.485, 1908).[12] Later, commenting on the Bergsonian conception of philosophy manifested in James's *A Pluralistic Universe* (1909b [1977]), Peirce was even more critical: "I thought your *Will to Believe* was a very exaggerated utterance, such as injures a serious man very much, but to say what you now do is far more suicidal.... [P]hilosophy is either a science or is balderdash..." (Perry 1935/1936: II, 438; letter to James, March 9, 1909).[13] Peirce insisted that pragmatism is not a *Weltanschauung* but "a method of reflexion having for its purpose to render ideas clear" (CP 5.13 n1, c. 1902). In a letter to the Italian pragmatist Mario Calderoni, Peirce, having made the distinction between pragmatism (among whose representatives he mentioned Schiller, James, Dewey, and Royce) and pragmaticism, noted that pragmaticism is "not a system of philosophy" but "only a method of thinking" (CP 8.205–6, c. 1905).

It was already in 1897, after having received James's *The Will to Believe*, dedicated to him, that Peirce reflected on the relation between his old and more recent conception of pragmatism in a letter to James (March 13, 1897; cf. also CP 8.255–6, 1902):

That everything is to be tested by its practical results was the great text of my early papers; so, as far as I get your general aim . . . I am quite with you in the main. In my later papers, I have seen more thoroughly than I used to do that it is not mere action as brute exercise of strength that is the purpose of all, but say generalization, such action as tends toward regularization, and the actualization of the thought which without action remains unthought. (CP 8.250)

This contains, *in nuce*, the difference between James's and Peirce's pragmatisms, as Peirce saw it. While it is not clear that James should be interpreted as having favored mere "brute exercise of strength," it is fairly accurate to say that he considered action or "doing" the main purpose of life. This is something that Peirce, impressed more by self-reflective habits and regularized action than individual actions, could not accept. "[T]he end of thought," he wrote, "is action only in so far as the end of action is another thought" (CP 8.272, 1902). Thus, Peirce thought that his fellow pragmatists, overemphasizing what he called "secondness," did not really understand what his categories were all about (CP 8.263, 1905). He also considered James's terminology unclear: in addition to accusing James of having misdescribed "pragmatism," he remarked that James's "pure experience" (James 1912 [1976]) "is not experience at all and certainly ought to have a name," because it is "downright bad morals so to misuse words, for it prevents philosophy from becoming a science" (CP 8.301, 1904). But then again, James hardly wanted philosophy to become a science.

A metaphilosophical opposition between Peirce and James can be observed in their conceptions of the role of philosophy in human life. While some Peirceans – e.g., Misak (1994, 2000) – have found support from Peirce's notions of truth and inquiry in defending moral realism, there is some evidence for the contention that Peirce did not consider our "practical affairs" or matters related to "the conduct of life" philosophically important.[14] He condemned, in his Cambridge Conferences Lectures (1898), "with the whole strength of conviction the Hellenic tendency to mingle Philosophy and Practice," and remarked that in philosophy, "the investigator who does not stand aloof from all intent to make practical applications, will not only obstruct the advance of the pure science, but[...]will endanger his own moral integrity and that of his readers" (RLT: 107). He claimed that pure science has nothing to do with action, that nothing is "vital" for science, that "pure theoretical knowledge, or science, has nothing directly to say concerning practical matters," and that we cannot serve "the two masters, *theory* and *practice*" (RLT: 112–13; cf. CP 1.642).[15] Yet, a simple theory/practice distinction is too crude to have been Peirce's considered view. We must remember the context of Peirce's claims: He protested against James's suggestion that he should give lectures about "vitally important topics" rather than technical logical questions.[16]

While pointing out that there "appears to be no slight theoretical divergence" between James's definition of pragmatism and his own, Peirce said that that divergence, "for the most part, becomes evanescent in practice," and that "the discrepancies [between James and him] reside in other than the pragmatistic ingredients of our thought" (CP 5.466, c. 1906). He remarked that James does not restrict "meaning," or "the ultimate logical interpretant," to a habit, as he does, but allows percepts to play this role; and that, if he (James) is willing to do this, he need not give any room to habit. "But practically, his view and mine must[...]coincide, except where he allows considerations not at all pragmatic to have weight" (CP 5.494, c. 1906; see also EP 2:421, 1907). Now, in a sense, practice is what pragmatism is all about. If there is no "practical" difference between Peircean and Jamesian pragmatisms, then there is all the more reason to see pragmatism as one single tradition with somewhat different overtones.

It is, then, overhasty to regard Peirce's and James's pragmatisms as fundamentally opposed to each other. Even the standard division between James's "nominalistic" and Peirce's "realistic" pragmatism turns out to be problematic, as Haack (1977: 392–393) shows: the difference is not that Peirce accepted and James denied the reality of universals but that Peirce denied that real universals can be reduced to particulars, while James thought that they can. Perry (1935/1936: I, 547) observes that James, recognizing the significance of "general ideas," "was never (in spite of Peirce's strictures) a thoroughgoing nominalist" and even "approached the 'realistic' position" in his mature writings, especially in *A Pluralistic Universe*. James "never became a nominalist," for he always found some way "to provide for universals, generals and concepts, however much he might disparage them" (Perry 1935/1936: II, 407). This is an important point, still insufficiently discussed. As Seigfried (1990: 267) also notes, James did not exclude "the modality of possibility," for he affirmed the need for "general rules," even though the emphasis was on the particular consequences experienced in the future. "Peirce's well-known criticism of James as a nominalist rather than a realist could not be further from the textual record," she concludes, "and yet it is uncritically repeated to this day" (399n5).[17] As Rosenthal (2000: 94) puts it, Peirce opposed a nominalistic pluralism of "discrete units," while James's pluralism was closer to Peirce's own synechism, the doctrine of continuity.

James argued that philosophical abstractions must do some real work: pragmatism "has no objection whatever to the realizing of abstractions, so long as you get about among particulars with their aid and they actually carry you somewhere" (James 1907 [1975]: 40). "We are like fishes swimming in the sea of sense [sensible facts], bounded above by the superior element [abstract ideas], but unable to breathe it pure or penetrate it" (64). It is questionable whether this even amounts to a reductionist conception of abstractions and generalities in relation to concrete facts. James seems to have maintained that we need abstractions in order to act in the world of particular experiential facts and that this is all we need them for, but he did not say, at least not explicitly, that the former are nothing but complexes of the latter. Perhaps the more important conflict is between Peirce's strict antipsychologism and James's more psychologically oriented admission of general ideas. For James, general ideas were human beings' classifications of reality through their practices, and thus dependent on or emerging from human purposive action, not anything ready-made in reality itself. For Peirce, undoubtedly, this was little more than nominalism, because the independent, nonpsychological reality of generals was not accepted by James. In any case, the differences Peirce found between his views and James's, though genuine and important, should not be overemphasized.[18]

Moreover, Peirce and James both held an extremely rich, inclusive conception of experience, according to which we experience "external things as external," interactions between them, their sensory impacts upon us, and "law-governed interactions – mediated transitions – between things we experience, and real continuity in the ways that processes develop" (Hookway 2000: 292; see Pape 2000). While both were empiricists, urging that our knowledge is based on experience, they rejected the passive, atomistic conception of experience consisting of scattered individual sensations assumed in much of the empiricist tradition.

4. INTERPRETATIONS OF THE PRAGMATIC MAXIM

While Peirce distanced his pragmatism from James's, James tended to diminish the differences. Specific references to Peirce by James can be found in *The Will to Believe* (1897b [1979]), the *Varieties* (1902 [1985]), *Pragmatism* (1907 [1975]), and *The Meaning of Truth* (1909a [1978]), as well as in manuscripts and lecture notes. These are in most cases to the pragmatic maxim, though James did teach Peirce's evolutionary metaphysics in his courses at Harvard, as his *Manuscript Lectures* (1988) show. In the *Varieties*, James (1902 [1985]: 351) mentioned "the principle of Peirce, the principle of pragmatism," referring to "How to Make Our Ideas Clear" (1878) and applying the principle to a discussion of God's metaphysical attributes. The same article by Peirce was already quoted in James's "The Function of Cognition," read before the Aristotelian Society in 1884 and published in *Mind* (vol. 10, 1885). That paper later formed the first chapter of *The Meaning of Truth*.[19] Later James reports:

The term ["pragmatism"] is derived from the same Greek word [$\pi\rho\alpha\gamma\mu\alpha$], meaning action, from which our words 'practice' and 'practical' come. It was introduced into philosophy by Mr. Charles Peirce in 1878....Mr. Peirce, after pointing out that our beliefs are really rules for action, said that, to develop a thought's meaning, we need only determine what conduct it is fitted to produce: that conduct is for us its sole significance.... To attain perfect clearness in our thoughts of an object, then, we need only consider what conceivable effects of a practical kind the object may involve – what sensations we are to expect from it, and what reactions we must prepare. Our conception of these effects, whether immediate or remote, is then for us the whole of our conception of the object, so far as that conception has positive significance at all....

To take in the importance of Peirce's principle, one must get accustomed to applying it to concrete cases. (James 1907 [1975]: 28–9)

Peirce's original text reads as follows: "Consider what effects, which might conceivably have practical bearings, we conceive the object of our conception to have. Then, our conception of these effects is the whole of our conception of the object" (CP 5.402/W 3, 266, 1878).[20] When presenting Peirce's principle in his California address in 1898, James said "it should be expressed more broadly than Mr. Peirce expresses it" (James 1898: 124). Attempting to do this, he appears to slide from acknowledging Peirce's notions of *possible* differences and *conceivable* effects to the stronger requirement that those differences or effects should be actualized in our concrete experiences or practices.

James demanded the practical consequences of our conceptions to be, above all, *particular* (James 1909a [1978]: 124; Perry 1935/1936: I, 458; II, 410–11). This, though little more than a corollary of his insistence that abstract ideas ought to be put to work among the actual facts of our world, conflicts with Peirce's focus on generality and habits, as Peirce consistently emphasized – instead of any particular, actualized bearings – the *"conceivably* practical bearings" in which "the entire meaning and significance of any conception" lies (EP 2:145, 1903). The Peircean formulation allows that conceptions, though always conceptions of "conceivable practical effects," "reach far beyond the practical"; it is only required that we maintain a connection with some possible practical effect (CP 5.196/EP 2:235, 1903). Thus, Scholastic realism, the principle that generality is operative in nature (and that modalities are thus interpreted realistically), is a central background assumption of pragmatism. It is not required that certain specific, particular consequences be actualized; it is enough that some general habitual patterns can be connected with all of our meaningful ideas.

Peirce remarked in a letter in December, 1904, that James's "Humanism and Truth" (reprinted in *The Meaning of Truth*) had distorted his views:

You have a quotation from me which greatly astonishes me . . . : "The serious meaning of a concept lies in the concrete difference to some one which its being true will make."[21] . . . I do not think I have often spoken of the "meaning of a concept" whether "serious" or not. I have said that the concept itself "is" *nothing more* than the concept, not of any concrete difference that *will* be made to someone, but is nothing more than the concept of the *conceivable* practical applications of it. (Perry 1935/1936: II, 432–3)

Peirce was somewhat happier with the way James interpreted him in *Pragmatism*, though he wished that James had learned to think "with more exactitude" (Perry 1935/1936: II, 436–7). It is, clearly, in the "applications" that James's pragmatism takes a turn away from Peirce's. James did not pay much attention to Peirce's later developments of pragmatism; the logical spirit of Peirce's thought remained alien to him. This is something that James admitted, referring to his "non-mathematical" mind and "slight interest in logic" (Perry 1935/1936: II, 427; letter to Peirce, June 5, 1903). He wrote: "Your mind inhabits a technical logical thicket of its own into which no other mind has as yet penetrated" (Perry 1935/1936: II, 427n7; letter to Peirce, July 10, 1903; see also Perry 1935/1936: II, 680). Peirce agreed that James's failure to appreciate his (Peirce's) pragmatism resulted from his (James's) weak mathematical and logical capacities: James "had no head for logic at all" and thus "made the man in [the] street get some notions of what pragmatism was" (NE 3/1: 192, 1911).[22]

The oppositions between Peirce and James can be seen as emerging from their different formulations and applications of the pragmatic maxim. Peirce's Scholastic realism, emphasis on community, antipsychologistic view of logic, and emphasis on pragmatism as a logical principle conflicted with James's nominalism, individualism, psychological orientation, and psychologistic interpretation of pragmatism.[23] These conflicts are not unrelated to how they viewed the notion of practical consequences: for instance, in a note added in 1893 to the 1878 paper (CP 5.402n2), Peirce remarked that the maxim, understood as an application of the Biblical rule, "Ye may know them by their fruits," ought to be interpreted collectively, not individualistically. The emphasis on the collective nature of science, and of the habitually evolving rationality that human action manifests, extends through virtually everything that Peirce wrote. The individualistic overtones of James's pragmatism were as alien to him as James's psychologism. These differences are especially clear in Peirce's 1903 Harvard Lectures, one of the most significant documents of how Peirce resisted the psychologization of pragmatism.[24] He said that his own formulations of the 1870s were too psychological and that he no longer considers it satisfactory "to reduce such fundamental things [as the pragmatic maxim] to facts of psychology," because "man could alter his nature" (EP 2: 140; see also CP 5.28).

In these lectures, Peirce was concerned with demonstrating the truth of pragmatism as a method of thought and inquiry, connecting the maxim with almost all other branches of his philosophy (i.e., phenomenology, the categories, logic of relatives, theory of probability, the normative sciences – logic, ethics, and aesthetics, theory of inference, semiotics, and scholastic realism).[25] Regarding the "truth" of pragmatism, James's view may, however, have been more consistently pragmatic than Peirce's. Arguably, James applied pragmatism *to itself*, treating the pragmatist principle as pragmatically true (cf. Conant 1997, Pihlström 1998a). No logical demonstration of its truth, independently of pragmatism, was needed or even possible for him; the pragmatic efficacy and the truth of pragmatism were (*pace* Turrisi 1997b: 28) pretty much the same thing for James, though not for Peirce. The maxim that ideas ought to be tested practically in the course of experience covers this pragmatist idea itself.

This metaphilosophical difference over the status and provability of the pragmatic maxim was a corollary of the opposition between the logical and psychological orientations of Peirce and James, respectively. We may say that for James the evaluation of the philosophical role of generalities or abstract ideas was among the applications of the pragmatic maxim, whereas for Peirce the reality of generals was a presupposition making pragmatism possible. James could have argued that any such presupposition must again be pragmatically assessed. Peirce also thought that the pragmatic maxim had pragmatic consequences; he, too, in his own way applied pragmatism to itself. But the point is that James was willing to let practical consequences – which for him constituted a more open and inclusive class than the scientifically focused consequences Peirce emphasized – determine the philosophical value of pragmatism in a pragmatic manner, independently of any *prior* logical demonstration. Peirce's pragmatism was subordinated to logic; according to James, whatever philosophical value logic had it was to be explained on a pragmatic basis.

Some of these differences may hide a more basic similarity. The fact that, in Peirce's view, theory must be distinguished from practice and philosophy cannot help us in "matters of vital importance," might be considered a key difference to James, but it might also express a partial agreement. Peirce thought, with James rather than against him, that vitally important issues should be resolved by instinct and sentiment rather than mere intellectual reflection or theorizing. Even so, the distance from James is considerable here. For James (as well as for Dewey), matters of vital importance do require something like "inquiry," because "inquiry" is defined in highly general terms, more broadly than "scientific inquiry." On the other hand, even Peirce may be interpreted as having held the view that "the method of science" can be applied to "all respectable subject-matters" (Hookway 2000: 76–7). There is perhaps a tension in Peirce's position in this respect.[26]

Another interesting comparison, not unrelated to the pragmatic maxim, results from the question of whether Peirce's presuppositions of inquiry – e.g., that there are real things independent of what we think about them – should be interpreted as transcendentally established truths or mere *hopes* (cf. Hookway 1998: § 10; 2000: 6–7, 39, 109–10, 185–6, 190, 296). Hookway observes that, from Peirce's point of view, the fact that something is a presupposition of inquiry, experience, or thought only provides a reason for hoping, not for believing, that it is true. Now, James's pragmatism might lead us to reject the distinction between these two attitudes as practically idle. What we *have to* adopt as a sincere hope on the basis of what our inquiries or experiences presuppose is, James would have urged, for us *ipso facto* pragmatically true. There is, in James's pragmatism, no pragmatically solid distinction to be drawn between hopes and beliefs in the Peircean way. This is especially clear in the "will to believe" doctrine and in James's "faith ladder" (as formulated in *A Pluralistic Universe*): the status of sincere hopes is pragmatically indistinguishable from their status as convictions we need in our lives, convictions that are, for this reason, pragmatically true *for us*.

Here James was a more radical pragmatist with respect to truth than Peirce. One might argue against him by saying that hopes or regulative assumptions are not true or false and should be distinguished from beliefs. Calling something a regulative assumption is "to make a statement about a practice," about some practice (e.g., inquiry) requiring "for its sensible continuation" certain assumption(s) by those who engage in it (e.g., inquirers); this is not to claim that such assumptions are true (Misak 1991: 140). But one of the arguments characterizing James's pragmatism as a whole is that the boundary between the concepts of belief and hope is vague. It is part of James's "humanizing" of the concept of truth to insist that what we need to hope in our lives is true in the pragmatic sense. What we, *qua* agents engaging in a practice, cannot help assuming is, for us, true. As our needs and hopes may change, an element of mutability is introduced into the pragmatist conception of truth – something that horrified Peirce.

This disagreement can perhaps be expressed by saying that Peirce endorsed, while James denied, Kant's distinction between *praktisch* and *pragmatisch*.[27] The former, Kant thought, is concerned with a priori moral laws established through the practical use of reason; the latter, instead of being associated with morality, relates to the purposive nature of cognition in relation to sensibility and is closer to what Peirce had in mind in discussing the experimental procedures of inquiry. James saw no pragmatically meaningful difference here. He applied the same pragmatic method that he used in various philosophical problems more metaphilosophically to the dissolution of the contrast between *pragmatische* scientific experimental operations and *praktische* morally motivated considerations. From the Jamesian (but surely not from the Peircean) point of view, moral (practical) issues are always already at work in our pragmatic assessments of the conceptions of reality we operate with in our practices, scientific conceptions included. It is precisely those ethical consequences of our actions or habits of action that must be taken seriously in pragmatic evaluations. We should not, according to James, rely on any science vs. ethics dichotomy if we attempt to understand what pragmatism is all about.

For anyone willing to defend the role of philosophy in a rational consideration of ethical and political issues, the Jamesian route – inherited by Dewey and his followers – is a maturation rather than a distortion of pragmatism. The pragmatic maxim remains too narrow if confined to scientific methodology. This is the relevant *practical* difference between Peirce's and James's applications of their method. We can use the pragmatic method itself reflexively and metaphilosophically in order to determine what the difference is. It may be suggested that by thus applying pragmatism to itself we adopt a more Jamesian than Peircean approach. Since this proposal is vulnerable to a Peircean counterargument emphasizing the scientific need to state pragmatism more sharply as a logico-semiotic principle based on scholastic realism, no bottom line of the debate can easily be reached.

5. PEIRCE AND DEWEY

Our conception of the relation between Peirce and James can be enriched by studying the views of some other pragmatists. The obvious place to begin is Dewey's philosophy, variously labeled not only as "pragmatism" but, more often, as "instrumentalism" or "experimentalism." As in James's case, I shall focus not on the bulk of Dewey's writings but on what Dewey said about Peirce and on what Peirce said about him.

Dewey's (1923) essay "The Pragmatism of Peirce," supplementing Peirce's *Chance, Love, and Logic*, is still one of the best brief characterizations of Peirce's pragmatism.[28] Dewey compares James and Peirce, noting the standard differences (nominalism vs. realism about generals, individuality vs. emphasis on the social). Peirce, according to Dewey, emphasized "the method of procedure" more than James (307) and rejected the Jamesian "appeal to the Will to Believe – under... the method of tenacity" (308). In another paper discussing Peirce and James, Dewey (1922) pointed out that James, being a "humanist" rather than a logician, both expanded the pragmatic method by applying it to the theory of truth and restricted it by emphasizing particular instead of general consequences. Later, Dewey (1946: 156–7) referred favorably to Peirce's way of linking truth with the dynamics of scientific belief – against the idea of truth as a "fixed structure" – and called Peirce "the man who more than any other single person is the begetter in philosophy of an attitude and outlook distinctively American."

There are issues on which Peirce and Dewey were closer to each other than either of them was to James – in particular, the social orientation of pragmatism and the advancement of scientific knowledge.[29] However, regarding the issue of realism, Dewey was closer to James than to Peirce. Neither James nor Dewey could accept scholastic realism; nor did they accept Peirce's logical, nonpsychological interpretation of pragmatism.[30] As in James, Peirce found in Dewey the unfortunate tendency to psychologize what he had presented as logical and normative principles of scientific inference. On June 9,

1904, he wrote to Dewey: "You propose to substitute for the Normative Science which in my judgment is the greatest need of our age a 'Natural History' of thought or of experience. . . . I do not think anything like a natural history can answer the terrible need . . ." (CP 8.239). Since pragmatism was, for Peirce, a method for clarifying ideas and, because of its relation to the theory of inference, a maxim of logic, and since logic was a normative science, James and Dewey were from Peirce's perspective guilty of a conflation of logical and (socio) psychological issues.

Still, pragmatists like Dewey and Mead can be seen as developing further some basically Peircean themes, particularly the reflexivity of habits of action and of rationality (Kilpinen 2000: ch. 3). Dewey did not entirely reject Peirce's realism of generality: ". . . Peirce has laid the basis for a valid logical theory of universals. It is the business of leading principles, as formulae of operations, to guide us in the drawing of inferences. They accomplish this task by indicating what qualities of things are characteristic of the presence of a specified kind of object or event" (Dewey 1936: 532). But he insisted that the problem of the relation between universals and individuals is logical rather than ontological (533), resisting the metaphysics of real generality. Dewey (1946: 228) also approvingly remarked that Peirce was the first to draw attention to the importance of the principle that "[t]he generic propositions or universals of science can take effect . . . only through the medium of the habits and impulsive tendencies of the one who judges" and that they have "no *modus operandi* of their own."

One of the major differences between Peirce's and Dewey's conceptions of inquiry is related to their accounts of truth. As was observed, Dewey (like James) approved of Peirce's 1878 definition of truth as the ultimate opinion of inquiry; yet Dewey did not rely on the idea that there must be a *unique* limit to inquiry (Tiles 1988: 107). He conceived of the tasks of inquiry more pluralistically than Peirce did, remaining closer to James. Instead of Peircean "pure science," Dewey favored "socially responsible science" (Tiles 1988: 160). This basic position regarding the social and, more generally, human relevance of inquiry can be found in virtually all of his writings. Furthermore, Dewey (like James) was more idealistically or constructivistically oriented than Peirce in his quite explicit view that the actions of inquirers constitute the objects of knowledge instead of being answerable to pre-existing real things (cf. Dewey 1929; see Shook 2000).

It is undeniable that Peirce's community-driven conception of inquiry was a crucial background of Dewey's "instrumentalism" (cf. Dewey 1922); moreover, even within a Deweyan, more pluralistic conception of what our inquiries aim at one may retain the Peircean view that there is one definite answer to be arrived at regarding any particular question, provided that inquiry could be carried out long enough. The pluralism associated with James's pragmatism and his doctrine of the mutability of truth seems to be more extreme than the pluralism we can read into Dewey's account of inquiry.

6. PEIRCE AND OTHER EARLY PRAGMATISTS

Among the initial pragmatists, Josiah Royce was an important critic of James and developed a mixture of pragmatism and Hegelian idealism ("absolute pragmatism") that was closer to Peirce's views than were most other classical formulations of pragmatism. G. H. Mead was perhaps the one closest to Peirce among the early figures of the tradition, especially because of his interest in semiotics. C. I. Lewis, sometimes described as the last classical pragmatist, was also closer to Peirce than to James or Dewey. Lewis's "conceptualistic pragmatism," developed in *Mind and the World-Order* in 1929, perhaps lies between Peirce's and Royce's views (Fisch 1986: 300–1). These pragmatists remain outside the scope of the present inquiry.[31] I shall, in this section, focus on F. C. S. Schiller, the most radical subjectivist among the classical pragmatists.

Peirce did not approve of Schiller's manner of transforming pragmatism any more than he approved of James's: "... I, by no means, follow Mr. Schiller's brilliant and seductive humanistic logic, according to which it is proper to take account of the whole personal situation in logical inquiries." His reason for dismissing Schiller resembles his critiques of James and Dewey: "... I hold it to be very evil and harmful procedure to introduce into scientific investigation an unfounded hypothesis, without any definite prospect of its hastening our discovery of the truth" (CP 5.489, c. 1906; cf. also 5.494, c. 1906). Schiller was irresponsibly unclear about what he meant by "the *real*" (CP 5.533, c. 1905; cf. also CP 8.319, undated), as well as about his definition (influenced by James) of truth as something that is "satisfactory" (CP 5.552, 1906). In his review of the book

Personal Idealism (Sturt 1902), to which Schiller had contributed, Peirce noted that Schiller "does not believe that there are any hard facts which remain true independently of what we may think about them" (CN 3, 127). Although he did not criticize this position in any detail in the review, most of his writings on pragmatism and the scientific method defend such "hard facts." "Humanism," in particular, remained unclear and unscientific in Peirce's eyes:

[Schiller] does not wish us to devote any attention to the effects of conditions that do not occur, or at any rate not to substitute the solution of such a problem for the true problems of nature.... I think such talk shows great ignorance of the conditions of science. [As] I understand it, this Humanism is to be a philosophy not purely intellectual because every department of man's nature must be voiced in it.... I beg to be excused from having any dealings with such a philosophy. I wish philosophy to be a strict science, passionless and severely fair. (CP 5.537, c. 1905)

To ignore the conditions of science – especially scholastic realism, which draws attention to unactualized generalities – was, for Peirce, to ignore the central teachings of his pragmati(ci)sm. As he wrote to James: "The humanistic element of pragmatism is very true and important and impressive; but I do not think that the doctrine can be *proved* in that way. The present generation likes to skip proofs.... You and Schiller carry pragmatism too far for me. The most important consequence of it, by far,... is that under that conception of reality we must abandon nominalism" (CP 8.258, 1904; Perry 1935/1936: II, 430).[32] Apparently, Schiller, like James, applied pragmatism (or humanism) to itself, finding it a pragmatically valuable philosophy in human affairs, instead of seeking a proof available for nonpragmatists and pragmatists alike.

Apart from this metaphilosophical difference, Peirce's disagreements with James and Schiller were partly terminological. In another letter to James, Peirce noted that he would prefer the term "anthropomorphism" to Schiller's "humanism," especially if it implies theism (though he rejected the idea that the theistic God might be finite).[33] Furthermore, "[p]luralism," he said, "does not satisfy either my head or my heart" (CP 8.262, 1905; Perry 1935/1936: II, 434). Later, he mentioned "pluralism generally," along with the "will to believe" and the "mutability of truth," as an implication of James's and Schiller's pragmatism he did not accept (EP2: 457, 1911). As in the case of James and Dewey, Peirce felt that Schiller's psychologism and nominalism were the opposite of the true spirit of pragmatism: "When you say that Logical consequences cannot be separated from psychological effects, . . . you are merely adopting a mode of expression highly inconvenient which . . . can only confuse, any sound argumentation. It is a part of nominalism which is utterly antipragmatistic . . ." (CP 8.326; letter to Schiller, September 10, 1906).

Given Peirce's remarks on the indistinguishability of his views from James's, it seems that Peirce was more critical of Schiller than of James. Why? Is there a difference between James's pluralistic pragmatism and Schiller's personalistic humanism, although James often appeared to endorse Schiller's views on truth and on the constitution of reality through human practices?

This issue must be left for James and Schiller scholars to solve on another occasion. We can say that Schiller, even more radically than James, distanced himself from Peirce's logical, scientific pragmatism. He admitted that Peirce was the one who invented pragmatism, but added that "it would seem to follow from pragmatist principles that a doctrine belongs to him who makes an effective use of it" (Schiller 1903: 27 n1). Schiller (1907: ix–x) ignored Peirce's criticism of James's and his own views simply by remarking that Peirce's 1905 *Monist* papers "have shown that he had not disavowed the great Pragmatic principle which he launched into the world so unobtrusively nearly thirty years ago." Schiller (1907: 5) thought this principle was "the greatest truism": it is clear that the consequences of a claim are used to test the truth of the claim. "Humanism" is a broader doctrine than pragmatism (1907: 5 n1). Schiller added, though, that Peirce had privately assured him that "from the first he had perceived the full consequences of his dictum."

Neither James nor Schiller was responsive to the critique Peirce launched against them, although they, as leading figures of the movement founded by Peirce, perhaps ought to have been. This, one might speculate, may have been one of the reasons Peirce's pragmatism was only slowly received in the philosophical community.

7. PEIRCE AND LATER PRAGMATISM

Peirce and other classical pragmatists influenced later thinkers in many ways. Among central twentieth century philosophers, Ludwig

Wittgenstein is one of the most interesting in relation to the pragmatist tradition, although he was influenced more by James than by
Peirce. Peirce's influence on Wittgenstein has been shown to go primarily through Frank Ramsey.[34] Unlike Wittgenstein, postpositivist
philosophers of science, especially scientific realists, have been less
affected by James and Dewey and more attached to a Peircean doctrine of the final opinion of the scientific community as the measure
of truth (cf. Niiniluoto 1999). There are, furthermore, contemporary
pragmatists (e.g., Haack 1998; Rescher 2000) whose views can be
regarded as "Peircean," but despite the growing industry of Peirce
scholarship, it seems that the most original thinkers to be classified
as pragmatists today have been more strongly influenced by James
and Dewey than by Peirce (e.g., Putnam, Rorty, and others). Yet we
can find conflicting attitudes to Peirce even among these Jamesian–
Deweyan neopragmatists: there is a great gulf separating Putnam's
(1990: ch. 18) appreciation of Peirce's role as one of the founders of
modern logic from Rorty's infamous way of restricting his contribution to the pragmatist tradition to his having given it the name and
having stimulated James (see Rorty 1982: 160–161).

Putnam (1994, 1995a), like Rorty, sees James and Dewey as the two
great pragmatists he wishes to follow. He refers to himself as one who
attempts to revive the idea that truth is, "in some way (not in Peirce's
way, but in a more humanly accessible, modest way), an idealization
of the notion of warranted assertibility" (Putnam 1990: 223), and
points out that "Peirce was certainly wrong in thinking that truth
can be defined as what inquiry would converge to in the long run"
(Putnam 1994: 152). Still, there are Peircean elements in Putnam's
pragmatism: his attempt to define truth in epistemic terms (Putnam
1981, 1990) is not unlike Peirce's notion of the ideal limit of scientific opinion.[35] In Rorty's neopragmatism, such Peircean elements
have disappeared, since in Rorty we can hardly find any sincere concern with truth or inquiry. Rorty also misuses Peircean ideas by regarding the pragmatist tradition as based on what he calls "antirepresentationalism." It is odd to claim that the founder of semiotics
also founded an antirepresentationalist philosophy. Yet Rorty (1998)
maintains something from the Peircean account of truth: insisting
on the "cautionary" use of "true," he comes close to the kind of regulative "absolute" truth that James and Dewey considered valuable
in Peirce's philosophy, viz., a notion of truth whose point is that "it

is always possible (and frequently likely) that further inquiries will exercise their powers of 'retroactive legislation' and thus require us to abandon our current conclusions" (Hookway 2000: 69). We use the notion of truth partly in order to remind ourselves of our fallibility, since the notion of error seems to presuppose the notion of truth (see Misak 2000). We may always be mistaken in our opinions, and since (as Putnam, Rorty, and many others have argued) we cannot directly compare our beliefs and theories to an unconceptualized practice-, perspective-, and discourse-independent reality (to the world in itself), there is no higher authority than "our future selves" (to use one of Rorty's favorite expressions) to determine whether we have been mistaken or not.

The difference between Peirce's and Rorty's pragmatism is clear, however, when the Peircean inquirer points out that our fallible beliefs should address an *unlimited* community of inquirers (Hookway 2000: 70). Rorty has no use for such a notion, as he insists on the limited and contextual nature of human projects, including inquiries. Here Rorty is much closer to James and Dewey. Science was, for James, essentially instrumental, and the practical use to which scientific theories are to be put does not require that those theories be interpreted in terms of "absolute truth" (Hookway 2000: 73–74). Rorty appears to hold an equally instrumentalist conception.

Among contemporary Peirceans, Haack (1993, 1998) has most vigorously attacked Rorty's version of pragmatism. She argues that Rorty's neopragmatism amounts, in Peirce's terms, to a pseudo-inquiry carried on in a "literary spirit," or a "fake reasoning" rather than genuine truth-seeking. Thus, Rorty fails to follow Peirce's "first rule of reason," the rule that "in order to learn you must desire to learn" (see CP 1.135/EP 2:48, 1898). From Haack's perspective, Rorty's pragmatism is a vulgarization of Peirce's.[36] Peirce would hardly have any difficulties in judging Rorty as one of the abusers of the word "pragmatism," as one of those who misapply the term – and the doctrine – in "literary journals." Haack's and other Peirceans' critiques of Rorty are among the most important recent twists in the pragmatist tradition. Yet, had Peirce's original views never been extended, reinterpreted, and perhaps in some cases even misapplied, had pragmatist ideas concerning truth and reality never been carried into the Rortyan antirealist and ethnocentrist extremes, the

pragmatist tradition might be poorer than it is – although we cannot
know for sure.

8. CONCLUSION: REALISM AND IDEALISM

Only the future can show how much the Peircean conception of
philosophy as inquiry will be respected in the pragmatist tradition.
Peirce's pragmatism is of lasting value, but James and Dewey developed independent, though controversial, versions of pragmatism
that are less realistically biased. Their constructivistic and humanistic views can – contrary to what they themselves claimed – be
interpreted as variations of Kantian idealism, which perhaps cannot
be consistently done in Peirce's case. The idea that the objects of
knowledge are in a sense constructions by the knowing subject, or
by the subject's actions in the course of inquiry, an idea that Peirce
rejected but James, Dewey, and Schiller in some sense endorsed, is a
fundamentally Kantian idea.

In neopragmatism, it is the Jamesian–Deweyan standpoint that
dominates over the Peircean one, although Peirce's thought is more
influential in the philosophy of science, especially in the tradition
of scientific realism, as well as in semiotics and communication
studies.[37] Insofar as pragmatism is considered an important tradition today, it is largely because of its promise to take seriously the
vital questions of human life, rather than making the distinction between theory and practice that Peirce made. For example, James's
pragmatism offers a more promising agenda for philosophers of religion seeking to understand religious experiences and the possible
"pragmatic truth" (or warrant) of religious beliefs than Peirce's evolutionary metaphysics. And although the relevance of Peirce's pragmatism, especially its habitual conception of rationality, to social
theory has been emphasized (Kilpinen 2000), it is easier to find directly relevant social-theoretical views in Dewey than in Peirce.

Peirce's and his followers' interpretations of pragmatism are
united by certain questions their views seem to leave unsettled. In
particular, the problem of *realism vs. idealism* is unavoidable in the
pragmatist tradition. It is legitimate to object that this contrast is
not appropriate in a discussion of pragmatism, as pragmatists have
attempted to transcend the oscillation between realism and idealism

instead of defining their views in terms of it. But it is equally legitimate to use this traditional opposition to uncover the tensions that
remain in pragmatists' peculiar combinations of realism and idealism (even if we may in the end agree that the contrast has been tran-
scended). What makes pragmatism philosophically interesting is its
tendency to result in fruitful albeit not easily resolvable struggles between realism and idealism.[38] Neither Peirce's, James's, nor Dewey's
(nor their more recent followers') views can be simply described as
realistic or idealistic. They are as complex doctrines as Kant's, who
combined transcendental idealism with empirical realism.

In his essay on Peirce, Dewey concluded: "Do not a large part
of our epistemological difficulties arise from an attempt to define
the 'real' as something given prior to reflective inquiry instead of as
that which reflective inquiry is forced to reach and to which when
it is reached belief can stably cling?" (1923: 308) This suggestion –
that the "real" should *not* be defined as "something given prior to
reflective inquiry" – leads to the elusiveness of the contrast between
realism and idealism that can be found throughout the pragmatist
tradition. Does inquiry produce the real by being forced to reach
for it? How independently does the real exist before inquiry, if it
is not "given" prior to it? And how meaningful is this worry itself? Although we should not confuse the problems we encounter
in formulating the realism question with the openness of the question itself, the fact that a certain issue is hard to formulate is an
indicator of its genuine openness. Through pragmatists' writings,
the problem of realism is continuously transformed, but never fully
settled. For example, Putnam (1992a: 73) classifies Peirce's scholastic realism as a species of metaphysical realism, the unpragmatistic
view that we can discover Nature's own "joints" – a view whose
rejection he regards as a virtue rather than a vice in James and
Dewey.

Peirce and other pragmatists were presumably aware of their difficulties in reconciling the *prima facie* conflicting demands of realism
and idealism. Peirce characterized truth as "[t]he opinion which is
fated to be ultimately agreed to by all who investigate" and reality, or
"the real," as "the object represented in this opinion" (CP 5.407/W 3,
273, 1878). But the real, he always emphasized, must be thought of as
something that is "independent of the vagaries of me and you" (CP
5.311/W 2, 239, 1868; see also CP 5.405/W 3, 271, 1878; CP 5.430,

1905). Traditional realists require that the nature of reality be absolutely independent of our – even our most considered, collective, or "final" – opinions. Peirce thought that reality "depends on the ultimate decision of the community" (CP 5.316/W 2, 241, 1868). Claims like this seem to make his pragmati(ci)sm ambiguous between realism (connected with a correspondence analysis of truth, according to which the final opinion of inquiry corresponds to the way things are) and idealism (connected with a coherence or consensus account of truth). Peirce also said that reality, while being independent of "what you or I or any finite number of men may think about it," may not be independent "of thought in general" (CP 5.408/W 3, 274, 1878; cf. also CP 7.336, 1873).[39] This reference to "thought in general" in the constitution of reality in some sense makes him an idealist. Realizing the instability of his position, Peirce remarked that the claim that "[t]he object of final belief which exists only in consequence of the belief, should itself produce the belief" sounds paradoxical, but that this is not to say that the object of the belief "begins to exist first when the belief begins to exist" (CP 7.340, 1873). Even though the Peircean pragmatist characterizes inquiry nonpsychologically in illuminating the notions of reality and truth in terms of the final outcome of inquiry, it is not easy to make sense of the idea of inquiry as a genuine discovery, if inquiry, fated to lead to a consensus of opinion in the long run, constitutes the way the world is (Hookway 1985: 37–9).

The secondary literature is full of attempts to reconcile the tension between realism and idealism. For example, Carl Hausman (1993) endorses the idea that Peirce was a "metaphysical realist" (although preferably to be called an "evolutionary realist"), and defends this view against philosophers like Putnam. While Peirce rejected the "spectator theory of knowledge" (as all pragmatists did), he insisted that there are conditions of inquiry that were never made by us, that there is "resistance" in our experience (224–5). But is it possible to reject the spectator theory, denying that the object of knowledge is "given" to us, and yet claim that there is an external, independent world that is the object of knowledge? If the object of knowledge is constituted as the final outcome of inquiry, if truth is to be equated with belief that cannot be improved on through further inquiry, it is hard to see how the world can be totally independent of us in the sense in which realists claim it to be.

It would be too simple to say that the progressive dynamics of science – scientific inquirers' collective belief-fixation – decides, determines, or constructs the world. It would certainly be too simple to ascribe this view to any of the pragmatists. But it would also be too simple to say that reality exists in a ready-made form, as a "thing in itself," independent of the inquirers' habits of action. Peirce's pragmatism, and the countless post-Peircean versions of pragmatism, all the way up to and including controversial contemporary figures like Putnam and Rorty, deal with or try to undermine this opposition between realism and idealism. Perhaps the question, "Is Peirce assuming an external, objective world independent of inquiry, or is the world constituted through the process of inquiry?" is a bad question, but it remains to be determined exactly in what sense it is a bad question and with which questions it should be replaced. For instance, one may ask whether Peirce held a nonepistemic or an epistemic concept of truth.[40] Truth is epistemic in the sense of being necessarily tied to our inquiries but nonepistemic in the sense of being about a reality we did not build up. According to philosophers operating with traditional nonpragmatic dichotomies, this is hopelessly ambiguous; according to pragmatists, we do not have ambiguities here but complexity that cannot be avoided, if we wish to obtain an adequate conception of truth and realism.

Royce made an important point in 1881, when in a letter to James he asked, "Do you or do you not recognize this reality of which you speak as ... independent of the knowing consciousness?" observing the same hesitation and ambiguity in Peirce's 1877 and 1878 papers: "[He] seems to regard reality as for us merely the representative of our determinations to act so or so, and of our expectations that we shall succeed if we do so. ... Yet [he] is not content with this, but continually appeals to the transcendent reality as justifying our determination and our expectation" (Perry 1935/1936: I, 792). The issue Royce identified is, essentially, a Kantian one, reflecting the Kantian background of the pragmatist tradition. In a way Peirce, like most other pragmatists, was an empirical realist about the "real things" that are the object of the final scientific opinion, while remaining a transcendental idealist about the constitution of these things, and of their objectivity, grounded in the intersubjective action of the scientific community.[41]

Although (or because) no "solution" to our Kantian issue has been reached, I hope I have been able to produce a modest contribution to the pragmatist tradition characterized by the irreducible complexity of the realism vs. idealism opposition.[42]

NOTES

1. See CP 8.253, editors' note. James's lecture, often considered the beginning of the pragmatist movement, was published in the *University of California Chronicle* 1 (1898) and is most easily found as "The Pragmatic Method," in *Essays in Philosophy* (1978: 123–39) or as an appendix to *Pragmatism* (James 1907 [1975]: 257–70).

2. Nor am I concerned with the Metaphysical Club or with the broader historical background of pragmatism; cf. Menand (2001).

3. This is not, however, a historical study on the changes that took place in Peirce's philosophy. Such developmental questions are dealt with elsewhere in this *Companion*.

4. Another interesting, somewhat bitter passage is this: "To speak plainly, a considerable number of philosophers have lately written as they might have written in case they had been reading either what I wrote but were ashamed to confess it, or had been reading something that some reader of mine had read. For they seem quite disposed to adopt my term *pragmatism*. . . . I cannot find any direr fault with the new pragmatists than that they are *lively*. In order to be deep it is requisite to be dull. //On their side, one of the faults that I think they might find with me is that I make pragmatism to be a mere maxim of logic instead of a sublime principle of speculative philosophy." (EP 2: 134, 1903; cf. CP 5.17–18.) See also CP 6.482, 6.490, 1908.

5. For the "two pragmatisms" image, see Apel (1981), Mounce (1997), Haack (1998), Rescher (2000), and Misak (2000). According to these commentators, Peirce's pragmatism was gradually, through misapplications and distortions, transformed into Rorty's completely un-Peircean neopragmatism.

6. In order to obtain a good overall picture of pragmatism, it is advisable to focus on those pragmatists (James, Dewey, Schiller) whose views were different from Peirce's rather than on those (Royce, Mead, Lewis) who more or less agreed with him.

7. On these differences – realism vs. nominalism, truth, formulations of the pragmatic maxim, etc. – see Perry (1935/1936: II, ch. 75), Thayer (1968), and Hookway (2000).

8. For Peirce's formulations of Scholastic realism, see CP 5.430–3, 1905; 5.453 ff., 1905; 5.470, c. 1906; 5.528, c. 1905; 8.7–38, 1871, as well as the 1898 lectures, *Reasoning and the Logic of Things* (RLT). Only a part of Peirce's important 1905–1907 writings on pragmaticism (in which Scholastic realism is a major topic) can be found in the *Collected Papers*; a more comprehensive selection is included in EP 2: chs. 24–8. The equally important early Berkeley review (1871) can also be found in W 2, 462–87, and in EP 1: ch. 5. On the role of Scholastic realism in Peirce's thought, see Apel (1981), Skagestad (1981), Margolis (1993), Haack (1998), and Pihlström (1998b).

9. For discussions of Peirce's theory of truth, see Misak (1991) and Hookway (2000).

10. See Hookway (2000: 68–69); on the "Peircean strain" in James's theory of truth, see Putnam (1997: 167–71); on Dewey's approval of Peirce's definition, see Tiles (1988: 106) and Shook (2000: 130).

11. Cf., e.g., CP 5.504n1, c. 1905. Peirce refers to his 1868 writings in the *Journal of Speculative Philosophy* (cf. CP 5.213 ff.; these can also be found in W 2, chs. 21–3, and in EP 1: chs. 2–4; see also Fisch 1986: 118).

12. Such alertness was, however, hardly denied by James (cf. Pihlström 1998a: ch. 6).

13. James (1909b [1977]: 153–4) referred favorably to what he regarded as affinities between Peirce and Bergson. This must have annoyed Peirce (see also NE 3/2: 836, 1909).

14. See, however, Misak's contribution to this *Companion*, "C. S. Peirce on Vital Matters." A less Peircean version of pragmatic moral realism is defended in Pihlström (2003).

15. A similar – rather unpragmatic – theory/practice distinction is at work in Peirce's 1903 lectures. Cf. also Putnam (1992a: 55–8).

16. For relevant correspondence, see Perry (1935/1936: II, 418–21). Peirce noted on January 4, 1898, that his first lecture would be about "vitally important topics," "showing that where they are 'vital' there is little chance for philosophy in them" (421). Peirce's lectures were stimulated by James's will to believe theory (Houser 1998: xxi).

17. Seigfried's reference is to James (1907 [1975]: 18) and (1909a [1978]: 28).

18. This extends to their views on religion. Peirce may have thought, with James, that we have a humanly natural tendency to believe in God (see CP 6.487, 1908; Roth 1965). In a letter to James's son Henry after William's death in 1910, Peirce said that *The Varieties of Religious Experience* was the best of James's books (Perry 1935/1936: II, 286). There may even be a version of the "will to believe" doctrine in Peirce (see CP 5.60/EP 2: 156, 1903; cf. Gavin 1980; Hookway 2000: 19; Kilpinen 2000: 117). Gavin (1980) argues that Peirce employed such a doctrine in

his identification of the real and the knowable – in his rejection of an incognizable *Ding an sich* (CP 5.257/W 2, 208ff., 1868).

19. See James (1909a [1978]: 31).

20. See also CP 5.422, 1905; 5.438, 1905; 5.468, c. 1906; 6.481, 1908; 8.191, c. 1904. A longer formulation is the following: "Pragmatism is the principle that every theoretical judgment expressible in a sentence in the indicative mood is a confused form of thought whose only meaning, if it has any, lies in its tendency to enforce a corresponding practical maxim expressible as a conditional sentence with its apodosis in the imperative mood" (CP 5.18/EP2: 134–5, 1903). For discussions of Peirce's maxim, see Apel (1981: ch. 4), Skagestad (1981: ch. 3), and Hookway (1985: ch. 8); on James's interpretation, see Hingst (2000). Recent scholarship appears to show that Peirce had enunciated the pragmatic principle at the Metaphysical Club not later than November 1872 (see the editors' introduction to W 3, xxixff.).

21. As Perry (1935/1936: II, 432n11) notes, James does not in fact *quote* this passage. It is a paraphrase, though inaccurate by Peirce's lights.

22. Some of Peirce's long letters to James were full of logical and mathematical formalisms – apparently Peirce tried to teach his friend some mathematics (see NE 3/2: 788–878). The selection of Peirce's letters to James in EP 2:492–502 is focused on semiotics.

23. On pragmatism as a logical method, cf. further Turrisi (1997a, 1997b) and Hookway (2000: 286 ff.).

24. Turrisi (1997a: 9) remarks that the title of the lectures, *Pragmatism as a Principle and Method of Right Thinking* (see CP 5.14–212/EP 2: chs. 10–16), was given by James. James probably authored the *Harvard Crimson* announcement on Peirce's lecture on March 26, 1903, which defined pragmatism as a philosophical system viewing philosophical questions "primarily from the standpoint of their practical bearing upon life" (Turrisi 1997a: 10; 1997b: 23).

25. On the question of whether Peirce was able to "prove" pragmatism, see Houser (1998) and Hookway (2000: ch. 12).

26. See, again, Misak's contribution to this volume, which seeks to show how Peirce "builds instinct into the scientific method." Peirce argued not only that we should not trust science in vitally important matters but also that *believing* has no place in science (CP 5.60/EP 2:156, 1903). It is problematic to fit such a view with his own belief/doubt theory of inquiry. Cf. Hookway (1998: § 5; 2000: ch. 1).

27. See Kant (1781/1787: A800/B828, A823–4/B851–2); for Peirce's way of making the distinction, see Thayer (1968: 138–139).

28. Dewey also occasionally reviewed Peirce's writings, for example, the first volume of Peirce's *Collected Papers* in *New Republic* 68 (1932).

29. Dewey's and Peirce's affinities were noted early. The psychologist James Rowland Angell wrote to James in 1898 that Peirce's pragmatism is "surprisingly like what Dewey is driving at." (See the editors' notes to James 1907 [1975]: 146.)

30. Dewey also criticized (in a letter to James in 1903) Peirce's metaphysical "hypostatizing of chance" (Perry 1935/1936: II, 523).

31. Cf. the discussions of Peirce's relation to later pragmatists by Thayer (1968), Kilpinen (2000), and Rescher (2000). The influence of pragmatism became, after its major early classics, also geographically so dispersed that it would be impossible to give any even nearly exhaustive survey here. For example, in Italy, there were both Jamesian pragmatists (e.g., Papini) and Peircean ones (Vailati and Calderoni) (Fisch 1986: 295–6; see Perry 1935/1936: II, ch. 84; Shook 1998; and Peirce's own note, N 3: 233–4, 1905).

32. Here Peirce implies that pragmatism is a "conception of reality" (and not a mere method of thought). From James's or Schiller's perspective, these may be practically indistinguishable.

33. "William James and F. C. S. Schiller maintain that God and everything else is finite – a doctrine some people call *pragmatism*. To me it is as abhorrent as it is incredible." (NE 3/2: 786, 1906.) Peirce remarked to James that pragmatism does not require renouncing ideas about the Absolute (NE 3/2: 871, 1909). One of James's applications of pragmatism was his criticism of the notion of the Absolute.

34. On the relation between Peirce and Wittgenstein, including Ramsey's influence, see Thayer (1968: 304–5), Bambrough (1981), Gullvåg (1981), Nubiola (1996), and Crocker (1998). In addition to his conversations with Ramsey, Wittgenstein must have been acquainted with Peirce through his reading of James's *Varieties*.

35. For a comparison between Peirce and Putnam, see Hookway (2001). Hookway points out (1) that it is not necessary to interpret Peirce as subscribing to the idea of an "absolute conception of the world"; (2) that Peirce may be seen as sharing James's (and Putnam's) view that reality can be relative to human thought, interests, or desires, since the concepts by means of which we classify things are "sensitive to a distinctive human perspective"; and (3) that Putnam's (1994) "natural realism" is comparable to Peirce's "critical commonsensism." It is an open question whether Putnam's defense of common sense would be sufficiently "critical" by Peirce's lights.

36. Thayer (1996) suggests that a neopragmatism which sees objects as "social constructs" might have been regarded as an example of the "a priori method" of belief-fixation by Peirce – as one of the methods Peirce found inferior to the scientific method (CP 5.382 ff./W 3, 252ff., 1877).

37. Among major philosophers of science, Isaac Levi (1991), in his studies on the dynamics of scientific belief, has been one of the most important followers of Peirce. On Peirce's relevance for communication studies, see Bergman (2000).

38. Tensions like the one between realism and idealism may be considered *unfruitful*. I believe, however, that such tensions, dilemmas, and open issues are extremely important in philosophy. They keep our philosophical wonder alive. This attitude to philosophical questions requires that one values the questions themselves, their openness and even their unclarity, more than the "results" that may be achieved, in a way resembling scientific inquiry, in the course of philosophizing. See Pihlström (1998a).

39. See the drafts on the notion of reality in Peirce's 1872–1873 investigations of logic (W 3, 28–61). On Peirce's attempt to combine "semeiotic" or "discursive" realism with idealism, see Houser (1992).

40. Cf. Putnam (1981: ch. 3) and (1990).

41. While Peirce moved from a view resembling transcendental idealism to a more realistic position, he may have come closer to transcendental idealism in his latest thought (Hookway 1985: 117). I have discussed the Kantian nature of the pragmatist tradition elsewhere (Pihlström 1996, 1998a, 1998b, 2003). The common Kantian tension shared by the pragmatisms of Peirce, James, Dewey, Putnam, Rorty, and others is a good reason to reject the popular dualisms between "two pragmatisms." Some scholars who recognize the Kantian background of Peirce's thought – e.g., Christensen (1994), influenced by Apel – are committed to this simplistic picture, assuming that Peirce's pragmati(ci)sm is fundamentally different from the James–Rorty lineage.

42. I am grateful to Cheryl Misak for having invited me to contribute to this *Companion* and for her enormously useful comments on earlier drafts. I also wish to thank Mats Bergman, Susan Haack, Leila Haaparanta, Peter H. Hare, Erkki Kilpinen, Ilkka Niiniluoto, Jaime Nubiola, Sami Paavola, Richard S. Robin, and Kenneth R. Westphal, all of whom have taught me a lot about Peirce and pragmatism.

3 Peirce and Medieval Thought[1]

I

Introduction

Peirce's knowledge of and attitude toward medieval thought was clearly unusual among his peers,[2] and it contains some interesting surprises. His critical remarks, of course, while more colorful than most, are not unexpected.[3]

It is not worth our while...to ascertain what the schoolmasters of that degenerate age conceived mathematics to be. (CP 3.554, 1898)

[A] beastlike superficiality and lack of generalizing thought spreads like a pall over the writings of the scholastic masters of logic.... (CP 1.561, 1907)

Moreover, he seems to think the entire era was, with the possible exception of Roger Bacon, lacking in a scientific appreciation or outlook.[4]

Peirce's criticism of the later decadent scholasticism is of special interest for its reference to the followers of Scotus who had gained control of the universities and were given (by the humanists) the sarcastic title of "dunses" or "dunces" (CP 1.17–18, 1903; 2.166–8, 1902). They "set up their idle logical distinctions as precluding all physical inquiry" (CP 6.361, 1902). And while they were on the right side of the realist–nominalist issue, "their dunsical opposition to the new learning and their dreadful corruption of the university disgusted the new men" (CP 7.666, 1903).[5]

At the same time, Peirce's putdown of the humanists' reaction to the scholastics is if possible even more rude. The Dunses defended their position "with a logical accuracy, born of centuries of study, with which the new men were utterly incapable of coping"; they needed to formulate objections to the Dunses' positions, but it was "a business for which they were utterly unfitted" (CP 6.361).[6] The humanists, he says "were weak thinkers" (CP 1.18). "The *renaissance*...condemned the scholastic terms as not being Ciceronian, with the result of making *renaissance* philosophy as soft and savorless as a sage pudding" (CP 7.494 n9, c1898).

But, Peirce says, one should no more confuse the decadent scholastics with the work of the preceding high Scholastic period than link "the humanists" with the modern philosophy and science that followed them (CP 8.11, 1871). In fact, his praise of the high Scholastics can be extravagant. Duns Scotus is a genius (CP 2.166, 1902),[7] "one of the greatest metaphysicians of all time" (CP 4.28, 1893), and at least the greatest defender of realism, while Ockham is the greatest nominalist (CP 1.29, 1869).[8] And along with some later British logicians, Scotus and Ockham "can be used to lay a solid foundation on which to erect a new logic fit for the life of twentieth century science" (CP 7.161, 1902). Scotus is even singled out as in a class with Aristotle and Leibniz – and Peirce (!).[9]

When Peirce speaks of Scotus and Ockham as great logicians (CP 1.29), what he admired was not their logical theory but their rigorous application of a logical method.[10]

But [their] logic, relatively to the general condition of thought, was marvellously exact and critical. They can tell us nothing concerning methods of reasoning since their own reasoning was puerile; but their analyses of thought and their discussions of all those questions of logic that almost trench upon metaphysics are very instructive as well as very good discipline in that subtle kind of thinking that is required in logic. (CP 1.15, 1903)[11]

And:

[A]bove all things, it is the searching thoroughness of the schoolmen that affiliates them with men of science and separates them, worldwide, from so-called philosophers. The thoroughness I allude to consists in this, that in adopting any theory, they go about everywhere, they devote their whole energies and lives putting it to tests *bona fide* – not such as shall merely add a new spangle to the glitter of their proofs but such as really go toward satisfying their restless insatiable impulse to put their opinions to the *test*. Having a theory, they must apply it to every subject and to every branch of every subject to see whether it produces a result in accordance with the only criteria they were able to apply – the truth of the Catholic faith and the teaching of the Prince of the Philosophers. (CP 1.33, 1869)

The mix of criticism and praise in Peirce's attitude towards medieval thinkers is especially intriguing when it comes to authority; for he thinks the whole era was characterized by its respect for authority: "The most striking characteristic of medieval reasoning, in general, is the perpetual resort to authority" (CP 5.215n, 1893). The backhanded compliment he offers on this score offers no relief: the weight they attached to authority "would be excessive were not the human mind at the time in so uneducated a state that it could not do better than follow masters, since it was totally incompetent to solve metaphysical problems for itself ... " (CP 1.31).[12]

Given what Peirce has to say about the method of authority in "How To Make Our Ideas Clear" (CP 5.379ff, 1878), one must wonder that he did not dismiss the period entirely.[13] So it is a surprise when he gives a special twist to the Scholastics' dedication to authority:

The great object of the metaphysics of Duns Scotus is so to state the results of ordinary experience, that it shall not close any positive experimental inquiry, or pronounce anything possibly observable to be *a priori* impossible. In Scotus this naturally led to loyalty to Authority, then the recognized fountain of truth; in our day it will produce unfaltering faith in Observation. (CP 7.395, 1893)

This loyalty to authority meant that the medievals were less interested in originality than in consistency of interpretation; and they were remarkably free of "the vanity of cleverness" (CP 1.31, 1859). Peirce continues:

All these characters remind us less of the philosophers of our day than of men of science. I do not hesitate to say that scientific men now think much more of authority than do metaphysicians; for in science a question is not regarded as settled or its solution as certain until all intelligent and informed doubt has ceased and all competent persons have come to a catholic agreement. ... (CP 1.32, 1869)[14]

It is clear, I think, that Peirce has a moral to preach here as much about modern as about medieval thought. While his peers in the United States and Europe saw themselves as (critically) advancing the cause of modern philosophical thought, Peirce increasingly saw himself, if not in opposition, at least as proposing a radical overhaul. And perhaps nothing would get the attention of his readers so much as flagrantly lining himself up with the thought of a "backward" age and outlook.[15] But his remarks carry a substantive philosophical point as well. Consider:

The logical upshot of the doctrine of Scotus is that real problems cannot be solved by metaphysics, but must be decided according to the evidence. As he was a theologian, that evidence was, for him, the dicta of the church. But the same system in the hands of a scientific man will lead to his insisting upon submitting everything to the test of observation. (CP 4.28, 1893)

Peirce was writing at a time when grand system-building was prominent, and it would be part of his pragmatist outlook to insist that the real world does not reveal itself to armchair theorizing.[16] What he recognized in the medievals' respect for authority was a check on the penchant of philosophers to let their theorizing dictate what the world is really like.

II

In any event, it is from Peirce's explicit remarks that we have the clearest indication of his readings and the possible influence of medieval thought upon his own. I shall take up some of the more obvious aspects of that in Section III. But there are two other sources of evidence for possible medieval influences. The one has to do with what we can identify from references he makes to medieval texts and from hints for a reconstruction of Peirce's own library. The other has to do with similarities (acknowledged or not) to positions of medieval thinkers. None of the three sorts of evidence is without its problems, as I shall try to explain as I go along.

In fact – that is, as I see it – we may not yet be in a position to provide a definitive account of medieval influences on Peirce. It is extremely unlikely that there is a smoking gun yet to be discovered in the unpublished manuscripts, but there are some familiar enough factors that complicate the enterprise. One, of course, is the constant development within Peirce's own thinking. Another has to do with improvements in our own understanding of both Peirce and the medievals. What we (should) have learned from the good work that has been done in recent years is that the better we understand them the more we realize there is to know. Fortunately for my present purposes, we already know enough to allow some plausible remarks about where we are today.

A. A Little History[17]

Actually, Peirce seems to have had an interest in and a flair for the history of philosophy,[18] though it was motivated, I think, more by philosophical than historical concerns:

The chief value of the study of historical philosophy is that it disciplines the mind to regard philosophy with a cold and scientific eye and not with passion as though philosophers were contestants. (CP 1.28; cf., CP 8.9)

At a relatively early age, he had been forcibly immersed in Kant by his father, Benjamin Peirce (CP 3.405). And during his Harvard College education (and beyond) he seems to have read the texts in modern philosophy that would have been standard (Hookway 1985: 4–6, 12). But, sometime around the mid–1860s, perhaps dissatisfied with the logic texts of his time, he undertook a concentrated study of the history of logic.[19] It was that project that led him to read extensively in (ancient and) medieval sources and introduced him to the broader range of philosophical analysis in the later Middle Ages.

Peirce graduated from Harvard College in 1859 and had already written some metaphysical (but unpublished) essays around 1860 (Hookway 1985: 4). In 1863, he received (in effect) a graduate degree in chemistry. As a promising scholar (still only 25 years old), he was invited to give a series of lectures on the logic of science.[20] Hookway thinks they may have contained material that would appear in the anti-Cartesian/intuition articles of 1868–1869 (Hookway 1985: 6). Just where Peirce found the texts necessary for his early study of the medievals is not altogether clear (to me).[21] In any event, by the time of his teaching career at Johns Hopkins (1879–1884), Peirce had amassed an extensive library of medieval texts; and in 1880, he offered to sell it to the university library there.[22] Of course, Peirce had been traveling widely before this, and most of the books were purchased between 1866 and 1871 in various cities in Europe which would have provided a plentiful market for obtaining medieval (and other) texts.[23]

B. Peirce's Library

We know from the enthusiastic support for the purchase by the librarian at Johns Hopkins that the collection was a noteworthy one, apparently over two hundred items, though not all on medieval sources.[24]

Fisch gives a sketchy description of the works on the library's accessions list and, more importantly, of the rather sad history of the collection (Fisch, 1986: 52–3). Fortunately, the bulk of the collection is still in the Johns Hopkins library, including thirty-four incanabula. But in somewhat typical fashion, Peirce borrowed back a number of the books. He meant to repurchase the entire collection, but never had the money to do so. Some of the books he kept went to Harvard when they purchased Peirce's papers.[25] But others may have been burned when Peirce's widow died in 1934 (Fisch, 1986: 54).

C. Citations (of Medieval Authors)

When we turn to Peirce's own writings, we find a good number of exact quotations and even more specific references to ancient and medieval writers. Just working from the indices of the *Collected Papers*, and leaving aside his references to Aristotle and to Stoic and Epicurean logic, the list would include Augustine, Boethius, Cassiodorus, Scotus Eriugena, Anselm, Abelard, John of Salisbury, Alexander of Hales, Peter of Spain, William of Auvergne, Roger Bacon, Albert the Great, Avicenna and Averroes, Thomas Aquinas, Henry of Ghent, Duns Scotus, William Ockham, and Paul of Venice.[26]

Most of these citations appeared as entries in Baldwin's *Dictionary of Philosophy and Psychology*, which was published in 1901–1902. Peirce had before then "retired" to Arisbe in Milford, Pennsylvania; and while he may have retained accurate notes from earlier readings and conceivably even traveled to a library such as Johns Hopkins, the more likely implication is that he had (many of) the texts with him. A number of general allusions to medieval writers appear even earlier as introductions, by way of the history of the field, in drafts of his efforts to construct a comprehensive text on Logic.[27]

There are also some cases where, even without explicit citation, Peirce is clearly working with a medieval text: for example, in the review of Frazer's *Berkeley*, he has in front of him Scotus's treatment of universals from Book VII, q. 18, of the *Questions on the Metaphysics* (Duns Scotus 1997: II, 337–56).[28]

D. Similarities

Alan Perriah has suggested a further source of evidence for possible medieval influences on Peirce's thought: similarities in doctrine even if not explicitly identified by Peirce (Perriah 1989: 41–9). He suggests (but does not mean as exhaustive): the idea of modes of being and modes of propositions, the normative character of logic, the priority of dialectical reasoning, logic and probability, semantics of signs (e.g., signification and supposition), and of course the nominalist–realist debate. It is an interesting idea but I think it deserves a word of caution. One would like ideally to distinguish cases of influence on Peirce's thought from those where he simply found in the medievals positions that he liked.[29] It takes a trained eye to distinguish appearance and reality here (as elsewhere). In effect, one has to be familiar with both Peirce and the relevant medievals, and as I have suggested earlier, that would involve keeping up with the best of recent commentary.

Peirce's allusions to "speculative grammar" seem to me a case in point.[30] The 1639 Wadding edition of Scotus's works contained a number of works we now know were not written by Scotus,[31] one of which is *Grammatica Speculativa* by Thomas Erfurt. "Speculativa" simply means "theoretical," and medieval speculative grammar was an attempt to provide a formal grammar, in part from a study of natural languages and in part from logical structure. It is not hard to see why Peirce might not make great use of it,[32] for its "formal" character relies heavily on a subject–predicate analysis of Latin and Greek models.[33] But it should already be suspicious, I think, that while Peirce refers to the medieval work frequently, he never quotes from it or even gives exact citations.[34]

The key to Peirce's interest in the topic lies in his identifying speculative grammar with what he calls "Erkenntnislehre" or sometimes "Elementarlehre,"[35] an idea he more likely got from Kant than from Scotus/Erfurt. We can see what he had in mind from an important early article "On a New List of the Categories" (CP 1.545–59, 1867).[36] For Kant, very roughly put, categories can be derived from the logical forms of judgments and represent the ways the mind structures experience. Peirce was sympathetic to both these ideas,[37] objecting only (!) to Kant's having insufficiently generalized the basic nature of logical form; and the "New List" was his first effort to correct that (CP 1.560–4).

The "New List" is a very original work expressed in traditional terminology. Its three categories of Quality (reference to a ground), Relation (reference to a correlate), and Representation (reference to an

interpretant) mediate between "Substance" and "Being" (CP 1.555).
In the process, however, Peirce is able to set out his basic triad of
signs, likeness (later icon), index, and symbol (CP 1.558), and to de-
lineate his three types of inference, deduction, hypothesis (later abduction), and induction (CP 1.559). He even manages to hint at his
later most abstract characterization of categories in terms of valencies: i.e., monadic, dyadic, and triadic.

In the final analysis, however, the "New List" proves inadequate
to Peirce's purposes, in large part because the *way* he derives the
categories there essentially depends upon a subject–predicate (or "*S*
is *P*") form in its analysis of propositions.[38] Hookway (1985: 80–117)
has an extensive discussion of the "New List" and most importantly
of the transformation in Peirce's approach to the derivation of categories, both in the more abstract device of valencies and in the more
concrete "phenomenological" approach. I have a little something to
say about the latter toward the end of section III; but, fortunately for
me, the very complex and controversial topic of Peirce's mature category theory impinges only marginally on the question of medieval
influences.

To return to the immediate topic at hand, I am not suggesting
that speculative grammar, aka *Erkenntnislehre*, is not important for
Peirce, or that a study of the medieval treatises would not be valuable
in its own right. But I do not think one would learn a lot about the
former by examining the latter. That Peirce saw in it a forerunner
to his own interests seems to me a more likely hypothesis than its
having been an influence on his thought.

III

Peirce's Scholastic Realism

The best known and most commented upon case of medieval influence on Peirce is his self-ascribed "scholastic/Scotistic realism":[39]

I should call myself an Aristotelian of the scholastic wing, approaching Sco-
tism, but going much further in the direction of scholastic realism. (CP 5.77
n1, 1903)

No one doubts Peirce's claim that he was significantly influenced by
reading Scotus and other Scholastics, but there is some controversy

about when, how much, and what Peirce ultimately made of it. The answer to those questions, however, is complicated by, among other things, Peirce's own development, both in his logical theory (e.g., where he moved away from the subject–predicate form as basic) and in his mature, three-categoried ontology.[40] Still, one can make out the general lines of an answer. As for the details, however, I shall not try to give a full account of either Peirce's or Scotus's realism but will develop only enough of their positions to deal with questions of similarity and influence.[41] For reasons that should become clear in Section IV, I shall concentrate on Peirce's earlier formulations.

There are interesting and significant differences in the way medievals handled various semantic issues,[42] but from early on there was no confusion about what makes a term universal: i.e., not that it signifies a general entity but that it signifies many individuals. After all, were the term "donkey" to stand for some general entity, it would function rather as a proper name. We can call this one–many character of the signification of general terms "universality"; it is clearly a property of signs and not of the things they signify. But the dispute that came to be called the (sic) problem of universals had to do not with universality but with the objective status of natural kinds.[43] And in the medieval controversy at least, two conditions provide the context of that discussion; for while the Scholastics held that science is of the universal and necessary they took individual substances to be ontologically prior.[44] They readily talked of essences and/or natures as well as of abstract entities such as justice, but their tendency was to reject any realm of "separate" entities, an attitude reinforced by Aristotle's criticism of Plato. Even where they found a role for Plato's Ideas as examplars in the mind of God (i.e., patterns according to which God created things), these were distinguished from forms inherent in creatures.

Along with other Scholastic realists, Scotus proposes what we might call a "metaphysical" composition *within* things (or first substances),[45] in his case that of common nature(s) and haecceity (or "thisness").[46] He marshalls a set of arguments to show that the natures of things, as common, have a real but "less than numerical unity" which is required to ground the objectivity of our scientific knowledge.[47] And he is renowned for maintaining (against Aquinas and others) haecceity or thisness as a positive principle of individuation. Moreover, while he emphasizes the reality of common natures, he holds that the nature is "contracted to the mode of the individual" in actually existing things (CP 8.208, 1910).[48] This is important for a number of reasons, as we shall see, but for the moment it is enough to note that, for Scotus, the analysis into components is not reductive: they are not merely found in substance but are importantly dependent upon substance as primary being.

William Ockham, who is Peirce's favorite nominalist (CP 1.29), is equally committed to the priority of first substance, and he is perfectly clear that Scotus (like other realists such as Aquinas) was trying to protect the objectivity of knowledge without postulating an extramental general thing. But he thinks that the appeal to special components of things, forms (Aquinas) or common natures (Scotus), cannot avoid blurring a crucial boundary between what is real or outside the mind and what is conceptual or in the mind, thus making real things somehow relative to or dependent upon the mind.[49]

We might assume, then, that we are on familiar ground when in his earliest extended account of the nominalist–realist dispute, which occurs in his review of Frazer's *Berkeley* (CP 8.7–38, 1871), Peirce says:

The question, therefore is whether *man*, *horse*, and other names of natural classes, correspond with anything which all men, or all horses, really have in common, independent of our thought, or whether these classes are constituted simply by a likeness in the way our minds are affected by individual objects which have in themselves no resemblance or relationship whatsoever. (CP 8.12)

And in an earlier brief reference to the Scholastic outlook:

Objects are divided into figments, dreams, etc., on the one hand, and realities on the other. The former are those which exist only inasmuch as you or I or some man imagines them; the latter are those which have an existence independent of your mind or mine or that of any number of persons. The real is that which is not whatever we happen to think of it, but is unaffected by what we may think of it. (CP 5.311, 1868)[50]

But the reader is in for a surprise when Peirce goes on to explain what the dispute was really about. He begins it this way:

The current explanations of the realist–nominalist controversy are equally false and unintelligible[51] . . . Yet it is perfectly possible so to state the matter that no one shall fail to comprehend what the question was, and how there might be two opinions about it. Are universals real? We have only to stop and consider a moment what was meant by the word *real*, when the whole issue soon becomes apparent. (CP 8.12)

As it happens, Peirce's sense of the obvious is itself something to wonder at. For he devotes the next four or five pages to a discussion of the "two views of reality" in a way which at first glance seems to have more to do with idealism than realism. But while one cannot dismiss the idealist idiom, I think it may be something of a distraction. Peirce is not embarrassed about favoring idealism so he has no reason to hide that behind the Scholastics. It will be the main burden of my account here to show how this early (1871) account exhibits the central elements of what, for Peirce, is Scholastic realism.

In order to see that, one should begin with Peirce's description there of nominalism. On the nominalist view, he says, reality lies wholly "outside the mind" (or *extra animam*); it causes our sensations and through them our conceptions (which are *in anima*). These are not geographical locations, of course; what is "in the mind" is not a mental act, but something more like its content: being "in" the mind is rather like being "in" a picture or "in" a story. This insistence on a sharp "internal–external" distinction is, for Peirce, a nominalist fixation.[52] It is also something Peirce could well have learned about from Ockham for whom "the worst error in philosophy" is to confuse the properties of our representative system with the properties of real things.[53]

The point, for the nominalist, is that the real has to be wholly independent of the conceptual.[54] As Peirce will say later:

The heart of the dispute lies in this. The [nominalists] ... recognize but one mode of being, the being of an individual thing or fact, the being which consists in the object's crowding out a place for itself in the universe, so to speak, and reacting by brute force of fact, against all other things. I call that existence. (CP 1.21, 1903)[55]

Peirce comes to identify nominalism with the claim that "reality" and "existence" are synonymous (CP 5.503, 1905). While this description appears only after Peirce has developed an explicit theory of (three) modes of being,[56] the doctrine itself can be seen in the "nominalistic Platonism" he had identified already in the *Berkeley* review (CP 8.10): philosophers who wanted to preserve the objectivity of scientific laws but recognized only the one mode of being had to suppose that real generals were themselves individual things.[57] The Scholastics' rejection of that move, in favor of special constituents, is not what made them "moderate" in Peirce's eyes, but what made them realists. It is easy to miss this important point.[58]

In any event, Peirce thinks Ockham's (or any nominalist's) effort to maintain an ontological purity ultimately creates an unbridgeable gap between the way things really are and the way we conceive of them: not just between what is individual and what is general, but between the real condition of external things and the properties we conceive them to have.[59] From his nineteenth century perspective, Peirce describes this as making the real an unknowable thing-in-itself (e.g., CP 8.13). The idealist idiom continues in his description of the contrasting, realist conception, where the real is located not in what starts the thought process but in its result, which is the opinion that any inquirer (given the proper circumstances) would arrive at:

This final opinion, then, is independent, not indeed of thought in general, but of all that is arbitrary and individual in thought. (CP 8.12)[60]

And then:

It is plain that this view of reality is inevitably realistic; because general conceptions enter into all judgments, and therefore into true opinions ... It is a real which only exists by virtue of an act of thought knowing it; but that thought is not an arbitrary or accidental one ... but one which will hold in the final opinion. (CP 8.14)

And finally:

[W]hat Kant called his Copernican step was precisely the passage from the nominalistic to the realistic view of reality. It was the essence of his philosophy to regard the real object as determined by the mind. (CP 8.15)

One might well wonder how a nice, young Aristotelian Scholastic like Scotus could get mixed up with all of this! Before looking at Scotus more closely, however, a comment on Peirce's account here is in order. For it seems clear enough (if only from what he says later) that Peirce is not proposing a simple commitment to idealism, as if trying to make Scotus a precursor to the post-Kantians. After all, one could easily make out a "nominalistic idealism" on the model of "nominalistic Platonism." What makes for *Scholastic* realism is the appeal to "constituents,"[61] not to real things that are thoughtlike but rather to an aspect of things that must be real if our knowledge is objective. What Peirce sees in the Scholastics, I think, is an appeal to a *structure* in things that is analogous to the *structure* of thought.[62] Finally, Peirce will not maintain that a commitment to an existence independent of thought must be eliminated but that it be complemented with another mode of reality (CP 7.339, 1873).

To return to Scotus, then, what is unique to his position (among scholastics) is that he brings the two components, common natures and haecceity, under the "formal distinction *a parte rei*," a notorious device that at least creates a real distinction among commentators and alone could have earned him the title of "Most Subtle Doctor."

His theory of "formalities" was the sublest, except perhaps Hegel's logic, ever broached, and he was separated from nominalism only by the division of a hair. (CP 8.11) [63]

It is understandable that Scotus would want a distinction here that is something of an *entre deux*: i.e., not merely a logical distinction (as between the author of Rob Roy and the author of Ivanhoe), but also not a strong real distinction as between two things (*res et res*). But there are features peculiar to the formal distinction that would be attractive to Peirce even if they complicate the description of Scotus.[64]

The formal distinction requires a special sort of term: not forms, Scotus says, but *formalitates*, not *res et res* but *realitates*.[65] What we have then is not just a somewhat strange distinction between otherwise familiar sorts of things but rather (or more) a special distinction between somewhat strange sorts of thing. In cashing this in, moreover, one must balance the idea that the distinction is objective (that is, *a parte rei*) with an unavoidable reference to conceivability. Here is a recent interpreter's effort to characterize it:

A formal distinction is a distinction from the nature of the thing occurring between two or more really identical formalities, of which one, before the operation of the intellect, is conceivable without the others though inseparable from them even by divine power. (Grajewski 1944: 93)

That is, the distinction holds prior to the act of any intellect; but it is even so a matter of what *would be* conceived by a truly knowing mind.[66] It is not that formalities are to be confused with thoughts about them; but their being relative to thought goes beyond a psychological or epistemological claim that this is the only way *we* can describe them.[67]

In describing the formal distinction in Scotus, I have focused on the status of formalities or realities as *what would be conceived* because I think that is the background for Peirce's early (and continuing) approach to the nominalist–realist dispute in terms of views of "reality." That is to say, despite the idealist idiom, the emphasis in the *Berkeley* review on a realist conception of reality seems to me identifiably "Scotistic." Moreover, the ground for Peirce's later identification of (three) modes of being[68] can be found, even in this original presentation, in the genuinely "Scholastic" appeal to constituents, i.e., to a structure in things analogous to the structure of predication. These broad Scotistic/Scholastic elements are never abandoned by Peirce, though something needs to be said about the transformation they undergo in his developing metaphysics.[69]

From some of his later formulations of the categories, one might be led to think that Peirce means to be talking, as Scotus is, about aspects or features of the sorts of individuals that the medievals (and most of the rest of us) take as making up the familiar world in which we live. On this approach, Firstness, Secondness, and Thirdness could be seen as, say, the quality, brute existence, and lawlike behavior exhibited by first substances. Properly understood, however, familiar physical objects for Peirce are lawlike processes, systems, *constituted* by Firstness, Secondness, and Thirdness rather than being supportive of them.[70] But there are other changes as well.

Haecceity, to begin there,[71] may look as if it goes directly into Secondness for Peirce. But its primary ontological role for him is not at all to reflect the priority of familiar individual things as first substances. Secondness, which is haecceity transformed,[72] is something of a surd: it is the brute facticity of our encounter with an external world. It is not the content or intelligibility of that encounter but the pure resistance of, say, tugging at a stuck door (CP 1.324) or the shock of having one's reverie interrupted by being knocked to the ground (CP 1.431); hence its dyadic character. It is important for Peirce,[73] but not as a feature of physical objects, as if the latter were ontologically prior.

Firstness is variously described by Peirce (Hookway 1985: 106–7). It is "the mode of being which consists in a subject's being positively such as it is regardless of all else [which is] a positive qualitative possibility" (CP 1.25). In this case, the more abstract characterizations may help: it is monadic (and so is independent of any instantiation); and it is pure possibility and so different from potentiality which belongs to Thirdness.[74]

Thirdness is I think basic, as it were the first among three equals in Peirce's mature metaphysics. And though he will locate the real generality that concerned medieval realists under Thirdness, it is not so much the commonness of natures that Peirce thinks must be recognized in the objective discoveries of science as it is the reality of "would-be's" that are not exhausted by (or reducible to) any one or more actual events or Seconds (CP 1.422). It is to this that Peirce ultimately ascribes his own "extreme realism":

I myself went too far in the direction of nominalism when I said that it was a mere convenience of speech whether we say that a diamond is hard when it is not pressed upon, or whether we say it is soft until pressed upon. [Cf. CP 5.403, 1878] ... It is a real fact that it *would* resist pressure, which amounts to extreme scholastic realism. (CP 8.208, 1905)

As it happens, there is a Scotistic background for that development as well, though it is not so clearly acknowledged as such by Peirce. It is to be found less in Scotus's account of real generals than in his account of potentiality.[75] After all, while the nature "loses" its commonness in the individual substance for Scotus, potentiality can transcend its exercise. The potential house is "replaced" by the actual house that is built. But while he is an actual and no longer a potential builder when he is on the job, the builder's capacity for building houses is not displaced by that activity.[76]

Let me conclude this section with what is perhaps the most basic difference from Scotus, reflected in Peirce's complaint about "contraction":

Even Duns Scotus is too nominalistic when he says that universals are contracted to the mode of individuality in singulars, meaning as he does, by singulars, ordinary existing things. The pragmaticist cannot admit that. (CP 8.208, 1905)[77]

There are, I think, three things going on here. First, contraction for Scotus preserves the ontological priority of first substance; and Peirce means to deny that. While Firstness, Secondness, and Thirdness are never found apart from one another, they each have an independent status so that they are prior to and not brought together in or supported by a subject that is metaphysically prior. The second role of contraction for Scotus is that it grounds the activity of substances in their individual natures. For Peirce, as we have seen, the reality of Thirdness is located in objective "would-be's" which are not exhausted in any act or actual condition of things. The scholastics, of course, relied heavily on potencies in their explanation of the activities of things, but they still saw the ground for that activity in certain actual conditions (e.g., forms or natures) of individual substances.[78]

The third problem with Scotus's contraction is not something that Peirce calls explicit attention to, but it is basic for him; and it returns us to Peirce's early description of nominalism in the *Berkeley* review: contraction reintroduces a gap between the way things are and the way we conceive them to be. And it is that rather than a restriction on generality that I think Peirce finds "nominalistic." The gap is perhaps narrower in Scotus than in Aquinas, but it is something Peirce would be especially sensitive to.[79]

Conclusions

"[G]eneral principles are really operative in nature. That is the doctrine of scholastic realism" (CP 5.101, 1903). The form this takes in Peirce is a commitment not to a new sort of thing (individual) but to a new sort of constituent, the analogue of the predicate function in the expression of our thought. The status of that sort of constituent in his Scotistic realism is that of a formality or reality, which is what a truly knowing mind would conceive. If I am right, this general structure of Scholastic realism, as Peirce sees it in contrast to a nominalistic Platonism, is already in place in the *Berkeley* review. Whether the important concept of *potentia* should be seen as part of Scholastic realism or simply as another Scotistic/Scholastic influence is not crucial.

What needs emphasis is that the contribution of Scholastic realism is only one element in the development of Peirce's ultimate position.[80] For example, that reality, properly understood, is somehow thought-relative is not something new for Peirce even in

1871. It is early on associated with the idea of a community of inquiry; and it is not unfair to say that Peirce is still struggling at the end of his life with a scheme for grounding the objectivity of these thought-relative data.[81] Then, the Scholastic constituents, of course, are radically transformed as modes of being that constitute rather than depend upon individual substances. Even the identification of generals in "would-be's" goes beyond the Scholastic idea of potentiality.

Given the extent of these developments, is Peirce right to persist in calling himself a Scholastic realist? Commentators whose simple answers to that question are different may not always differ about the facts of the case.[82] Once one is clear about the details of his "Scholastic realism" and his "extreme realism," however, I do not see any profit in worrying over the labels.

IV

In making out a case for Peirce's "Scholastic realism," I have concentrated on its early appearance while noting some of the important transformations that accrue in the course of his developing logic and metaphysics. But something needs to be said about the place of realism itself in Peirce's development, brief and sketchy though it will have to be. It can perhaps serve as a kind of review.

In 1891, Peirce says that "never, during the thirty years in which I have been writing on philosophical questions, have I failed in my allegiance to realistic opinions and to certain Scotistic ideas" (CP 6.605). But in a very important article, Max Fisch claims that Peirce has located that allegiance about five years too early (Fisch 1986: 197–8). He places Peirce's intensive study of the medievals in 1868–1869,[83] though that would not preclude Peirce's holding a realist position without yet knowing that it was "Scholastic." More importantly, Fisch claims that, until he was 29 years old, Peirce was willing to call himself and be called a nominalist.[84] Fisch then argues that Peirce first runs up the realist flag toward the end of "Some Consequences of Four Incapacities" (CP 5.312, 1868), one of his anti-Cartesian (or anti-intuition) articles. But this "first step towards realism," Fisch claims, was actually only a "rider on his early idealism" (Fisch 1986: 193). Even the more fully developed account in the *Berkeley* review seems to Fisch only "a second step *towards* realism" (Fisch 1986:

188, italics mine), where Fisch is evidently thinking of the later realism that is fully developed in Peirce only after the turn of the century (Fisch 1986: 187–88).[85]

Fisch then points out that "for nearly two decades," from 1872 to 1890, Peirce is almost silent on the nominalism–realism issue while concentrating on major developments in the logic of relations, a revision of his theory of categories, his pragmaticist commitment to would-be's, and doing work on transfinite numbers that formed a preparation for his theory of real continuity (Fisch 1986: 188). Fisch sees these changes as a matter of Peirce's progressively abandoning recalcitrant "nominalistic" positions (e.g., on the material conditional in his early pragmatic maxim, and the definition of the possible).[86] And he suggests that it may have been while preparing for his contributions to the Century Dictionary that Peirce undertook a review of the history of philosophy that re-energized his interest in the medieval debate (Fisch 1986: 192).

In any event, after 1890, especially in drafts for the Grand Logic, references to realism become prominent again, for example in the first fully explicit account of three modes of being, where haecceity gets a new emphasis[87] and pragmatism is associated with realism (Fisch 1986: 195). Finally, Fisch claims that a late conversion to a doctrine of Immediate Perception (connected in part with the emphasis on Scotus's haecceities as Secondness) constitutes a rejection of idealism in favor of what is finally Peirce's ultimate position on "realism" (Fisch 1986: 192–6). These changes, he adds, opened up whole new lines of development which Peirce struggled with but never brought to completion before his death in 1914 (Fisch 1986: 196–7).

As is evident from the last section, I find a more substantial Scholastic realism in Peirce's 1871 formulations than Fisch (inter alia) does. But I have no quarrel with Fisch's account of the many developments that took place between that and Peirce's later return to the topic of realism. After all, it only reinforces my own emphasis on the limited (if important) influence of his Scholastic realism on the later realism. But I have my doubts about the "nominalism to realism" story as the best format for understanding Peirce's overall development. Of course, there may be no one story that would do the job.[88] But I will close my account with two comments on the picture Fisch offers.

To begin at the beginning, a youthful espousal of nominalism does not seem to me to provide a very solid base from which to view Peirce's subsequent development. At that time, being a nominalist was the politically correct stance for someone who wanted to give the impression of having a hard-headed and scientific outlook. It is unlikely, moreover, that even if Peirce held a number of "nominalistic" positions, he was committed at that time to anything like a developed theory of nominalism.[89]

The end of Fisch's story strikes me as even more problematic. Fisch claims that Peirce ultimately rejects his idealism because of the realism of his late doctrine of Immediate Perception.[90] What Peirce says is:

Every philosopher who denies the doctrine of Immediate Perception – including idealists of every stripe – by that denial cuts off all possibility of ever cognizing a relation. (CP 5.56, 1903)

But this is, I think, misleading. If the doctrine of Immediate Perception is supposed to be a form of Direct Realism, it is opposed to representationalism, which is not a peculiarly idealist position. Peirce may have at one time maintained a form of representationalism (CP 8.12),[91] but he seems to me all along to favor the broader sort of "objective idealism" which argues not that the immediate object of knowledge is our own ideas but (roughly) that if knowledge is possible, the real as the object of knowledge must be idea-like: cf. (CP 5.553, 1906).[92]

In fact, Peirce's doctrine of Immediate Perception is not a matter of perceiving ordinary physical objects as such, as an allusion to Direct Realism might suggest. It has to do with the brute encounter of Secondness; and we still need to introduce the aspects of Firstness and Thirdness to provide any intellectual content to the experience. But any experience that includes the latter will be woefully underdetermined by the brute encounter with Secondness, leaving us again with an appeal to the object of the final opinion to establish the objectivity of any empirical claim based upon it.[93] And that, to my mind, could even lead us into the issue of realism and antirealism.[94]

In sum, to try to bring realism-versus-nominalism and realism-versus-representationalism (and realism-versus-antirealism) under a single heading is more likely to be confusing than illuminating.[95]

For my present purposes, it may be enough to note that it takes us well beyond the topic of medieval influences.

NOTES

1. The rather bland title reflects my caution about claims of influence (on which more later). All my direct references to Peirce are from the *Collected Papers*. They are, however, chronologically challenged, so I have often included the dates of passages I cite.

2. He was in fact a perceptive reader of the history of ideas in the Middle Ages and his extended accounts, too long to quote here, are worth looking at: e.g., CP 4.1, 1829, 4.21–37, 1893, 8.9–11, 1871; see also CP 2.166–8, 1902 and 6.312, 1891. Though he should have known better than to lay the canard about angels dancing on the head of a pin onto Aquinas (CP 8.11). He also anticipates Panofsky's analogy of gothic architecture and Scholasticism (1957) with (to my mind) equally little effect (CP 4.27 and 8.11).

3. The entire era does not get off unscathed, but his harshest remarks are rarely directed at the figures of high Scholasticism and seem to be reserved mainly for the beginning and end of the period: i.e., before the twelfth century resurgence of learning and then the decadent Scholasticism of the sixteenth century. See CP 8.11 and 1.27n1.

4. "The schoolmen, who regarded Aristotle as all but infallible, yet to whom the ideas of a naturalist were utterly foreign . . ." (CP 6.357); and see CP 6.361, 1902 (this is a paragraph worth reading in its entirety); though for contrast: CP 1.32–3, 1869, CP 7.161, 1902, CP 7.395, 1893. For Roger Bacon, CP 1.29, 1869; CP 5.360, 1877.

5. See also CP 2.166–8, 1902, CP 3.509, 1896, CP 6.348, 1909.

6. "[Nominalists' protests] against much of the empty disputations of the medieval Dunces [amounted to] a protest against the only kind of thinking that has ever advanced human culture." (CP 3.509, 1896)

7. Cf. CP 1.3ff, 1890, 1.6, 1897, 6.328, 1909. Aquinas is the "psychologist" of the trio (CP 4.27).

8. One should not underestimate what Peirce learned from Ockham, positively and negatively; see my remarks in Section III and Boler 1980. F. Michael, who thinks Peirce began as a nominalist, is clear that the early nominalism was not from the Scholastics (Michael 1988: 317). But I am not persuaded by Michael's attempt to make out that Peirce then developed a more sophisticated nominalism under Ockham's influence (Michael 1980: 179–85).

9. "The only logicians who are in the same rank as I are Aristotle, Duns Scotus and Leibniz." (MS L 482, quoted in Fisch 1986: 250.)

10. On method: de Waal (1996: 440n11). On theory: "During the middle ages, purely formal syllogistic made no progress worth mentioning" (CP 1.567, 1805). Though he knows they worked more with the theory of consequence: CP 4.45; and on that topic, see Moody (1953). On their respect for logic, see, e.g., CP 1.29–33, 1869 and CP 2.12, 1902.

11. "Logic and metaphysics were studied with a considerable degree of minuteness and accuracy; so that in spite of a barbaric civilization and other unfavorable influences, sufficiently obvious, they reached an excellence which our generation has not been able to appreciate" (CP 2.12, 1902).

12. And a little further on: "the schoolmen, however, attached the greatest authority to men long since dead, and they were right, for in the dark ages it was not true that the later status of human knowledge was the most perfect . . ." (CP 1.32).

13. "When the method of authority prevailed, the truth meant little more than the Catholic faith. All the efforts of the scholastic doctors are directed toward harmonizing their faith in Aristotle and their faith in the church, and one may search their ponderous folios through without finding an argument which goes any further" (CP 5.406, 1878).

14. See note 11, above, and the whole of CP 1.29–33, 1869 for "the spirit of scholasticism." The connection with Peirce's idea of a community of inquirers is clear: "The real, then, is that which, sooner or later, information and reasoning would finally result in, and which is therefore independent of the vagaries of me and you. Thus, the very origin of the conception of reality shows that this conception essentially involves the notion of a COMMUNITY, without definite limits and capable of a definite increase of knowledge" (CP 5.311, 1868).

15. "The medieval universities were places of learning where ours are institutions for teaching" (CP 5.582, 1898).

16. Manley Thompson (1952: note 9) refers on this point to 5.436.

17. See Fisch, Kloesel, and Houser (1982) and more generally Hookway (1985:Introduction). Peirce gives his own account: CP 1.3–14, 1897, CP 1.560, 1907, and CP 4.2–4, 1898.

18. Peirce is an astute reader: e.g., he recognizes that Aristotle's agent causality is not about events (CP 6.66); he is familiar with the practice called *obligationes* (CP 5.340n, 8.118); he has accurate things to say about Aquinas on signate matter (CP 6.359–60), on angels (CP 3.403I), and on "species" (CP 8.18). And he has interesting bits on Greek and Latin terms for form and matter (CP 6.353), and on the shift in later medieval logic from the syllogism to the theory of consequence (CP 4.45).

19. Peirce says that in his study of Kant's categories, he realized that what was needed was a better logical basis: CP 1.560, 1905 and CP1.563, 1898; and that seems to have led to his studies in the history of logic. Fisch puts Peirce's "most intensive" study of the medievals in 1868–9 (Fisch 1986: 188); Popkin and Meyers think he could have been reading medieval texts as early as 1865 (Popkin and Meyers 1993: 610–11). The best account of the dating is E. Michael (1976: 48).

20. This was probably the Harvard lectures of 1864–5 and/or the Lowell lectures of 1866–7 (Hookway 1985: 6, 8).

21. He could have used the Harvard library; we know he came to make considerable use of Prantl (1955) and Cousin (1836). Among the Scotus volumes I examined at Johns Hopkins, one had the name of his father, Benjamin Peirce, on the fly-leaf.

22. As in so many other facets of Peirce studies, the basic work on this incident has been done by Max Fisch (Fisch 1986: 51ff). I follow his account.

23. Peirce kept a record of what he bought and where (Fisch 1986: 52).

24. Even granting that he was trying to "sell" the higher administration on buying the books, the librarian's enthusiasm is genuine: "It is doubtful whether a similar collection exists in any library in this country." (Quoted in Fisch 1986: 52.)

25. Goodwin (1961: 479–80) lists five volumes of Scotus that Peirce's widow later sold to Johns Hopkins.

26. Peirce made considerable use of certain secondary sources, especially Prantl (see note 21, above), of whom he is sometimes critical: CP 2.218, CP 323n, CP 361, CP 364, CP 391n, CP 393; CP 5.4, CP 83; CP 6.312.

27. CP 1.28ff, Lectures on British Logicians, given at Harvard in 1869. See also CP 4.21–37.

28. CP 5.312n is an explicit quote from *Quaestiones in Metaph.*, VII, q 18, n 8. It is not a matter of influence, but Murphey (1961: 117) points out that CP 5.213ff. takes after the form of a scholastic disquisition. These cases are different from the similarities discussed below.

29. Also, he learned a lot about medieval logic and logical and other terminology, but I do not count that as influence: see CP 2.225, CP 3.159, CP 7.494n9, CP 7.395.

30. E. Michael (1976) and Kloesel (1981) discuss Peirce's appeal to speculative grammar. For work on Thomas Erfurt, see Bursill-Hall (1971).

31. McKeon (1952: 241n5) notes that Peirce refers to other bits of pseudo-Scotus: e.g., at CP 1.549n1.

32. Even Kloesel (1981: 32) says Erfurt's work lacks the breadth and comprehensiveness of Peirce's theory of the nature and meaning of signs.

33. See CP 4.48 for Peirce on European grammar and the subject–predicate form. I mean by the latter, as I think others who use the phrase do, a basic propositional form consisting of two categorematic terms (subject- and predicate-terms) with a copula and the various syncategorematics that make up the familiar AEIO forms of Aristotelian logic. The "logic of relatives" which Peirce develops uses what we would desribe as predicate-functions within a quantificational scheme.

34. CP 1.191, CP 444, CP 559, CP 2.83, CP 206, CP 229, CP 332, CP 432, CP 438, CP 4.9, CP 8.342.

35. See for example, CP 2.60, CP 62, CP 64, CP 83, CP 229, CP 232, CP 3.432. See CP 2.206 for "Kant's *Elementahrlehre*."

36. In discussing the need to update it, Peirce describes the "New List" as speculative grammar (CP 2.332, ca. 1895). Murphey (1961) is in large part a detailed analysis of the article and its background.

37. The list of categories is "a table of conceptions drawn from the logical analysis of thought and regarded as applicable to being" (CP 1.300, ca. 1894). Whatever the medievals may have meant by speculative grammar, it is this analysis of the structure of thought through the structure of its expression that Peirce means by *Erkenntnishlehre*.

38. See note 33, above. As we know, it is easy enough to translate from "All S is P" to "For all x, if x is S then x is P" and vice versa. The problem arises with relational predicates whose structure is "buried" in the corresponding monadic predicates in S-is-P form. The latter, therefore, cannot support the classification of monad, dyad, and triad that is the structure of Peirce's mature category theory. See Hookway (1985: 97ff.).

39. All the book-length studies take up the topic. Among articles devoted to it, McKeon (1952), Moore (1952), Bastian (1953), and Goodwin (1961) are the earliest, though there are a host that follow. Mine is the only book so far specifically on this topic, though it needs qualification, as you can see if you read these articles. Among those that I do not refer to in other notes specifically, I would mention E. and F. Michael (1979), Forster (1992), H. Lee (1982), R. Lee (1998), Nesher (1981), Rohatyn (1983), and Rosenthal (1968)

40. "For as soon as you have once mounted the vantage-ground of the logic of relatives ... you find that you command the whole citadel of nominalism, which must fall almost without another blow" (CP 4.1, 1898). A number of commentators have noticed this and the importance of his three modes of being: e.g., F. Michael (1988: 329–35) and Raposa (1984: 151f.)

41. Among recent studies of Peirce, see Hookway (1985). For Scotus, see King (1992: 60 and 67) and (2001:especially Section 2.2); Marilyn

Adams's account of the dispute between Scotus and Ockham is very good (Adams 1987:chs. 1–2).

42. For example, on what is predicated; whether words signify things directly or only through concepts; whether "white" primarily signifies a property or the bearer.

43. Peirce recognizes the difference: "no great realist held that a *universal* was a *thing*" (CP 1.27n). And this may be why he distinguishes the earlier discussions from those of the thirteenth and fourteenth centuries: CP 8.11, and see note 3, above.

44. See Peirce CP 8.18. Ockham shows the courage of his convictions in holding that since science is of the universal, it is strictly about concepts, although they stand for real individuals (Ockham 1990: 11–12).

45. It is standard for most accounts of the Scholastics to describe this as "moderate realism" precisely because it has to do with special components (dependent on and posterior to first substance) rather than with a commitment to general "things." Plato is for them an "extreme" realist. As I shall explain below, Peirce thinks the appeal to constituents *constitutes* Scholastic realism as opposed to nominalistic Platonism; so that is not where he locates Scotus's moderateness (i.e., his being "too nominalistic").

46. I offer a plural on "natures" because Scotus allows a plurality of substantial forms (see CP 7.580) and includes among generals various "accidents": on formalities and multiple habits see Goodwin (1961: 482).

47. He marshalls seven arguments (King 1992: n 6) to the effect that there is a real but less-than-numerical unity that grounds our ascription of common terms.

48. King offers an interpretation that allows for both a contracted and an uncontracted nature in things (King 1992: 54–6), though I do not think it would have satisfied Peirce even so.

49. Peirce gives a brief but accurate enough account of the positions of Scotus and Ockham at CP 8.18–21, 1871. It is important to keep in mind, while talking about the changes Peirce makes to Scholastic realism, that he does not distort or manipulate the *medievals'* position to support his own. (Though see note 72, below.)

50. It is typical of Peirce to put the question of nominalism and realism as "whether *laws* and general *types* are figments of the mind or are real" (CP 1.16). And it is easy to assume he means to contrast things inside the mind with what is unequivocally outside. But the contrast has to do with the objects of two kinds of thought; and the real, as he says elsewhere, is not independent of thought.

51. "As [usually] stated, the question was whether *universals*, such as the Horse, the Ass, the Zebra and so forth were *in re* or *in rerum natura*.

But that there is no great merit in this formulation of the question is shown by two facts: first, that many different answers were given to it, instead of merely yes and no, and second, that all the disputants divided the question into different parts" (CP 4.1, 1898). Note the parallel in CP 8.12, quoted just above, where one might have thought Peirce meant this as just the way to describe the dispute.

52. "The gist of all the nominalist's arguments will be found to relate to a *res extra animam*, while the realist defends his position only by assuming that the immediate object of thought in a true judgment is real" (CP 8.17).

53. See Boler 1985: 121–3.

54. "Roughly speaking, the nominalist conceived the *general* element of cognition to be merely a convenience for understanding this and that fact and to amount to nothing except for cognition, while the realists, still more roughly speaking, looked upon the general not only as the end and aim of knowledge, but also as the most important element of being. Such was and is the question" (CP 4.1, 1898).

55. "[T]he sectators of individualism, the essence of whose doctrine is that reality and existence are coextensive ... go along with you in holding that "real" and "existent" have the same meaning, or *Inhalt*" (CP 5.503, 1905).

56. The three modes of being are the categories of Peirce's later theory: Firstness, Secondness, and Thirdness. See the discussion in Hookway (1985: 80–117). As I suggest below, they are what the Scholastics' "constituents" become in Peirce's mature metaphysics: see CP 1.22–3. As Fisch (1986: 194) points out, Peirce does not use "mode of being" talk until much later (around 1896, for example at CP 1.432ff and CP 1.51ff); and he cites Thompson (1953: 182) who finds only two mentions of modes of being before 1902. Once nominalism is understood as the denial of all but one mode of being, it is less surprising that Peirce should extend his pejorative use of the label so that the mark of the beast is on any failure to acknowledge the full range (viz., three) of modes of being (see CP 5.79).

57. CP 5.502–4, 1905. For a full discussion of nominalistic Platonism, see Anderson and Goff (1998: 165–78). It sounds a bit odd, of course, but it is not unreasonable to see Plato as a nominalist. The Ideas are not generals. They are not predicates and "participates in," which is the canonical predicate, has no corresponding Idea.

58. See note 45, above.

59. F. Michael also emphasizes the "gap" (1980: 185).

60. See CP 5.311, quoted in note 14, above.

61. Goodwin (1961: 489) recognizes formalities as constituents.

62. "The question of realism and nominalism [is] the question of how far real facts are analogous to logical relations" (CP 4.68). And: "That which any proposition asserts is *real*, in the sense of being as it is regardless of what you or I may think about it. Let this proposition be a general conditional proposition as to the future, and it is a real general such as is calculated really to influence human conduct; and such the pragmaticist holds to be the rational purport of every concept" (CP 5.312). F. Michael emphasizes this (1988: 330–4).

63. See also CP 8.19–20 and CP 1.549n1.

64. In interpreting Scotus, one might well want to play down the talk of conceivability: see King (1992: 60; and 2001: Section 2.2). In describing Scotus from Peirce's point of view, however, I want to bring out the "reality–conceivability" connection as lying behind his account in *Berkeley*.

65. Peirce claims Scotus brought the term "real" into common use (CP 8.319), and I think that is related to *realitates*: see CP 4.28, CP 5.430, CP 6.328 and CP 495, and CP 8.14–18.

66. For a careful account of the formal distinction, see Adams (1987: 22–9).

67. That reality does not have to do with concepts, for Peirce, is clear in his rejection of conceptualism which he sees as just a confused form of nominalism: 1.27.

68. See note 56, above.

69. As I said earlier, I cannot do justice here to Peirce's theory of the categories or modes of being. His "phenomenological" approach can be seen in CP 1.284–353 and CP 5.41–65. The three categories are also described in Hookway (1995: chs. 3 and 4).

70. For "systems," see Raposa (1984: 161). For some, the difference is enough to justify the claim that Peirce gives up on Scholastic realism: McKeon (1952: 247ff), Thompson (1952: 133, 136f), Bastian (1953: 246–9), with Moore's reply (Moore 1953: 250–1), Murphey (1961: 138ff., 401), Pihlstrom (1998d: n 47). Goodwin (1961: 509) seems to me to have a sensible approach to the problem.

71. Peirce does not: 1890 is his first use (Murphey 1965: 131). McKeon (1952: 245) cites CP 1.458, 1896, but says it is different from Scotus. See CP 6.95, 1903, on Scotus and Kant; and CP 6.319, 1908 on "what Scotus should have meant." I think Peirce comes back to haecceity from his (later) interest in Secondness. In 1901, Fraser produced a new version (not merely a re-edition) of the works of Berkeley, and Peirce reviewed it in the *Nation*. While he mentions Scotus in connection with haecceity, his concern here is to criticize the sort of absolute idealism that takes insufficient (or no) notice of the brute encounter with the existent (N 3, 36, 1901). DiLeo devotes an article to haecceity (1991: 79–107).

72. For other references to thisness/haecceity: CP 1.405, CP 408, 1890, CP 458; CP 3.434, CP 460–2, CP 475, CP 479, CP 535, CP 543, 1896. There is a terminological problem here. I am calling attention to the difference between Scotus's haecceity and Peirce's Secondness. But Peirce tends to coopt "haecceity," making it synonymous with "Secondness"; see CP 6.319 quoted in note 71, above.

73. Especially in his criticism of absolute idealism: see note 71, above.

74. Fisch finds Firstness more important in Peirce's development, the scholastic realism involved in Thirdness having got Peirce only halfway out of the clutches of nominalism (Fisch 1986: 228; and see CP 6.201). I admit to not having a very firm grip on Firstness.

75. Timothy Potts pointed this out in an early review of Boler (1963): (Potts 1965: 362). Peirce says that "the general has an admixture of potentiality" (CP 1.420). "Its mode of being is *esse in futuro*" (CP 2.148; cf., CP 5.48 and McKeon (1952: 239)). It is central, of course, in Peirce's notion of the would-be: e.g., CP 3.527, CP 5.77n1, CP 428 & CP 527, and CP 6 Bk.1, chs. 1&2. On the thing as a bundle of habits/powers: CP 1.414. See: Goodwin (1961: 497–507), Olshewsky (1981: 87), Engel-Tiercelin (1992: 51–82); and it is the theme of Raposa (1984: 147–68). For Scotus, see King (1992: 67).

76. A more radical modification in Peirce's realism is the emphasis on continuity: it is what generality becomes in the logic of relatives (CP 5.436, CP 6.172), as I tried to explain in my book (Boler 1963: ch. 3). See also Hookway (1985: 174–80). On the importance of the change from a subject–predicate logic to the logic of relatives, see Murphey (1961: 401), Olshewsky (1981: 87,92), F. Michael (1988: 329–34), Raposa (1984: 151f., and note 68), and Short (1996: 420).

77. Presumably this is what Peirce means by Scotus's "halting realism" in CP 6.175, 1905.

78. Fr. Bastian may not have paid enough attention to the way in which an Aristotelian form resembles a higher level power: a power of powers (as, e.g., in the intellectual soul which grounds the many powers that humans exhibit). But he is surely traditional in insisting that in the hylomorphism of the Scholastics, potentiality is grounded in the essence or substantial form (Bastian 1953: 246–9, espec. 249). McKeon (1952: 249) cites CP 6.361, where Peirce rejects form (and presumably anything other than Thirdness itself) as the ground for dynamical power in agents.

79. Aquinas says explicitly that the mode of understanding does not have to match the mode of being: *Summa Theologiae* I, q. 84, a. 1.

80. Peirce's realism is not a simple doctrine (F. Michael 1988: 336). While Peirce himself seems to attribute his realism to a close reading of Duns Scotus, there may have been other factors even in his earlier idea of

"Scholastic realism." There is evidence, for example, that Francis Abbott may have been a strong and more proximate influence than the scholastics at some point in the process (O'Connor 1964: 543–64). For a very positive account of the importance of Peirce's extreme realism along with its scholastic elements, see (Haack 1992).

81. Short (1996a: 419) and Murphey (1961: esp. 123–50) in their own ways make a similar complaint. And see Thompson (1952: 138).

82. See note 70, above.

83. See note 19, above.

84. Roberts disputes Fisch's evidence, holding that Peirce was a realist all along (Roberts 1970: 67–83). F. Michael defends Fisch on the early nominalism (1988: 339) and Short returns to its criticism (Short 1996b: especially 416–20). Both Michael and Short think Fisch's "first step" is really only a change of labels, though (if I have them right) Michael claims that Peirce's "early realism" was nominalistic (1988: 339) while Short holds that his "early nominalism" was realist (1996b: 416–22).

85. I would have said that Peirce's *Scholastic realism*, already evident in the *Berkeley* review, was only a first step toward his *later realism*. But this might upset Fisch's storyline. He is clear that Peirce does not *retreat* from the position in the *Berkeley* review (Fisch 1986: 198n3).

86. There may be a spectrum stretching from nominalism to realism, where one could see Peirce as basically a nominalist gradually giving ground in the face of realist concerns or as basically a realist gradually working out the implications of realism. On the "half-full or half-empty" analogy, the labels do not make all that much difference. The issue is doctrines, of course, and not labels. The problem with the labels is that different people (Peirce included) have different ideas about what the various "isms" amount to. Hausman (1991: 475–500) tries to sort out some different senses of realism and idealism.

87. See note 71, above.

88. Fisch recognizes other storylines: (1986: 390). Among leading contenders, I would have picked the developments in his logical theory, the troubled journey from objective idealism to the real as object of a (real or fictional) community of inquiry, or perhaps the transformation (or replacement of) the New List with the three modes of being.

89. His advice that one should start with nominalism and accept realism only when forced to (CP 4.1) suggests more that a theory is being developed than one abandoned. He says that nominalism is an "undeveloped state of mind" (CP 5.121, 1903). Here, as in moral assessment, there is an important difference between a young person still in the process of acquiring a moral outlook and a mature person undergoing a change of heart.

90. "The novel doctrine of these lectures, so far as concerns realism, is the theory of Immediate Perception. It is in this connection that he first makes it quite clear that his realism is now opposed to idealism as well as nominalism" (Fisch 1986: 195.) For a detailed account of the doctrine in Peirce, see Bernstein (1964).

91. Olshewsky (1981: 87, 90) finds Peirce's mature semeiotic theory to be representationalist; and if that is right, the issue of his epistemological realism is complicated. My only point is that it does not involve the realism opposed to nominalism.

92. '[T]hat to which the representation should conform is itself something in the nature of a representation or sign – something noumenal, intelligible, conceivable and utterly unlike a thing-in-itself" (CP 5.553, 1906). This is three years later than CP 5.56 (quoted just above) and it seems to me still to have an idealist ring.

93. See note 81, above.

94. Fortunately, the latter issue is not my topic, for I am not clear about just where Peirce finally stands on the matter. But both Altshuler (1982: esp. 38–46) and Hookway (1985: 37ff.) see him as an antirealist; though apparently the latter has changed his mind on that (Hookway 2000).

95. O'Connor (1964: 552ff.) claims that Abbott convinced Peirce that epistemological and ontological realism stand or fall together. Engel-Tiercelin (1992: 52) tries to tie the two "realisms" together. I still see it as changing the subject.

4 Reflections on Inquiry and Truth Arising from Peirce's Method for the Fixation of Belief

My paper of November 1877, setting out from the proposition that the agitation of a question ceases when satisfaction is attained with the settlement of belief... goes on to consider *how the conception of truth gradually develops* from that principle under the action of experience, beginning with willful belief or self-mendacity, the most degraded of all mental conditions; thence arising to the imposition of beliefs by the authority of organized society; then to the idea of settlement of opinion as the result of fermentation of ideas; and finally reaching the idea of truth as overwhelmingly forced upon the mind in experiences as the effect of an independent reality.

CP 5.564, "Basis of Pragmatism." 1906. (italics not in original)

The third philosophical stratagem for cutting off inquiry consists in maintaining that this, that, or the other element of science is basic, ultimate, independent of aught else, and utterly inexplicable – not so much from any defect in our knowing as because there is nothing beneath it to know. The only type of reasoning by which such a conclusion could possibly be reached is *retroduction*. Now nothing justifies a retroductive inference except its affording an explanation of the facts. It is, however, no explanation at all of a fact to pronounce it *inexplicable*. That, therefore, is a conclusion which no reasoning can ever justify or excuse.

CP 1.139 "The First Rule of Logic." 1899

Abduction consists in studying facts and devising a theory to explain them. Its only justification is that, if we are ever to understand things at all, it must be in that way.

CP 5.145 "Harvard Lectures on Pragmatism." 1903

[Scientific procedure] will at times find a high probability established by a single confimatory instance, while at others it will dismiss a thousand as almost worthless.

Frege 1884: 16

I

"The Fixation of Belief" was published in 1877 as a popular essay. But Peirce must have attributed to it not simply the literary felicity that we find in it, but high philosophical importance. For in the ensuing decades he constantly returned to this paper as a focus for the clarification of his thoughts, either entering corrections and amplifications or else adapting it to new philosophical initiatives. Some of the amendments were designed to adjust the essay to the projects of "The Grand Logic" and "The Search for a Method." Our chief concern here will be with the essay as Peirce came to reread and rewrite it, rather than with the essay in its original condition. The first of our epigraphs, which is dated 1906, is surely the product of one of these rereadings.

Not only does "Fixation" appear at least as important as Peirce supposed. There radiate from it some of the grandest themes of modern philosophy – the nature of truth, for instance, and the relation truth has to meaning when meaning is operationally or pragmatically conceived; inquiry and the ethics of belief; the epistemic status of perceptual experience; and the proper aspiration or aspirations of hypothesis. Once it is seen in proper conjunction with other Peircean claims into which it leads, the essay will even promise a line of response to Hume's doubts about the rational basis of our efforts to argue from the known to the unknown.

What has prevented philosophers from investing the paper with the sort of importance in connection with truth that we find Peirce attributing to it in our first epigraph? Maybe the tendency to read the paper itself as a phase in a one-issue philosophical campaign to demystify the idea of truth by *redefining it* as the eventual, if not predestinate, opinion of those who open-endedly and resolutely pursue the business of inquiry. Only for a small minority who still espouse some sort of verificationism or "prope-positivism" (Peirce's term) could such a campaign be interesting or convincing.

Recently, Peircean scholars[1] have pointed to the implausibility of attributing to the exponent of a theory of signs and signification as special as that of Peirce the project of offering an analytical decomposition of the concept of truth (or of any other concept). In the light of this doubt, it will no longer do to suppose that, at any time, let alone in 1906, by which point he had recanted the worst exaggerations of "How to Make Our Ideas Clear" (1878), Peirce would have approved a report, *given in our language as used by us*, to the effect that Charles Sanders Peirce thought that an opinion's being true and its being the eventual opinion were simply, analytically, or necessarily one and the same thing. Not only is that a questionable report. Unless some quite peculiar sense is attached to "the eventual opinion," it appears inconsistent with that which we read toward the end of "The Fixation of Belief" and read again in Peirce's subsequent reports of its content (e.g., that quoted from 1906). It is time to supersede the form of words that Peirce took the risk of using when he wrote: "The opinion which is fated to be ultimately agreed by all who investigate is what we mean by truth, and the object represented in this opinion is the real" (CP 5.407, 1877). For, if Peirce's ideas are to reach again into the bloodstream of philosophy, then we need not only fresh studies of his texts but speculative transpositions of these ideas – transpositions recognized as speculative but given in language that can be understood without any reference to special or peculiar stipulations. (To the extent that our chosen vehicle of expression is philosophical language, let us confine ourselves to such portions of it as are securely cantilevered from the everyday language of those who are wont to listen to what they are saying.)

Under the transposition I shall propose here, the exact meanings of "ultimately" and "end of inquiry" will no longer be any great issue, and the relation between truth and inquiry will be a degree or two more indirect than Peirce was accustomed to allow. Another Peircean preoccupation we shall abandon is Peirce's thought that proper conduct of inquiry not only comprises the motive and means for correcting its own conclusions but is *bound in the long run to iron out every error*. This perilous claim will be no part of the core

Peirceanism that is here to be consolidated and defended. What then will remain? Above all, the idea of inquiry, seen always as a process that gathers rational strength as it gathers force and gathers force as it gathers rational strength, a process at once communal and personal, in which participants receive benefits that are indefinitely divisible among them and reciprocate, in the light of their own experiences and reflections, however they can or are permitted to do.

II

Peirce says in "Fixation" that, with respect to any question that concerns us, belief or opinion is the state we seek to attain and doubt (not knowing what to think about this or that) is the disquieted, dissatisfied state that we seek to end. The essay reviews four different but developing methods: the method of dogmatism or tenacity, the method of authority, the a priori method, and the method of experience, which Peirce himself approves and commends to his reader. This last method embraces logic, in the broad nineteenth-century sense of the term. The "distinction between good and bad investigation . . . is the subject of the study of logic. . . . Logic is the doctrine of truth, its nature and the manner in which it is to be discovered" (CP 7.320–1, 1873). In Peircean usage, logic is the general art of reasoning – nothing less than everything which "The Fixation of Belief" opens out into – and it subsumes the art of making inferences from the known to the unknown. Logic embraces not only deduction, not only induction, which is the testing of hypotheses, but also abduction, which is the framing of explanatory hypotheses. "Reasoning is good if it be such as to give a true conclusion from true premisses and not otherwise [good]," (CP 5.365, 1877) Peirce wrote. Later, he amended this sentence to say "Reasoning is good if it be dominated by such a habit as generally to give a true conclusion from true premisses" (CP 2.11, 1902).

Nineteenth- and twentieth-century conceptions of the province of logic are interestingly different. Each conception insists, however, on the incompleteness of the canon that we shall recognize at any point for good reasoning. Twentieth-century logicians have stressed the essential incompleteness of canons of provability, an incompleteness demonstrated for purposes of strictly deductive logic by meta-mathematical investigation initiated in the nineteen-thirties.

For Peirce, the incompleteness of logic in his broader sense is made manifest in constant extensions of the methods of scientific argument and the concomitant renewal of the abductive initiative of a community of inquirers. "Each chief step in science has been a lesson in logic" (Fixation, W3, 243, 1877)."[2] In so far as a Peircean philosophy of truth will elucidate truth by reference to inquiry itself and inquiry by reference to a struggle against doubt (= not knowing what to think about this or that) which finds its final fruition in the dispassion of a pure science of unbounded aspiration, it is not to be expected that the elucidation will have the effect of circumscribing truth itself or limiting it to that which is discoverable by any particular research method or aggregation of research methods.

The insatiability of the inquiring mentality, like the ordinary discomfort (from which the scientific outlook originates) of not knowing what to think about some particular question, is one part of the background for the very idea of belief or opinion. So too is the calmness and satisfactoriness of knowing what to believe. Christopher Hookway[3] has been troubled that Peirce should at once have condemned psychologism in logic and intruded psychological facts into his account of inquiry. But if we see these background facts as conditioning the emergence of fully fledged opinion or belief – if we see the concern for truth as latent already within the nature of opinion and belief themselves, inquiry being the expression of that very concern – then I hope we can exempt Peirce from the charge that he allows mere contingencies to corrupt his conceptions of logic and truth themselves. These are not mere contingencies. They are the enabling facts for the existence of belief itself – and of any normative science of that which *deserves* (however tentative and fallible) belief.

III

It might be questioned how exactly and faithfully, dating from 1906, our first epigraph reflects Peirce's intentions of 1877.[4] But it matters far more for present purposes – and it matters especially for the Peircean conception of truth – how Peirce himself, in his full maturity, wanted to read or reread or rewrite "Fixation" and what place he came to want it to occupy within the context of his mature position. If "Fixation" read with the emphases Peirce suggests in 1906 can help us to see the conception of truth "gradually" and "under the action of experience" emerge from the abandonment of dogmatism and authoritarianism, and make us see it emerge thence by virtue of the workings of the principle that the agitation of a question ceases when satisfaction is attained with the proper settlement of belief, then the next task for the philosopher of inquiry will be to speculate what it is about the notions of truth and belief that fits them to cohere and consist with one another in this way. For beliefs, truth must be the first dimension of assessment of their goodness and badness (of their eligibility, so to speak), even as true opinion must be our preeminent aspiration if we ask "What shall I believe about such and such or so and so?" These are normative claims of a sort, conceptually founded. Under both aspects, they are more or less indispensable to the correctness of Peirce's conception of inquiry – and, in so far as plausible, supportive of it.

IV

Our first epigraph recapitulates "Fixation," but a longer commentary is needed. This may usefully begin with Peirce's claim that belief or opinion is the state we seek to attain and doubt the state of irritation we seek to end. The latent complexity of this simple-seeming declaration may be brought out by an analogy.

Suppose that someone has appealed to me for my help, I make an excuse, and then I feel ashamed of letting them down. Finding it hard to live with this failure, I try at first to forget all about the matter. (After all, I didn't owe the person any help, rather the reverse perhaps. And there are all sorts of other people they could have appealed to.) Suppose that, within my own mind, this doesn't work and I start to wonder why I haven't had a simpler, more straightforward thought: oughtn't I to go back to the person and see if there is anything left that I still can do? Suppose that, pursuing that very thought, I minister directly to the object of disquiet and then, like a cloud, the disquiet itself disappears.

Mutatis mutandis, compare now the disquiet/dissatisfaction of not being sure what to think about whether . . . (some particular question, that is). Should such disquiet be remedied by attention to the state of mind, vexatious as it is, or to the object of the state? If Peirce had been asked this question – and what a pity he wasn't – then how would he have replied? I don't know. But I think his reply ought to have been this: the first two of his methods of fixation seek to work directly upon the state; the third method is transitional; the fourth works directly upon the object of the disquiet. As we review the four methods, however, let the reader verify this for himself or herself.

Concerning the method of tenacity or dogmatism, Peirce says that the social impulse, which comprises the inner compulsion to pay anxious heed wherever others think differently from oneself, practically guarantees the total ineffectiveness of this method to implant or maintain conviction or forestall the disquiet of not knowing what to believe.

The second method is the method of authority, consisting of dogmatism supported by the repression of social impulses that unsettle prescribed opinion. Here Peirce's prescription is this:

Let [men's] passions be enlisted, so that they may regard private and unusual opinions with hatred and horror. Then, let all men who reject the established belief be terrified into silence. (W 3, 250 "Fixation," 1877)

[L]et it be known that you seriously hold a tabooed belief, and you may be perfectly sure of being treated with a cruelty less brutal but more refined than hunting you like a wolf. (W 3, 256 "Fixation," 1877)

Even though this method holds better promise for the end of doubt than the first, and its past triumphs are manifest, Peirce then declares – in passages which seem in the light of recent events in Eastern Europe not only prophetic but vividly illustrative of why, under those kinds of conditions, things will almost inevitably tend to work out in a certain way – that such a policy will be powerless in the end to counter the irritation of doubt or to stabilize opinion:

[N]o institution can undertake to regulate opinions upon every subject. Only the most important ones can be attended to, and on the rest men's minds must be left to the action of natural causes. (W 3, 251 "Fixation," 1877)

For that reason, Peirce holds, once some people are led by unregulated convictions to reject that which is officially prescribed for general belief, more and more others will come to think that their own adherence to this or that approved opinion may be owed to "the mere accident of having been taught as [they] have." Where people are already tending toward doubt, the beliefs that they think they owe to this source are bound to come adrift.

Evidently then,

a new method of settling opinions must be adopted, which shall not only produce an impulse to believe, but shall also decide what proposition it is which is to be believed. Let the action of natural preferences be unimpeded, then, and under their influence let men, conversing together and regarding matters in different lights, gradually develop beliefs in harmony with natural causes. (W 3, 252 "Fixation," 1877)

Peirce calls this third method, the a priori method, new. But all that "new" needs to mean (I suggest) is that he has put it next after tenacity and submission to authority in his enumeration of remedies for doxastic disquiet. For he says of the a priori method "so long as no better method can be applied, it ought to be followed" because "it is the expression of instinct, which must be the ultimate cause of belief in all cases." Under this aspect, the a priori method is only a resumption of protorational ways of information gathering. Self-evidently, then, even when dignified as a method for "the fermentation of ideas," (CP 5.564, 1906) the method can only restore the state where we were before we turned to these other expedients. It is not surprising then if (as Peirce claims)

its failure has been the most manifest. It makes of inquiry something similar to the development of taste; but taste, unfortunately, is always more or less a matter of fashion ... [And] I cannot help seeing that ... sentiments in their development will be very greatly determined by accidental causes. Now, there are some people, among whom I must suppose that my reader is to be found, who, *when they see that any belief of theirs is determined by any circumstance extraneous to the facts, will from that moment not merely admit in words that that belief is doubtful, but will experience a real doubt of it, so that it ceases to be a belief.* (W 3, 253, "Fixation," 1877 my italics)

The last sentence is one of the most important sentences in Peirce's whole essay. It suggests *inter alia* that those who practice the first or second methods have misunderstood the nature of the disquiet or irritation of not knowing. Once they understand this better, they will return to the *object* of their disquiet, namely the particular thing not known. Would that Peirce had said more here, and would that he had attended separately to the aspects of the matter that appear to the individual inquirer and those that appear under a collective aspect. But the last sentence quoted is the point of transition to Peirce's fourth method of countering our disquiet at not knowing or not knowing for sure:

> To satisfy our doubts, therefore, it is necessary that a method should be found by which our beliefs may be caused by nothing human, but by some external permanency – by something upon which our thinking has no effect.... [That external permanency] must be something which affects, or might affect, every man. And, though these affections are necessarily as various as are individual conditions, yet the method must be such that the ultimate conclusion of every man shall be the same. Such is the method of science. Its fundamental hypothesis, restated in more familiar language, is this: There are real things, whose characters are entirely independent of our opinions about them; those realities affect our senses according to regular laws, and, though our sensations are as different as are our relations to the objects, yet, by taking advantage of the laws of perception, we can ascertain by reasoning how things really and truly are, and any man, if he have sufficient experience and reason enough about it, will be led to the one true conclusion. The new conception here involved is that of reality. (W 3, 253–4 "Fixation," 1877)

Here, in so far as we are influenced by the gloss of 1906, we shall understand Peirce to say something like this: that anyone who has the idea that the proper response to their doubt or disquiet about this or that is to work on the particular object of their dissatisfaction and initiate some careful inquiry is in a position to discover that this apparently simple aim *must*, if they are to escape their disquiet, comprehend within it nothing less than this: that any opinion or belief they arrive at to the effect that p should be determined by circumstances that are not extraneous to the fact that p. Meanwhile, the philosopher of inquiry, reflecting on the aim that an ordinary inquirer will have if he feels the dissatisfaction of not knowing what to believe, must be tempted to think that this need of the inquirer's, this wanting his or her belief to be determined in just such a way, is exactly what is needed for us to begin to understand the idea of "a reality" to which the belief that p is answerable.

Here it helps to distinguish very deliberately the roles of inquirer and of philosopher of inquiry. Normally, when we engage as inquirers in some investigation, we do not think, in the abstract, about methodology. The Peircean philosopher of inquiry knows that. But if, even as inquirers submit to experience, they do reflect abstractly about their procedures and the rationale of what they do, then,

according to Peirce, the thing they are bound to find they have discovered is the ideas of truth, of fact, and of a reality or (as Peirce
rewrote some passages of "Fixation" to say) "a Real." The corresponding role of the philosopher of inquiry is to make the however
inexplicit working ideas of inquirers *more* explicit, thus harvesting
the outcome of the apparently meager resources that the methodology of inquiry starts out with.

Amid this harvest, once it is properly examined, along with the
ideas of truth, fact, and reality (Real), the theory or philosophy of
the practice of inquiry will also find "the fundamental hypothesis,"
which speaks of our taking advantage of our perceptions and the
"laws of perception," in order to ascertain "by reasoning how things
really and truly are."[5] Consideration of this hypothesis will force
upon a philosopher of inquiry the task of arriving at a proper conception of experience. For experience is that by which we can and do
expose our minds to realities/Reals and make our beliefs answerable
to realities/Reals. The forcible element in our experience is what
Peirce calls "secondness."[6] "It may be asked," Peirce notes, "how
I know that there are any realities [Reals]." To this question Peirce
gives four replies, of which the most striking, interesting, and con-
clusive is this one:

The feeling which gives rise to any method of fixing belief is a dissatisfaction
at two repugnant propositions. But here already is a vague concession that
there is some one thing to which a proposition should conform. Nobody,
therefore, can really doubt that there are realities [Reals], or, if he did, doubt
would not be a source of dissatisfaction. The hypothesis, therefore, is one
which every mind admits. So that the social impulse does not cause me to
doubt it. (W 3, 254 "Fixation," 1877)

There is more to say about realities (Reals) (see Section IX) and
reality and there is more to be said also about the extent of Peirce's
commitment to causal realism (see Section VI), but such in bare outline is Peirce's doctrine. Before we can convert any of this into a distinctively Peircean contribution to the philosophy of truth, however,
some further explanation and defense is needed of Peirce's conception of belief, of the abductive coloration that he gives to the idea
of experience, and of his idea of abduction itself. We shall attend to
each of these things, in Sections V, VI, and VII.

V

At the outset, Peirce says that belief in a particular proposition is a calm and satisfactory state. It is a state "we do not wish to avoid, or to change to a belief in anything else. On the contrary, we cling tenaciously not merely to believing but to believing just what we do believe." (CP 5.372, 1902–03) In the same tenor he writes,

With the doubt...the struggle begins, and with the cessation of doubt it ends. Hence, the sole object of inquiry is the settlement of opinion. We may fancy that this is not enough for us, and that we seek, not merely an opinion, but a true opinion. But put this fancy to the test, and it proves groundless; for as soon as a firm belief is reached we are entirely satisfied, whether the belief be true or false. And it is clear that nothing out of the sphere of our knowledge can be our object, for nothing which does not affect the mind can be the motive for a mental effort. The most that can be maintained is that we seek for a belief that we shall *think* to be true...and, indeed, it is a mere tautology to say so. (W 3, 248 "Fixation," 1877)

From this conclusion about the thoughts first-order inquirers can have Peirce derives three attractive corollaries, corollaries that maintain the impossibility *cum* pointlessness, in the absence of real and living doubt, of any general project or plan of exposing everything to question. (Contrast Descartes.) I like that and shall return to one aspect of its most distinctive importance in Section XV. But one ought not to permit the claim that the sole object of inquiry is the fixation of belief to escape criticism just because it delivers conclusions that we have other reasons to find attractive. So the claim needs more extended comment. Indeed it requires emendation.

The directive "seek a true belief," Peirce seems to argue, has no more practical content than "seek a belief you think true." And then he continues, "we think each one of our beliefs is true. It is a mere tautology to say so." If doubt irritates us, Peirce seems to say, his advice to us is "seek for a belief," not "seek for a true belief."

This does not look right. If it is wrong, moreover, room can and must be made in our transposition of Peirce's theories of inquiry and truth to correct the mistake. The defect of Peirce's way of arguing becomes very evident as soon as we recall that similar claims used to be made to the effect that there is no practical difference between the directives "do your duty" and "do what you think is your duty."

Makers of such philosophical claims always paid too little attention to the fact that it is not without consequence which of these directives you second. One who fails to think hard what his duty is but does what he *takes* to be his duty obeys the directive to do what he thinks is his duty, but he does not necessarily do his duty. In Peirce's manner of argument about seeking a belief, there is a closely parallel oversight. One wishes he had not said what he says. It will miss the point, though, to insist too much upon it. For, as we have already seen, it becomes clear slightly later in Peirce's essay – see the transition from the third to the fourth method – that he is deeply impressed by a particular and special point about belief and the conditions that are constitutive of belief, namely that the belief that *p*, once challenged, is a state which needs, on pain of extinction, to see itself as a state *not* "determined by circumstances extraneous to the facts [concerning whether or not *p*]." By its nature, belief is a touchy, uncomplacent condition of the mind, a disposition which will not and cannot stay around on just any old terms. This is one of the things that bring into being the normative science of logic.

Once we absorb these points, charity will suggest that we should see Peirce's insistence that the sole object of inquiry is the settlement of opinion as tantamount to his saying this: "Believe what you will – end the irritation of doubt however you like – only provided that the belief with which you conquer doubt will *stick*, provided it really *will* conquer doubt."[7] So understood, the prescription suggests that, given the *exigence* that Peirce finds latent in the state of belief and given the *object-directedness* of the disquiet of not knowing, the injunction to get oneself a belief in order to end the irritation of some doubt can never be satisfied by possessing oneself of just any opinion or just any substitute for a belief that gives dissatisfaction or disquiet. Once a question arises that one cares about, one can only be satisfied by an answer to it that one takes oneself to have acquired in a manner that is proper to the content of the answer.[8]

What then ought Peirce to have said was the whole aim of inquiry? It would have been better, and much less open to misunderstanding, if he had said that the whole aim of inquiry was to end the irritation of not knowing (whether/who/when/what/....) by bringing into being the proper conditions for the settlement of opinion with respect to the matter that is in question. The whole aim is to secure *everything that it takes* to obtain this settlement. Once we say that, let it be noted, there is scarcely any temptation at all to make Peirce's mistake of saying that there is no difference between seeking an opinion and seeking a true opinion. No doubt the notion of truth lurks within the notion of the "proper condition for the settlement of opinion." But we are already prepared for any disappointments this holds for the project of philosophical analysis. Analysis as such is not the only possible aim. See Sections I and XII.

VI

So much for belief. Now let us continue the description of Peirce's fourth method, and fill out the account of the fundamental hypothesis, of realities (Reals), and of that "external permanency upon which our thinking has no effect" which will under the right conditions prompt beliefs to us.

When Peirce speaks of "realities/Reals affect[ing] our senses according to regular laws" or speaks of anyone with sufficient experience and willingness to reason "taking advantage of the laws of perception" in order to "ascertain by reasoning how things really and truly are," the cases that first come to mind as illustrations of this strange – seeming doctrine are singular empirical judgments relating to the past and present as treated by the causal theories of memory and perception. It would be a pity if these were the only cases that were tractable by Peirce's theory of inquiry. Nevertheless, let us start in the area that is easiest for the doctrine and begin by asking what kind of reasoning it is that leads there to that ascertaining, and how, in the most straightforward perceptual case, Peirce envisages its workings.

The answer to the question is that this reasoning is abductive or retroductive, though in a special way. Even for the normal case, of perception or memory, Peirce offers no systematic account of the relation between perception and abduction or memory and abduction. We do, however, get some indications of the link he saw between hypothesis or abduction and states such as memory or perception:

I once landed at a seaport in a Turkish province; and as I was walking up to the house which I was to visit, I met a man upon horseback, surrounded by four horsemen holding a canopy over his head. As the governor of the province was the only personage I could think of who would be so greatly honoured, I inferred that this was he. This was an hypothesis.

Fossils are found; say, remains like those of fishes, but far in the interior of the country. To explain the phenomenon, we suppose the sea once washed over this land. This is another hypothesis.

Numberless documents and monuments refer to a conqueror called Napoleon Bonaparte. Though we have not seen the man, yet we cannot explain what we have seen, namely, all these documents and monuments, without supposing that he really existed. Hypothesis again.

As a general rule, hypothesis is a weak kind of argument. It often inclines our judgment so slightly toward its conclusion that we cannot say that we believe the latter to be true; we only surmise that it may be so. But there is no difference except one of degree between such an inference and *that by which we are led to believe that we remember the occurrences of yesterday from our feeling as if we did so.* (W 3, 326 – 7, "Deduction, Induction, and Hypothesis," 1878, my italics.)

This is the case of memory. For the case of perception, we have the following:

... abductive inference shades into perceptual judgment without any sharp line of demarcation between them; or, in other words, our first premisses, the perceptual judgments, are to be regarded as an extreme case of abductive inferences, from which they differ in being absolutely beyond criticism. The abductive suggestion comes to us like a flash. It is an act of *insight*, though of extremely fallible insight. (CP 5.181, 1903)

What did Peirce have in mind when he claimed that perception and memory were abductive? Any adequate answer for the case of perception would need to cohere with two other Peircean doctrines (the first not, in the light of our earlier mention of "secondness," unexpected):

... this direct consciousness of hitting and getting hit enters into all cognition and serves to make it mean something real (CP 8.41, c.1885)

and, second,

The chair I appear to see makes no professions of any kind, essentially embodies no intentions of any kind, does not stand for anything. It obtrudes itself upon my gaze; but not as a deputy for anything else nor "as" anything. (CP 7.619, 1903)

A full reconstruction of Peirce's doctrine would not only have to cohere with these clues and with his fallibilism (which suggests that what is "beyond criticism" must be not a perceptual belief but the perceptual state itself which may or may not *sustain* a belief). It would also need to cohere with Peirce's numerous but sketchy hints about the distinct roles in perception of *percept, percipuum,* and *perceptual judgment.* In lieu of such a reconstruction, I offer an interim statement. It is intended to respect most of these constraints, but it is not given in Peircean language.

Suppose object and perceiver encounter one another in perception. Then independently of will or reason, the perceiver may be moved to report what he sees by uttering the words "Six windows obtrude, it seems, upon my gaze." No abduction yet. But for the perceiver to *take* what he is confronted with *for* six windows just is – whether he knows it or not – for him to take it that the best explanation of his perception is that *there are* six windows there. *Mutatis mutandis* it will be the same for the remembering case. From remembering (or its being as if one remembers) the messenger giving one a letter yesterday, one concludes that the messenger did indeed give one a letter yesterday. Nothing else (here) will explain (here) one's conviction that he did. Again, whether one knows this or not, the conclusion is abductive. Rather it is a limiting case of abduction, or so Peirce supposes. In so far as one *takes* oneself to remember, one is committed to accept the conclusion of an abduction of course, this is a third person remark about the legitimacy of what the inquirer does, not a reconstruction of his thoughts.

Can we generalize this? Well, it seems the relation of experience and belief must be this: that the experience creates, by its nature as experience, a fallible presumption that what we are moved to report that we see or remember is that which accounts for our being so moved to report. Rather than attribute thoughts of this kind to ordinary percipients or intellectualize that which needs not to be intellectualized, one might say that the acceptability of abduction is quietly and tacitly *institutionalized* in our exercise of our faculties, in our practice and in the title that perceivers could claim that the use of senses or memory affords for them to make empirical claims. Echoing a formulation that appealed at one time to A. J. Ayer, the philosopher of inquiry can say that it is the outcome of the exercise of these faculties which, with respect to certain indispensable judgments, gives ordinary inquirers in ordinary circumstances *the right to be sure*. Such normative claims as this are undergirded by nonnormative laws whose special dependability would legitimate an abduction.

VII

Here ends the interpretation and explication of "The Fixation of Belief" (at least with respect to judgments conforming to the easiest empirical paradigm). Indeed, in one way, we are well beyond the end of the paper itself. But we are not yet at the end of expounding the fourth method, the method of experience, which is still in the condition of a program needing to be worked out. The fourth method depends on abduction, not only in the (limiting) perceptual case but for almost everything else that we can then build upon perception. In order to enlarge upon the method, we now have to set out certain details that Peirce gives in other writings that he devoted to logic and his theory of inference.

Peirce classifies inferences as deductive/analytic/explicative and as synthetic/ampliative. And the synthetic/ampliative he subdivides into (1) abduction, hypothesis, or retroduction (these terms are close to synonymous in Peirce) and (2) induction.

Let us begin with induction:

Induction is where we generalize from a number of cases of which something is true, and infer that the same thing is true of a whole class. Or, where we find a certain thing to be true of a certain proportion of cases and infer that it is true of the same proportion of the whole class. (W 3, 326, "Deduction, Induction and Hypothesis," 1878)

Hypothesis, on the other hand,

is where we find some very curious circumstances, which would be explained by the supposition that it was a case of a certain general rule, and thereupon adopt that supposition. Or, where we find that in certain respects two objects have a strong resemblance, and infer that they resemble one another strongly in other respects. (W 3, 326, 1878)

Or as Peirce describes abductive thought elsewhere:

The first starting of a hypothesis and the entertaining of it, whether as a simple interrogation or with any degree of confidence, is an inferential step which I propose to call *abduction*. This will include a preference for any one hypothesis over others which would equally explain the facts, as long as this preference is not based upon any previous knowledge bearing upon the truth of the hypotheses, nor on any testing of any of the hypotheses, after having admitted them on probation. I call all such inference by the peculiar name, *abduction*... (CP 6.525 "Hume on Miracles," 1901)

Here the restrictions we see Peirce start to draft may need very careful statement. For we shall also need to prevent this form of inference from allowing into the place of a hypothesis – into the place marked by "A" in our next citation – suppositions that are contrary to things in the reasoner's evidential background or that are gratuitous relative to that background. The thought that some such preclusion is needed becomes even more evident when abduction is set out as starkly as it is here:

The hypothesis cannot be admitted, even as an hypothesis, unless it be supposed that it would account for the facts or some of them. The form of inference, therefore, is this:

The surprising fact, C, is observed;
But if A were true, C would be a matter of course;
Hence, there is reason to suspect that A is true.

Thus, A cannot be abductively... conjectured until its entire content is already present in the premise, 'If A were true, C would be a matter of course.' (CP 5.189, 1903)

When the form of this reasoning is set out in this way, the question that takes shape is whether (subject to the restrictions Peirce gives in 6.525, cited) just any supposition, any supposition at all which would make "C" a matter of course, should be permitted to count as a hypothesis, and as something ready to move up to the next stage of being subjected to confirmation/disconfirmation.[9] Must there not be criteria for the interrogation and selection of things that shall count as hypotheses?[10] And where do *they* spring from? Do they entirely spring from the need to stabilize belief on belief's own terms, etc.? How much does it help to reflect that, in hypothesizing, "man divines something of the secret principles of the universe, because his mind has developed as a part of the universe and under the influence of these same secret principles"? I shall not answer these questions here.

According to Peirce's doctrine, retroduction or abduction (however we enlarge upon it) is a distinctive mode of thinking. It is reducible neither to deduction, whose role is the ancillary one of drawing out the consequences of hypotheses, nor yet to induction, to which Peirce assigns the special role of testing (refuting or supporting) the hypotheses that are submitted to it by abduction. Induction itself, as Peirce sees it (and note that Peirce does not deny that there is any such thing as reasonable induction), can *support* generalizations but, pace Nicod, it does not license us, in or of itself, to go from positive instances of an arbitrary putative generalization toward the assertion of that generalization. Before that can happen, the generalization has to enjoy the status of a hypothesis. It can only attain that status if, in the right way, it renders less surprising something else that has seemed surprising or wanted explaining. From this it follows that no methodological paradoxes such as Hempel's (of the ravens, etc.) or Goodman's (of "grue," etc.) can gain any purchase on the Peircean account of inquiry. For there is nothing in that account that corresponds to Nicod's postulate. If a white shoe really did confirm to some degree that "all nonblack things are nonravens" – this would be the effect of Nicod's postulate – then it would have to confirm to the same degree its contrapositive equivalent "all ravens are black." And that, in any normal setup, is absurd. Here a thousand confirmatory instances are worthless. In Peirce's conception of inquiry, appostioning work in the way it does between induction and abduction, there is no place for Nicod's postulate.[11]

VIII

How does a putative subject matter need to be if Peirce is to allow that it constitutes a proper field of genuine inquiry? A similar (or equivalent?) question: to what standard must a putative subject matter attain, and what must be its condition, for the judgments it throws up to count as properly answerable to Peircean realities/Reals?

Suppose there is a mode of thinking, neither purely perceptual nor relating only to what is remembered, that is well enough manageable for the following to hold: if you engage in the form of thinking in question, then "secondness jabs you perpetually in the ribs" (CP 6.95, 1903). Suppose that, practicing this mode of thinking, you can reach by patient labor a complex and many-layered state of readiness and then arrive, when jabbed, at a belief. This is to say that, at some crucial point in your thoughts or explorations, something that is not up to you but is of the right sort to do this can bring it about that you are convinced, fallibly but fully. Suppose that in this field you can arrive at a belief (as Leibniz would say) *malgré vous*. Then, whatever the distance at which this form of thinking lies from the perceptual case or the memory case, your search cannot help but represent a genuine form of inquiry – a form within which the judgment that you arrive at can be answerable for its correctness to some reality/Real. Or so it seems. If Peirce's accounts of the fourth method and of secondness have any generality at all, then the only doubt there can be concerning whether there is any such reality/Real is a doubt relating to the credentials themselves of the form of thinking that purports to invoke the Real in question.

Such is the distance that it appears one can put between Peirce's theory of inquiry and any uniformly causal picture. Support might also be mustered here from Peirce's philosophy of mathematics, where Peirce describes the sort of secondness that can arise from experimenting by pencil and paper with a representative diagram, running through all possible cases and finding (say) that some apparent plurality of alternatives reduces to one case. See, for instance, CP 4.530, 1905 3.516, 1896. Nevertheless, it may be said, there is an objection. Consider Peirce's own phrase "determined by circumstances not extraneous to the facts." What can these words mean, it will be asked, unless Reals are items with a distinctively causal role?

If this objection is right, then either we must abandon every kind of thinking that trespasses outside the paradigm furnished by the causal theories of memory and perception (as arithmetical thinking surely does) or else we must try to unpack the phrase "determined by circumstances not extraneous to the facts." The second response seems more promising. Nor are we the first to think this. In the course of one of his rereadings of "Fixation," Peirce made an annotation against the words (already quoted in Section IV) "To satisfy our doubts, it is necessary that a method be found by which our beliefs may be caused by nothing human, but. ... by something upon which our thinking has no effect." Peirce's annotation requires the word "caused" to be replaced by the word "determined."[12] It suggests that he wanted to construe "[beliefs or opinions] determined by circumstances not extraneous to the facts" in a way that *allowed but did not require* such determination to be simple causal determination.

In order to set out some of the options that this creates for the different kinds of case that Peirce needs to accommodate here (they are far too many for comfort, but let us see whether anything at all can be said at this level of generality), we must begin with a concession to causality. Opinions arise from thoughts and thoughts are produced by earlier thoughts. "If we mount the stream of thought instead of descending it, we see each thought caused by a previous thought" (W 3, 34, 1872). Taking our cue from this dictum and tracing the sequence from later to earlier, let us accept that the opinion or conviction that a thinker reaches at the end will be the product or effect of some secondness experience (as one might say). Let us allow too that, at the earlier point, the secondness experience itself must be traced back to its proper ancestry in some reality that it presents. These ancestries will come in different varieties, however.

In an ordinary causal case, there is a causal-*cum*-perceptual transaction between (say) the Cathedral at Chartres and a conscious, properly recipient subject S; and then, on the strength of this event, S believes justifiably and correctly that the Cathedral at Chartres has two spires. Here it is by virtue of the causal perceptual transaction that the Real consisting in the cathedral's having two spires determines S's belief that the cathedral has two spires. (In a fuller treatment one would attend separately of course to the cases of seeing x and of seeing that x is φ.)

That is the familiar case. But now suppose that the initiator of belief was not perception but some "elaborative process of thought" (W 3, 42), one leading into a gradual accumulation of reasons that culminated at the moment of secondness in the thinker's finding nothing else to think but that (...). Here the thing which brought the thinker to the point of conviction was not just any causal effectiveness. Still less was the thinker's finding that there was nothing else to think but that (...) the outcome of some reality's/Real's causally effective agency.[13] Rather the reason why the thinker was unable to find anything else to think but that (...) was that *there is nothing else to think*. If there is nothing else to think, no wonder the thinker thought that! You can say, if you wish, that some reasonable being's finding himself unable to discover anything else to think causally explains his finally arriving at the opinion that (...). But at the temporally first link in the chain, the *reasonableness* of the thinker and the *reasoned* character of his thought is essential to the explanation. It is in this essentially normative way that we satisfy Peirce's requirement that the inquirer's opinion that (. . .) should be determined by a circumstance not extraneous to the facts. It is satisfied because the circumstance of there being nothing else to think but that (. . .) is not something extraneous to the facts. Rather, this circumstance bears a (so to speak) constitutive relation to the reality/Real that consists in the fact that (. . .).[14]

IX

I hope that the proposal just offered is in the spirit of Peirce's annotation and correction. It shows how the purely causal case need only be one among many others. Elsewhere, I have tried to illustrate the formal pattern given in the previous section. I shall give again here two examples, doubtful though it is that Peirce would have approved of the second.

(A) Peter believes that $7 + 5 = 12$. He has learned this neither by rote nor yet by reading that famous passage of Kant's *Critique of Pure Reason* where $7 + 5 = 12$ serves as an example. Why then *does* he believe it? Well, the explanation begins with the fact that all the other answers to the question "what is the sum of 7 and 5?" are blocked or excluded. In a full version of the explanation, this exclusion could be proved by reference to the calculating rules. In a maximal version, one would also rehearse the irresoluble difficulties attaching to proposals for different rules. Once so much was set down, the explanation might continue as follows. Peter knows those calculating rules. Moreover, in espousing the answer 12, Peter is going by the rules. So no wonder it is his opinion that $7 + 5 = 12$. So, in this case, Peter's belief that $7 + 5 = 12$ *is* determined (as Peirce requires) by a circumstance not extraneous to the fact that $7 + 5 = 12$. His reasoning summarily recapitulates the very reason why seven plus five *is* twelve. Indeed the full explanation of Peter's belief precisely vindicates Peter's belief.

(B) Paul believes, let us suppose, that slavery is unjust and insupportable. Suppose that, in seeking to explain why Paul believes this, we inquire into his reasons for thinking this, and suppose we then look for further amplifications and elucidations of those reasons, drawing on the whole ethical background that we share with Paul. This will take a long time, but suppose that, as we proceed, it appears more and more clearly that the only way to think anything at variance with the insupportability and injustice of slavery is to opt out altogether from any moral viewpoint that can make sense of asking the question "What is one to think of the supportability or justice of slavery?" For suppose that at some point, in heaping consideration onto consideration, we find we have *enough* and it becomes apparent that *there is simply no room* in which to form another opinion. No doubt there will be many ethical cases where we do not reach this point and we do not know how to close off every avenue. But, in the case where we really can see Paul's belief as downwind of reasons like the convincing ones that we have imagined someone's eventually rehearsing about slavery, surely we can say "No wonder Paul believes what he believes! There is nothing else to think." In other words, Paul's belief about slavery is determined by circumstances (namely the considerations that we are supposing to have been rehearsed and to impinge on one who understands the moral question) not extraneous to the fact that slavery is unjust and insupportable. For Paul's reasons for thinking what he thinks do summarily recapitulate that in virtue of which slavery *is* wrong and insupportable.

Peirce would have been sceptical, I fear, whether our example (B) could be worked out in the way I have imagined. He could not object in principle, though, to the idea that a mass of considerations can culminate in conviction. For he speaks in other connections of reasons "not form[ing] a chain which is no stronger than its weakest link but a cable whose fibers may be ever so slender provided they are sufficiently numerous and intimately connected" (W 2, 213, 1868).

X

It is evident – and a search for more examples would make it even more evident – that the generality to which Peirce aspires in his theory of inquiry involves us in a bewildering and indefinite variety of different ways in which thinkers in different areas of concern can satisfy the Peircean requirement on which we have laid such stress. It is no less evident, though, that in so far as we want to persist at that level of generality, the answer we give to the question proposed at the beginning of Section VIII, will have to be as follows: the thing that is minimally required in order to secure pragmatic content to a subject matter is this: that there, in that subject matter, a belief to the effect that p can be determined by circumstances not extraneous to the fact that p.

More generally, the conclusion to which we are drawn is that for any genuine belief, whether true or false, there has to be something it is answerable to and sensitive to. This last may as well be called a Real. But instead of rushing into a new ontology of Reals, let us look carefully to the status of our familiar form: *whoever sincerely inquires whether p seeks to ensure that any belief of theirs to the effect that p be determined by circumstances not extraneous to the fact that p.* This is only a schema. Reals are not here objects quantified over. The sentence letter "p," being not a variable, functions by holding a place for a sentence in use. On these terms, the minimal claim about the formation of the belief that p is a notionally simultaneous assertion of all instances of the italicized sentence form with all possible sentential fillings for the letter "p." In putting forward this schema, we *gesture* (if you like) at something entirely general, something that would be gestured at by these countless assertions. But we only gesture. For, strictly speaking, there is only a pattern here, nothing more. If we do proceed in this way, though, there is another advantage. We can also give notice that not all these assertions work in the same way. The secondness requirement, the nonextraneousness condition, and the other requirements on the determination of the inquirer's belief are to be understood in the divers ways that are appropriate to different examples. If what Peirce says about Reals is interpreted or elucidated, logically speaking, in this way, then the philosophical effect is that the schema is grammatically and philosophically filled out for different kinds of cases according to the subject matter – and in the light of whatever Peirce's logic can add to his characterization of the fourth method.

XI

If the fourth method as now explained and enlarged upon is the only method of satisfactorily settling opinion (albeit fallibly, always fallibly), what conception of truth do theorists of inquiry have to see as animating and constraining the epistemic efforts of those who practice the method? And how are theorists further to elaborate or elucidate this conception?

Let us begin with some of the materials of "Fixation" itself. In a footnote to a passage that I quoted in Section V, continuing that passage into an afterthought dated 1903, Peirce writes:

1. CP 5.375: [T]ruth is neither more nor less than that character of a proposition which consists in this, that belief in the proposition would, with sufficient experience and reflection, lead us to such conduct as would tend to satisfy the desires we should then have. To say that truth means more than this is to say that it has no meaning at all.

This is the kind of statement that has given pragmatism such a bad name. Apart, however, from the warnings already urged in section I, there are other reasons to be careful here. If I say that the character of being red is nothing more nor less than the character of being the color thought by blind people to be well grasped by a comparison with the sound of a trumpet, does my claim have to be interpreted as a definition? If, in addition, we take the characterization in passage (1) to be a definition of truth that is intended to bring out what is so good about truth, then we misunderstand Peirce even more unfairly. Not only do we attribute to him a cynical instrumentalism that is utterly alien to his actions, his character, and his expressed views of science and life itself. We interpolate into his theories something that is entirely alien to the later sections of "Fixation." It is true that, in other places, Peirce gives a pragmatic reinterpretation of the notions of "reality"/"Real"/"external permanency" that play such an important role in "Fixation." But that reinterpretation is precisely not intended to *blunt the force* of the later sections of "Fixation." The intention (whether successful or unsuccessful) is rather to explicate these notions – in the spirit of "look[ing] to the upshot of our concepts in order rightly to apprehend them" (CP 5.3, 1901).

We need more Peircean testimony, testimony beyond that already displayed in Section IV, about the idea of truth:[15]

2. CP 2.135, 1902: You certainly opine that there is such a thing as Truth. Otherwise reasoning and thought would be without a purpose. What do you mean by there being such a thing as Truth? You mean that something is SO . . . whether you, or I, or anybody thinks it is so or not. . . . The essence of the opinion is that there is *something* that is SO, no matter if there be an overwhelming vote against it.

3. CP 5.553, 1905: That truth is the correspondence of a representation with its object is, as Kant says, merely a nominal definition of it. Truth belongs exclusively to propositions ... the proposition is a sign ... thought is of the nature of a sign. In that case then, if we can find out the right method of thinking and can follow it out – the right method of transforming signs – then truth can be nothing more nor less than the last result to which the following out of this method would ultimately carry us. In that case, that to which the representation should conform, is itself something in the nature of a representation, or sign – something noumenal, intelligible, conceivable, and utterly unlike a thing-in-itself.

CP 554: Truth is the conformity of a representamen to its object, *its* object, ITS object, mind you. ... Here is a view of the writer's house: what makes that house to be the object of the view? Surely not the similarity of appearance. There are ten thousand others in the country just like it. No, but the photographer set up the film in such a way that according to the laws of optics, the film was forced to receive an image of this house. ... So, then, a sign, in order to fulfil its office, to actualize its potency, must be compelled by its object. This is evidently the reason of the dichotomy of the true and the false. For it takes two to make a quarrel, and a compulsion involves as large a dose of quarrel as is requisite to make it quite impossible that there should be compulsion without resistance.

4. CP 5.565, 1901, "Truth and Falsity and Error": Truth is that concordance of an abstract statement with the ideal limit towards which endless investigation would tend to bring scientific belief. ... Reality is that mode of being by virtue of which the real thing is as it is, irrespectively of what any mind or any definite collection of minds may represent it to be. The truth of the proposition that Caesar crossed the Rubicon consists in the fact that the further we push our archaeological and other studies, the more strongly will that conclusion force itself on our minds forever – or would do so, if study were to go on forever. An idealist metaphysician may hold that therein also lies the whole *reality* behind the proposition; for though men may for a time persuade themselves that Caesar did *not* cross the Rubicon, and may contrive to render this belief universal for any number of generations, yet ultimately research – if it be persisted in – must bring back the contrary belief. But in holding that doctrine, the idealist necessarily draws the distinction between truth and reality.

5. CP 5.416, 1905: [A truth is] that to a belief in which belief would tend if it were to tend indefinitely to absolute fixity ...

Let us begin with (2). (2), like the beginning of (3), effectively reinforces the manifest purport of Peirce's rationale for the fourth method. It reinforces the concluding message of "Fixation" but does not carry us beyond.

In (3), the object of a representamen must surely be the very same thing as its Real. The analogy with one view or aspect, as given in the photograph of Peirce's own house, echoes a sentence (CP 5.549, 1905) where Peirce claims that a fact is something "so highly prescissive[16] that it can be wholly represented as a simple proposition." But, however striking the analogy may appear that we find in (3), and however helpful this may promise to be, the ontology that it imports is full of difficulty. The problem is familiar. We think a proposition should be true by satisfying its truth-condition. But, if we think that, then we need to be able to state the truth-condition in such a way that the proposition can be false as well as true. Peirce claims that "a proposition is true if it conforms to its object," and he indicates in the passage cited in (3) (which I have abbreviated) that here he is reaching beyond the correspondence theory. But then we must ask what to say, according to the account he is developing, if the proposition is false. For in that case there will be no such thing as ITS object.[17] There will be nothing the proposition has failed to be "compelled by." On the other hand, if the proposition is true, its object will exist and there will be no need to enter further into questions about conformity or compulsion. For its object exists and that alone will be enough.

"Corresponds to the facts," as the correspondence theory has it, where "facts" is plural, appears to be a merely stylistic variant on "true." Understandably, this provokes us to try to find a proper relation here between a proposition and some one thing, its representatum, so to say (CP 5.384). But the auguries are not good, it has already appeared, for the theory which we see Peirce picking his way toward in our citation (3). The counterattractions will be further evident of the approach we adopted in Section X. On that approach the schematic letter, by standing hostage in each case for a sentence that is reality-involving, does a sort of justice to the realism of Peirce's view of the search for truth. But it does this without ontological commitment to facts, realities, or Reals and it dispenses entirely with all relations of conformity and compulsion between a belief and a particular item, whether fact or object. This may seem to suggest the possibility of replacing Peirce's effort in CP 5.554 (cited earlier) with some scheme for truth that is more anodyne, less troublesome, and entirely general. But I have tried to show in another place that, here too, no general account of truth itself is to be had – at best a thought which, consistently and sincerely pursued, leads straight into paradox.[18]

The proposals (4) and (5) bring us closer to the formulation from "How to Make Our Ideas Clear" which we rejected in Section I. Proposals (4) and (5) are intended to give the effective or pragmatic meaning of the manifestly correct "merely nominal" conceptions expressed in proposals (2) and (3). In (4), such pragmatic proposals, even the idealist ones, are defended from the charge of losing the distinction between truth and reality. So far, so good; and no doubt these proposals also have other merits. Nevertheless, when read literally, they all seem to depend for their acceptability upon the supposition that no information of the kind that would be needed to test plausible guesses already made or discover truths as yet unknown (e.g., concerning that which is past or is presently hidden) *ever perishes* or becomes unavailable to inquiry. For if, always and constantly, such information is being lost, then it is neither here nor there that inquiry can be constantly renewed, constantly corrected, and open-endedly prolonged. Moreover, such perishing, as Hilary Putnam points out, is not only a fact but a fact that is implied by modern physics.[19]

Peirceans may respond to this crippling objection by reading proposals (4) or (5) less literally. But then the construal will need to lean heavily on our understanding of that which (4) and (5) purport to define/explain/elucidate. It is also worth remarking that, once the reference of "that to which inquiry would tend," etc., is sufficiently carefully distinguished from any particular set of propositions that has been redacted or will have been redacted at any particular point in the future, the phrase "that to which inquiry would tend," so far from distilling an effective or pragmatic meaning from the truisms that figure in (2), is a form of words that stands in radical need (as radical a need as any expression ever could) of pragmatic elucidation!

XII

Is all then entirely lost so far as truth is concerned? Can it be that truth waits in the wings, is latent in the inquirer's project of deciding what to think (see again our first epigraph), can be clearly seen emerging in the thoughts of someone who moves through the first, second, and third methods into the method of experience, abduction, and the rest – and yet is a character that defies all identification or elucidation? No. Surely we can find for Peirce some form of words that fastens down and promises in due course to help elucidate, in terms that essentially involve the business of inquiry and the method of "experience," the nature of that property, namely truth, which (unless we are complete strangers to opinion or doubt) is already familiar to any or all of us. Once we allow ourselves to speak of a property that is already known to us, and once we dissociate ourselves from Peirce's numerous and uniformly unsuccessful attempts to arrive at the property from pragmatist would-be determinations of the extension of "true," several suitable forms of words stare us in the face:

6. Truth is the property that it is the aim of inquiry as such to find beliefs possessed of.

7. Truth is the character which, if only we follow the fourth method of inquiry, we may *justifiably hope* will be enjoyed by beliefs that survive however long or far inquiry is pursued or prolonged.

8. Truth is the property that anyone will want for his or her beliefs who sincerely inquires whether p (or not) and who seeks to ensure that any belief of his or hers to the effect that p (or not p) should be determined by circumstances not extraneous to the fact that p.

Such formulations might not have pleased Peirce, but they hold a place for a view to which he could lay claim if he wanted.

XIII

Suppose that, in the cause of further elucidating[20] the property of truth, we were to deploy the identities given in (6), (7), and (8) and we were to elaborate the plurality of linkages holding between truth, on the one side, and inquiry, experience, secondness, hypothesis, . . . , on the other. Suppose that, proceeding in this way, we were to present our findings as the marks, in Frege's sense,[21] of the concept *true*, and suppose that, in the same effort, we tried to explore the logical properties of the concept of truth (ascertain what properties the property of truth implies, excludes, etc. in a thing thought or said). Then what would follow from the fact the whole basis on which this elucidatory exercise was conducted was a link between a notion of truth awaiting further specification and the notion of inquiry that is already developed (cp. IV, V, VI) and is partially definitive of pragmaticism as a philosophical position? If, proceeding in the way indicated and adducing our understanding of inquiry, we look in this spirit of pragmaticism "to the upshot of our conception [of truth] in order rightly to apprehend [it]," then what do we learn about that conception? Will our findings have the effect of subverting the ordinary ("realist") presumption that the truth is perfectly independent of us (except, of course, in so far as some judgment that is in question relates to doings of ours, or relates to the effects of such doings)? Will the pragmaticist outlook have the effect of undermining the ordinary idea – compare citation (2) – that the truth is "there anyway," definitely and determinately? Will it move us toward the position that Michael Dummett has called antirealism?[22]

It is hard to find very much in Peirce's texts that conforms to these expectations. Nor is there any anticipation in any logical writings by Peirce of the classic antirealist position developed by Michael Dummett under the influence of mathematical intuitionism and the strong emphasis that intuitionism places on the relation between grasping a proof of a proposition and understanding it. (The intuitionist emphasis is philosophically akin to the logical positivists' foundational idea that to understand a Satz is to know the method of its verification.) The antirealist whose position Dummett develops is one who affirms the laws of noncontradiction (no statement is true and false) and of *tertium non datur* (no statement is neither true nor false) while *withholding assent* from the principle of bivalence (every statement is either true or false). Such assent is withheld by virtue of the absence of any assurance that, with regard to every well-formed assertion, either it or its negation can be proved or established to be true. (Dummett points out that, for the same sort of reason, the positivists would have been well advised to withhold that assent.)

Things seem very different with Peirce. In all his logical explorations, he never raises doubts or questions of principle about the status of the law of double negation elimination. Since double negation elimination elides the subtle difference between *tertium non datur* and bivalence, committing anyone who accepts the former to the latter, it would appear that Peirce can have had no premonition at all of an antirealism such as Dummett's. It is true that, in a more philosophical context, Peirce writes (using the name excluded middle where modern antirealists might prefer bivalence) that "Logic requires us, with reference to EACH question we have in hand, to hope some definitive answer to it may be true. That HOPE with reference to EACH case as it comes up is, by a SALTUS, stated by logicians as a law concerning ALL CASES, namely the law of excluded middle. This law amounts to saying that the inverse has a perfect reality."[23] But the hope Peirce speaks of here relates to truth, not to proof or verification; and the substance of the hope surely relates to truth as ordinarily conceived. For, as I shall try to show in the next pages, the confidence that Peirce speaks of as presupposed by the logical principle in question smacks more of Peirce's confidence in the significance or Sinn of declarative sentences that are properly answerable to experience or experiment than it can of any faith of Peirce's in declarative sentences or their negations all having proofs or verifications. At least in Dummett's sense, Peirce is not an antirealist. In Peirce, the key to having significance or sense (and to grasping significance or sense) is not the actual prospect of proof/disproof or verification/falsification but proper engagement with the business of inquiry and of *reaching for* verification or falsification.

If (as I venture to think) pragmaticism leaves truth just as it was, what then is the real purport of pragmaticism in its connection with truth and meaning? What is the intended import of such dicta as these? –

There is no conception so lofty and elevated that it cannot be fully defined in terms of the conceptions of our homely, instinctive everyday life (MS 313 p. 29, quoted in Misak 1991: 119)

or the familiar foundational claim

Consider what effects that might conceivably have practical bearings we conceive the object of our conception to have. Then our conception of these effects is the whole of our conception of the object.[24] (CP 5.402, "How To Make Our Ideas Clear," 1877)

According to the transposition of Peirce's thoughts that I offer in these reflections, the real purport is relatively simple. Even though Peirce is a realist about truth, he is an operationalist about meaning. There is no specifically pragmaticist conception of truth,[25] but there is a pragmaticist conception of sense/significance/Sinn. A Peircean pragmatist, a pragmaticist (as Peirce was led to say in order to make room for the differences between William James and himself), will scarcely think it worth saying that there is more to reality than could ever be put into however many propositions – that, truth being what it is, there are all sorts of truths we shall never formulate and never could. His key concern is with the propositions we *shall* ourselves arrive at, express, affirm, or believe. It is with the real purport or meaning of our actual utterances, and the illusions we so easily fall into about what we can mean by what we say. The pragmatist's chief contribution to these questions, and the source of his critique of "vagabond ideas that tramp the public roads without any human habitation" (CP 8.112, 1900), lies where the citation last given indicates that it does. It lies in Peirce's account of the grades of clarity that can be attained in our understanding of the terms that enter into meaningful sentences and in our grasp of the concepts that enter into the propositions that such sentences express. Where concept-terms are concerned, we have the first grade of clarity, according to Peirce, if we can apply the term to things in our experience. We have the second grade when we can produce the kinds of explanation that pass muster as dictionary definitions or the like. At the third grade, if we are to attain that, our recognitional capacity must have been elaborated into a further and better state of practical readiness, a fully operational state, so to speak, one that engages with inquiry, experience, secondness, guessing, retroduction... with these things as they are or can be in life. See again the recently displayed citations. The practical conceptions mentioned in the second relate to habits of action. They also involve a rather specific orientation toward possible or actual future experience. (Compare CP 8.194.) It is at the third grade (presupposing and not superseding the first and the second) that the grasp of sense/significance/Sinn of a symbol has to be made complete.

The third grade of clarity can only be attained if, independently of any particular person's efforts, there awaits one who seeks to grasp the meaning of a given term some publicly completed or completable meaning for a sufficiently determined thinker to grasp. Peirce offers no unitary or full answer to the question what it is that completes this meaning or saturates the Sinn of the symbol. (See Misak 1991: 12–35). Supposing, though, that somehow this saturation has been achieved or is in the process of being achieved, we may expect the proposition expressed by a sentence comprising such symbols to depend on the Sinn of its constituent parts. Thinkers' corresponding grasp of the proposition and its truth-condition, arrived at through their understanding of a sentence's mode of composition, may *or may not* put them into a position to verify or falsify the proposition expressed by the sentence. Where thinkers can verify or falsify, it needs to be no accident that that is so. But being placed to verify or falsify is not the general form of the kind of readiness which Peirce is concerned with.

XIV

Such in outline is the semantic operationalism which, using language more current than the language of Peircean semeiotic, I speculatively reconstruct for the author of "Fixation" at the time of the rereadings and rewritings recorded in our first epigraph. Leaving intact the ordinary ideal of truth, the position counsels, no doubt, that often the best we can hope to achieve is approximation to truth – and nothing wrong with that. If, on the one side, there is truth itself (truths themselves), which propositions seek to track down, then on the other side there are propositions, and the senses of sentences in use. These are our artifacts. As such, they depend on us for their completion. The properly significant sentence, by being the sentence it is and having its sense determined by whatever senses with which we contrive for the senses of its constituents to be saturated, sets itself a goal that it either attains or does not attain. Whether this goal is attained or not is in no way up to us. But what sentence it is that has been propounded, with what sense, and engaging in what way with inquiry, this *is* up to us. It is a highly nontrivial achievement on our collective part for a sentence to set itself such a goal. It is an achievement not contrivable at all unless the conditions for truth are coordinated with the demands that are placed on an inquirer to avail himself or herself, in the right way, of experience. Such realism and such operationalism are made for one another.

One word more, about bivalence. Suppose that in a context c there is a sentence S each of whose components has a sense that is lexically and contextually fully determinate, operationally complete, and ready and waiting in c for the comprehension of any thinker who is ready to attain to the third grade of clarity with respect to it and ready to grasp the Sinn of the sentence that all these components make up. Suppose that the proposition expressed by S in c will be true if and only if..., where "..." is a fully determinate condition (determinate in c, even if not necessarily verbally completely explicit). If so, then the proposition conveyed by S will be so determinate that it is determinate what it is for things to be *otherwise* than they are when.... In that case, given such determinacy for S, nothing obstructs the full determinacy of the sense of the negation of S. For whatever in c circumscribes the sense of " ... " will determine the sense of "things are otherwise than they are when...." Such a form of stipulation seems ideally suited to the rule Peirce gives at CP 4.492 for his system of existential graphs, to the effect that two SEPS (signs of exclusion), "the one enclosing the other, but nothing outside that other, can be removed." (See CP 4.490–8, 1903 and 4.572, 1905) This is equivalent to the law of double negation.[26] An antirealist might demur, but Peirce himself entertains no doubts at all about the pragmatic meaning of a SEP-sign that conforms to such a rule.

XV

Inquiry conducted along the lines of Peirce's fourth method, inheriting as it does the merits of various predecessors, is a process that gathers rational strength, we have claimed, as it gathers force and gathers force as it gathers rational strength. On the proper understanding of this process, we have said, truth is conceived as the property that we can hope to steer our enquiry to home upon; the beliefs that inquiry furnishes to us are beliefs that it is rational for us, however fallibly, to persist in until specific grounds for doubt present themselves; and the method of inquiry makes room for any or all modes of research or criticism, whether commonsensical or scientific, that promise to reach beliefs by routes not extraneous to the facts they are concerned with. One who conducts himself on these principles will be no more eager to define "rational" than he is to circumscribe legitimate methods of exploration and discovery; but such a person will surely insist that the method of inquiry is a fully rational way of arguing from the known to the unknown – that it is a paragon of rationality.

Such an attitude will appear to conflict with something commonly regarded as one of the great insights of David Hume. Hume points out in *Enquiry Concerning Human Understanding* that all reasonings concerning matters of fact are founded in the relations of cause and effect, and the foundation of our understanding of these is experience. But here he claims to find a problem. How may I rationally infer from past bread-eatings' *having* nourished me that similar eatings *will* nourish me? If there is such an inference it is not *intuitive* (knowable without demonstration); nor yet is it *demonstrative*. What is it then?

It is *experimental*, Hume imagines your saying. But to this he replies that experimental reasonings already presuppose that the future will resemble the past. How then, presupposing this, can they show or even suggest that the future will resemble the past? Hume infers that it is not reasoning that engages us to suppose the future will resemble the past. It is habit, not reason.

What ought Peirce to say? Peirce would begin by agreeing that inference from the known to the unknown is a matter of habit and is not demonstrative. But habits, he would insist, can be good or bad. And good habits can exemplify a distinctive form of reasonableness. (See Section II.) After all, we *need* to argue from the known to the unknown. If we need to, then it is reasonable for us to do so (intuitively rational you can say, if you wish) and it is irrational for us not to do so – provided that we do not entrust ourselves to a particular policy that there is reason for us to regard as reckless (as exposing our vital needs to risks there is no necessity for us to incur) or as ill-calculated to bring us to beliefs we shall accept for reasons nonextraneous to the facts. If Hume wants to make a point about habit, let him make it as a point about the relevance of habits to the science of logic. It is a good point, and Peirce would second it. (Cp. Section II.) But it is no excuse for an assault on reason as such – unless Hume's aim is to put himself at the center of a long-running controversy.

It is easy to imagine that, if he were allowed a response, Hume would still press upon the question how Peirce can argue non-question-beggingly from past nourishings by bread to future nourishings by bread, if this presupposes the *general* claim that the future will resemble the past – which is something yet harder to establish than future nourishings by bread.

To this Peirce would surely reply (here anticipating Popper) that good arguments from the known to the unknown had better *not* presuppose that the future will resemble the past. For it is not even true that it will!

Nature is not regular.... It is true that the special laws and regularities are innumerable; but nobody thinks of the irregularities, which are infinitely more frequent. (W 2, 264)

Moreover, when we argue from past nourishings by bread to future nourishings by bread, we are *not*, according to Peirce, simply extrapolating a past regularity. That is never, in his view, a valid procedure. If that was what Hume was attacking, then Hume was right, Peirce will say, but far short of the conclusion that Hume was aiming for. When we extrapolate a regularity, there has to be another reason to do so beside the fact that the regularity has held so far. Even in the special case of the "particular methods" beloved of the inductive reliabilists, Peirce would say, it would be utterly invalid to argue from the mere past success of a method to its future success. With any method, there has to have been something else to commend it. And here is the role of abductive thought. (Compare Section VII.)

Let us distinguish here two cases. The first is that of the ordinary person with an ordinary need not to starve, who wants to prolong life and needs some determinate way, here and now, of sorting the nourishing from the nonnourishing. Any such sorting must either deploy existing categorizations such as "bread" or deploy improvements upon the categorizations the person already has. There is nowhere else for him to work from. In so far as "bread" is one of the categorizations on which the person habitually relies and on which he acts, he is committed to think that there is something about bread – a substance that he can identify where necessary with some precautionary care – which would explain why it nourishes. Under interrogation he would appear to be committed to think there is some generalization about bread and nourishing (one he may not know how on demand to formulate very carefully or articulately) which would not, if it were tested, be falsified. (Compare our discussions of perception and memory at Section VI.) If the question were raised why, once formulated or reformulated, any such generalization should be relied upon, the person might reply first that faith in this is a much more reasonable faith than faith in the future's resembling the past; and second that *some* such generalization has to be relied upon if life is to go on. There is no alternative. It would be irrational then not to act on the basis he is acting on. Criticize that basis and he will look for something better, for something that is adequate for the matter in hand. But the only point of departure in the search for something better is the place where we are. Cp. Plato *Phaedo* 10 1D (ad fin.); Aristotle *Nicomachean Ethics* 1095^{b2}.

As one makes more and more explicit that which an ordinary person might say in defense of his habit of taking bread to be nourishing, one converges on the case where a more theoretical answer is to be given. That theoretical answer is not, according to the pragmatist, essentially different, only more discursive. It begins in the same place. If we are to do what we are naturally committed to do and argue in this case from the known to the unknown, then we must begin by trying to understand the thing that is known. So the thing we must understand better is bread. The problem of understanding or singling out this particular kind is not, however, one we need to solve on its own, or without any reference to the state of our inquiries into other empirical questions. We can only approach it from where we are at any given point in our inquiry. Looking at things from where he is, the inquirer notices the remarkable phenomenon that some have nothing to eat and starve and die while others who eat, and eat bread among other things, sustain their life. (See the third epigraph.) If bread nourished then it would be a matter of course that those who ate it sustained life. So it seems, according to the abductive hypothesis, that bread nourishes. This is a generalization worthy to test; and in the interim it is one to live by, pending any refinement or refutation that it may suffer.

Hume or his followers will notice that the Peircean strategy leans here upon the fundamental hypothesis. So they are bound to inquire what grounds the fundamental hypothesis itself. One tempting answer is: "Nothing holds or is so or obtains but that there is some reason why it is so." Readers of Leibniz will recognize the thought.[27] It is true that the claim is quite as general as the claim that the future will resemble the past, but it is a far better candidate to be the regulative assumption of inquiry. At least it suggests nothing that is *manifestly* false. Still better, it scarcely needs to be thought of as an empirical generalization about reality. It proposes rather a certain attitude toward reality – an attitude that it would be unreasonable for us not to share in if we are to do that which we shall perish by not doing.

What then is the connection between Sufficient Reason and the twofold procedure that Peirce commends to us? Suppose our methodological stand is that nothing holds unless there is a reason why it should. Then we are committed to think that, if some phenomenon C obtains, something must be true which explains why C obtains. But then it must be possible for us to argue backwards, against the current of deductive sequence, and to infer from C's obtaining whatever *best* explains why *C* obtains. But here we come back to abduction, which supplies selected materials to induction. (See VII end.) If stuffs like bread nourish, there must be something or other about them in virtue of which they do that.... Of course "bread" may be the wrong basis for an abduction and ensuing generalization. But this is a question that we can only attempt from the midst of a large background, already given, of collateral beliefs, nonarbitrary suspicions, conjectures, questions, and the rest. The label "bread" is our provisional place-holder for some stuff or other that makes a difference to life's being sustained. (Cp. CP 4.234, 1902) "Bread" provides us with the materials for a hypothesis that can be tested, qualified, reformulated, tested again, and so on. In practice and so far, some hypotheses have stood up. When they fail, we will start repairing them. It would be arbitrary to proceed in any other way and worse than arbitrary not to proceed in this one. Of this, indeed, we can be *intuitively* certain.

None of this proves that bread will continue to nourish. Such a proof was not what Hume took himself to be entitled to ask for. What he asked was what kind of reasonable inference it is that gives the conclusion (however fallible) that bread will nourish. The answer to his question is that it is a fallible extrapolation, which we should be practically irrational not to attempt, from an abductive hypothesis that we should have been practically irrational not to try to formulate and test, an abductive hypothesis arrived at from wherever we actually are, and made in accordance with the branch of thinking that the nineteenth century called logic. Except in so far as it subsumes the science of deduction, it is not the business of such logic, and it does not need to be its business, to furnish infallible directions by which to argue from the known to the unknown[28] – only directions that it would be unreasonable not to employ. Let those who are expert in the classification of forms of reasonableness now classify the various elements of this response to Hume's challenge and let them assign them variously to the intuitive, the demonstrative, and the experimental.[29]

NOTES

1. See Misak (1991: ch. 1, for instance), who alerts us to the consistently and strictly pragmatic signification of Peirce's use of words such as "mean."

2. See Short (2000: 2, and n3). Another citation given by Short: "The method of science is itself a scientific result" (CP 6.428, 1893).

3. Hookway (1985: 52f).

4. The importance of this citation is pointed out by Skagestad (1981: 141).

5. It is worth comparing the indispensability of this hypothesis with one of the several roles of Leibnizian Sufficient Reason. For all these roles, see Wiggins (1996: 117–32).

6. Here there is rich collateral evidence of Peirce's intentions. Especially, perhaps, we should take note of a manuscript of 1893–5 that Cheryl Misak draws to our attention:

> As for the experience under the influence of which beliefs are formed, what is it? It is nothing but the forceful element in the course of life. Whatever it is ... in our history that wears out our attempts to resist it, that is experience.... The maxim that we ought to be "guided" by experience means that we had better submit at once to that to which we must submit at last. "Guided" is not the word; "governed" should be said. MS 408, p. 147, 1893–95, quoted in Misak (1991: 83)

7. An analogy may be helpful. Augustine wrote *"Dilige [deum] et quod vis fac."* The exhortation "Love God and do what thou wilt" may seem to be utterly permissive. It seems so until you reflect that such an injunction requires you to desire nothing God would not wish you to desire (or nothing you think he would not wish you to desire). It does not entail that you should do whatever you will. (There is no doubt how Augustine's double direction is to be understood. No doubt it is a question whether our "imperative logic" would need general modification lest "conjunction elimination" destroy the sense of such double commands. Better though to show the dispensability of imperative logic.)

8. In something he wrote before "The Fixation of Belief," Peirce had already noted that there is an important difference between the settlement of opinion which results from investigation and every other such settlement. Investigation "will not fix one answer to a question as well as another, but on the contrary it tends to unsettle opinions at first, to change them and to confirm a certain opinion which depends only on the nature of investigation itself" (CP 7.317, 1873). By the time someone has reached for the fourth method, he will be fully prepared for this.

9. Peirce sometimes talks like this: "Abduction commits us to nothing. It merely causes a hypothesis to be set down upon our docket of cases to be tried" (CP 5.602, 1903). Elsewhere, he is troubled by the fact that "it is well within bounds to reckon that there are a billion hypotheses that a fantastic being might guess would account for a given phenomenon." See Peirce (1929:269–83). For his response to this difficulty, see the sentences from "Guessing" cited at the end of the paragraph to which the present note attaches.

10. See Misak (1991: 99).

11. On Nicod, see Hempel (1945).

12. See Short (2000: n 9).

13. Here one is eager to allow on Peirce's behalf for the full force of a remark that he made in 1902 – I owe the reference to Skagestad (1981: 39) – "In reasoning, we have the singular phenomenon of a physiological function which is open to approval and disapproval" (CP 2.152).

14. Compare "[T]he truth of the pure mathematical proposition is constituted by the impossibility of ever finding a case in which it fails" (CP 5.567, 1901). We shall supersede in the next section the apparently relational mode of discourse adopted in the sentence to which the footnote is annexed.

15. Useful collations of sources on truth will be found in Haack (1997: 91–107) (which sets out some wicked, curious, and instructive contrasts between her two subjects) and in Migotti (1999).

16. That is to say that the fact that p *prescinds from* the aspects of reality with which it is not concerned.

17. Compare P. F. Strawson (1965).

18. See Wiggins (2002).

19. See Putnam (1995b).

20. In order to elucidate a predicate (without necessarily defining it or giving necessary and sufficient conditions for its application) one deploys the predicate and puts to use the concept that it introduces in ways that exhibit the character of the concept and reveal its connection with other concepts that are established, coeval, or collateral with it, and already intelligible in their own right. (For the pedigree of the term elucidation, see Wittgenstein 1921: 3.263, 4.026, 4.112.)

21. For various attempts of my own to pursue this line of inquiry, see the article cited in note 18 and the bibliography there.

> *Marks.* The marks of the (first level) concept *horse* are the (first level) properties possessed by all things that fall under the first level concept *horse*. Thus we arrive at the marks of the concept *horse* by asking, of things that share the property of being a horse, what properties they have. The answer in this case will be the properties of having a head, four legs, a solid hoof, a flowing mane and tail, a voice that is a neigh.... Similarly then, what properties do things have that possess the property of truth?

22. See Misak (1995: 121, 125, 127).

23. NE 4.xiii, undated, emphasis as cited in Misak (1991:157).

24. Cp. "We must look to the upshot of our concepts in order rightly to apprehend them" (CP 5.3, already cited).

25. As we saw in the first epigraph, Peirce thinks that truth is *identifiable by reference* to the concept of inquiry. In Section XII, I have exploited that very thought. But truth is *not* for that reason an epistemological

or inquiry-based notion. It is a misunderstanding of the nature of elucidation to suppose that the concept of truth had to be epistemological *just because* one elucidatory route to truth was through the concept of inquiry. The method of elucidations neither retraces a prior process of contagion nor yet leaves contagion in its tracks.

26. In a comparable formulation devised in the service of a different conception of assertion, Dummett says that "a statement, so long as it is not ambiguous or vague, divides all possible states of affairs into just two classes. For a given state of affairs, either the statement is used in such a way that a man who asserted it but envisaged that state of affairs would be held to have spoken misleadingly, or the assertion of the statement would not be taken as expressing the speaker's exclusion of that possibility" (Dummett, 1959: 149–50). For Dummett this claim is part of the build-up for a proof of *tertium non datur*. ("If a state of affairs of the first kind obtains, the statement is false; if all actual states of affairs are of the second kind, it is true. It is thus *prima facie* senseless to say of any statement that in such-and-such a state of affairs it would be neither true nor false.") One part of Dummett's dialectical framework here is the verifiability principle to the effect that "a statement cannot be true unless it is in principle capable of being known to be true." For that reason Dummett holds that his own dichotomy principle falls short of implying bivalence. In the absence from Peirce's thought as we have reconstructed it of any such verifiability principle, it is hard to see what could prevent Peirce's semantic operationalism from delivering full bivalence. An illuminating critical commentary on Dummett's argument will be found in Ian Rumfitt (forthcoming).

27. Leibniz puts the claim to a theological use. Indeed, he sometimes tries to prove by its means the existence of God. But Sufficient Reason itself is neither theological nor teleological in its original purport. For more on some of these matters, see note 4.

28. Or even to furnish procedures that "will, if persisted in long enough, assuredly correct any error concerning future experience into which [they] may temporarily lead us" (CP 2.769, 1905). Peirce does make such claims, but they are inessential to his contribution to the "problem of induction." (On the status of these Peircean claims, see Misak (1991: 111, 115). See also Sections I, XI.)

29. Peirce refers to Hume rather infrequently. But see CP 6.500, 1906 6.605, 1891 5.505, 1905.

5   Truth, Reality, and Convergence

I. INTRODUCTION

Most contemporary philosophers who are sympathetic to pragmatism are anxious to distance themselves from Peirce's pragmatic clarification of the concept of truth as 'the opinion which is fated to be agreed to by all who investigate'. This reluctance is found both in those who follow Dewey and James in giving little role to a 'realist' notion of truth in accounting for our cognitive evaluations and in those who do not take this direction. Why does the suggestion that truth is a matter of fated convergence of opinion seem so unpromising to pragmatists other then Peirce?

One problem concerns 'buried secrets' or 'lost facts'. It seems evident that there are many truths which, we are sure, would not be discovered, however long we inquire into them. Another is that it seems to yield a strange view of what makes some propositions true: whether it is true that an inch of rain fell on the morning of the Battle of Hastings depends upon what evidence will turn up in the future rather than upon meteorological conditions in southern England nearly a thousand years ago. It is also charged that Peirce's theory obscures an insight which many find central to what makes pragmatism attractive. James's pluralism suggests that our practical concerns and aesthetic interests have a role in determining whether a system of beliefs agrees with reality; perhaps there are different versions of reality which answer to different practical concerns and are not in competition. Since Peirce identifies the truth with what anyone is fated to believe, if she only inquires for long enough, it is natural to conclude that his account of reality depends upon identifying a single fundamental aim for inquiry, that of contributing to the growth of finished knowledge. If truth were not characterised by reference to such a general interest, why should we expect *all* inquirers to discover it?

This line of thought led Hilary Putnam to suggest that Peirce's account of truth commits him to what Bernard Williams has called the absolute conception of reality. This is a view of 'the world as it is there anyway independently of our experience'. Such a view will abstract from anything that belongs to a specific perspective and will avoid dependence upon features of our cognitive apparatus that are specifically human: it is a conception which is 'to the maximum degree independent of our perspective and its peculiarities'. Thus it provides an account of reality which omits secondary qualities such as colours, which omits values, and which makes no use of such concepts as those of artefacts which answer to specific human interests. For Williams, this view of reality expresses an ideal of objectivity which is sought by the (physical) sciences: an account of reality which is not relative to any particular perspective, and which is in principle available to any creature that investigates the nature of reality (1978, 1985). Humans, extraterrestrials, and robots might all be included in this fated convergence of opinion.[1]

Describing Williams's position, Putnam writes: 'any conceivable species of intelligent beings (if they frame hypotheses correctly, perform the appropriate experiments) can "converge" toward agreement on the laws of ideal physics, in the fashion first envisaged by C. S. Peirce' (1992b: 84). Elsewhere, he refers to the 'Peircean idea of truth ... as a coherent system of beliefs which will ultimately be accepted by the widest possible community of inquirers as a result of strenuous inquiry' (1990: 221); and to the idea (shared by Peirce and metaphysical realists) that scientific inquiry will converge to 'one ideal theory' (1994: 353); to 'one complete and consistent theory of everything' (1990: 223).

Exploring how far this is true will help us to understand the development of Peirce's ideas about truth and reality. The passages which appear to suggest a commitment to the 'absolute conception' come from before 1880. Even these, I shall argue, need not be interpreted as carrying that commitment. Later writings, which emphasise that secondary qualities such as colours are real, and that kinds of artefacts (such as lamps) are real kinds, fit very poorly with it. There is even an argument urging that the contribution of religious belief to our personal fulfilment and to the success of our scientific inquiries provides 'evidence' which reinforces our natural (and often unacknowledged) belief in the reality of God. It is also striking that, in some later passages, the insistence that sufficient well-conducted inquiry is fated to take us to the truth is considerably qualified.

It is important that Peirce's pragmatic account of truth was formulated in order to clarify the concept of *reality*: 'The opinion which is fated to be ultimately agreed to by all who investigate, is what we mean by the true, and the object represented in that opinion is the real' (W 3, 273, 1878). His strategy was to provide an explanation or 'clarification' of truth, a concept he thought of as *logical*, and then use this to explain what we mean by reality: the real is the object of a true proposition. The account was required to vindicate the verbal definition of reality as 'that whose characters are independent of what anyone may think them to be' (W 3, 271, 1878); 'that mode of being by virtue of which the real thing is as it is, irrespectively of what any mind or definite collection of minds may represent it to be' (CP 5.565, 1901). So what recommended the view of truth as convergence was that it promised a pragmatic clarification of this idea of reality being independent of thought. Explaining the origins of the conception of *reality* in 'Some Consequences of Four Incapacities' (1868), Peirce described the real as 'that which, sooner or later, information and reasoning would finally result in, and which is therefore independent of the vagaries of me and you' (W 2, 239). After 1880, he had a new way to explain the concept of reality: we directly perceive external things *as external*, and (by 1903) when I perceive a red book, that independently existing book is the *immediate* object of my perception.[2]

After considering how we should understand the absolute conception of reality and the connections between truth and a fated convergence of opinions (Section 2), we turn to Peirce's writings, arguing that it is unclear whether the early writings involve the commitment to the absolute conception that some of Peirce's critics suggest. His writings from after 1880 certainly do not involve such a commitment. Moreover (Section 4), these later writings distinguish the concepts of truth and reality, suggesting that metaphysics is more independent of logic than he initially supposed. This reflects a new way of thinking about reality (Section 5). Finally (Section 6) we note that it may be a mistake to think of the convergence thesis as a traditional 'theory' of truth at all. This helps us to see how Peirce avoids the problem of buried secrets.

2. TRUTH, CONVERGENCE, AND THE ABSOLUTE CONCEPTION

When a proposition is true, 'anyone who investigates' is fated to arrive at belief in it. Now 'investigates' is a transitive verb. So anyone who investigates what? When this is spelled out, a variety of distinct theses emerge.

(1) If a proposition is true, then anyone who inquires 'into the nature of reality' (well enough and long enough) is fated to believe it.

(2) If a proposition is true, then anyone who investigates some question to which that proposition provides the answer is fated to believe it.

The 'traditional' reading of Peirce, the reading that leads to the claim that he is committed to an absolute conception of reality, suggests that he accepts (1): *any* truth is, in principle, accessible to *any* inquirer. (2) need not lead to such an interpretation of his views. It is compatible with the recognition that a particular inquirer might be fated never to confront a question to which some true proposition provides the answer, perhaps even with the admission that some inquirer could never even understand such a question. Whereas (1) suggests that any serious inquirer could eventually reach a stable belief in any true proposition, if only she pursued her inquiries for long enough and with sufficient diligence, (2) leads only to a conditional claim: *if* an inquirer investigates a question to which a given proposition provides the correct answer, then, granted that her inquiries are conducted well enough and continue for long enough, she is fated to arrive at belief in this proposition. (2) is compatible with rejection of the absolute conception of reality, for it is compatible with the view that our different perspectives are reflected in the varying ranges of questions that we can understand or take seriously. It is thus compatible with allowing that there are truths that some inquirers would never discover, even truths that some inquirers *could* never discover, no matter how much effort they put into their investigations. And we should note that this could arise in two ways. First, it is possible that they would never (or indeed could never) consider any questions to which those truths provide the answers. And second, even if they considered such questions, it is possible that they could never inquire into them either long enough or well enough. Comparing (1) and (2) enables us to see that the texts in which Peirce applies his pragmatist principle to the clarification of truth are compatible with a range of different views of varying strengths. And, if we arrive at an interpretation that fits (2) without entailing (1), there may be no reason to anticipate any close connection between Peirce's theory of truth as convergence and the absolute conception of reality.

The example of secondary qualities helps us to see the difference between these positions. Suppose we grant that possession of colour concepts (*green, blue,* and the like) is available only to those with a distinctive kind of visual apparatus, or, perhaps more plausibly, that it is only available to those who either possess such visual apparatus or can communicate with (and defer to) those who do so. Colour concepts are 'response-dependent' and are thus only available to those familiar with the appropriate kind of response – something is red only if it produces appropriate sensations in 'normal' observers in 'normal' circumstances. Unless we think that all inquirers must possess visual apparatus like ours or that they will inevitably encounter creatures that possess such visual apparatus, position (1) will entail that colour propositions cannot be true and that their objects are not real. Position (2) has no such entailment: it requires only that those capable of understanding questions about colours are capable of finding their answers. This too may be a problematic claim – and indeed I shall question whether Peirce actually endorsed it below. But what is important here is that, unlike (1), it does not involve a commitment to the absolute conception of reality.

So is Peirce committed to the absolute conception of reality? There are passages which, we may suppose, are hard to reconcile with accepting (2) but rejecting (1). For example: Reality is independent of the 'vagaries of you and me' (1868); its characters are 'independent of what we think them to be'(1877–1878). Do such claims suggest that colours, for example, are not part of reality? Whether 'things whose characters are independent of what we take them to be' are the same as 'things whose characters would be contained in a view of the world which, to a maximum degree, was independent of my perspective and its peculiarities' is very uncertain. If not, then Peirce's view of reality can be distinguished from the absolute conception. Of course, Peirce did not draw these distinctions, and his texts often leave it unclear what stance he would have taken had he done so. However, if we are to understand and evaluate his views of truth and reality, we must keep these differences in mind and consider the different positions that are compatible with what he says.

3. SOME DEVELOPMENTS IN PEIRCE'S VIEWS

In this section, we examine a number of passages from different stages in the development of Peirce's views in which he discusses truth, reality, and the convergence of opinion. We start with material from before 1880 that is often taken to manifest a commitment to something like the absolute conception, but that I shall argue does not do so. We then consider a number of later discussions that show that, after 1880 at least, Peirce had no such commitment.

(a) 1877–1878

Putnam, and other commentators who find the absolute conception in Peirce's writings on truth, refer to the clarification of truth and reality in 'How to Make Our Ideas Clear' and the passage we cited from 'The Fixation of Belief'. The first of these passages employs an example:

[All] the followers of science are fully persuaded that the processes of investigation, if only pushed far enough, will give one certain solution to every question to which they can be applied. One man may investigate the velocity of light by studying the transits of Venus and the aberration of the stars; another by the oppositions of Mars and the eclipses of Jupiter's satellites; [etc.] . . . They may at first obtain different results, but, as each perfects his method and his processes, the result will move steadily towards a destined centre. So with all scientific research. Different minds may set out with the most antagonistic views, but the process of investigation carries them by a force outside themselves to one and the same conclusion. This activity of thought by which we are carried, not where we wish but to a foreordained goal, is like the operation of destiny. No modification of the point of view taken, no selection of other facts for study, no natural bent of mind even, can enable man to escape the predestinate opinion. This great law is embodied in the conception of truth and reality. (W 3, 273)

Although consistent with it, this illustration does not require convergence thesis (1).[3] It requires only that the destined opinion will be reached by those who seek an answer to a particular question, in this case those trying to measure the velocity of light. Although the example is not worked out in any detail, it is left open whether those who reject that scientific framework are destined to investigate the question and reach the correct answer.

For a philosopher sympathetic to realism and anxious to explain reality by reference to a fated convergence of opinion, two possibilities are particularly disturbing. We might all accept permanently some proposition that is, in fact, false; and we might reach no destined convergence at all upon some matter where there is a truth. Realism surely demands that we allow for these possibilities; but Peirce's account of truth and reality appears to find no room for them. Immediately after giving his clarification of truth and reality in 'How to Make Our Ideas Clear', Peirce confronts this issue: 'Our perversity and that of others may indefinitely postpone the settlement of opinion; it might even conceivably cause an arbitrary proposition to be universally accepted as long as the human race should last' (W 3, 274). However, he insists, this shows only that we have not carried our investigations 'sufficiently far': if, after the extinction of our race, another should arise with faculties and disposition for investigation, the true opinion must be the one which they would ultimately come to (presumably unless they too were 'perverse' in their investigations). Thirty years later, in 'What Pragmatism Is' (1905), Peirce returned to his earlier claims about truth and reality. After explaining the 'destined opinion' as one which is 'controlled by a rational experimental logic' and 'does not depend upon any accidental circumstances', he once again allowed that the 'perversity of thought of whole generations may cause postponement of the ultimate fixation' (CP 5.430).

What 'perversity' means here is unclear: is there a connotation of cognitive failure or malfunction on the part of inquirers? The later reference to 'accidental circumstances' suggests that, perhaps through bad luck, relevant evidence may escape our attention and we may thus fail to reach the truth. Whatever he has in mind, reflection on one of Peirce's own examples will help us to see that his apparent confidence that, if only we keep inquiring for long enough, the effects of perversity and bad luck will be overcome, is misplaced. The description of the convergence about the velocity of light emphasised that many inquirers, using different methods, would arrive at the same result. The convergence thesis requires something stronger: that there were none who would not have reached the correct answer had they continued for long enough. If, as Peirce suggests, reaching the correct answer depends upon revising one's techniques and improving one's methods, it will depend upon the reliability and completeness of the background knowledge that shapes these improvements. If we are sent down the wrong path by faulty background knowledge, there is no guarantee that we shall recover the straight and narrow, no matter how careful we are in our inquiries.[4] As we shall now see, Peirce's formulations of the convergence thesis after 1880 qualify his apparent confidence that we shall always eventually reach a fated convergence.

(b) Convergence and Hope

In discussing some views of Schroeder's about the presuppositions of inquiry in 1896, Peirce began with a straightforward formulation of the convergence thesis:

[As] to an inquiry presupposing that there is some one truth, what can this possibly mean except that there is one destined upshot to inquiry with reference to the question in hand – one result that when reached will never be overthrown. (CP 432)

The passage continues

Undoubtedly, we hope that this, *or something approximating to this*, is so, or we should not trouble ourselves to make much inquiry. But we do not necessarily have much confidence that it *is* so.

This suggests a considerable weakening of the claims from 1877–1878. Transforming the commitment to convergence into a hope, a regulative ideal, is a pervasive feature of his later writings. Indeed when Peirce planned to republish 'How to Make Our Ideas Clear' in 1903, he proposed two changes to the passage from (W 3, 273).

The first sentence was revised so that it began '...all the followers of science are *animated by the cheerful hope*...'; and the conclusion was 'This great *hope* is embodied in the conception of truth and reality' (CP 5.407; italics added). Murray Murphey has emphasised that sometime between 1880 and 1890, Peirce's earlier constitutive principle linking reality and the destined final opinion was weakened to a regulative one which held that 'in order to make certain that agreement will be pursued, it is necessary to hope that ultimate agreement will come' (Murphey 1961: 301).[5]

Second, note that this hope is focused on 'the question in hand', suggesting convergence thesis (2) rather than (1). In the same spirit, 'What Pragmaticism Is' declares that: 'every man of us *virtually assumes* that [the convergence thesis is true] *in regard to each matter the truth of which he seriously discusses*' (italics added). 'Virtually assumes' may be a simple alternative to 'hopes'. And the thesis is restricted to matters the truth of which we seriously discuss: it is irrational to inquire into something unless we think there is a serious chance that we are destined to reach the correct answer and can escape being diverted down the wrong road by faulty background knowledge or flawed techniques of inquiry. So long as we are not seriously concerned to inquire into some matter, it seems, we need neither believe nor even hope that further inquiry into the matter would take us to a fated convergence. Thus:

It is rational to make some question the object of an inquiry only if we can (at least) rationally hope that we will reach a solution that would also be reached by anyone who inquired into the same manner (and whose inquiry was not hampered by perversity or by unpropitious 'accidental circumstances').

This view is also manifest in a response to Paul Carus who, to Peirce's apparent surprise, had interpreted Peirce's talk of fated convergence as suggesting that our reaching the truth was something 'inevitable'. He responded that convergence was 'a *hope* that such a conclusion may be substantially reached concerning the particular questions with which our inquiries are busied' (CP 6.610).

As Peirce's philosophy developed after 1878, he soon came to give his account of truth a regulative status: we hope we will converge on the truth if we inquire long enough and well enough. And many of his illustrations and formulations suggest that the thesis should be formulated with respect to particular questions or matters for discussion. When we claim that some proposition is true, we (virtually assume) that any well-conducted, sufficiently long inquiry into the truth value of that proposition would end up admitting that it was true. And when we inquire into some question, we hope that there is an answer to it which any nonperverse investigation which is unaffected by accidental circumstances would eventually accept. Thus (2) is employed rather that (1); but it is interpreted as a regulative principle rather than as a 'law' or a substantive truth. This weaker version can be expressed as follows:

(3) It is rational for someone to assert that p, or to inquire into whether p, only if it is rational for her to hope that anyone who inquired into whether p (long enough and well enough) would be fated eventually to arrive at a stable belief in p.

(c) Secondary Qualities and Reality

Let us now return to the issues about secondary qualities that were raised in Section 2. Since our concepts of secondary qualities are relative to our human sensory apparatus, and our concepts of artefacts are relative to our needs, interests and capacities, they would have no place in the absolute conception of the world. If Peirce is committed to that conception, he must deny the reality of such conceptions. In that case, it is revealing that, after 1900, Peirce challenged the 'virtual assumption that what is relative to thought cannot be real' (CP 5.430, 1905).

Ontological metaphysicians usually say that 'secondary sensations,' such as colours, are delusive and false; but not so the Pragmaticist. He insists that the rose really *is* red; for *red* is, by the meaning of the word, an appearance; and to say that a Jacqueminot rose is red means, and can mean, nothing but that if such a rose is put before a normal eye, in the daylight, it will look red. (CP 8.194, 1904; a much fuller discussion, claiming that colour is 'external' and so the denotations of colour terms are real, is found in CP 6.327-8, from 1909)

Whether he would have denied the reality of *red* in the 1870s is unclear, although the interpretation of him as defending the absolute conception of reality would have required him to do so.

In *The Minute Logic* (1902), Peirce examined the notion of a 'real', 'true', or 'natural' class. Having defined a *class* as 'the total of whatever objects there may be in the universe which are of a certain description', he claims that a class is 'natural' or 'real' when its members 'owe their existence as members of the class to a common final cause'. He continues 'In the case of lamps we know what that cause is: that instinct which enables us to distinguish human productions and to divine their purpose informs us with a degree of certainty which it were futile to hope any science should surpass' (CP 1.204). The class of lamps is 'real' because it corresponds to a distinctive human purpose. (Although Peirce then points out that biological classifications are not answerable to *purposes*, he insists that they still reflect final causation of a different kind, and he makes clear that he thinks that classes of artefacts are 'true', 'real', or 'natural'.)

This example shows that, in 1902, Peirce shared James's view that reality can be 'relative to thought' or to human interests, capacities, and desires. Whether something is red, or a lamp, is 'external' and 'independent of what anyone thinks it to be' even if the concepts in question are sensitive to a distinctive human perspective and could not be understood by anyone who was unable to enter that perspective. It is also used to illustrate the pervasiveness of vagueness in our thought about reality, something which requires further qualification of the claim about convergence. In view of the variety of uses to which we put lamps, there may not be a single purpose or desire that unifies the class of lamps. Instead, that class may be held together by a set of loosely similar 'desires' which correspond to these different uses. Lamps can be subdivided into different kinds that can answer to more specific needs and purposes (CP 1.205); and even these more specific desires will be vague, varying along a number of dimensions (CP 1.206). Judgement is thus required when we rank lamps or decide whether some object answers the interests that makes us want a lamp on a particular occasion; we must be sensitive to the balance of purposes and interests that are relevant in the context (CP 1.207). Within real or natural classes, 'objects actually will cluster about certain middling qualities, some being removed this way, some that way, and at greater and greater removes fewer and fewer objects will be so determined' (CP 1.207). 'And it may be quite impossible to draw a sharp line of demarcation between two classes, although they are real and natural classes in strictest truth' (CP 1.208). Our interpretation of Peirce's convergence thesis must allow for the fact that inquirers with different interests may arrive at a different judgement about whether some object is a lamp. At best we must *hope* that different people will exercise judgment in harmonious ways whenever it is important that there be agreement.[6]

Some readers will wonder how someone who explains reality in terms of the fated convergence of opinion can endorse these claims. In the remainder of the chapter, I shall argue that they reflect a change in Peirce's philosophical position, but it is a change in how he thought about *reality*, not a change in how he thought about *truth*. It is a consequence of this that the account of truth comes to have a very different role in his philosophy. Moreover his new way of thinking about reality embraces ideas that some of Peirce's critics would identify as pragmatist insights which Peirce himself failed to embrace.

4. THE CONCEPTS OF TRUTH AND REALITY

As we have seen, Peirce's earlier formulations of the convergence thesis all form part of his search for an explanation of the concept of *reality*. The immediate corollary of the claim that true propositions are those we are destined to believe is that reality is the object of this fated opinion. The way to capture the idea that reality is external, that it is independent of what we think it to be, is to insist that *any* inquirer who investigated for long enough would be bound to acknowledge the truth of an opinion that was properly descriptive of reality. Reality is independent of thought because it is independent of what any individual may think at any particular time (W 2, 467–70). This is, if you like, his constitutive account of *reality*: he saw it as the only way to make sense of how reality is independent of our opinions without succumbing to scepticism by turning this independent reality into an unknowable thing in itself. In this section we consider some passages that show that *truth* and *reality* were less intimately connected after 1880.

The first is taken from a manuscript and thus may not represent a lasting theme in Peirce's thought. It concerns the tensions between the convergence thesis and fundamental logical principles such as the law of bivalence. Unless we accept, implausibly, that every proposition (or its negation) will be the object of a fated convergence, Peirce's account of truth should lead him to question the principle that each proposition is either true of false. However

consider this passage which suggests a way of reconciling a version
of the convergence thesis with bivalence:

[Every] proposition is either *true* or *false*. It is false if any proposition could
be legitimately deduced from it, without any aid from false propositions,
which would conflict with a direct perceptual judgment, could such be had.
A proposition is true, if it is not false. Hence, an entirely meaningless form
of proposition, if it be called a proposition, at all, is to be classed along with
true propositions. (EP 2: 284–5)

Although this is closely related to the truth as convergence thesis,
it is formulated as a definition of *falsity*: truth is then defined as
anything that cannot be refuted. Since Peirce would not want to
conclude that the object of 'an entirely meaningless form of proposition' is real, his flirtation with this strategy – even if only briefly –
suggests that he is questioning the idea that the object of any true
proposition is real. Second, the definition is flawed. The qualifications introduced in his explanation of falsity suggests that he was
aware that widespread ignorance or error in our background beliefs
might prove a permanent obstacle to the convergence of opinion. But
to try to repair his account by saying that our refuting (or failing to re-
fute) some proposition must not depend upon any false propositions
renders his explanation of *falsity* circular.

The decisive evidence of his abandoning his analysis of reality
as the object of a true proposition is found in Peirce's definition
of truth for Baldwin's 'Dictionary of Philosophy and Psychology' in
1902. Truth is still explained in terms of convergence: 'Truth is that
concordance of an abstract statement with the ideal limit to which
endless investigation would tend to bring scientific belief' (CP 5.565).
Reality is now explained as 'that mode of being by virtue of which
the real thing is as it is, irrespectively of what any mind or definite
collection of minds may represent it to be' (CP 5.565). And he now
takes seriously the possibility that there might be truth where there
is no reality, and, indeed, reality where there is no truth.

How might there be reality where there is no truth? Vagueness
might offer one example. The vague proposition 'X is bald' may be
neither true nor false even if the underlying reality (the distribution
of hairs on the person's head) is fully determinate. Peirce's own example, tentatively put forward, supposes that 'if in respect to some
question – say that of freedom of the will – no matter how long the

discussion goes on, no matter how scientific our methods may become, there never will be a time when we can fully satisfy ourselves either that the question has no meaning, or that one answer or the other explains the facts, then in regard to that question, there certainly is no *truth*' (CP 5.565). Peirce is explicit that the metaphysical question then remains open. 'Even if the metaphysician decides that where there is no truth there is no reality, still the distinction between the character of truth and the character of reality is plain and definable.' If the metaphysician can produce a defensible account of the mode of being of the freedom of the will, one that perhaps explains why we could not resolve the question, then we *may* admit that there is a reality to which no truth conforms.[7]

Peirce also has examples of how there can be truth without reality. He considers a 'moralist' who describes an ideal of a summum bonum, in circumstances in which 'the development of man's moral nature will only lead to a firmer satisfaction with the described ideal'. It may be a consequence of this that, with time, anyone who thinks about the matter long enough and carefully enough will be led to share this view of the good (CP 5.566). This appears to be enough to render propositions about the good and bad *true*. There may be a fated consensus on the acceptability of such claims. Is there any *reality* corresponding to such truths? The passages, noted above, in which Peirce grants that reality might be 'relative to thought', suggest that there is: that realities should be 'relative to' our sentimental dispositions and moral nature need disparage their reality no more than the fact that colours are relative to our sensory apparatus should lead us to question their reality. If the example is genuinely to offer a case where there is truth but no reality, we need to understand how the role of the moralist and the reinforcement of the moral ideal through time somehow makes its acceptance dependent upon what some finite group of individuals think. Perhaps its general acceptance depends upon the charismatic powers of the moralist: if a different moral leader has seized the limelight, a different moral proposition would have been true.

In the 1860s and 1870s, Peirce aimed to derive metaphysical conclusions from logic. Hence an account of *truth* as a logical concept – one which was explained by reference to its role in inquiry – yielded an analysis of *reality*, which some might suppose to be a metaphysical concept. During the 1880s and 1890s, Peirce addressed problems that led him to search for a system of scientific metaphysics that, inter alia, would describe the different modes of being that realities could have. Peirce's discussion of the freedom of the will example shows that, by 1901, questions of reality could be addressed by metaphysicians which were not settled by appeal to a logical analysis of truth. When we regard a proposition as true, we hope for (and perhaps expect) convergence upon it. When such convergence occurs, we should expect an explanation of it: why do we come to agree on colours, on our moral judgements, on our beliefs about the physical world? For different kinds of truths, different kinds of explanation may be appropriate – consider the differences between moral truths, mathematical truths, biological truths, etc. The 'modes of being' of mathematical objects, moral facts, and scientific matters will be reflected in the kinds of explanations of convergence that we find appropriate. Peirce considers the proposition that Caesar crossed the Rubicon. Its truth 'consists in the fact that the further we push our archaeological and other studies, the more strongly will that conclusion force itself on our minds forever'. An idealist metaphysician may hold that the corresponding reality consists in – or is constituted by – the fact the inquiry is fated to take this path. Where opinion will not converge, reality would be indeterminate. But we might also explain convergence by showing how experimental interaction with an independently existing reality will suffice to ensure that reality makes itself manifest to us. Thus even if we decide that Caesar's crossing the Rubicon is something real, something independent of thought in the required sense, there is scope for a variety of metaphysical accounts of what its reality consists in, of what makes the corresponding proposition true. Similarly, although it is uncontroversial that many statements of mathematics are true, the supposition that mathematics deals only in hypothetical structures leaves room for it to be controversial whether a realist understanding of the subject matter of mathematics is defensible (CP 5.567). And even if a realist account *is* accepted, there are open questions about the modes of being of the objects of mathematical truths.

It is important to distinguish some of the different points being made in this section. Issues of 'realism' concern the mind-independence of the factors that determine whether particular propositions are true or false. Mathematics is mind-independent in at least this respect, that whether it is true that four plus five equals nine does not depend upon whether anyone actually believes that it is true. We would not explain its truth as grounded in the fact that some particular person (or group of people) accepts it. If a subject matter is mind-independent in this way, we can say that satisfies 'basic realism'.

The first point is that the fact that a proposition satisfies basic realism leaves the *metaphysical* character (the 'mode of being') of its objects open. Terms such as 'lamp' collect things together that embody forms of thirdness that are mind-dependent, while natural kind terms collect things together that satisfy the same mind-independent laws. Physical objects manifest real secondness; 'ideal' or 'hypothetical' objects such as numbers do not manifest real secondness. Perhaps we can think of basic realism as a sort of logical doctrine rather than a metaphysical one. And then examples such as that of the lamp show just how various and complex the issues about mind-independence are. Certainly basic realism leaves open most of the different options that have been discussed by philosophers who have debated realism about mathematical objects, external things, values, laws, causation, and the like.

The second point is that once we clarify the concept of truth by saying that a proposition is true if anyone who inquired into it would eventually arrive at a stable belief in it, then, although the application of the concept of truth to a proposition might guarantee basic realism about its objects, all these further metaphysical questions will remain open. This might be expressed by saying that the concept of truth is a logical concept and is metaphysically neutral. Saying this does not necessarily prevent our defining 'the real' as 'the object of a true proposition'. If truth guarantees basic realism, and ordinary talk of 'the real' and 'reality' is concerned with the requirements of basic realism ('There really are prime numbers between two and ten'), then the application of the concept of reality will be just as metaphysically neutral as the application of the concept of truth. But this clarification of the concept of reality would not equip us to understand and inquire into important metaphysical questions about the reality of secondness and thirdness (for example). A richer understanding of mind-independence is needed before we can investigate whether these things are real.

But there is a third point. Peirce's example of the moralist suggests that the application of the concept of truth does not always entail basic realism. And if that is correct, the concepts of truth and reality come apart; once this example is accepted, then we cannot simply define the real as the object of a true opinion. In that case the concept of truth will be neutral in a way that the concept of reality is not: it does not even entail the truth of basic realism. And that would mean that a new start is needed on clarifying the concept of reality.[8]

We now face an important problem. For a pragmatist like Peirce, concepts should be explained by reference to experience: we explain what it is for something to be hard by showing how our actions upon hard things have different empirical consequences from similar actions upon soft things. The early theory thus held that, if something is real, then inquiry into whether it is real will have an observable consequence, the convergence of opinion. Moreover this convergence will result from our regulating inquiries in the light of experience. If *reality* and *truth* are to come apart, or if reality *requires* more clarification than the early theory provided, then Peirce needs a new way of linking our thought about *reality* to experience. What is this? Experience is richer that many philosophers suppose and it contains the materials for explaining externality and independence of thought.[9]

5. EXPERIENCE AND REALITY

In his writings from the 1870s, Peirce's 'realism' about laws and about the external world depended crucially upon his claim that propositions about the external world, and propositions descriptive of laws of nature, would form part of a fated convergence of opinion. I have been suggesting that in the final three decades of his philosophical life, his realism received a different formulation. External things and law governed changes are objects of 'immediate' experience: our experience manifests secondness and thirdness and this is explained by reference to secondness and thirdness in the behaviour and interactions of external things. In turning to the philosophy of perception in thinking about realism, he resembles Hilary Putnam who, in his 1994 Dewey Lectures, came to insist that the theory of perception held the key to problems about realism (1999: 13–14).

Crucial developments in the 1880s and around 1900 involve insisting that we have a direct perceptual awareness of independent external things. One of the first of these developments, perhaps the most important, is found in Peirce's (unpublished) review of Josiah Royce's *The Religious Aspect of Philosophy*, which he read as challenging his account of truth and as suggesting that he could make no sense of the possibility of false belief (see Hookway 2000: Chapter four). He claimed that Royce relied upon the mistaken view that we can only refer to an object as whatever fits some individual concept or description; and he proposed that the most fundamental form of reference is indexical:

When I say I mean my discourse to apply to the real world, the word "real" does not describe what kind of world it is: it only serves to bring the mind of my hearer back to that world which he knows so well by sight, hearing, and touch, and of which those sensations are themselves indices of the same kind. Such a demonstrative sign is a necessary appendage to a proposition, to show what world of objects, or as the logicians say, what "universe of discourse" it has in view. (W 4, 250)

In his review, Peirce emphasized that the same was true of ordinary perceptual judgements: I judge that *that* is a black computer, that *this* is red book. And in making such judgements, we are aware of such things *as external*. In picking things out indexically, we are aware of them as existing independent of our thoughts about them, as something external with which we interact.

This was very explicit in the lectures on "Pragmatism" that were delivered in Harvard in 1903. Describing his experience of seeing a yellow chair with a green cushion, and having introduced the term 'percept' for what is immediately present to the mind in perceptual experience, he insists that the chair *is* the percept: 'The chair I appear to see makes no professions of any kind, essentially embodies no intentions of any kind, does not stand for anything. It obtrudes upon my gaze; but not as deputy for anything else, nor "as" anything' (CP 7.619, 1903; for further discussion, see Hookway 1985: 155ff). In earlier writings he had supposed that thinking of reality as the cause of our experiences would drive us towards admitting unknowable things in themselves. If the fact that we perceive external things as external is manifest within the content of the experience itself, this danger disappears. Moreover it is easy to see that this development makes it easy to loosen the connection between truth and reality: there might be a fated convergence upon matters that do not manifest externality or independence in this way. The presence of convergence upon an opinion does not guarantee that its objects will be experienced as external things that interact with us. It also leaves open the possibility that there may be other ways for real things to be independent of thought: this requires 'metaphysical' study and cannot be grounded solely in accounts of the structure of inquiry and the fated convergence of opinion.

Another development in Peirce's thought may have reinforced his realism. Appeal to the defeasible authority of common sense was an enduring feature of Peirce's thought and, after 1905, he was happy to describe his position as 'critical common-sensism'. Common sense, he tells us, suggests direct realism about the objects of perception (CP 5.444, 5.539), and critical commonsensism endorses common sense claims once they have been questioned and refined in the interests of constructing a theory that meets our philosophical needs.[10] Peirce's critical commonsensism allows for a qualified endorsement of our everyday realism.

As we noted above, similar developments occurred in Peirce's thought about laws and generality. In his earlier writings, the question of realism about natural laws is formulated as a question about whether sentences formulating such laws will form part of a fated convergence of opinion among those who investigate. During the 1880s, he developed a metaphysical account of laws as real habits, describing the forms taken by 'thirdness' in different disciplines (Hookway 2000: Chapter 6). And by the turn of the century, when he sought a phenomenological defence of his system of categories, he claimed that (external) 'mediation' and other forms of necessity were directly manifested in the *continuous* patterns that were present in our experience. So our concept of reality reflects both the presence of external law governed processes in experience, and a metaphysical account of the modes of being of laws and external things.

This change is inevitably liberating. If experience reveals law-governed patterns and changes in the colours that things display (or in the behaviour of artefacts), there is no longer any need to question the reality of secondary qualities and properties such as that of being a lamp. If experience (and our metaphysical story about reality) reveal complex patterns of continuity and mediation, there is no longer any logical obstacle to giving a role to our practical interests and aesthetic sensibilities in identifying some of these patterns as salient to our purposes and in employing particular idealisations in *describing* the structure of reality. So long as these 'reals' are 'external' and are not created by our beliefs that they obtain, it is no obstacle to their reality that they are relative to our perspectives and their peculiarities.

In the 1860s and 1870s, Peirce's approach to questions about reality was to pick out a distinctive set of signs or sentences, those that we are fated to accept if we inquire sufficiently well, and then to define reality as the objects of these sentences. This, he thought, was the only way to give pragmatic sense to the concept of reality. By the 1880s, he was already embarked upon a journey that would offer him an independent empirical handle on the idea of a reality that is external to us and independent of our thought. And there is no reason to think that this way of articulating his realism would commit him to any version of the absolute conception of reality.

6. PRAGMATIST 'THEORIES' OF TRUTH

The suggestion that Peirce's theory of truth has metaphysical implications as a result of committing him to a version of the absolute conception of reality has been made by a number of his readers. This paper has tried to throw doubt on these claims. The passages that support the diagnosis are all relatively early, dating from a time when Peirce tied the concepts of truth and reality together much more closely than after 1880. Peirce's later writings about truth and reality generally conflict with this interpretation of his views. Moreover even the early writings that appear to support these attributions are compatible with a weaker view that incorporates a different idea of convergence. I shall conclude by questioning another common assumption about Peirce's writings on truth: this is that he offers a theoretical account of what truth consists in, a rival to other 'constitutive theories of truth' such as the correspondence and coherence theories.[11]

As I have argued in "Truth, Rationality, and Pragmatism" (Hookway, 2000, Chapter 2), pragmatic clarifications of concepts and propositions are best seen as accounts of the (experiential) commitments we incur when we assert or judge the proposition in question. The account of truth as convergence reflects the belief that when I commit myself to the truth of a proposition, I must be confident that (or at least hope that) any disagreement on the part of others can be put down to lack of information on their part; possession of misleading information on their part; cognitive failings on their part; perhaps differences in the ways in which we have resolved the pervasive vagueness of natural languages, fixed universes of discourse, or interpreted ceteris paribus clauses; and so on. Similarly, when I investigate some question, I rely upon the confidence or hope that an answer can be found to which this sort of commitment is appropriate. Peirce is not offering an account of what it is for a proposition to be true. Instead he is clarifying:

(1) What commitments we incur when we take a proposition to be true.
(2) What commitments we incur when we seek truth in some area.

Such clarifications can ignore propositions that we do not take to be true and propositions whose truth value is not something that we can make an object of serious inquiry. And, as we have noticed, our commitment may be to no more than the reasonableness of *hoping* that inquiry will produce convergence.

Consider the proposition that Caesar sneezed three times on the morning that he first crossed to England. The principle of bivalence suggests it has a truth-value – although the vagueness of 'morning' and perhaps even of 'sneeze' may lead that to be qualified. The mature Peirce should admit that there is a determinate reality: it fits poorly with our metaphysical views that there was a gap in the history of the universe; and we believe that there were real events which had real effects, but which have not affected our current cognitive states. But is there any 'truth'? We take no checkable risks when we assert this proposition rather than the proposition that he sneezed four times; we incur no commitments that might reveal that we were mistaken. We could not reasonably hope that inquiry would make such commitments possible – although, of course, evidence *might* turn up. It is easy to understand how Peirce might conclude that there is no truth here. But, if so, this is because his account of truth has a different sort of aim from more traditional kinds of theories.[12]

NOTES

1. Note that this is a conception whose value (and indeed whose intelligibility) Putnam rejects (1992b: Chapter 5).
2. My use of terms such as 'explanation' and 'clarification' to describe Peirce's account is intended to leave open the question of whether it

is intended as a traditional kind of philosophical analysis. In the final section of this paper, I shall suggest that pragmatic clarifications should not be viewed as ordinary analyses, as statements of the necessary and sufficient conditions for applying problematic concepts.

3. The morals that Peirce actually draws from this example are three. First, that if a proposition is true, different inquirers, working relatively independently, will come to agree upon it. Second, that if it is true, different investigative techniques, different methods of inquiry, will normally arrive at the same answer to the target question. And third, that when different inquirers and different methods or techniques of inquiry appear *not* to provide the same answers to the question, this is usually a short-term phenomenon that will disappear once our techniques have been refined.

4. Robert Brandom has suggested in conversation that Peirce's theory of truth is refuted by the fact that ignorance and error can permanently block this fated convergence.

5. Most scholars would agree with Nathan Houser that Peirce's reflections on Royce's *Religious Aspects of Philosophy* played an essential role in that transition (see W 5, xlvi).

6. Compare here: 'Although it is true that "Any proposition you please *once you have determined its identity*, is either true or false"; yet *so long as it remains indeterminate and so without identity*, it need neither be true that any proposition you please is true, nor that any proposition you please is false' (CP 5.448, 1905)

7. This may already lead us to question whether Peirce's account is a *constitutive* account of truth.

8. I am aware of only the one place in which such examples are used to make this point, so the reader should beware that it may not represent an enduring theme in Peirce's thought. Moreover, the example may be problematic. It seems to involve a case where, even if not consciously, convergence in opinion is secured through using a variant on the method of authority, a method which Peirce rejected in 'The Fixation of Belief'. If it can be argued that Peirce's clarification of truth identifies it with belief on which there would be fated convergence among those who use the method of science, then this may not be an example of a true proposition: the convergence in opinion is secured in the wrong way.

9. This provides part of the explanation of why Peirce came to link his pragmatism to James's radical empiricism (Hookway 1997).

10. This might represent a further parallel with Putnam's writings: the Dewey lectures embraced 'natural realism' as a starting point for philosophical reflection (Putnam 1999).

11. See, for example, Putnam's paper on William James's theory of truth (1997).
12. This chapter builds on a reading of Peirce's account of truth that is defended in Chapters 2–4 of *Truth, Rationality, and Pragmatism* (Hookway, 2000) and in (Hookway, 2002). I am grateful to Hilary Putnam for very helpful comments when some of this material was presented to a conference on his work in Munster in 2000, to Leif Wenar for his advice on an ancestor of this piece, to Cheryl Misak for a number of helpful suggestions, and to Danielle Bromwich for helping me to identify some confusions in an earlier version of Section 4.

6 C. S. Peirce on Vital Matters[1]

I. INTRODUCTION

C. S. Peirce argued that a true belief is the belief we would come to, were we to inquire as far as we could on a matter. A true belief is a belief which could not be improved upon, a belief which would forever meet the challenges of reasons, argument, and evidence.

Peirce initially put this idea in the following unhelpful way: a true belief is one which would be agreed upon at the hypothetical or 'fated' end of inquiry (See W 3, 273, 1878). It is this formulation which is usually attacked by those who see little value in the pragmatist view of truth. But a much better formulation is this: a true belief is one which would withstand doubt, were we to inquire as far as we fruitfully could into the matter. A true belief is such that, no matter how much further we were to investigate and debate, it would not be overturned by recalcitrant experience and argument (CP 5.569, 1901, 6.485, 1908). I have argued elsewhere (Misak 2000:49f) that this formulation, unlike the first, is not vulnerable to the standard objections to the pragmatist account of truth.

I have also argued (Misak 2000) that this formulation is very friendly to cognitivism about morals – very friendly to the idea that moral judgements fall within the scope of truth, knowledge, and inquiry. Our ethical beliefs might well aspire to truth, as do our beliefs in science, mathematics, and discourse about ordinary middle-sized objects.

At times Peirce appears wholeheartedly to embrace the cognitivist view I would like to attribute to him – he happily extends his view of truth and inquiry to moral judgements. Here are two passages in which his cognitivist intentions are apparent. In the first, after saying that a true belief is one that would survive the rigours of inquiry, he says that beliefs in ethics can be true or false. In the second, he suggests that moral judgement draws on experience – experience which is not identical to that which is found in science, but experience nonetheless.

(i) But what else, when one considers it, can our 'truth' ever amount to, other than the way in which people would come to think if research were carried sufficiently far? That would seem to be all that *our* truth ever can be. So good morals is the kind of human behavior that would come to be approved if studies of right behavior were carried sufficiently far. Would it not be a good idea to begin a text-book of ethics... with this definition: Ethics is the theory of how to do as one would like if one had considered sufficiently the question of what one would find satisfactory? (MS 673, pp. 12–13, 1911)[2]

(ii) Ethics as a positive science must rest on observed facts. But it is quite a different thing to make it rest on special scientific observation... The only solid foundation for ethics lies in those facts of everyday life which no skeptical philosopher ever yet really called in question. (CP 8.158, 1901; see also 1.600, 1903)

But, as is usually the case with interpreting Peirce, matters are not quite so straightforward. When I first set out a pragmatist account of how moral judgement might be truth-apt, I said that Peirce himself had only unhelpful things to say about ethics (Misak 2000:48). He was frequently keen to insist that in 'vital' matters, which includes ethical matters,[3] one must eschew reason in favour of instinct, for in vital matters, we need to reach a definite conclusion promptly. Science, on the other hand, 'has nothing at stake on any temporal venture but is in pursuit of eternal verities... and looks upon this pursuit, not as the work of one man's life, but as that of generation after generation, indefinitely' (CP 5.589, 1898). Science is thus concerned with truth and ethics is not. The flip side of the point, he suggests, is that 'really the word belief is out of place in the vocabulary of science' (CP 7.185, 1901). Science concerns itself with a 'formula reached in the existing state of scientific progress' – not with a belief upon which to act.

Peirce appears to offer us here an extreme kind of noncognitivism, where matters of ethics do not fall under the scope of truth, knowledge, and inquiry. Ethics requires quickly formed beliefs upon which we can act and hence is a matter for gut-reaction. The preservation of the status quo seems inevitable. Indeed, Peirce is clear that this view, which he at times calls 'sentimentalism', 'implies conservatism' (CP 1.633, 1898). Ethics, he sometimes says,

is in fact nothing but a sort of composite photograph of the conscience of the members of the community. In short, it is nothing but a traditional standard, accepted, very wisely, without radical criticism, but with a silly pretence of critical examination. (CP 1.573, 1905)

We seem to have here the view that our cognitivist practices – debating and reasoning about moral matters, trying to improve our views, trying to weed out mistakes and prejudices, etc. – are based on an error, as Mackie (1977) would say.

I shall try to resolve this tension in Peirce's work by setting out the background to the cognitivist thoughts expressed in passages (i) and (ii). My argument shall be that if one looks at Peirce's epistemology, about which he did not waver, one can see that his remarks about instinct can be folded into the cognitivist view. That is, the odd-sounding view that ethics must go on instinct is, once we understand the place of instinct in Peirce's view, perfectly consistent with the cognitivist view. And we shall see that saying that belief is out of place in science is not the best way Peirce could have put his point. What Peirce was getting at when he made these odd remarks is that the scientist must keep his eye on the fallible nature of belief.[4]

2. TRUTH AND INQUIRY

Peirce famously argued (in, for instance, 'The Fixation of Belief') that inquiry begins with the irritation of doubt and ends with a stable doubt-resistant belief. If we were to have a belief which would always be immune to doubt – which would forever fit with experience and argument – then that belief would be true. Since we can never know when a belief is like that, our beliefs are fallible. Any one of them might be shown to be false.

Fallibilism, however, does not entail that we ought to follow Descartes and try to bring into doubt all beliefs about which error is conceivable. Such doubts would be, Peirce argued, 'paper' or 'tin' – not the genuine article. He says:

... there is but one state of mind from which you can 'set out', namely, the very state of mind in which you actually find yourself at the time you do 'set out' – a state in which you are laden with an immense mass of cognition already formed, of which you cannot divest yourself if you would ... Do you call it doubting to write down on a piece of paper that you doubt? If so, doubt has nothing to do with any serious business. (CP 5.416, 1905)

Our body of background beliefs is susceptible to doubt on a piece-meal basis, if that doubt is prompted by surprising or recalcitrant experience. We must *regard* our background beliefs as true, until some surprising experience throws one or some group of them into doubt. The inquirer

is under a compulsion to believe just what he does believe ... as time goes on, the man's belief usually changes in a manner which he cannot resist ... this force which changes a man's belief in spite of any effort of his may be, in all cases, called a *gain of experience*. (MS 1342, p. 2, undated)

So on the Peircean epistemology, an inquirer has a fallible background of 'common sense' belief which is not in fact in doubt. Only against such a background can a belief be put into doubt and a new, better, belief be adopted. All our beliefs are fallible but they do not come into doubt all at once. Those which inquiry has not thrown into doubt are stable and we should retain them until a reason to doubt arises.

Peirce links the scientific method to this epistemology. It is the method which pays close attention to the fact that beliefs fall to the surprise of recalcitrant experience. Inquiry 'is not standing upon the bedrock of fact. It is walking upon a bog, and can only say, this ground seems to hold for the present. Here I will stay till it begins to give way' (CP 5.589, 1998). Accepted hypotheses and theories ('established truths') are stable and believed until they are upset by experience.

The scientific method is also the method which leads to the truth. We aim at beliefs which would be forever stable – we aim at getting the best beliefs we can. We have in our various inquiries and deliberations a multiplicity of local aims – empirical adequacy, coherence with other beliefs, simplicity, explanatory power, getting a reliable guide to action, fruitfulness for other research, greater understanding of others, increased maturity, and the like. When we say that we aim at the truth, what we mean is that, were a belief really to satisfy all of our local aims in inquiry, then that belief would be true. There is nothing over and above the fulfillment of those aims, nothing metaphysical, to which we aspire. Truth is not some transcendental, mystical thing which we aim at for its own sake.

This epistemology and its accompanying view of truth is entirely general, despite the fact that Peirce calls it the method of science. That is, what Peirce calls 'science' is extremely broad. Any inquiry that aims at getting a belief which would forever stand up to experience and argument abides by the method of science. We shall see that Peirce thought that metaphysics (when it is well-conducted) and mathematics are legitimate aspirants to truth. And so is moral deliberation. He thought, that is, that metaphysics, mathematics, and morals might satisfy his pragmatist maxim – the maxim that a genuine belief must be linked to experience. I have elucidated elsewhere both the semantic and the epistemological arguments in this thought's favour[5] – in the next section, I will simply gesture at them.

3. EXPERIENCE: MATHEMATICAL, METAPHYSICAL, AND MORAL

Peirce thought that the motto 'Do not block the way of inquiry' 'deserves to be inscribed upon every wall of the city of philosophy' (CP 1.135, 1899; see also 7.480, 1898). A hypothesis which had no consequences, which was severed from experience, would be useless in inquiry. It would be, as Wittgenstein put it, a cog upon which nothing turned. Investigation into such hypotheses is bound to be barren and to direct attention away from worthwhile pursuits.

We can accept the idea that a belief must be responsive to experience without committing ourselves to anything as strong as the verificationism of the logical positivists. For Peirce takes the kind of experiential consequences required of various beliefs to be very broad indeed. Perception or experience is anything that is forced upon one. It goes far beyond what our ears, eyes, nose, and skin report:

...anything is, for the purposes of logic, to be classed under the species of perception wherein a positive qualitative content is forced upon one's

acknowledgement without any reason or pretension to reason. There will
be a wider genus of things *partaking* of the character of perception, if there
be any matter of cognition which exerts a force upon us.... (CP 7.623, 1903;
see also 6.492, 1896)

Peirce takes anything that is compelling, surprising, brute, or impinging to be an experience, regardless of what causes us to feel
compelled and regardless of whether we can identify the source of
the compulsion:

The course of life has developed certain compulsions of thought which we
speak of collectively as Experience. (CP 8.101, 1900)

Experience just is whatever prevents someone from believing exactly
what he *wants* to believe – it is what keeps us in check (MS 1342,
undated; see also MS 408, p. 146, 1893–1895).

Peirce argues that there are two kinds of experience – 'ideal' and
'real'. The latter is sensory experience and the former is experience
in which

... operations upon diagrams, whether external or imaginary, take the place
of the experiments upon real things that one performs in chemical and physical research. (CP 4.530, 1905; see also 3.516, 1896)

This sort of thought experiment or diagrammatic experiment or experiment in the imagination is, Peirce argues, the core of mathematical and deductive inquiry. 'The mathematician, like every other
inquirer, begins by a conjecture, which usually is that a certain transformation of his icon [diagram] will lead him to, or towards, the end
of his inquiry. He then performs that experiment....'[6] He draws
subsidiary lines in geometry or makes transformations in algebraic
formulae and then observes the results. Those results might be surprising, and since surprise is the force of experience, such reasoning
is an experiment. This sort of experiment

is truly observation, yet certainly in a very peculiar sense; and no other kind
of observation would at all answer the purpose of mathematics. (CP 1.240,
1902)

Similarly, in valid deductive reasoning, we are compelled to accept
a conclusion – the facts stated in the premises could not be, if the
fact stated in the conclusion were not. The conclusion is, in the first
instance, irresistible. It comes upon the mind before one can control

it. Only later do we critically compare the conclusion to our norms and ideals.[7]

Peirce sometimes articulates his point about the breadth of experience by saying that everyone inhabits two worlds – the inner and the outer. We react with the outer world through the clash between it and our senses, and we react with the inner world – the world of mathematics, logic, and reasoning – by performing thought experiments. Inquiry, Peirce says, has

two branches; one is inquiry into Outward Fact by experimentation and observation, and is called *Inductive Investigation*; the other is inquiry into Inner Truth by inward experimentation and observation and is called *Mathematical* or *Deductive Reasoning*.[8]

The distinction between the two different sorts of experiments is that the results of diagrammatic experimentation exerts a comparatively slight compulsion upon us and we can change the construction of those diagrams, whereas the outer world is full of irresistible compulsions and is hard to change (CP 5.474, 1907, 5.45, 1903). But nonetheless, 'the inner world has its surprises for us, sometimes' (CP 7.438, 1893). He intends to leave the difference between the two sorts of experience vague:

We naturally make all our distinctions too absolute. We are accustomed to speak of an external universe and an inner world of thought. But they are merely vicinities with no real boundary between them. (CP 7.438, 1893)

Perhaps the contrast between the two sorts of experience is best made by Peirce's distinction between practical and theoretical belief. In the 1902 manuscript 'Reason's Rules' (CP 5.538–45), he says that a practical belief such as 'anthracite is a convenient fuel' will manifest itself in a disposition to behave on the part of the believer. All things being equal, she would sometimes use anthracite were she in need of a fuel. In addition, 'sensible' or empirical consequences can be derived from the hypothesis. For instance, if (*ceteris paribus*) you were to light it, it would burn. On the other hand, a 'purely theoretical' belief has to do not with 'habits of deliberate action' or with sensible consequences, but with 'expectations'. As examples of theoretical hypotheses Peirce offers 'there is an imaginary circle which is twice cut by every real circle' and 'the diagonal of a square is incommensurable with its side'. Of the latter, he says that although it is 'difficult to see what experiential difference there can be between commensurable and incommensurable magnitudes', there are nevertheless expectations:

...a belief about the commensurability of the diagonal relates to what is expectable for a person dealing with fractions; although it means nothing at all in regard to what could be expected in physical measurements.... (CP 5.539, 1902)

The pragmatic maxim asserts that if it is not to be 'metaphysical jargon and chatter', a belief must have a link with experience – it must issue in expectation for practice or theory. If there is an expectation, then the unexpected can surprise the believer. The difference between a practical and a theoretical belief, says Peirce, is that the former involves sensation that is 'muscular' and the latter involves sensation that is not muscular (CP 5.540, 1902).

Thus Peirce thought that hypotheses in religion must issue in expectations. In 'A Neglected Argument for the Reality of God' he sets himself the task of showing how the hypothesis of God's reality gives rise to expectations. In each of the three drafts of the paper, he breaks off in frustration. Each time he begins to talk about 'tracing out a few consequences of the hypothesis', he abruptly changes the subject. (See, for instance, MS 842, p. 127.) All he can come up with is that if 'God is real' were true then we would expect there to be a tendency towards 'growth and habit-taking' and we would expect that things would be harmonious in the world.[9] At the end of the 1910 'Additament' to the paper, he rather disingenuously says 'The doctrine of the *Ens necessarium* has a pragmaticist meaning, although I will not here attempt to sum up the whole of its meaning' (MS 844, last page; see also CP 6.491, 1910).

Clearly many wrinkles in Peirce's brand of pragmatism need to be worked out. Nonetheless, it is clear that we do not need to say, with the logical positivists, that only beliefs in the physical sciences meet the pragmatist standard. Will hypotheses about what is right or wrong, or just or unjust, meet the demand – can they be shown to be sensitive to experience so that they are candidates for belief and for truth-values? Do they set up expectations which can be met or unmet? We saw in the introduction that Peirce sometimes very clearly said that moral judgements are linked to experience or 'observed facts'. These are the 'observations of everyday life', observations which do not require special training or equipment.

Those who are familiar with Peirce's writings will immediately see that these thoughts are remarkably similar to his statements about metaphysics. Metaphysics, he says, is thought to be inscrutable 'because its objects are not open to observation'. But the blame for the 'backward state' of metaphysics cannot be laid there, as metaphysics is indeed an 'observational science' (CP 6.5, 1898). It 'really rests on observations...and the only reason that this is not universally recognized is that it rests upon kinds of phenomena with which every man's experience is so saturated that he usually pays no particular attention to them' (CP 6.2, 1898). Observations in the special sciences require special instruments, precautions, and skill because they are remote from everyday life (CP 1.242, 1902). Other phenomena, such as that which metaphysics studies, are 'harder to see, simply because they surround us on every hand; we are immersed in them and have no background against which to view them' (CP 6.562, 1905, see also 1.134, 1901). They are commonplace and banal, but they are observations nonetheless.

There certainly is *prima facie* reason to think that Peirce is right in thinking that the practice of moral deliberation is responsive to experience, broadly construed. For when we deliberate about what we ought to do, we take ourselves to be sensitive to reasons, argument, thought experiments, and first-person experience. We try to put ourselves in the shoes of others, to broaden our horizons, to listen to the arguments of the other side. That is part of what it is to make a moral decision and part of what it is to try to live a moral life. It wouldn't be a moral life – it would not be engaged with the complexities of moral requirements – if we simply made our decisions about how to treat others by following a oracle, or an astrologer, or the toss of the dice.[10]

Of course we must be prepared for the possibility that, as Bernard Williams thinks, 'ethical thought has no chance of being everything it seems' (1985:135). But the commitment to keeping philosophy in touch with experience and practice is such that we should not be too quick to jump to this conclusion.

4. THE TENSION BETWEEN VITAL MATTERS AND SCIENCE

We now have a sketch of how Peirce's epistemology might be friendly to the idea that moral judgements are candidates for truth. But we have yet to resolve the tension in Peirce's work. How can we handle Peirce's statements that science, but not ethics, goes on the hope that 'the truth may be found, if not by any of the actual inquirers, yet ultimately by those who come after them and who shall make use of their results' (CP 7.54, 1902)? How can we handle the thought that in vital matters, we do not aim at getting the answer in the long run, but rather, we follow instinct, convention, and common sense in order to get an answer here and now?

There is no use denying that the distinction between vital and scientific matters was dear to Peirce. But it is far less damaging for the cognitivist position than it first appears. Once we understand what Peirce means by 'instinct', 'experience', and 'common sense' and once we understand their roles in what he calls scientific inquiry, we can see that vital matters are indeed matters for scientific inquiry.

Peirce builds instinct into the scientific method – the method of abduction, deduction, and induction. Abduction is a matter of coming up with (Peirce sometimes says 'guessing at') an explanation for a surprising experience. Once abduction has provided a hypothesis, one deduces consequences from it and tests it by induction. Abduction provides science with new ideas and thus science advances by 'the spontaneous conjectures of instinctive reason' (CP 6.475, 1908, 5.604, 1901). That is, when a surprising phenomenon needs explanation, instinct plays a central role. It provides the fallible starting points of the scientific method – the hypotheses whose consequences are then tested by induction. That is one way in which instinct, rather than being set against science or inquiry which is aimed at truth, is a part of it.

Another way in which instinct is a part of science is as follows:

when one fact puts a person in mind of another, but related, fact, and on considering the two together, he says to himself 'Hah! Then this third is a fact', ... it is by *instinct* that he draws the inference. (MS 682 p. 19, 1913)

If you feel that an inference is correct, that feeling is an 'instinct' and is very much like the feeling that something is red. You have no *reason* to accept the judgement – it just comes upon you. It is thus a kind of experience or perception. This is not to say that this sort of instinct is infallible – it is as fallible as all kinds of experience (See CP 1.404, 1890).

Peirce also makes this kind of point by saying that instinct is aligned to our habits of reasoning: in Peircean terminology, our

logica utens. Reasoning 'is the principal of human intellectual instincts . . . reasoning power is related to human nature very much as
the wonderful instincts of ants, wasps, etc. are related to their several natures' (MS 682 p. 8–9). Our instinctive and habitual cognitive
skills, as Hookway (2000:255) puts it, guide our inquiries. Of course,
these habits can be flawed, but we nonetheless rely upon them until
they are shown to be flawed – until we have evidence that they lead
us astray or until we can explain what is wrong with them. If we are
to continue to inquire, we must assume that our stock of habitual
cognitive skills is reliable. Peirce is crystal clear that something's
being such a regulative assumption of inquiry does not mean that
it is true. But something's being a regulative assumption of inquiry
does entail that we should believe it and that we should construct
our philosophy in such a way as to make room for its truth.

And finally, instinct is, for Peirce, also aligned with that which is
not doubted – that which forms our 'common sense' fallible background body of beliefs. Writing in an entirely general way about belief
and inquiry, Peirce says '. . . the pragmatist will accept wholesale the
entire body of genuine instinctive beliefs without any shade of doubt,
tossing aside the toy doubts of the metaphysician as unworthy of a
mature mind'.[11]

That is what Peirce means when he says that in ethics we must
go on instinct or on the status quo. Even if you think, generally, that
trusting instinct is 'treacherous and deceptive', if you don't doubt
something and have never doubted it, you will believe it. Thus: 'that
which instinct absolutely requires him to believe, he must and will
believe it with his whole heart'. If something seems perfectly evident,
you can try as you will to criticise it, but you will eventually be
obliged to believe it. By 'common sense' and 'instinct', Peirce means
'those ideas and beliefs that a man's situation absolutely forces upon
him'. (CP 1.129, 1905) Instinct is that which we have no choice but
to rely upon. Instinct is just what the whole of past experience has
put into place.

In Peirce's Cambridge Lectures of 1898, one of the places in which
the problematic gap between science and vital matters is most stark,
we have this thought:

We do not say that sentiment is *never* to be influenced by reason, nor that
under no circumstances would we advocate radical reforms. We only say that

the man who would allow his religious life to be wounded by any sudden acceptance of a philosophy of religion or who would precipitately change his code of morals, at the dictate of a philosophy of ethics, – who would, let us say, hastily practice incest, – is a man whom we should consider *unwise*. The regnant system of sexual rules is an instinctive or Sentimental induction summarizing the experience of all our race. (CP 6.633/RLT: 111)

Parker (1998:50) notes that we also find these thoughts in James's work.[12] In 'The Moral Philosopher and the Moral Life', James extends Peirce's view of truth to ethics, saying '. . . there can be no final truth in ethics any more than in physics, until the last man has had his experience and his say' (1897a [1979]:184). He argues that society may be seen as a long-running experiment aimed at identifying the best kind of conduct. Its conventions thus deserve respect. Our background beliefs, while remaining fallible, capture the experience of generations (1897a [1979]:206). James thinks that 'ethical science is just like physical science, and instead of being deducible all at once from abstract principles, must simply bide its time, and be ready to revise its conclusions from day to day' (1897a [1979]:208).

Peirce is in agreement with James here. The ethical deliberator might be hesitant to revise her beliefs and this hesitation can be justified. But it is not always justified:

Like any other field, more than any other [morality] needs improvement, advance. . . . But morality, doctrinaire conservatist that it is, destroys its own vitality by resisting change, and positively insisting, This is eternally right: That is eternally wrong. (CP 2.198, 1902)

For both Peirce and James, moral judgements are connected to experience in the way that all of our genuine judgements are: 'just as reasoning springs from experience, so the development of sentiment arises from the soul's Inward and Outward Experiences' (CP 1.648, 1898). As with every other kind of experience, '[t]hat it is abstractly and absolutely infallible we do not pretend; but that it is practically infallible for the individual – which is the only clear sense the word "infallibility" will bear – in that he ought to obey it and not his individual reason, *that* we do maintain' (CP 1.633, 1898).

We have seen that, for Peirce, this holds for any domain of inquiry: we take our body of background belief to be practically infallible, until the course of experience weighs in against it. Instinctual and common sense beliefs are subject to revision, but they are held firm until experience prompts that revision (CP 5.444, 1905). That is the Peirce I want to focus upon. Ethics and science are in the same boat, relying on deeply held, but revisable, background beliefs and habits. Instinct has a positive and essential role to play in science and in morality.[13]

Enough said about how reliance on instinct does not distinguish ethical matters from other matters. Now we need to focus on the other aspect of the point – the contentious view of science, in which belief is out of place. Let us look at the source of the talk that, while the scientist can wait for an answer and thus does not believe his theories, the deliberator in ethics needs an immediate answer and thus has *beliefs* on which to act. One source is Peirce's 1902 application to the Carnegie Institute, pleading for funds so that he could write his grand work on logic. There are many drafts of this application in the Peirce Papers and some of these drafts show very clearly that Peirce did not have a settled view about the matter in question. Perhaps his doubts are best expressed on p. 54 of some of the drafts, where we have him saying that the scientist is in a bind – a 'double position':

As a unit of the scientific world, with which he in some measure identifies himself, he can wait five centuries, if need be, before he decides upon the acceptability of a certain hypothesis. But as engaged in the investigation which it is his duty diligently to pursue, he must be ready the next morning to go on that hypothesis or reject it . . . he ought to be in a double state of mind about the hypothesis, at once ardent in his belief that so it must be, and yet not committing himself further than to do his best to try the experiment.[14]

What a wonderful statement of the problem. The inquirer (*any* inquirer) must be ready to believe and to act on the belief, knowing full well that it might not be true. Belief is not *out of place* in science – it is just tempered by fallibilism. The scientist must believe, but be constantly aware that her belief might be overturned. This is a perfect statement of the tricky path on which the critical common sense philosopher must tread.[15]

Similarly, in the 1898 'Detached Ideas on Vitally Important Topics', it turns out that Peirce's statement that there is no belief in science is not as alarming as it first seems. It is here that we find the nice metaphor that science is walking upon a bog. The reason it can only say 'this ground seems to hold for the present. Here I will stay till it begins to give way' is that science always starts with an abductive inference. For Peirce, the conclusions of abductive inferences aren't to be believed: they are mere conjectures. But

After a while, as Science progresses, it comes upon upon more solid ground. It is now entitled to reflect: this ground has held a long time without showing signs of yielding. I may hope that it will continue to hold for a great while longer (CP 5.589).

We can now use the hypothesis or conjecture in practice – we can act on it. For it no longer rests upon a mere abduction. It has been inductively supported. Peirce says 'In other words there is now reason to believe in the theory, for belief is willingness to risk a great deal upon a proposition'. The scientist, however, will still be concerned about whether in fact the theory will continue to survive the trials of induction: he will keep his eye on whether the hypothesis will in the long run survive the trials of inquiry. Nonetheless: 'We call them in science established truths, that is, they are propositions into which the economy of endeavor prescribes that, for the time being, further inquiry shall cease' (CP 5.589).

Another source of the contentious view is Peirce's Cambridge Lectures of 1898 (RLT). These lectures are not the best place for discerning Peirce's considered view about science and vital matters. He was extremely irritated at James, who had charitably set up the lectures so that Peirce might quite literally be able to put a bit of food on his plate. Upon learning that Peirce intended to address technical questions of logic, James asked him to 'be a good boy and think a more popular plan out'. Perhaps he could rather speak about 'separate topics of a vitally important character'.[16] Peirce, struggling no doubt with the shame of having to be rescued by James and having been shut out of an academic job by Harvard, pours scorn on the Harvard philosophers for their lack of training in logic and sarcastically says that he will indeed restrict himself to 'vital matters'. The drafts of the lectures are more scathing than the lectures actually delivered, showing that Peirce thought he ought to try to hold his anger in check, but he does not altogether manage it. It is in this context that he makes the extreme remarks about reasoning being out of place with respect to vitally important topics. Reasoning, he sneers, seems not to be necessary for worldly success.

These remarks simply cannot be taken seriously once it is seen that Peirce was wounded about being told, in such an offensive way, to excise the hard reasoning and logic from his lectures. After James had died, Peirce clearly felt bad about having been so rude. Unwilling to give up on the point that his dear friend had an 'almost unexampled incapacity for mathematical thought', he nonetheless promises to endeavour 'to substitute a serious and courteous' tone for 'the tone I used at Harvard' (CP 6.182, 1911).

And finally, in the Cambridge Lectures, we find Peirce see-sawing in the same breath between the idea that belief has no place in science and the idea that it does. First he says:

> I would not allow to sentiment or instinct any weight whatsoever in theoretical matters, not the slightest. . . . True, we are driven oftentimes in science to try the suggestions of instinct; but we only *try* them, we compare them with experience, we hold ourselves ready to throw them overboard at a moment's notice from experience. (CP 1.634/RLT: 111)

This is the 'no belief in science' side of the see-saw. We are not ready to act on belief in science. Science

> merely writes in the list of premises it proposes to use. Nothing is *vital* for science; nothing can be. Its accepted propositions, therefore, are but opinions at most; and the whole list is provisional. The scientific man is not in the least wedded to his conclusions. He risks nothing upon them. He stands ready to abandon one or all as soon as experience opposes them. (CP 1.635/RLT: 112)

But in the next breath, Peirce says that some of the scientist's conclusions are called 'established truths' – 'propositions to which no competent man today demurs' (CP 1.635/RLT: 111). Established truths are the background beliefs which we take for granted – the beliefs against which we judge new hypotheses. They are what the critical common sense philosopher focusses upon. Peirce does indeed think that belief has a place in science.

If we have to choose, on their own merits, which of Peirce's opposing views of science to accept, the choice is easy. As Duhem, Quine, and Kuhn have gone so far to show us, no scientific theory is overthrown in a flash by a lone experience. Scientists tend to insulate their theories from rogue experiences unless the theory can bear such insulation no more. It would be an odd scientist indeed who abandoned a well-supported theory on the basis of one contra-dictory experiment. Peirce just makes a mistake here – one that has irritated many a contemporary pragmatist.[17] He at times fails to see how the background theories of scientists are accepted as true until recalcitrant experience overwhelms them. But of course, at times he sees this very clearly.

If we drop Peirce's contentious thought about science, we can discern a coherent and very sensible position. In both scientific and moral matters, we have cherished beliefs which are nonethe-less responsive to experience. In ethics, as in science, we act on our experience-driven background beliefs, while realising that they might yet be overthrown by further experience.

5. A MORE PRODUCTIVE TENSION

I have argued that Peirce's thoughts about ethics and science can be brought into harmony – that we ought to see Peirce as holding that vital matters fall under the scope of truth, knowledge, and what he calls the scientific method of inquiry. As in science, we hope or assume that there will be an upshot to our moral deliberations. But there is another tension in Peirce's thought about science and ethics which we would do well to leave in place. For any cognitivist position which fails to incorporate the tension is, I propose, simpleminded.

At one point Peirce distinguishes disagreement in moral matters from disagreement about taste: 'However it may be about taste, in regard to morals, we can see ground for hope that debate will ul-timately cause one party or both to modify their sentiments up to complete accord' (CP 2.151, 1902). That is the cognitivist thought which I have been trying to preserve for Peirce. But he then delivers the apparently anticognitivist thought that 'Should it turn out oth-erwise, what can be said except that some men have one aim and some another? It would be monstrous for either party to pronounce the moral judgments of the other to be *bad*. That would imply an appeal to some other tribunal' (CP 2.151, 1902).

At first glance, this looks like a straightforward contradiction. But Peirce here is rehearsing his rather subtle position on bivalence – a position which is especially suited to moral judgement. He thought that the principle of bivalence – that every statement is either true or false – is not a law of logic, but a regulative assumption of inquiry. If it were the case that, no matter how far we were to push our inquiries, there would be no upshot to the question at hand, then we must say that there is no truth of the matter at stake. The hope or regulative assumption of inquiry – that our inquiries will have an upshot – would here not be fulfilled. So we frequently have him saying, in an entirely general fashion:

It is true that we cannot know for certain that experience, however long and full, ever would bring all men to the same way of thinking concerning the subject of inquiry. But that is the only result that can satisfy us, so that we must forever continue in the hope that it will come, at last.[18]

We must hope, for any question into which we inquire, that bivalence will hold. And here is the point to which any cognitivist must be alert: we expect that bivalence will fail more often in moral inquiry than in chemistry and less often than in matters of taste.

A particularly helpful text regarding bivalence and morals is 'Truth and Falsity and Error'. Here Peirce considers the possibility that for some questions, no answer would be forthcoming, no matter how long the discussion were to go on and no matter how advanced our methods of inquiry were to become. Perhaps the question of whether there is free will is like that:

Then in regard to that question, there certainly is no *truth*. But whether or not there would be perhaps any *reality* is a question for the metaphysician ... Even if the metaphysician decides that where there is no truth there is no reality, still the distinction between the character of truth and the character of reality is plain and definable. (CP 5.565, 1901)

After drawing the distinction between truth and reality, Peirce very carefully says that it holds not just for science, but also for ethics (CP 5.566, 1901) and for mathematics (CP 5.567, 1901). All of these inquiries aim at the truth:

Now the different sciences deal with different kinds of truth; mathematical truth is one thing, ethical truth is another, the actually existing state of the universe is a third; but all those different conceptions have in common something very marked and clear. We all hope that the different scientific inquiries in which we are severally engaged are going ultimately to lead to some definitely established conclusion, which conclusion we endeavour to anticipate in some measure. Agreement with that ultimate proposition that we look forward to, – agreement with that, whatever it may turn out to be, is the scientific truth. (CP 7.187, 1901)

There will of course be differences between kinds of inquiry: the mathematician, the chemist, and the inquirer into what is the morally right thing to do will not use identical methods. Nor will they find that their aspirations have identical prospects. Nor will they all be talking about the same sort of reality. As Hookway puts it:

We might agree that mathematical propositions, ethical propositions, propositions from the more theoretical reaches of science can all be assessed as true or false. Each, we might suppose, can be tested or 'compared with reality'. This might involve looking for a proof, considering how the ethical proposition would appeal to someone who took up a distinctive disinterested viewpoint on things, or making explanatory inferences about what best systematises our other theoretical beliefs and experimental results. (Hookway 2000:97)[19]

That is, comparing hypotheses with 'reality' is bound to take different forms in different inquiries. And Peirce is a realist about kinds of reality that are not physical.

Peirce goes on to make the point that I have been stressing: what is central in these various inquiries is the surprise of experience, against a background of stable expectation or belief. He says: 'Thus it is that all knowledge begins by the discovery that there has been an erroneous expectation. ... Each branch of science begins with a new phenomenon which violates a[n] ... expectation'. (CP 7.188, 1901)

Let us look at the mathematical case, about which Peirce is exceptionally clear. In 'Truth and Falsity and Error', he says that

[t]he pure mathematician deals exclusively with hypotheses. Whether or not there is any corresponding real thing, he does not care. His hypotheses are creatures of his own imagination; but he discovers in them relations which surprise him sometimes. A metaphysician may hold that this very forcing upon the mathematician's acceptance of propositions for which he was not prepared, proves, or even constitutes, a mode of being independent of the mathematician's thought, and so a *reality*. But whether there is any reality or not, the truth of the pure mathematical proposition is constituted by the impossibility of ever finding a case in which it fails. (CP 5.567, 1901)

Peirce argued that mathematics does not answer to a *physical* reality – it is not concerned with physical objects, but with possibilities (CP 4.234, 1902, CP 3.527, 1896) or the forms of relations (CP 4.530, 1905). Peirce of course thinks that reality does go beyond the physical – generals and potentialities, for instance, are real. But, as he says, that is a further question for the metaphysician – it goes beyond the basic pragmatist elucidation of truth.

Whatever your metaphysics might be, mathematics aims at the truth in the same way other kinds of inquiry aim at the truth. A true belief would be the best belief, were we to pursue our inquiries as far as they could fruitfully go, and what makes a belief best in mathematics might differ from what makes a belief best in science, or in morals.

'Truth and Falsity and Error' is thus a wonderful text for the cognitivist pragmatist. We have Peirce saying that a belief can be sensitive to experience even if there is no underlying physical reality. Experience, for Peirce, just *is* a surprise. Perhaps a domain of inquiry which rests on an underlying physical reality will have more statements which are bivalent. But some kinds of inquiry, such as mathematics, will be full of bivalent statements and yet they are such that there is no underlying physical reality.

Morality is an especially interesting domain of inquiry with respect to these questions. In yet another grand proposed book on logic, where Peirce is outlining his view in a systematic way, he says what surely any cognitivist must accept: morality is somehow both subjective and objective. Morality arises from human predicaments and history – it 'has its roots' in 'human nature' (CP 2.156, 1902). Yet it is such that we aim to get a right answer. Unlike taste, which seems to be mostly subjective, morals 'has a subjective and an objective side' (CP 2.153, 1902). There is a continuum here: 'taste, morality, rationality, form a true sequence in this order', with taste being 'purely subjective'.

Peirce's elaboration of this thought takes us further into the subtle moves required of moral cognitivism. It often happens, he says, that a man seriously considers what his duty is in a certain case, but then draws a mistaken conclusion: it is 'quite the reverse of that which he would reach if certain aspects of the case had not escaped him'. Yet he is right to do what seems to him to be his duty, despite the fact that he is mistaken. It would be very odd to suggest that he *not* follow 'the dictates of his conscience'. He must act and he must act on what, after careful consideration, he takes to be his duty. If he 'carried his self-discussion further', he might have discovered the truth about what his duty was. But he cannot but do what he thinks is right. There *is* a right answer to the question 'what is my duty?' even if I do not reach it. 'It seems right to me' comes apart from 'it is right', as it must in any objective matter. As in science, we go on the best beliefs, given the available evidence and argument, knowing that further evidence and argument might prove us mistaken.

Then Peirce calls for a correction in moral philosophy: 'It is true that the majority of writers on ethics in the past have made the root of morals subjective; but that best opinion is very plainly moving in the opposite direction' (CP 2.156, 1902). It cannot move too far in the objective direction, for the only ground we have for our moral judgements is feeling: 'our aversion for and horror of' incest 'is simply felt' (CP 2.171, 1902). The kind of experience relevant to moral judgement is likely to be much less uniform than the kind of experience one finds relevant to belief in logic and in science.

Peirce thus presents us with an extremely sophisticated cognitivism. We ought to expect bivalence to fail more often in ethics than in physical science, but moral deliberation nonetheless aims at the truth. We can see that the reality to which ethical judgements fit is not physical reality, yet ethical deliberation is still guided by the surprise of experience. Ethics falls somewhere in between the highly subjective domain of taste and the much more objective domain of the physical sciences. We have moved very far indeed from the thought that Peirce had only silly things to say about ethics.

6. THE NORMATIVE SCIENCES AND THE FORCE OF EXPERIENCE

On the outline of Peirce's view which we have in hand, it would seem that experience, not religion, not some set of philosophical principles delivered to us by utilitarianism or Kantianism, is the lifeblood of moral deliberation. The pragmatist cognitivist should, by and large, stay away from a *theory* of morality and take insight from wherever it is to be found (See Misak 2000: 122f).

Many a Peirce scholar will be wondering at this junction why I have been silent about what appears to be Peirce's theory of morality – his outline of the normative sciences. So I will conclude by very briefly looking at how the focus on experience fits with this late aspect of Peirce's thought.

Peirce makes the bold claim that logic is dependent on ethics and ethics is dependent on aesthetics. The claim, once unpacked, looks less startling than it does at first. We do not have here the bizarre thesis that logic is based on morality and that morality is based on art.

Peirce thought that the normative sciences (aesthetics, ethics, and logic), although they have often been mistaken for practical sciences, are really theoretical. They study what ought to be, not what will be or what is (CP 1.281, 1902, CP 2.156, 1902). All three pronounce some things good and some things bad. All three study forms of voluntary, self-controlled conduct, aimed at an ideal or end. They set out rules which ought to be followed if our aims are to be attained. They investigate the 'laws of the relation of Phenomena to *Ends*, that is, perhaps, to Truth, Right, and Beauty' (CP 5.121, 1903).

Aesthetics asks what is possible to admire unconditionally. This is of course not how we usually think of aesthetics. The science of aesthetics, Peirce thinks, 'has been handicapped by the definition of it as the theory of beauty' (CP 2.199, 1902). It is limited to matters of taste only if we include under the umbrella of taste 'forming a taste in bonnets...or...a preference between electrocution and decapitation, or between supporting one's family by agriculture or by highway robbery' (CP 1.574, 1905). And in forming these preferences, self-control and criticism is important. One doesn't just go on one's whims – one goes on one's considered and disciplined feelings, experiences, and thoughts.

Ethics, he says, is based on aesthetics, as we cannot know how we should aim to behave or know what is possible to adopt as an ultimate end until we know what is most admirable (CP 5.130, 1903). And logic is based on ethics. Logic is normative: it is thought which is under self-control (CP 1.606). 'Thinking is a kind of action, and reasoning is a kind of deliberate action; and to call an argument illogical, or a proposition false, is a special kind of moral judgment' (CP 8.191, 1904).[20]

So what does Peirce think that we can admire unconditionally? His rather unhelpful answer is 'concrete reasonableness' – reason and the growth of reason (CP 1.615, 1903). That is the *summum bonum* or the highest good to which all of our actions, intentions, and projects must answer.

When Peirce asks how self-control manifests itself in ethics, he says exactly what one would expect of someone who holds that a true belief is one which best accounts for experience, broadly conceived. He says that we criticise our own conduct, compare that conduct to a standard, ask whether our actions accord with our intentions, ask whether we are satisfied or dissatisfied with our actions, absorb lessons, and review our ideals (CP 1.591–9, 1903). 'The experience of life is continually contributing instances more or less illuminative' (CP 1.599).

We are thus quickly returned to the parallel between Peirce's view of ethics and his general epistemology:

Just as conduct controlled by ethical reason tends toward fixing certain habits of conduct, the nature of which...does not depend upon any accidental circumstances, and *in that sense* may be said to be *destined*; so, thought, controlled by a rational experimental logic, tends to the fixation of certain opinions, equally destined, the nature of which will be the same in the end, however the perversity of thought of whole generations may cause the postponement of the ultimate fixation. (CP 5.430, 1905)

Here again we have an excellent statement of Peirce's cognitivism. When we inquire about how we ought to control our conduct, we are 'destined' to reach the truth. That is, our reaching a permanently settled belief does not depend on accident – we are destined to reach the truth in the sense that experience and argument would, we hope, lead to a belief which would not be overturned. This is a thought which appears again and again in Peirce's epistemology and theory of truth. We may go badly wrong for generations, but we hope that there is an answer to the question at hand which would fit with all the evidence and argument, were we to have so much of it that further inquiry would be fruitless. The beauty of the above passage is both in making clear the modest sense of 'destined' and also in drawing the explicit parallel between ethics and other kinds of deliberation. In ethics we aim at getting an answer which would satisfy our aims in inquiry: which would forever meet the challenges of reasons, argument, and evidence. Peirce's view of truth is indeed a friend of cognitivism, despite certain of his assertions about vital matters.

NOTES

1. This paper has been improved by comments from Thomas Short.
2. This manuscript, titled 'A Sketch of Logical Critic' is a gem, as it also contains a statement of considerable importance for Peirce's view of belief: 'But it is one of the essentials of belief, without which it would not *be* belief, that it brings peace of mind, or at least relief from the struggle of doubt; so that a man could hardly be considered sane who should wish that, though the facts should remain lamentable, he should believe them to be such as he would wish them to be' (p. 11; see also the variant MS 675, p. 8). See Misak (1991:59ff) and Wiggins (1999) for the significance of this thought.
3. As Chris Hookway pointed out to me, a vital matter, for Peirce, is any urgent question about what we ought to do. The category of the vital is wider than the category of the ethical.
4. The resolution offered here is, in essence, the resolution offered in note 12 of Chapter 2 of Misak (1991).
5. Misak (1995), especially pp. 59ff, 97–127, 152–62, 171–8.
6. MS 328, p. 43, 1905. See also CP 3.363, 1885; see also 4.233, 1902, 1.322, 1903, 5.162, 1903, 6.568, 1905.
7. MS 453, loose sheets, 1903. See also CP 2.96, 1902, 6.497, 1906.
8. MS 408, pg.150, 1893–1895; see also CP 3.527, 1896.
9. CP 6.490, MS 842, p. 16, MS 843, unmarked page, 105 pages from the end of the manuscript. Hookway (2000:273f) suggests that Peirce backed off from the idea that one must find evidence for God's reality, suggesting that the model of abduction, deduction, and induction is being stretched to fit the religious question. I think that Peirce just couldn't find such evidence and only then did he back off from the idea that he must find it. See (CP 1.91, 1896) for the claim that whether prayers are efficacious is a question 'open to experimental inquiry'.
10. See Misak (2000) for a sustained discussion of these issues.
11. MS 329 p. 12, 1904. See also CP 5.445, 1905 and Short (2001) for the idea that common sense beliefs are of the nature of instincts. Hookway points to a similar connection between common sense background beliefs and vital matters: 'We begin with a folk physics and a folk psychology and a commonsense view of morality ...' (2000: 198, 205). It is important to see that once the Peirce scholar thinks of instinct as falling within Peirce's critical commonsensism, my central thesis follows. That is, the fact that Peirce thinks that vital matters must be driven by instinct does not make vital matters special. For Peirce takes all of our inquiries to rely on a background of 'instinctive' undoubted belief – belief upon which we act, until experience prompts us to revise it.

12. It is, however, not clear whether, in the end, James can be described as a cognitivist about any kind of belief.

13. As Trammell (1972) tells us, Peirce did at times innocuously oppose reason and vital concerns. First, the more emotionally committed one is to a vital belief, the harder it is to reason in an unbiased way about it. He also sometimes suggests that inductive reasoning requires a kind of detachment from immediate concerns, as it depends on the notion of a long run. And sometimes he suggests that highly theoretical or technical science is such that instinct is less reliable than it is in less abstract and less technical inquiry. These points are of course fine by me – my argument is that Peirce did not flat-out set instinct against reason, experience, and inquiry. Rather, he allowed a role for instinct in all kinds of reasoning. Instinct is not out of place in science and it is not out of place in morals. Both aim at the truth, using the method of experience and reasoning. (Hookway (2000:228), by the way, notes that the sharp distinction between theory and practice was confined to the 1880s.)

14. MS L75, p. 53–5 of the first 88-page variant.

15. See Misak (1991: 50ff) for a more detailed description of this path.

16. Trammell (1972) presents an excellent account of this dispute. See also Hookway (2000: 23f).

17. See, for instance, Levi (1983), (1984) and Hookway (2000: 210).

18. MS 1342, p. 2 of variants, undated. See also MS 408, p. 147, 1893–1895.

19. I prefer this statement of Hookway's position, rather than the following: 'Some truths can be understood in a "realist" manner, as dealing with a mind-independent reality, while others deal with matters whose character bears more marks of our interests, sentiments or constructive activities' (2000:77). For this latter way of putting the point makes it seem as if there are different kinds of reality, some of which are deserving of the title 'realist' and others not. Then the question must be whether those downgraded forms of reality ought to count as reality. In the same vein, notice that, despite Peirce's language, there are not different kinds of truth – each kind of inquiry aims at getting an answer that will not be overturned by subsequent experience. *That* is the pragmatist elucidation of truth.

20. Peirce also argues that logic is based on ethics in the following way: 'logic requires, before all else, that no determinate fact, nothing which can happen to a man's self, should be of more consequence to him than anything else. He who would not sacrifice his own soul to save the whole world, is illogical in all his inferences, collectively' (W 3, 284, 1878). Peirce's claim here is that in order to make sense of the notions of truth and probability, we need to refer to an extended community of inquirers.

When he says that 'it is impossible for a man to be logical unless he adopts certain high moral aims', his argument is 'extremely simple'. It is: 'All positive reasoning depends upon probability. All probability depends upon the supposition that there is a "long run". But a long run is an endless course of experience...' (MS L75 p. 13–14, variants, 1902). Logic doesn't require that someone be capable of the heroism of self-sacrifice; it just requires that we recognise the possibility of it. It requires that we see that our inferences are valid if they would be accepted by the hero. One has to 'refer his inferences to that standard' (W 3, 284). See Misak (1991: 108ff) for a sustained discussion.

7   Peirce's Common Sense Marriage of Religion and Science

In 1905 in a letter to F. C. S. Schiller, Charles Peirce responded to Schiller's attempt to define "pragmatism": "I would let it grow and then say it is what a certain group of thinkers who seem to understand one another think, and thus make it the name of a natural class in the Natural History fashion" (MS L390 p. 3). We might follow Peirce's suggestion in giving an account of pragmatic philosophy of religion. If we do so, we find Peirce's work marking out a middle position among the work of the other American pragmatists. At one extreme we find John Dewey who, in *A Common Faith*, defended a minimal notion of religiosity in which "God" stood for the power of actualizing human ideals. Dewey explicitly rejected both supernaturalism and the church. Next on the spectrum we find William James who likewise downplayed the importance of the church. However, in *The Varieties of Religious Experience* and elsewhere, James described and defended the importance of traditional kinds of individual religious experience. At the other extreme position stands Josiah Royce, whom both Schiller and Peirce included among the pragmatists (MS L390 p. 2). Royce's "absolute pragmatism" initially provided philosophical argumentation in defense of a religious outlook; later, in *The Problem of Christianity*, Royce, working under the influence of Peirce, developed the importance of the church as a "beloved community." In this "natural class" Peirce's philosophy of religion stands somewhere between those of James and Royce. In this essay, I would like to mark out some of the defining features of this mediating position and to show that it is a fitting piece of Peirce's philosophical architectonic.

Peirce did not write any single text that he identified as his philosophy of religion. But over the course of his career he generated a basic outlook on religion by exploring the relationship between what he called the spirit of science and the spirit of religion. The spirit of religion, which for Peirce is driven by instinct, feeling, and common sense, aims directly at guiding the conduct of life. Because of its focus on practice, Peirce believed, the spirit of religion tends to be – and needs to be – somewhat conservative. The spirit of science, on the other hand, is such that science is open to change. When science is properly understood not as a stagnant body of beliefs but as "a living and growing body of truth," we see its natural inclination to freedom, change, and liberality (CP 6.428). As Peirce argued in 1898, the difference between the two spirits is reasonable since in practice we must act, for the most part, on the basis of our funded experience and in theory we must allow ourselves to be as flexible and creative as the information we gather allows. "Thus it happens quite naturally," Peirce said, "that those who are animated with the spirit of science are for hurrying forward, while those who have the interests of religion at heart are apt to press back" (CP 6.430).

However natural this difference between the two kinds of inquiry, Peirce believed it was often pushed to an extreme by both scientists and religionists. In 1911 he reasserted that "no two spirits (tendencies) not downright conflicting can well be more opposed than the spirit of science and the spirit of religion" (MS 851, p. 1). He went on to point out that this often leads to an animosity between the two. Difficulties arise when the novelties of science encounter the natural conservatism of religion. "In this way," he argued, "science and religion become forced into hostile attitudes" (CP 6.431). It is easy to see that this has been a common problem in the developing histories of science and religion. But we need to note the phrase "not downright conflicting" in the 1911 passage. Although science and religion place their emphases and develop their tendencies in different directions, they are not, as Peirce saw it, "downright conflicting." Thus, the historical conflicts are in principle mendable – the opposing spirits should be able to live together. How such a "marriage" of science and religion might be effected was a theme of Peirce's thinking both early and late in his career. Peirce often chided scientists for not being more tolerant of religious belief. In his 1908 essay "A Neglected Argument for the Reality of God," he even went so far as to maintain that religious experiences such as his "humble argument" for the reality of God might be incipient scientific experiences. The "humble argument" was simply a natural affinity for believing in God as the creator or sustainer of the cosmos. As such, Peirce suggested, it "is nothing but an instance of the first stage of all such [scientific] work, the stage of observing facts, or variously rearranging them, and of pondering them until, by their reactions with the results of previous scientific experience, there is 'evolved' (as we chemists word it) an explanatory hypothesis" (CP 6.488). Nevertheless, most of Peirce's efforts were directed toward reconstructing our understanding of a religious life – we might call it his pragmatizing, or pragmaticizing, of religion.

ORIGINS AND AIMS OF RELIGION

As did William James, Peirce downplayed rational or philosophical argumentation as a source of religious belief. For Peirce, religious belief was most often exemplary of instinctive or commonsensical belief. In his "Neglected Argument" he made this explicit in his discussion of belief in the reality of God. There he argued, in trying to make sense of Galileo's conception of "simplicity," that "the simpler Hypothesis in the sense of the more facile and natural" is "the one that instinct suggests" (CP 6.477). Thus the "humble" belief in God's reality was an initially strong hypothesis because it excited the "peculiar confidence" that instinctive beliefs create "in the highest degree" (CP 6.477). Religious belief is directly experiential and therefore bears the strength of immediacy; it is what Peirce occasionally called "practically indubitable." Peirce often equated instinctive and common sense beliefs with feeling and perception, further amplifying the originary power that religious experience displayed.[1] In his eighth Lowell lecture of 1903, Peirce indicated that instinct suggested a kind of direct experience or perception:

Ordinary ideas of perception, which Descartes thought were most horribly confused, have nevertheless something in them that very nearly warrants their truth, if it does not quite so. 'Seeing is believing, says the man of instinct.' (CP 5.593)

In 1896, Peirce had already drawn the connection between religious belief and perception, hinting at its instinctive or commonsensical nature. In one of his many attacks on nominalism as unscientific, he brought perception into the religious arena:

Where would one find such an idea, say as that of God, come from, if not from direct experience? Would you make it a result of some kind of reasoning, good or bad? .... No: as to God, open your eyes – and your heart, which is also a perceptive organ – and you see him. [CP 6.493]

In short, philosophy is not the origin of most religious belief – such belief is felt, perceived, or experienced. This has several implications. First, the power of instinctive belief seemed to Peirce exemplified by religious experience, thus providing a solid basis for the commitments necessary to the conduct of life. Second, it meant that the contents of such beliefs were invariably vague, general, and unfinished. And finally, this indefiniteness meant that religious beliefs required philosophy, science, or theoretical inquiry for their development – their unfinished state needed explication and interpretation. Thus, the instinctive – perceptual origin of religious belief made it useful for its primary aim – conducting life. But at the same time, it made it susceptible to misuse and abuse, for which the only antidote could be an openness to ongoing theoretical inquiry concerning its meaning.

The "most distinctive character of the Critical-Common-sensist," Peirce remarked, "lies in his insistence that the acritically indubitable is invariably vague" (CP 5.446). The instinctiveness of the ideas of religious belief thus entails their indeterminateness in vagueness and generality.[2] It is important to note that this is a strength of instinctive beliefs, as Peirce saw it, not a weakness. The vagueness of the common sense or instinctive beliefs allows them to provide a direction or heading for our conduct without foreclosing on the variety of ways in which that direction might be developed. In religious belief specifically, it allows for a variety of religious experiences that are tethered only by vague, working conceptions of God, love, and the *summum bonum*. In short, vague and general conceptions are good enough for the conduct of life, that is, for most of our practical concerns. Such a view lies at the heart of Peirce's "Neglected Argument." There the "God" hypothesis is understood "as vague yet as true so far as it is definite" (CP 6.466; see also CP 6.494). In a 1905 letter to William James, Peirce made the point in similar fashion: "The idea [of a "living" God] is a *vague* one but is only the more irresistible for that. Subtile distinctions are out of place; the truth of common sense is that little as we can comprehend the author of all beauty and power and thought, it is really impossible, except by sophisticating the plain truth, to think otherwise than that there is a living being" (MS L224: n.p., 7/26/05). Peirce saw the directness of religious experience as a kind of knowledge by acquaintance, the way we might know, say, physical suffering through participation in a contest of endurance. He seemed to indicate that though the definiteness of such ideas is limited, we have a closeness to them through this direct acquaintance such that they are easily employed in guiding everyday practices: "No words are so well understood in one way, yet they are invariably vague; and of many of them it is true that, let the logician do his best to substitute precise equivalents in their places, still, the vernacular words alone, for all their vagueness, answer the principal purposes" (CP 6.494). Thus, for religious practice, vagueness is a virtue not a vice; as Potter points out, "it is vagueness which allows our notions to be about God" (Potter 1972: 249).

The spirit of religion is to conduct our lives under the guidance of instinctive, common sense beliefs in such a way as to ameliorate human existence. To establish this is the aim of the first of the three nested arguments in the "Neglected Argument," the "humble argument" noted above: "any normal man who considers the three Universes in the light of the hypothesis of God's Reality, and pursues that line of reflection in scientific singleness of heart, will come to be stirred to the depths of his nature by the beauty of the idea and by its August practicality, even to the point of earnestly loving and adoring his hypothetical God, and to that of desiring above all things to shape the whole conduct of life and all the springs of action into conformity with that hypothesis" (CP 6.467). This seems a tall order at first glance, but Peirce believed he was simply reflecting an experience that had been common among human cultures and histories. Across time and cultural space, there seems to be a general consensus of the "goodness" of those who act from love and caring toward the interests of others. As Kelly Parker suggests, for Peirce, those "who are affected by the religious sentiment will be attuned to the benevolent, just, and wise aspects of the world, and will mold their lives so as to contribute to these tendencies in society and in the order of things" (Parker 1990: 198). In such attunement there is a natural conservatism, a humble affinity for the acritical instinctive and common sense beliefs. However, the spirit of this conservatism is directed toward moral action and is not antagonistic to the spirit of science. It is innocent rather than ignorant. It is, as it were, not yet awake to the spirit of science. No theorizing, interpreting, or precising of the instinctive beliefs is yet at stake.

The origin of the religious life is, from Peirce's angle of vision, adequate to the aim of religion's practical task. Our vague notions of God and *agape*, or cherishing love, are sufficient for us to get on with the project of bettering human existence.[3] Nevertheless, Peirce routinely worried about the dangers – to science, to morality, and to religion itself – whose germs lay at this juncture of religious belief and practice. The conservatism, if taken to the extreme, could stand in the way of any quest for truth. Thus, the way of life guided by religious belief was always on trial; we are in fact always carrying out experiments on our beliefs in the ways we live. This marks the clearly Jamesian side of Peirce's pragmatic philosophy of religion: "Even for the greatest saints, the active motives were not such hopes and fears [of heaven and hell], but the prospect of leaving behind them fertile seeds of desirable fruits here on earth" (CP 6.451).[4] The consequences of our actions are, in part at least, the pragmaticistic test of the truth of our instinctive beliefs. The beliefs take on a life in human history and remain open, to growth, development, and change. Thus, for Peirce, the "reasonable" religious person

will see that the hypothesis [of a real, loving God], irresistible though it be to first intention, yet needs Probation; and that though an infinite being is not tied down to any consistency, yet man, like any other animal, is gifted with power of understanding sufficient for the conduct of life. This brings him, for testing the hypothesis, to taking his stand upon Pragmaticism, which implies faith in common sense and instinct, though only as they issue from the cupelfurnace of measured criticism. In short, he will say that the N. A. [Neglected Argument] is the First Stage of a scientific inquiry, resulting in a hypothesis of the very highest Plausibility, whose ultimate test must lie in its value in the self-controlled growth of man's conduct of life. (CP 6.480)

Peirce's conception of the religious life thus shares James's and Dewey's meliorism. The difference is that Peirce makes a much stronger commitment to the regulative ideals of truth and goodness.

This commitment requires an openness to the growth and development of religious beliefs as with all beliefs – religious belief must be open to reflection and inquiry. For Peirce, this meant that the spirit of religion must find a way to marry itself to the spirit of science. However, he believed that another mode of theorizing about religious belief stood in the way of this proper union.

THEOLOGY AND THE THEORIZING OF RELIGIOUS BELIEF

As a good Aristotelian, Peirce did suggest that it was natural for persons to want to theorize about the world and about their religious beliefs. He maintained that religious ideas "are easily doubted" and we know that for him doubt was the mainspring of inquiry. So, the question, especially given his critical commonsensism, was not whether one can inquire into religious ideas or into other ideas that might have a bearing on religion, the question was *how* one is to do this. Theology, as Peirce understood it, employs the wrong kind of theorizing and leads to a vicious conservatism that threatens both science and religion.

The failure of religions, from a pragmatic point of view, has by and large been a function of their engaging in theology. Peirce believed that theology masqueraded as a science while it was, in essence, antithetical to the spirit of science. It indeed brought logic to bear on religious beliefs, but it mistakenly treated religion as a closed deductive system of ideas. Since "theology pretends to be a science," Peirce argued in 1898, theologians "must also be judged as scientific men" (CP 6.3). Judged in this way, theologians invariably and miserably fail because instead of seeking truth through open inquiry, they take as their "principal business ... to make men feel the enormity of the slightest departure from the metaphysics they assume to be connected with the standard faith" (CP 6.3). Theology poses as an exploration of the natures of God, creation, and the cosmos. But it is antiscientific just insofar as it is tenacious and authoritative. Instead of actually exploring the possibilities, it begins with a dogmatic platform and seeks to insulate it from criticism. It is at best an uncritical commonsensism. Indeed, theology need not even be common-sensical, since the theologian may – and often does – arbitrarily adopt any belief as the origin of his or her deductive work. More often than not, theology becomes a practical instrument for narrow aims – an instrument that is neither scientific nor theoretical.

Theology's method, if it is a method, is to express and defend tenaciously and authoritatively some specific version of religious ideas. To do this, it tries to specify the ideas so particular rules and interpretations can be nailed down. For example, the vernacular "God" is replaced with a named being or beings who are historically located, embodied, or otherwise definitely described. Likewise, the "good" is reduced to a narrow formula of behavior, a set of rules that curtails human variety and flexibility in dealing with life situations. In short, theologians produce and defend creeds and doctrines. Under the method of theology "the Church requires subscription to a platform – a Creed" (CP 6.450). By way of this version of theorizing religion, Peirce argued, we cannot "hope that any body of priests should consider themselves more teachers of religion in general than of the particular system of theology advocated by their own party" (CP 6.427). Theology thus embodies all that Peirce resisted: tenacity, authority, closure of inquiry, and absence of growth. It has repeatedly proved itself a danger to humanity, and, as Parker aptly states, theologians are "to be chastised as much for muddying the waters of religion as they are for obstructing the scientific spirit" (Parker 1990: 196); theology as a way of theorizing about religious belief is not only unscientific, it is antagonistic to religion itself.

The waters of religion get muddied in at least three ways: (1) theology makes religion exclusionary and antithetical to the principle of love, (2) theology overlooks and/or rejects religious perception and sentiment, and (3) theology's overdetermination of religious ideas leads to an inquiry it cannot satisfy. This last way also marks the point at which theological credalism antagonizes the spirit of science.

As we have just noted, Peirce believed theology's primary task was to demand adherence to a specific doctrine and to reject, usually in an articulate fashion, any deviation from this doctrine: "religious truth having been once defined is never to be altered in the most minute particular" (CP 1.40). The upshot is that theological practice is fundamentally exclusionary and establishes the basis for warring among different religious outlooks. Because Peirce identified God with love and took *agape* to be the instinctive basis of a religious attitude, he found the exclusionary practice to be fundamentally irreligious and immoral (see CP 6.441). Consequently, in "What Is Christian Faith?" he asked that we "[d]iscountenance as immoral all movements that exaggerate differences, or that go to make fellowship depend on formulas invented to exclude some Christians from communion with others" (CP 6.445). In short, Peirce was radically antifundamentalist. Since the aim of religion is to guide the conduct of life melioristically, theology, because it is essentially fundamentalist, is both immoral and irreligious.

The second problem Peirce found in theology was its obscuring of religious experiences and the religious sentiment. On the one hand, because theology is primarily the deductive explication of a set of dogmatic premises, the theologians need not have any direct acquaintance with religious sentiment or sensibility: "a man," Peirce said, "may be an accomplished theologian without ever having felt the stirring of the spirit, but he cannot answer the simple question at the head of this article [What is Christian faith?] except out of his own religious experience" (CP 6.435). On the other hand, theology, in enforcing closure on the content of belief, often openly challenges the very origin of religious belief. Those who disciple themselves to a theological doctrine become automata following rules rather than believers inspired to produce a better life through love. Instead of looking to the efficacy of love in daily life, theologians generate argumentation that unnecessarily politicizes the religious life:

Then, after a religion has become a public affair, quarrels arise, to settle which watchwords are drawn up. This business gets into the hands of theologians: and the ideas of theologians always appreciably differ from those of the universal church. They swamp religion in fallacious disputations. Thus, the natural tendency is to the continual drawing tighter and tighter of the narrowing bounds of doctrine, with less and less attention to the living essence of religion, until, after some *symbolum quodcumque* has declared that the salvation of each individual absolutely and almost exclusively depends upon his entertaining a correct metaphysics of the godhead, the vital spark of inspiration becomes finally quite extinct. (CP 6.438)

Thus, the vicious conservatism of theology moves beyond the working conservatism of religious belief and works to destroy the religious life out of which it grew.

This vicious conservatism also reveals theology's final distortion of a genuinely religious life. As we noted earlier, for Peirce, religious belief worked effectively with vague ideas – the ideas generated by instinct or common sense. Theology's aim, however, is always to give concrete determination – Peirce would call it overdetermination – to the vague ideas. But, as Potter points out, the more overdetermined these ideas become, the more doubtable they become: "To the extent that some particular formulation of an instinctive belief is definite (nonvague), that formulation is open to doubt and demands critical review" (Potter 1972: 225). This is the point of Peirce's critical commonsensism. The beliefs move from the role of practical guides to that of hypotheses in an inquiry. Theology routinely fails to draw this distinction.

For Peirce there is a clear division of labor. Religion can initially effect its practical work with its vague beliefs. However, as natural curiosity leads us to inquire about these ideas, we move from religion to science, from practice to theory. Thus, when theology's narrow determination of religious beliefs creates doubt and generates inquiry, we must turn to the spirit and the method of science. But theology is unable to make the transition. The height of its reasoning is explicative deduction. It can only return to its dogmatic doctrine and authoritatively repeat its arguments. It circles its wagons and conservatively holds its ground.

For Peirce, however, a genuinely religious outlook would understand the limitations of its aim and would know to relinquish the responsibility of inquiry to the scientific spirit.[5] If religious life is to ameliorate the world, it must, Peirce believed, hold an abiding respect for truth. Such respect involves an openness to growth, to development. Thus, as ideas develop through the community of inquirers, they will have a gradual effect on religious belief and subsequently on religious practices: "I do not say that philosophical science should not ultimately influence religion and morality; I only say that it should be allowed to do so only with secular slowness and the most conservative caution" (CP 1.620). A Peircean religion must act through its commitments at the same time that it remains open to self-development and self-revision. Peirce put it this way when he wrote to James in 1897: "'Faith,' in the sense that one will adhere consistently to a given line of conduct, is highly necessary in affairs. But if it means you are not going to be alert for indications that the moment has come to change your tactics, I think it is ruinous in practice" (MS L224, p. 2).

Peirce thus envisioned religion in a reciprocal dependence with science; the two must engage in an ongoing dialectical relationship. An idea that is effective as a religious belief, if it is to be theorized about, must turn itself over to scientific inquiry, to criticism. A theologically driven religion is unable to do this and thereby becomes, on Peirce's terms, irreligious. Theology simply opens up the need for an inquiry that it cannot deliver. Richard Trammell sees this point made manifest in Peirce's discussion of musement in the "Neglected Argument": "This argument shows that the same course of meditation which, for practical purposes, produces a living belief in God, from another point of view is the first stage of a theoretical inquiry" (Trammell 1972: 19). For Peirce, a theological religion has no route to genuine inquiry and therefore makes the spirits of science and religion fundamentally antagonistic. A critically commonsensist religion, on the other hand, while acknowledging the different spirits of science and religion, brings them into union through a mutual dependence. Consequently, as Michael Raposa points out, Peirce "thought it altogether reasonable that certain religious beliefs should be revised or even discarded as a result of new scientific discoveries" (Raposa 1989: 13).

CHURCH AS A COMMUNITY OF LOVE

In examining Peirce's thorough rejection of theology for its irreligiosity and its antagonism toward science, we might expect him to join James and Dewey in rejecting churches, or organized religions, in general. James and Dewey shared Peirce's rejection of credalism and vicious conservatism. James blamed a church's apparent need to manipulate and control its members for ruining the beneficial effects of individual religious experience. Dewey simply rejected religions altogether, arguing that they had caused too many problems historically with their supernaturalisms to be redeemed. Peirce, however, did not follow suit. Instead, he turned in the direction of Royce, defending the central importance of a church for the religious life's task of ameliorating human existence in this world. Through his peculiar – and admittedly tense – marriage of science and religion, he argued for the possibility of a nontheological church.

We noted earlier that for Peirce as for James religion begins in personal experience. However, because religion's importance is found in guiding the conduct of life, it immediately discloses that it has social consequences. "Man's highest developments," Peirce argued, "are social; and religion, though it begins in a seminal individual inspiration, only comes to full flower in a great church coextensive with civilization. This is true of every religion, but supereminently so of the religion of love" (CP 6.493). The church leads us out of ourselves, as *agape* requires, and generates concern for others. It is this move toward selflessness – which Peirce also took to be a central feature of the spirit of science – that makes our lives "social" and not just mechanically interactive. "The *raison d'etre* of a church," Peirce believed, "is to confer upon men a life broader than their narrow personalities, a life rooted in the very truth of being" (CP 6.451). Not only does the church enable a "broader life," it also serves as a vehicle for the social work that the principle of love requires.

Peirce's descriptions of the church's reason for being are rooted in his agapasm – his belief that love is an effective force in the evolution or development of the universe. Whatever one thinks of it as a cosmological speculation, agapasm can be convincing as a normative theory of how human history can develop in a meliorative fashion.[6] It is agapastic love that overcomes self-interest and self-love and turns to the interests of others and ultimately to the interest of the truth of God's cosmos. Peirce often admitted to having caught a dose of Schellingian romanticism and it no doubt reveals itself here. Nevertheless, his outlook is reasonably in line with his realism, his commitment to inquiry toward truth, and his belief in the possibility of a genuine community of inquirers – his defense of an agapastic church is not merely a hopeful addendum to his other work. It is a development of his own critical commonsensism. The principle of love expressed common-sensically in the Golden Rule, he maintained, "does not, of course, say, Do everything possible to gratify the egoistic impulses of others, but it says, Sacrifice your own perfection to the perfectionment of your neighbor" (CP 6.288). Thus, the church's function is to disseminate the principle of love to combat the specific "evils" generated by self-love and self-seeking.

Just as the community of inquirers was needed to move science forward, the church, as a beloved community, was required for the ameliorative work of religion. The church cannot be merely an institution for "getting together," a kind of social club. "A religious organization," Peirce asserted, "is a somewhat idle affair unless it be sworn in as a regiment of that great army that takes life in hand, with all its delights, in grimmest fight to put down the principle of self-seeking, and to make sure the principle of love is triumphant" (CP 6.448). The triumph sought cannot be a matter of getting persons to sign on, in theological fashion, to a creed. The principle of love must be disseminated through actions that are themselves governed by love. This, again, is the pragmatic test of Peirce's version of religion and of a church. In "the Marriage of Science and Religion" he made this point at length:

> But religion cannot reside in its totality in a single individual. Like every species of reality, it is essentially a social, a public affair. It is the idea of a whole church, welding all its members together in one organic, systemic perception of the Glory of the Highest – an idea having a growth from generation to generation and claiming a supremacy in the determination of all conduct, private and public. (CP 6.429)

To pursue this Roycean dimension of his philosophy of religion, Peirce needed to alter his church to meet the concerns expressed by James and Dewey. In being a church of love, his church must be "universal," it must confidently turn theory over to the spirit of science, and, consequently, it must be strong enough to learn from and grow through its own failures. In short, Peirce's church was to be a direct answer to the dangers he located in theological approaches to religion.

Peirce's agapastic church requires universality in both its origin and its aim. Because it is generated by instinctive or common sense beliefs, it is open to and accessible by everyone from the "clodhopper" to the scientist: "it has always seemed to me reasonable to suppose that, if He [a God in whom religious people of all creeds believe] really is, there must be some good reason for believing so, otherwise than on authority of some kind, which should appeal to the lowliest mind..." (MS 842, p. 8–9). Thus Peirce's church is universally open to all who would pay attention to common sense and instinct.

The church's aim must likewise be inclusive. Actions under the guidance of *agape* must reach out to the interests of all persons through a concern for their "perfectionment." Persons are brought together not by a forced agreement to some doctrine but by a genuine acceptance of their importance. Love must be transformative: "Love, recognizing germs of loveliness in the hateful, gradually warms it into life, and makes it lovely" (CP 6.289). At the political level, Peirce's nontheological church must not act so as to divide believers, but must seek "to patch up such peace as might be with the great religious world" (CP 6.447). Thus, Peirce's church not only accepts everyone, it attends to everyone.

The bidirectional universality of the agapastic church places extraordinary demands on it – demands not altogether unfamiliar to those who would join Peirce's community of inquirers. A thoroughgoing selflessness must become an ordinary habit. The church also needs the strength to contend with its own finitude and unfinished state. It must, on the one hand, be willing to act through its commitments to its vague, instinctive beliefs out of which it is generated. At the same time, it must know that its beliefs – "working creeds" we might call them – are open to criticism, to refinement, and to growth. The universal church's practices are to be tempered by an abiding respect for truth – an avenue of humility that was not open to theological churches. Peirce demanded that his church be conservative in its practice and liberal in its theory. In this way, it allows itself to grow, to revise itself in pragmatic fashion – a process that for different reasons James and Dewey did not think possible. Insofar as the universal church can live with this tension, it can keep alive the religious attitude that is its life's blood. Peirce believed the church could learn from the spirit of science "to become more and more perfect" instead of suffocating itself with doctrines until the "vital sentiment that gave it birth loses gradually its pristine purity and strength" (CP 6.430). In a much more systematic way than Emerson and Thoreau, Peirce defended the American transcendentalists' desire for a "living religion."

The lynchpin to the success of Peirce's universal church is this fundamental respect for truth. A church of love must also be a church of truth. To act with concern for others is to act, so far as we can, in line with the way things are – from a religious perspective, after all, it is God's world, not ours. A blind and ignorant love is likely to fail to achieve its purpose. And since for Peirce truth is always "on the way," the church must confidently respect change and development that result from inquiry. In an 1898 manuscript he entitled "Religion and Politics" Peirce recounted learning this lesson from a moment in politics. A Democratic senator had left his party because its platform became "contrary to his convictions" (MS 894 p. 1). The newspapers in New York "expressed contempt" for the senator's action. Peirce agreed that the senator had a commitment to his party, but argued that he had an even greater commitment to the whole community of citizens and therefore might be right in rejecting his party. A church is, Peirce suggested, analogous to the party – it has some platform to which we owe some allegiance. Nevertheless, "owe what one may to the Church, the truth claims permanent allegiance" (MS 894, p. 2; CP 6.450; see also CP 6.426). In its allegiance to the truth, the universal church must recognize its need for the spirit of science.

Peirce's church, as a community of love, does not produce a "religion of science" in which one simply rejects instinctive and common sense beliefs. These beliefs remain the "bedrock" of any reasoning. But his church must be critically commonsensist and must accept his peculiar marriage of science and religion:

The man whom religious experience most devoutly moves can recognize the state of the case. While adhering to the essence of religion, and so far as possible to the church, which is all but essential, say, penessential, to it, he will cast aside that religious timidity that is forever prompting the church to recoil from the paths into which the Governor of history is leading the minds of men, a cowardice that has stood through the ages as the landmark and limit of her little faith, and will gladly go forward, sure that truth is not split into two warring doctrines, and that any change that knowledge can work in his faith can only affect its expression, not the deep mystery expressed. (CP 6.432)

Religion and science work together toward Peirce's *summmum bonum*, the growth of concrete reasonableness – the realizing and actualizing of purposes and meaning (CP 5.3, 5.433). What, Peirce asked, "is man's proper function if it be not to embody general ideas in art-creations, in utilities, and above all in theoretical cognition?" (CP 6.476). Science is to be neither rejected nor romanticized; its spirit is to work in concert with the spirit of religion as a critical measure of religion's instinct and common sense. Together they generate the possibility of a living religion and a living science.

CONCLUSION

Peirce's pragmatic – or pragmaticistic – philosophy of religion holds to a tenuous middle ground. As for James and Dewey, individual religious experience is the origin of any religiosity. And as for Royce, a community – ultimately a universal community – of religious believers is essential to the ameliorative conduct that religious practice requires. To this point, I have sought primarily to sketch a description of Peirce's mediating outlook, not to defend it. It is, of course, not without its difficulties. Deweyans will continue to wonder if the dangers of religions and churches do not outweigh any possible benefits. Some will with Christopher Hookway raise questions concerning Peirce's claim that belief in God, vague or otherwise, is instinctive (Hookway, 2000: 269–72). Likewise, there are difficulties of internal consistency lurking within Peirce's overall description.

Nevertheless, Peirce's pragmatic philosophy of religion is both provocative and suggestive. It is provocative in part because it is Peirce who developed it. Many who have been attracted to Peirce because of his work in logic, the philosophy of science, and semeiotic find his work on religious issues disconcerting. It was this provocativeness, I think, that in part inspired Thomas Goudge's well-known suggestion that there were two incompatible Peirces: a reasonable scientific Peirce and a less reasonable transcendentalist Peirce. What I have tried to show here is that Peirce's philosophy of religion is not fundamentally opposed to, but works in concert with his theory of inquiry and his pragmaticism. This is useful if one is interested in the viability of both science and religion. Along these lines, Peirce's work is suggestive. One virtue of his outlook is that both as a religious believer and as a scientific inquirer he can face all criticisms directly; he can look down the road toward the consequences of his own confrontation with criticisms to see how his own views have developed or grown and how they might be further revised. His religiosity is not an ongoing death-rattle and his science is not a dogmatic nominalism terminating in an equally dogmatic materialism. In a firm but articulate manner he claims a plague on both houses: fundamentalist religion and dogmatic scientism.

Moreover, like many philosophers of religion, Peirce wants to see the best of religious experience express itself through a universal church. But he does not universalize in patchwork fashion by trying to meld or syncretize the various world religions. Instead, he throws religion back onto its instinctive beliefs in all their vagueness, asking that we take them as "good enough for now," while we together work out truth in the long run. Interestingly, Peirce's pragmatic and scientific religion not only makes room for the incorporation of new scientific truths, it opens us to the growth and development of specific moral insights under the direction of our vague and general instinctive beliefs. The principles of love and justice are open to extension beyond whatever historical bounds they at anytime rest. Peirce's evolutionary love can underwrite humanity's growing resistance to slavery, to sexism, to racism, and to simple abuse wherever it occurs; its central aim is to struggle with whatever particular evils it encounters. Peirce's answer to the historicist is that the vital sentiments of religion are true insofar as they are vague and general. What is human-made are the ways in which we implement them, and these remain open to criticism and development. Moral development – ameliorating conduct – is a real possibility in Peirce's pragmatic conception of religion.

If we are to try to bring the variety of human experiences together, not reductively, but as they are lived, then Peirce's common sense marriage of science and religion is instructive. The middle is not excluded; we can live toward truth without having certainty. We can act with commitment without becoming totalizing. These seem to Peirce to be the best features of religion and science in a world in which truth is on the highway. And he offers us a way of living one life with both in hand.

NOTES

1. The details of the relationship Peirce tried to establish between perception and instinct require another inquiry. In the 1903 pragmatism lectures he raised the issue explicitly and suggested the possibility of perceiving "thirds." So far as this is true, Peirce held an earlier and even more radical "radical empiricism" than that of James. This would help underwrite his claims that "God" is perceivable in some fashion and is no doubt linked to his strong Scotistic realism. However, it also seems to create problems for distinctions he might want to make between conceiving and perceiving.

2. For a detailed discussion of these and how they are relevant to Peirce's conception of "God," see Potter 1972.

3. It is important to note that Peirce often equated "God" and "love." *Agape* is God's mode of agency.

4. Indeed, Peirce thought of human immortality in light of his realism. Our habits and personalities leave behind real effects; it is by way of these that we "immortalize" ourselves.

5. I should note that for Peirce this does not mean that religion must simply capitulate to some dogmatically held set of "scientific" views. The spirit of science is in its method, not in any particular historical set of beliefs.

6. In his essay "Evolutionary Love," Peirce describes both ways of employing agapasm. In its cosmological form it serves primarily to mark out a world in which neither sheer contingency nor sheer determinism reigns. In its social use, the one in which I am here interested, agapasm is offered as a model for how humanity might work towards its own perfection. See CP 6.287–6.317.

8   Peirce's Pragmatic Account of Perception: Issues and Implications

Peirce's understanding of perception is crucial in situating his philosophy within a broad range of issues. Yet a cursory reading of Peirce seems to indicate that what he says about perception is both incomplete and inconsistent, leading both to an early neglect of his account of perception and to widely varying interpretations of his claims, as interest in them began to grow. The following analysis of Peirce's view of perception will try to resolve the ambiguities by bringing into focus the systematic completeness of Peirce's understanding of the process of perceiving and the object of perception, at the same time showing its relevance for a range of contemporary issues.

Peirce holds that the scientific method is the only genuine method of fixing belief, for it is the only method by which beliefs must be tested and corrected by what experience presents (CP 5.384). And the very first stage of scientific inquiry requires human creativity. Peirce calls the process of creative hypothesis formation 'abduction' to distinguish it from the inductive process of data collection. He rejects the claims of British Empiricism, that knowledge begins with first impressions of sense. He also rejects the claims, such as that put forth by Descartes, that it begins with immediate cognitions or indubitable intuitions. All knowledge begins with perception, but perception is not the having of brute givens. Rather, there is a creative element in perceptual awareness, an interpretive creativity brought by the perceiver.

Exactly how deeply this interpretive element runs in Peirce's account of perception is open to confusion because of the seemingly contradictory characterizations he gives of the various "ingredients" in perceptual awareness. Thus, while in recent years a good deal of attention is beginning to be focused on Peirce's understanding of perceptual judgments in relation to the contemporary issue of foundations for knowledge, there are widely conflicting claims as to whether he is a foundationalist or an antifoundationalist. These conflicting claims tend to stem from conflicting understandings of Peirce's account of the percept, the perceptual judgment, and what he calls the percipuum. For example, Christopher Hookway holds that the percipuum fuses the percept and perceptual judgment into a single whole and represents Peirce's attempt to reject foundationalism, though he never attempts to explicate why this is so.[1] On the other hand, David Gruender, in his discussion of the interrelation of observation and theory in Peirce's philosophy, tends to interpret what is given in the percept along foundationalist lines.[2] Similarly, Jeremiah McCarthy argues that Peirce is led to a foundationalist position because perceptual judgments are immune to doubt.[3] Carl Hausman recognizes dual meanings of the perceptual judgment in Peirce's philosophy, but links them to a seemingly univocal meaning of the percipuum.[4] The ensuing analysis will attempt to bring into focus Peirce's understanding of the dual senses of the percept, the perceptual judgment, and the percipuum in the logic of perceptual awareness, in order to show the unique and fruitful position he holds.

The percept is that sensory element which is presented in perceptual awareness. It in turn instigates the formation of the perceptual judgment, which involves a creative interpretation placed upon the percept or presented sense content or, in other terms, an abduction which yields a hypothesis as to what the content is (CP 5.115). Peirce is not here asserting that we first observe the percept and then proceed to interpret it in a judgment. Nor is he asserting that the percept and the content of the perceptual judgment are physically, metaphysically, or numerically distinct. He does not hold that what we are aware of is sense data of some sort rather than a physical object. Rather, the percept as interpreted *is* what we immediately perceive and *is* the reality (CP 5.568). But Peirce characterizes both the percept and the perceptual judgment in quite different, often contradictory, ways. For example, on the one hand he characterizes percepts as specifically individual (CP 7.633), as insistent and forcing themselves upon us (CP 6.541). At the same time he holds that percepts incorporate generality (CP 4.542). and involve processes which are "for all intents and purposes mental" (CP 7.624). And conflicting claims abound in Peirce's depictions of perceptual judgments. He at times claims that they are infallibly true statements about what is perceived (CP 5.55), but also states that perceptual judgments are fallible, for there is no infallible truth (CP 5.544). Further, he at times holds that perceptual judgments yield claims about the way things appear (CP 7.626), and at other times that they yield claims about the way things are (CP 7.636n).

The clarification of the way these seemingly conflicting statements refer to different senses of the percept and the perceptual judgment operative in perceptual awareness can best proceed by turning to the nature of the percipuum. It will be seen that Peirce uses the term 'percipuum' in two different senses, a wide sense and a narrow sense. And, when his various characterizations exemplified above are understood in the light of his broad and narrow senses of the 'percipuum,' or outcome of the perceptual judgment, it can be seen that Peirce uses both 'percept' and 'perceptual judgment'[5] in a wide and narrow sense, corresponding to the two sense of the 'percipuum': the percipuum in its wide sense as actually experienced in the flow of experience (CP 7.657; 7.676), and in its narrow sense is an analytical or logical abstraction indicating a "stopping" point prior to anticipatory expectations within the percipuum.

The term, percipuum, within the perceptual situation seems to have been first used by Peirce in a manuscript of 1903 (CP 7.642–81). He there proposes "to consider the percept as it is immediately interpreted in the perceptual judgment, under the name of the 'percipuum'" (CP 7.642). Though the term is introduced late in Peirce's career, and may seem to many to be representative of the unnecessary obscurity often found in his writings, it will in fact help bring into focus the distinctions toward which he seemed to be groping throughout his career, as well as the novel position these embody, in a way which would be obscured or misinterpreted by the use of more traditional philosophical terms.

Peirce states that "There is no Percipuum so absolute as not to be subject to possible error" (CP 7.676). However, Peirce is here using the term "percipuum" in its wide sense, a sense intended in the context to show that time is not composed of a series of discrete instants. As he there states, "The percipuum is not an absolute event" but rather occurs in a span of time which includes memory and expectation (CP 7.657). Here Peirce is concerned with emphasizing the

continuity of time or the passing temporal spread in which the percipuum looks to both the past and the future. Yet, within the wide
sense of the percipuum, Peirce makes several distinctions which are
abstractions for the purpose of analysis. The percipuum in its wide
sense, as it actually occurs in the so-called specious present, contains
several analytical distinctions,[6] one of which is the percipuum in its
narrow sense (CP 7.648).

These are intended to indicate that the very grasp of sensory
content as recognized content which in turn can activate habits of
response involves interpretive elements. For this grasp requires a
synthesized criterion for grasp of presentation as repeatable content.
Indeed, it is the interpretive process of grasping the individual unique
percept as a repeatable content, as "that which has been seen before
and may be seen again," which allows for the activation of habits of
anticipation involved in the perceptual judgment in its wide sense.
This primitive interpretive process involves the formation of a perceptual judgment in the narrow sense, yielding a percipuum as the
outcome of its interpretive process. It is this percipuum which in
turn becomes the percept for the perceptual judgment in the wide
sense, yielding the percipuum in the wide sense. The only type of
"reference to future experience" implicit in the percipuum in its
narrow sense is the possibility of future presentations of graspable
content which, for purposes of clarity, can perhaps best be termed
"possibility of repetition" rather than possibility of future experience. It provides "sameness of type" (MS p. 740) but "contains no
assertion of a fact" (MS p. 740). It is that by which one is able to grasp
a content which, in becoming a repetition of previous content, can
instigate anticipations or "activate" a habit.

This percipuum is the outcome of the perceptual judgment in its
narrow sense and yields "repeatable content" which serves to activate habit though, as an analytical stopping point, it provides no
anticipation of future experience. The perceptual judgment in its
narrow sense is the primitive abductive hypothesis of a present repetition of past experiential content, and the content in fact becomes a
repetition of previously experienced contents only as the perceptual
judgment does assimilate it to those contents in the abductive process of recognition. Or, as Peirce notes elsewhere, "The percipuum
is a recognition of the character of what is past" (CP 7.677). The percipuum is grasped by means of the character of what is past and, as an

analytical abstraction for purposes of analysis, it contains no reference to future experience. As Peirce states, "What two things can be more disparate than a memory and an expectation?" (CP 2.143). Yet, while the perceptual judgment in its narrow sense does not include anticipations of future-activities, the very character of past assimilation incorporates assimilation of that which has been partially constituted in action. Even the percipuum as the repeatable content which activates habit is not the product of a purely passive assimilation. Human creativity and activity enter into every dimension of perceptual awareness.

Thus as an analytical stopping point in the analysis of perception one finds a recognized content or percipuum which is totally devoid of reference to future experience yet which, as a recognized content, is dependent upon and is in fact the outcome of a judgment – the perceptual judgment in its narrow sense. Thus, the "sensing dimension," as it enters the structure of human awareness, is not an absolute given but a taken. The content of this analytical stopping place is difficult to indicate, for even the narrow percipuum in its purity can be expressed neither in the language of objectivity nor in the language of appearing. It is a spontaneous qualitative immediacy in that "it cannot be articulately thought," for it loses its "characteristic innocence" in the very attempt. Yet this content is there as an analytical element of the perceptual situation, serving as the basis for our full predictive meanings asserted in the perceptual judgment in the wide sense.

The attempt to explicitly grasp this percipuum yields apprehension of appearance. But even appearances are apprehended as appearances of objectivities and expressed through the language of objectivities because appearances, as grasped through interpretive habits, reflect, in their very emergence, the structurings of objectivities; they reflect the structurings of the very anticipations which one is attempting to withhold in focusing on the appearance qua appearance. Ordinarily, when actions or anticipations are not inhibited because of a questionable situation, we perceive appearing objects, not appearances. When an interpretive expectation does not work, when "what is there" requires reinterpretation, then the focus is turned to "what appears." Appearances are not the building blocks of perception, as held by phenomenalist positions of various sorts, but rather a level brought about by a change of focus when a problem arises.

And, as we reinterpret the objective situation, we no longer "see" the appearance of what we mistakenly took to be there, but a new appearing object. Thus, appearances themselves incorporate meanings, irreducible meanings which function to verify the application of objective meanings in the ongoing course of experience. The following focus on Peirce's claims can best be understood in terms of the apprehension of appearances as the closest one can come in the ongoing course of experience to the percipuum in its narrow sense as the abstraction of a "stopping point" in the logical analysis of perception.

Though Peirce speaks of the percipuum as the percept immediately interpreted in the perceptual judgment, he elsewhere states that "Perhaps I might be permitted to invent the term 'percipuum' to include both percept and perceptual judgment" (CP 7.629), since "the differences are so minute and so unimportant logically that it will be convenient to neglect them" (CP 7.629). As he clarifies, "The forcefulness of the perceptual judgments falls short of the pure unreasonableness of the percept only to this extent, that it does profess to represent the percept, while the perfection of the percept's surdity consists in its not so much as professing anything" (CP 7.628). The percept, in its surdity, is infallible because it does not profess anything. And the perceptual judgment is infallible because "to say that the perceptual judgment is an infallible symptom of the character of the percept means only that in some unaccountable manner we find ourselves impotent to refuse our assent to it in the presence of the percept, and that there is no appeal from it" (CP 7.628). Thus the percept by itself professes nothing, while the perceptual judgment professes the presence of the percept as a recognized content. Both are infallible because neither professes the existence of any objective fact or the anticipation of any possibilities of future experience. Future experience cannot show the perceptual judgment in its narrow sense to be in error, since it makes no reference to future experience. Thus Peirce, in replying to the objection that a perceptual judgment is not so utterly beyond all control or check as he says, since it may be revised, states that the "perceptual judgment can only refer to a single percept which can never re-exist; and if I judge that it appears red when it did not appear red, it must, at least be acknowledged that it appeared to appear red" (CP 7.636).

In distinguishing percept and perceptual judgment, Peirce observes that perceptual judgments are as unlike the percept "as the printed letters in a book, where a Madonna of Murillo is described, are unlike the picture itself" (CP 5.54). This example may easily lead one to view the relation between percept and perceptual judgment as analogous to the relation between nonlinguistic experience and language. Though Peirce's example is ill chosen, he clearly indicates elsewhere that the perceptual judgment is "a higher grade of the operation of perception" (CP 7.634).

The distinction between the perceptual judgment in its wide and narrow senses can gain further clarity if we turn to Peirce's discussion of the fallibility of memory, which is perhaps not so clear cut as it first appears.

> Now let us take up the perceptual judgment "This wafer looks red." It takes some time to write this sentence, to utter it, or even to think it. It must refer to the state of the percept at the time that it, the judgment, began to be made. But the judgment does not exist until it is completely made. It thus only refers to a memory of the past; and all memory is possibly fallible and subject to criticism and control. The judgment, then, can only mean that so far as the character of the percept can ever be ascertained, it will be ascertained that the wafer *looked* red. (CP 5.544; italics added)

In just what sense does Peirce mean that memory is subject to criticism and control? As Peirce notes in the paragraph immediately following the quotation above, "Perhaps the matter may be stated less paradoxically" (CP 5.545). And Peirce proceeds to do this in a discussion which concludes that "to say that a body is hard, or red, or heavy, or of a given weight, or has any other property, is to say that it is subject to law and therefore is a statement referring to the future" (CP 5.545). It is evident that in the above discussion Peirce has switched from the term "looks" to the term "is" and that the character of the percept is ascertained by reference to the future; in this way, then, by the test of future experience, memory is subject to criticism and control.

However, in confounding the percipuum in its wide sense and apprehensions of appearances Peirce does make an important point concerning appearances. Though he never explicitly discusses the point, its significance is to be found among the confused statements of the two passages cited above. "All memory is possibly fallible," yet "so far as the character of the percept can ever be ascertained, it will be ascertained that the wafer looked red" (CP 5.544). If one does not go on to Peirce's "less paradoxical" statements of the issue, this can be taken not as a confused statement concerning future verification but rather as a statement concerning the nature of the content of the "seeming" statement. If, as Peirce explicitly states, all memory is fallible, it is difficult to see how that which is indicated by the seeming statement can provide the bedrock of certainty. The reliability of memory must be questioned not only in regard to what can be predicated based on the present content but in regard to the recognition of the present content itself. Memory is involved in the very recognition of that content which has been seen before and may be seen again, a grasp which allows the content to become the basis for predictive meaning. This basis, then, is not certain but rather subject to the error of memory and incapable of providing an indubitable bedrock of empirical knowledge in any foundationalist sense of the term.

What is provided is not the absolute certainty of foundationalist claims but "pragmatic certainty." The apprehension of an appearance is indubitable in the sense that its falsity is inconceivable. It is beyond conceivable doubt, because to doubt it in the sense that one thinks it may be proven wrong is senseless; indeed, literally so. To doubt it is to put into question something for which there is no tool for getting "behind" or "beneath" it to compare it with anything more fundamental. For us, it must itself be the final court of appeal. The apprehension of an appearance is not certainly true as opposed to possibly false. It is "certain" in the sense that neither truth nor falsity is applicable to it. The perceptual judgment in its narrow sense cannot even be labeled certainly correct as opposed to possibly incorrect. There is no correct or incorrect recognition involved at this level, for what the percipuum is is determined only in its recognition and can be determined in no other way. It becomes a "repetition" of previous contents only by being assimilated to those contents in the perceptual judgment.

In relation to more traditional views, this conclusion is surely more paradoxical than the conclusion that the perceptual judgment, in its wide sense, is fallible because it can be proven wrong by reference to future experience. Perhaps the novelty of the former conclusion, coupled with his own failure to clarify the conceptual distinctions towards which he was groping, led Peirce subtly to switch in his attempt to make his position seem "less paradoxical." However, apart from such speculation, it does seem that Peirce's confused discussion stems from a careless slipping back and forth between two concepts which he later clearly distinguished.

Peirce's use of the perceptual judgment in its narrow sense has been discussed in detail because it is the "more paradoxical" and less emphasized of the two senses. That this is so is no doubt due both to Peirce's brief and late exposition of a distinction in levels of judgment and to the assumption that what is the outcome of a judgment must be capable of being shown to be true or false. Bernstein points out that if the perceptual judgment cannot be true or false it is not a judgment,[7] and again, that if there is a hypothetical element involved in every perceptual judgment, then every perceptual judgment is fallible and subject to future tests.[8] Conversely, it is McCarthy's acceptance of the claim that perceptual judgments are immune to doubt which allows him to hold that Peirce makes use of an observation–theory distinction which turns him into a foundationalist.[9]

The perceptual judgment in its narrow sense does have a hypothetical element, [10] for the judgment is a hypothesis that a content is "the same as" that which has been seen before or "appears as" (W 1, 471). However, the above analysis has shown that the perceptual judgment in its narrow sense is not fallible and subject to future tests, for it makes no references to future experience. As Peirce states, its surdity is almost complete. It cannot be characterized as true or false for, as indicated above, we have no more fundamental perceptual tool by which to assert its truth or falsity. To deny the term "judgment" to that which can be characterized as neither true nor false is one way to avoid the frequent confusions which pervade Peirce's analysis of perception because of his dual uses of this term, and it allows one to follow a more conventional terminological procedure. It is not, however, to offer an objection to that concept which Peirce intends by the term.[11] By characterizing this primitive synthesis in terms of a perceptual judgment which yet cannot be true or false, he brings home more forcefully the radical novelty of his rejection of foundationalism. What is "given" at the most fundamental level of perceptual awareness is in fact a "taken," and it incorporates both the nature of the taking and the nature of what is taken.

The perceptual judgment in its wide sense is indubitable, not in the sense that the discovery of its falsity is inconceivable, for its truth or falsity may be ascertained by future experience, but rather in the sense that there are no positive grounds to stimulate doubt present in the perceptual situation. As Peirce has stressed in his rejection of Descartes' universal doubt, we cannot feign doubt (CP 5.265). Unless some positive ground for doubt is given in the perceptual situation, perceptual judgments and certain vague beliefs (CP 5.442) must be taken as indubitable, for they cannot seriously be doubted – though they are eminently fallible, since they are subject to the test of future experience. Thus, we arrive in a broad sense at Peirce's "fallibilism."

The fallibility of the perceptual judgment in its wide sense, as it actually occurs in the passage of the present and makes a claim about an objective state of affairs, lies in the fact that it will be rejected as false if it does not fit with future experiences anticipated by its claim. The indubitability at this level enters in the sense that the formation of the perceptual judgment cannot be controlled and is beyond logical criticism in its formation. While we cannot critically control the judgment, however, we can criticize its results and conclude, based on future experience, that it is false. Underlying the very possibility of these common sense indubitables which may turn out to be false, there has been seen to lie an indubitability to which neither truth nor falsity is applicable, which is "pragmatically certain." David Savan aptly characterizes this type of distinction when he notes the difference between indubitables which cannot conceivably be doubted and indubitables which are so only because there is no positive ground to stimulate doubt.[12] Underlying the very possibility of these testable perceptual judgments which may turn out to be false, however, there has been seen to be an indubitability to which neither truth nor falsity is applicable, which is "pragmatically certain." Yet, this pragmatic certainty is the product of interpretive activity, it is about a "taken" rather than a "given." Peirce's stress on certitude, then, far from indicating his alliance with foundationalism, in fact leads to the radical, novel nature of his rejection of it.

It has been seen that perception is infused with meanings structured by possible purposive activity. The role of purposive activity in thought and the resultant appeal to relevance and selective emphasis which must ultimately be justified by workability are key tenets of Peirce's understanding of the nature of experience as experimental. And, interpretive activity begins at the most primordial level of the formation of repeatable content which can activate habits of anticipation. What is yet to be examined is the way in which this understanding of perception involves temporality.

Peirce makes clear that verification instances are themselves possible only because our perceptual meanings contain activity and temporal reference in the very heart of its internal structure. As Peirce stresses, "There is no span of present time so short as not to contain . . . something for the confirmation of which we are waiting" (CP 7.675). But this "peculiar element of the present, that it confronts us with ideas which it forces upon us . . . is something which accumulates in wholes of time and dissipates the more minutely the course of time is scrutinized" (CP 7.675). Or, as Peirce sums up this sense of temporality at the heart of perceptual awareness, "if we wish to know what the percipuum of the course of time is, all we have to do is abstain from sophisticating it, and it will be plain enough . . ." (CP 7.649). This temporal awareness present in our common sense perceptions is also the basis for our sense of the continuity within experience. Thus in a claim parallel to the above one, he states that "So long as we trust to common sense, the properties of a true continuum are a matter of course," while through our abstract elaborations "we founder from quagmire into quicksand" (MS 137, p. 10). He stresses that this temporally rooted percipuum makes nominalistic maxims futile. As he elaborates, "But it is remarkable that in case we do not accept the percipuum's own account of itself . . . then it would seem that there is nothing that empirical truth can mean except accordance with what is given in those instants, which in this case, in no way testify concerning one another or in any way refer to one another" (CP 7.671). The same temporally rooted, dispositionally organized sense of expectation which is at the heart of perceptual claims is at the heart, also, of the very possibility of pragmatic evidence and is rooted in our common sense perceptual awareness of the sense of temporality and continuity. Thus Peirce states of the pragmatist, "That he will have no difficulty with Thirdness is clear enough because he will hold that conformity of action to general intentions is as much given in perception as is the element of action itself, which cannot really be mentally torn away from such general purposiveness" (CP 5.212).

Until this point the major emphasis has been on the interpretive elements which enter into our perception of the world in which we live, even at the rudimentary level of what is "given" in experience. It may begin to seem that Peirce, in rejecting foundationalism, has indeed sided with the other alternative. But Peirce, with equal force-fulness, rejects the claims of antifoundationalism, for he holds that there is a "hard" reality with which we interact and which provides the workability for our interpretations. For Peirce, our perceptual awareness is a direct grasp, though not a spectator grasp, of a hard external reality. To understand this interaction between the creative and constraining forces involved in perceptual awareness, it will be helpful to turn to Peirce's understanding of the world that is grasped in our perceptual awareness.

Peirce never explicitly clarifies his understanding of "the real world," though he refers to it frequently throughout his writings. One thing that is clear is that "the real world" fits inadequately within the confines of the labels, 'realism,' 'idealism,' or 'phenomenalism,' for it is a distinctively pragmatic world. The following discussion proposes to show that Peirce, in rejecting the role of humans as spectators, in understanding experience as a unity of interaction between humans and that facticity which gives itself within experience, can hold at once that the real world is the perceived world, that the real world has an independence from mind, and yet that the perceived world is partially dependent upon the noetic act and is thus relative in its nature to the mind. The supposed incompatibility of these three characteristics of the relation of perception to the world stems the failure to radically and once and for all reject the presuppositions of a spectator theory of knowledge.[13] Peirce's absolute and radical rejection of the spectator theory of knowledge gives rise to, and is in turn brought into clearer light by, his pragmatic concept of world.

That the real world is the perceived world is clearly indicated by Peirce in several succinct passages. He states that "The real world is the world of sensible experience" (CP 3.527); or, in other terms, the real world is the world of "insistent generalized percepts" (CP 8.148), which are not representative of any underlying reality other than themselves[14] (CP 2.143). Such a world is a consistent system of facts rigorously obeying the laws of noncontradiction and excluded middle, for, as he states, "Dichotomy rules the ideal world" (CP

3.529), and "it is part of the process of sensible experience to locate its facts in the world of ideas" (CP 3.527). Such a grasping of the sensible world in terms of a system of ideas is of the very essence of the sensible world. As Peirce stresses, "This is what I mean by saying that the sensible world is but a fragment of the ideal world" (CP 3.527). Further, the system of ideas or meanings limits the facts which may occur "in the world," for, as Peirce states, "We know in advance of experience that certain things are not true, because we see they are impossible ... there is no room for (them) even in that ideal world of which the real world is but a fragment" (CP 3.527). Thus, what can occur "in the world" must conform to the possibilities allowed for by the world of ideas or the system of meanings in terms of which we approach it. This claim does not lead to a conventionalism, for Peirce stresses that the real world is that special part of the ideal world which sufficient experience would tend to compel us to acknowledge as having a being independent of what we arbitrarily, or willfully, create (CP 3.527).

So, for Peirce, dichotomy rules the real world, because it rules the ideal world of which the real world is a part. Yet, his view of the nature of the real as independent of the human mode of grasping it indicates that such hard discrete exactitudes do not exist, for reality, according to Peirce, is a continuum which "swims in indeterminacy" (CP 1.171–2) because of its indefinite richness. For this reason, he holds that the principle of continuity, which pervades the independently real, is "fallibilism objectified" (CP 1.171). Further the independently real as a continuum of events is precisely that to which neither the law of noncontradiction nor the law of excluded middle is perfectly applicable.[15] The relation between the continuum of qualitative events which constitutes the character of the metaphysically real independently of the human mode of grasping, and the system of facts which constitutes the real world, finds its analogue in Peirce's distinction between an occurrence as a slab of the universe in all its infinite detail, and a real fact as that which is extracted from the universe by the power of thought (MS 647, p. 8). Thus Peirce holds that the real world can be characterized, also, as the world of perceptual facts, for "what I carry with me" of the percept "is the perceptual facts" (CP 2.141).

Here lies the significance of Peirce's claim that "Nature, in connection with a picture, copy, or diagram does not necessarily denote an object not fashioned by man, but merely the object represented as something existing apart from the representation"(CP 3.420). Mill's failure to recognize this mind-relatedness of worldly nature, according to Peirce, led him astray in his analysis of the "uniformity of nature" (CP 6.67). Peirce indicates the above position from a slightly different direction in his claim that "There is no *thing* which is in itself in the sense of not being relative to the mind, though things which are relative to the mind doubtless *are*, apart from that relation"(CP 5.311). Or as he elaborates, a "this" is an object selected by a subject from the continuum of possibility (MS 942, p. 16). Reality independent of our thinking exerts an influence on our ways of thinking about it, but what facts and objects it contains is partially dependent upon the conceptual framework in terms of which perceived objects and facts can emerge within the backdrop of a world. Indeed, according to Peirce "External Fact" can change in accordance with the way human minds "feel, think, or suffer" (MS 642, p. 16). Peirce offers a helpful clarification about his limited intentions in his numerous statements concerning the independence of real objects, claiming that, the real object can be "an object shaped by thinking...; but so far as it is Real, it is not modified by thinking about it (MS 634, p. 9).

The above analysis has attempted to show that the perceived world is ontologically one with independent reality as an infinitely rich continuum of qualitative events. Yet, the perceived world is dependent upon the meaning system which grasps in a way in which reality as independent is not. The perceived world, though concrete, is nonetheless selective in the sense that a world, as the concrete content denoted by a system of meanings, is a way in which the concreteness of reality can be delineated or "fixed." A system, once chosen, limits the alternatives possible within it, but alternative systems may be possible. As Peirce notes, "Truly natural classes may, and undoubtedly often do, merge into one another inextricably" (CP 1.209), and thus boundary lines must be imposed, although the classes are natural (MS 427, p. 40–1). The continuity is there; where the "cut" is imposed is, in part, our decision. Like the boundary lines of natural classes, the "boundary lines" that constitute our world of perceptual experience may have been differently drawn, giving rise to different possibilities within the world.

What appears within experience, then, is also the appearance of the independently real; there is no ontological gap between appearance and reality. As Peirce observes, "Synechism . . . will not admit a sharp sundering of phenomena and substrates. That which underlies a phenomenon and determines it thereby is, itself, in a measure, a phenomenon"(CP 7.629). Further, it is at the same time "to me" to whom it appears and reflects my intentional link with the externally real. Thus Peirce can say that "Perhaps it may reconcile the psychologist to the admission of perceptual judgments involving generality to be told that they are perceptual judgments concerning our own purposes"(CP 5.166). The epistemic and ontological unity of these two dimensions can be seen from Peirce's position that though the generality of perceptual judgments reflects our own purposes, yet "since no cognition of ours is absolutely determinate, generals must have a real existence" (CP 5.312). Peirce further indicates the above position in his cryptic claim that "The inkstand is a real thing. Of course in being real and external, it does not in the least cease to be a purely psychical product, a generalized percept"(CP 8.261). For Peirce, these are "two sides of the same shield" (CP 1.420). Or, as he eloquently summarizes his position, though "everything which is present to us is a phenomenal manifestation of ourselves," this "does not prevent its being a phenomenon of something without us, just as a rainbow is at once a manifestation both of the sun and of the rain" (CP 5.283). For Peirce, then, perceptual facts at their very core emerge neither from mind alone nor from the dynamic reality of the universe alone, but rather from the interaction of the two which constitutes experience. This unification undercuts the dichotomy of foundationalism or nonfoundationalism and along with it, the closely related dichotomies of realism or antirealism and objectivism or relativism since each of these dichotomies, in its own way, represents the alternatives of an absolute grounding of knowledge or skepticism.

This interactive unity at the heart of experience clears the way for a fuller understanding of the verification of our perceptual claims in the ongoing course of experience. The extent of the radical conflict of interpretations concerning Peirce's theory of truth in the literature is perhaps best captured in Robert Almeder's claim that the literature on Peirce contains "no fewer than thirteen distinct interpretations of

Peirce's views on the nature of truth."[16] Within Peirce scholarship, the acceptance of convergence and the final ultimate opinion is not dependent on one's stance in the realist – idealist controversy, though the understanding of the nature of the final ultimate opinion as that toward which inquiry on any subject will converge will vary according to camps. Thus, as has been stated from the backdrop of a coherence theory of truth, the true bedrock of pragmatism is "ultimately the entire framework of objective logic and objective idealism."[17] On the other hand, a realist interpretation holds that "The opinion reached in the final opinion, unlike opinions reached earlier, shall never be overthrown although the degree to which the final opinion *corresponds* to fact admits of indefinite, (but not substantial) refinement."[18] John E. Smith refers to Peirce's theory of truth as a conform theory, which has a distinct advantage over the term 'correspondence' in that it can avoid much of the historical baggage attaching to the term 'correspondence,' but it operates nonetheless within a framework of realism and ultimate convergence.[19] Before examining Peirce's theory of truth in relation to traditional alternatives of correspondence or coherence, it will be helpful at this point to clarify the type of realism which is intertwined with the correspondence theory of truth, and to which Peirce's pragmatic position is opposed. This can perhaps best be approached by Almeder's espousal of Peirce's "epistemological realism." He proceeds by showing that Peirce is not a phenomenalist and not an idealist, and that Peirce offers a defense of belief in the existence of an external reality, a reality, moreover, with which the knower is in direct contact.[20] With these points the present interpretation agrees. But, what this realism also includes for Almeder, as well as for most who accept the realist label, is that the sense in which the real external world we know "is dependent on mind turns out to be *trivially* true and necessary for any epistemological realism wherein it is a necessary condition that the external world be knowable."[21] Or as such a realism is elsewhere characterized, "There is a world of *objects* whose properties are neither logically nor causally dependent upon the noetic act of any number of finite minds."[22] Precisely what is denied by Peirce is the "furniture realism" which holds that there is a world of objects or facts whose character is in no way dependent upon human noetic activity. It is these generally held assumptions associated with the realist label that are denied in denying that Peirce is a realist, for, as seen above, the world and the objects within in are partially dependent upon the noetic acts of finite minds.

Thus, while Peirce cannot be called an idealist[23] or a phenomenalist, neither can he be adequately labeled a realist. For, though Peirce holds we are in direct contact with an external "brutely there" reality which limits our interpretations, thus showing he is not a coherence theorist, yet the relation of the knower to this known external reality cannot be understood in terms of correspondence. And, although it may well be an oversimplification to say that coherence theories of truth belong to idealism while correspondence theories of truth belong to realism, an interpretation of Peirce as an epistemological realist in the above sense indicated by Almeder and accepted by most others using this label, leads to the view that at least the ideally true and final opinion on any matter would involve a relation of correspondence.[24] To the question, what alternative remains when one rules out realism as well as idealism or phenomenalism, the answer is, the pragmatic alternative. Peirce's pragmatic theory of truth is ultimately intertwined with the entire gamut of his unique pragmatic epistemology and metaphysics which interweave in his pragmatic understanding of the perceptual world.

Because for Peirce the hereness and nowness of events and the real connections they display is independent of, yet enters directly into interaction with, our conceptualizations and the possibilities they allow, coherence or consistency is not a sufficient criterion for the truth of empirical assertions. There is an ontological dimension to what appears within experience which limits our interpretations in terms of workability.[25] But, true knowledge, even ideally true knowledge, could not be correspondence, for the nature of our creatively interpretive, interactive link with reality, and the nature of reality as a continuum which "swims" in indeterminacy, makes the relation of correspondence literally senseless. Rather, in Peirce's words, a true thought is one which *answers*, which leads to thoughts in harmony with nature (MS 934, p. 24). The relation of "answering" is ultimately two-directional. Reality answers our questions, and determines the workability of our interpretations, but what answers it gives is partially dependent on what questions we ask, and what interpretive meanings work is partially dependent upon which ones we bring. Truth is always worldly truth, for Peirce claims "nothing else than a Fact possibly can be a 'witness' or 'testimony'" (MS 647,

p. 26), and facts, it will be remembered, are always relative to the framework of a discriminating mind. Yet he stresses that the witness of a fact is the real, "since it is truly in that which occurs" (MS 647, p. 9).

Worldly truth is thus perspectival, and other perspectives are always possible. Truth involves convergence, but convergence within a common world which we have partially made, and continually remake in various of its aspects. Thus Peirce, in speaking of truth, whether scientific, moral, metaphysical, or common sense (CP 5.565–8), states that "the perfect truth of a statement requires that it should involve the confession that the perfect doctrine can neither be stated nor conceived" (CP 5.565–8). Again, Peirce claims that an essential ingredient of truth includes a confession of its "one-sidedness" (CP 5.566). That this is intended not as a factual limitation on present knowledge but as a theoretical limitation due to the nature of knowledge is found in Peirce's comparison of the ideal limit of convergence, the ideal of a "final ultimate opinion," to the ideal limit of pi. It is "an ideal limit to which no numerical expression can be perfectly true" (CP 5.565). It is an unattainable ideal not only in fact but by the very nature of that which sets the ideal limit (CP 5.565). Thus, Peirce can present the following hypothetical situation:

"Suppose our opinion with reference to a given question to be quite settled, so that inquiry, no matter how far pushed, has no surprises for us on this point. Then we may be said to have attained perfect knowledge about that question. True, it is conceivable that somebody else would attain to a like perfect knowledge which should conflict with ours. This is conceivable" (MS 409, p. 112). Peirce then goes on to say that though it is theoretically possible it is not practically possible "considering the social nature of man," for we would "compare notes; and if we never do compare notes, and no third party talks with both and makes the comparison, it is difficult to see what meaning there is in saying we disagree" (MS 409, p. 112). That Peirce is not using the term "perfect knowledge" in a loose common sense way can be seen from his explicit distinction between it and "practically perfect belief" (MS 409, p. 112).

Thus, even the ideal of convergence to a final ultimate opinion, to perfect knowledge, is always convergence within an accepted framework or perspective. And, there are always other and possibly better ways of cutting into reality, of delineating the context within which convergence can occur. This is implied by the very nature of reality as a continuum which swims in indeterminacy because of its indefinite richness which "overflows" the rigidies of our interpretive structures. Thus, Peirce states that convergence toward one final truth is "a regulative principle, an intellectual hope," and such a rule of hope must be followed, for "despair is insanity" (CP 1.405). Yet, even such a rule of hope, the "cheerful hope" which animates the followers of science involves, in his words, "something approximating" only (CP 3.432), for the "indeterminate" nature of reality may mean that concerning "*the* answer, that is, the final answer . . . there is none"[26] (CP 4.61). The objects within our world do not copy the independently real but rather emerge through our modes of grasping the independently real. Nor do the modes of grasping via which emerge the objectivities within our world copy the independently real but rather they serve as conceptual tools for "cutting the edges" of the independently real continuum of events which "swims" in indeterminacy. The ideally true opinion would be that opinion which would perfectly work in anticipating possibilities of experience, and would work not because it adequately copied, but because it adequately "cut into" the independently real. Finally, the world within which specific meanings and beliefs arise, and within which objects or facts emerge for conscious awareness, is not a copy of an independent reality, nor is it identical with an independent reality in its character as independent. Rather, such a world is the encompassing frame of reference or field of interest of organism–environment interaction, the ultimate backdrop of rationality within which emerging facts are situated. We discover truths about our world only because we have first prescribed contours for our world. True beliefs are true before they are actually verified, but the very possibility of verification emerges from the backdrop of the transformation of the indefinite richness of reality into worldly encounter. Truth is truth relative to a context of interpretation, not because truth is relative but because without an interpretive context the concept of truth is meaningless.

What this essay has attempted to show in some detail is that for Peirce the perceptual field, as it arises in the context of human activity, is an ontologically thick, resisting field of objects which are essentially related to the interactional horizons of our world and which allow for the very structure of the sensing which gives access to them. In its emergence, the world grounds all levels of experience and knowledge, at the same time giving meaningful access to the independent reality of the natural universe. Such a view undercuts a long tradition of standard dichotomies which are increasingly seen to be unsustainable.

NOTES

1. Hookway (1985: 166).
2. Gruender (1983: 181–287).
3. McCarthy (1990: 63–113).
4. Hausman (1990: 271).
5. Hausman's analysis of two meanings of the perceptual judgment in Peirce's philosophy does not correspond with the distinction being made here (Hausman 1990: 271–308).
6. All these distinctions are discussed by Rosenthal (1969) in some detail, but the others need not be introduced here.
7. Bernstein (1964: 175).
8. Bernstein (1964: 173).
9. McCarthy (1990: 63–113). His highly perceptive analysis goes astray here because he remains too general in his discussion of perceptual judgments.
10. Thus Peirce states that both conceptions and sensations involve hypothetical inferences.
11. Gruender (1983: 281–7), in his foundationalist interpretation of Peirce's position, views the interrelation of observation and theory in Peirce's philosophy in terms of types of language, and seems to place the infiltration of the theoretical into what is given at a more sophisticated level than is indicated here. Thus, he may well object both to the terminology and the concept which it indicates.
12. Savan (1965: 40–1).
13. This point is discussed in some historical detail by C. I. Lewis (1929: 154) in relation to the development of his own position. Although Kant is considered the beginning of "the rejection of the spectator," he himself was not immune to some of its presuppositions. Thus, in accepting the latter two characteristics, he rejected the first.
14. Of course there is a sense in which other "worlds" are real. For example, the ideal world is a real ideal world.
15. Peirce asserts that the general is that to which the law of the excluded middle does not apply, while the vague is that to which the principle of noncontradiction does not apply (CP 5.448). He then explicitly identifies continuity with generality (MS 137, pp. 7–12). And, for Peirce, whatever

is general or continuous is to some degree vague. See Buchler's (1966: 25) comments on this point. Thus, neither the law of noncontradiction nor the law of excluded middle is perfectly applicable to the continuous.

16. Almeder (1985).
17. Esposito (1980: 229).
18. Almeder (1980: 52–57).
19. Smith (1978: 5off.).
20. Almeder (1975b: 3–17).
21. Almeder (1975b: 14). Italics not in text.
22. Almeder (1975b: 9). Italics not in text.
23. The Idealism under discussion here is of course epistemological rather than metaphysical idealism, though the two are certainly not unrelated.
24. This is precisely the conclusion reached by Almeder (1975a).
25. Some type of coherence theory of truth operates within the framework of ontological phenomenalism as well.
26. Thayer's (1968: 132) characterization of Peirce's concept of truth as having the function of Kant's regulative ideas "serving as a working standard of criticism" would apply here, but at a more radical level than that intended by his characterization. See also Murphey (1961: 302).

9   The Development of Peirce's Theory of Signs

Early and late, Peirce analyzed thought as a process of sign-production and sign-interpretation. But his early doctrine of "thought-signs" was deeply flawed and, therefore, he revised it drastically, changing its basic principles and greatly extending its scope. As he did that in several stages over many years – often in letters or unfinished manuscripts – what we now possess is little more than a sequence of contradictions, a series of ambitious yet unfinished sketches of elaborate but mutually incompatible structures. And yet, Peirce's work on signs cannot be ignored; for his pragmatic theory of inquiry and his synechistic account of the mind are incomplete without it. This essay traces the development of Peirce's theory of signs, or semeiotic, culminating in the mature, or post-1906, version of that theory. To speak of this mature theory at all is to speak hypothetically: it has to be constructed from the surviving manuscripts of Peirce's last years plus all that is consistent with them from his earlier writings.

I. THE EARLY THEORY: THE DOCTRINE OF THOUGHT-SIGNS (1866–9)

In 1866, when he had just turned 27, Peirce wrote that a representation is something that *stands for* something *to* someone who so interprets it – more precisely, *to* the "interpretant,"[1] which that person forms in response to the sign and which is a second representation of the same thing (W 1, 466). Already, then, we have Peirce's fundamental, unchanging conception of a sign (or, in earlier days, "representation" and, sometimes, "representamen"), as being one of three relata – sign, object, interpretant – of a single, triadic relation.

That makes interpretation essential to signhood. Significance is not a direct relation of sign to object; instead, the significance of a sign is determined by the interpretant which that sign elicits. But we have also the thesis that characterizes the early period of Peirce's semeiotic thought and that was dramatically reversed in his later years: that in every case the interpretant of a sign is another sign of the same object.

Peirce's early period culminated in the 1868–9 series of three articles in the *Journal of Speculative Philosophy* that introduced the concept of the "thought-sign" (W 2, 193–272). Every thought, Peirce therein maintained, interprets a preceding thought and is interpreted in a subsequent thought (W 2, 225). The thought-signs that a given thought, T, interprets determine T's referent, or object. And the thought-signs in which T is interpreted determine T's meaning, or what it represents about its object. For example, my startled attention is drawn to a shadowy shape: (A) "Something is in that alley." (B) "Maybe a mugger!" (C) "I'd better cross the street." The thought, B, is not about muggers in general: its object is presented in the thought, A, of which B is an interpretation, viz., the something that is in the alley. And what B represents about that object is interpreted in C, wherein a mugger is taken to be a form of danger best avoided. (Obviously, other subsequent thoughts can draw other meanings from "mugger.")

If this same sort of analysis applies to each thought, then every thought is both a sign and an interpretant. Hence, each is but a moment in an infinite *regressus* and infinite *progressus* of thought-signs. That thought begins and ends in time is accounted for by its being a continuum, packing an infinity of infinitesimal thoughts into a finite flow of thought.[2] Among much else, this entails that there is no cognition not determined by a previous cognition, hence, that none is determined directly by its object. If no cognition is determined directly by its object, then there is no intuitive knowledge. To establish that theorem and deduce its consequences was the main burden of the 1868–9 articles. But, apart from its explicitly anti-Cartesian intention, what led Peirce into this strange doctrine? Why oppose Descartes by positing a continuum of thoughts interpreting thoughts?

Peirce's philosophical studies began with Kant and centered around the Kantian problem of knowledge. As a generic term for any mental content, Kant had adopted Wolff's *Vorstellung* but he provided no discussion or definition of *Vorstellungen* in general (George, 1982: 31–4). Peirce was led from Kant back to the British empiricists; and almost certainly his term "semeiotic" is a transliteration of the Greek word Locke introduced, at the end of his 1690 *Essay*, to name a new "doctrine of signs." This, Locke explained, is to be "another sort of logic . . . than what we have been hitherto acquainted with," by which to study ideas as "signs the mind makes use of for the understanding of things" and words as "signs of ideas"(Locke, 1690 [1965], v.2: 309–10). This, apparently, is where Peirce's semeiotic analysis of thought began.

It should be emphasized, however, that Peirce's concept of thought was Kantian, not Lockean: thought, for Peirce, is always conceptual, hence, general in content. And he developed this idea in a distinctly contemporary (though also Platonic) way, by identifying thought as internalized discourse. Thought is a species of semeiotic behavior, generally but not exclusively verbal, on a par with speech and writing; our capacity to think is dependent on our having learned a language. To conceive of thought as a sign thus presupposes that words and sentences are signs.

But what makes something a sign? Aristotle's plausible view was that words signify thoughts by convention or custom and *thereby* signify the things of which thoughts are "likenesses" (*DeInt.*1). But if thoughts themselves are in words, then they are not likenesses. If thoughts are words, then Aristotle's account, thus modified, would imply that ideas signify things by signifying ideas of things – and so on, *ad infinitum*. Strangely enough, Peirce's early theory of signs is much like that. Thoughts are signs; signs signify through thought; therefore, thought-signs signify through other thought-signs.

What Peirce added to this combination of Kant and Locke with Aristotle was the idea of the continuum. By making the translation of thought by thought proceed *ad infinitum*, but in a continuous flow, he shifted the emphasis from individual thought-signs to the process – the movement of thought – itself:

It may be objected, that if no thought has any meaning [i.e., in itself, apart from its being interpreted], all thought is without meaning. But this is a fallacy similar to saying, that, if in no one of the successive spaces which a body fills there is room for motion, there is no room for motion throughout the whole. At no one instant in my state of mind is there cognition or representation, but in the relation of my states of mind at different instants there is. (W 2, 227)

In short, since meaning cannot be located in any thought-sign, it must be found in the very process by which one thought interprets another.

2. THREE FLAWS FATAL TO THE EARLY THEORY

Many commentators assume that Peirce never subsequently abandoned his 1868–9 doctrine of thought-signs. However, that doctrine faced at least three problems, any one of which would have been sufficient reason for him eventually to have abandoned it.

First, Peirce's attempt to explain how thoughts signify fails. He supposed that significance depends on interpretation, but then explained interpretation as consisting in signs. Thus, the problem of accounting for significance is not solved but is merely handed on, from one sign to the next. Nor does it matter that the process of interpretation continues *ad infinitum*. That merely postpones an answer *ad infinitum*.[3] Peirce anticipated this objection in the long passage quoted above. However, that response contains no explanation of how the translation of one thought-sign into another produces significance. Merely asserting that it does is not enough. The assertion that meaning is to be found in the movement of thought rather than in individual thoughts is unsupported by argument. And, as Peirce's analogy to physical motion is questionable for the same reason that the doctrine it is intended to save is questionable, that analogy is of no help whatsoever.

Peirce's failure to explain how thoughts signify is accompanied by another failure: to explain how sense can be distinguished from nonsense. The fact that "Possibilities pander to prodigious plentitude" can be translated into other languages or into other English phrases, and those into still others, and so on, *ad infinitum*, does not prove that it says anything. In fact, it says nothing. And since thought can be formed in such words, it follows that thoughts, like speech, can be nonsensical. But on Peirce's theory, this nonsense, being translatable, is not nonsense. Peirce's theory entails that certain phrases that signify nothing signify something; and, therefore, his theory is mistaken.

Second, Peirce assumed that every thought must actually be interpreted, that its interpretant must be actual and not merely potential; for why else hold that each thought occurs in an actual but infinite progression of thought-signs? But since the interpretant determines a sign's meaning, it follows that significance is nothing more or less than the way in which a sign is actually interpreted. Hence, erroneous interpretation is impossible: significance is entirely subjective.

There is an alternative that Peirce did not clearly articulate at that time, which is that significance is a potentiality for a specific sort of interpretation – a potentiality grounded on something that would justify interpretants of that type. If significance is grounded interpretability, then it is possible for something to be misinterpreted – namely, when an interpretant is not grounded in the sign's ground.

Why did Peirce, in this early period, identify significance with being interpreted, rather than with being interpretable? One might as well ask why, ten years later, he denied that there is any real difference between a hard and a soft thing before they are actually exposed to pressure. (The latter occurs famously in "How to Make Our Ideas Clear," at W 3, 266–7.) In both cases, it is evident that Peirce then lacked a definite concept of potentiality. His occasional use of expressions, such as some involving the word "would," that seem to represent potentialities, and even his occasional explicit assertions of potentialities, is no proof that he could accommodate them in his philosophy. Thus Peirce could not admit that a dispositional property like hardness consists in what *would* happen, as distinct from what *does* happen; and the same applies to a sign's significance.

Third, Peirce's infinite *regressus* of thought-signs is as unsatisfactory as is his infinite *progressus*. Each cognition is determined by a preceding cognition that establishes its object. But that object is not the preceding cognition itself; rather, it is the object of the preceding cognition. Thus the object is never to be found in the series of cognitions at all, but stands outside the series, approached but never reached as we trace thought-signs back to preceding thought-signs. For reasons we have no room here to explore, Peirce in the 1860s viewed this external object as, *qua* external, unknowable. But, on a principle announced in these same essays, that the incognizable is inconceivable (W 2, 208), this means that the object cannot be admitted as real or even as possibly real. As Peirce put it:

At any moment we are in possession of certain information, that is, of cognitions which have been logically derived by induction and hypothesis from previous cognitions which are less general . . . and so back to an ideal first, which is quite singular and quite out of consciousness. This ideal first is the particular thing-in-itself. It does not exist *as such.* (W 2, 238, Peirce's emphasis)

Peirce went on to argue that the object of thought *is* real, *insofar* as it is represented in cognition, and he concluded that "There is nothing, then, to prevent our knowing outward things as they really are" (W 2, 239). However, as the outwardness of the outward thing is by Peirce's argument unreal and, indeed, inconceivable, it is not clear how any reality or any object of knowledge could be identified as an "outward thing."

Notice that existence external to the mind is not all that is denied: individual existence is as well. This follows from the preceding plus Peirce's Kantian conception of cognition as invariably general. For, by that doctrine, the individual must lie outside the entire series of cognitions, and, thus, if the external is unreal, so is the individual. Yet, from his earliest philosophical writings through his 1877–8 papers on "The Fixation of Belief" and "How to Make Our Ideas Clear," Peirce never gave up the hypothesis that there is an external, individual cause of sensation. He merely attempted, in various ways, to combine that idea with the idea that the real is as inquiry tends eventually to represent it to be. That none of those attempts was successful is attested to by their number, and by the fact that, beginning in 1885, Peirce took a radically different approach.

3. THE THIRD FLAW CORRECTED (1885–1903)

By 1883, Peirce and his student, O. H. Mitchell, had discovered quantification (independently of Frege). In first order predicate logic, quantifiers bind individual variables, and the latter function as relative pronouns; together, quantifier and variable refer to some or to all of the individuals in a given set of individuals. Though these formal developments are neither necessary nor sufficient for the purpose, they appear in fact to have led Peirce, by 1885, to recognize a type of sign – the "index" – that is not general yet plays an essential part in cognition:

...generality is essential to reasoning....But [general terms] alone do not state what is the subject of discourse; and this can, in fact, not be described in general terms; it can only be indicated. The actual world cannot be distinguished from a world of imagination by any description. Hence the need of pronouns and indices.... The introduction of indices into the algebra of logic is the greatest merit of Mr. Mitchell's system. (W 5, 163–4)

Peirce applied this argument not only to discourse about particular individuals but to general statements as well, and to statements in mathematics and logic (CP 2.310–12, 336–7, 357, 4.56–9, 8.368 n23).

As Murray G. Murphey remarks, Peirce used the term "index" in the late 1860s, but not to refer to signs devoid of general meaning:

The index "It" of the "New List" is a concept – namely, the concept of "the present, in general"...The use of the term "index" to mean a sign which refers not to a concept but to an individual directly does not appear until 1885...It is at this point that the notion of individuality becomes important for Peirce. (Murphey 1961:299–300)

Thus, by 1885, Peirce can accept the individual thing[4] as real without qualification, not merely ideal, because, by that time, he saw that its conceptual apprehension – descriptive, general – is complemented by a more direct form of experience. "The index," Peirce wrote, "asserts nothing; it only says 'There!'" It "forcibly directs" our eyes, or otherwise our attention (W 5, 163). A pointing finger is the prime example.

Notice that Peirce did not say that indices operate outside of contexts created by other signs; much less did he assert that indices by themselves convey knowledge. He only asserted that indices are related to their objects directly, unmediated by general conceptions, and that it is by being connected with indices that general conceptions are applied to individual objects. Peirce's conception of the index requires careful explication.

The index "signifies its object solely by virtue of being really connected with it. Of this nature are all natural signs and physical symptoms" (W 5, 163). The relation of index to object is sometimes causal or physical; it will often be compulsive (as a sharp poke in the back calls one's attention to its as yet unidentified cause); but in any case it consists in a particular or existential relation between individuals.

But indices are rarely pure. Instinct, custom, or convention draws our attention to the extended arm and rigid finger and tells us to look along the line it defines; without that instinct, custom, or convention, index fingers would less often be rigid, for then there could be no intention "to point" (and the rigidity would not be called "pointing"). Nonetheless, the line that the finger defines depends on nothing but the fact that it is extended at this time in this place in this way. Instinct or convention calls attention to the line but does not make that line.

Furthermore, indices are interpreted in light of other signs with which they occur ("See that man I'm pointing at ?") or in light of background knowledge about indices of their type. Higher than normal bodily temperature is called "fever" and is taken to be a symptom of infection only because we know that generally such a condition is caused by infection. Nonetheless, the individual instance of fever picks out an individual instance of infection by virtue of being causally connected to it, and that causal relation is independent of any ideas we may have about it. Thus we can distinguish the indexical element of signification within these examples, even though it is effective only in combination with other, more general, elements.

Peirce's discovery of the indexical sign enabled him to relinquish the thesis that every cognition must be preceded by a cognition, *ad infinitum*. A cognition combines indices and concepts. The index picks out a particular of an otherwise signified type, which is then made the subject of a predicate (quantification extends this analysis to general statements). It follows that if the index is directly connected to its object, then so is the cognition, through the index it contains. Thus, a cognition does not have to be the interpretant of a preceding cognition in order to have an object.

In his 1903 Harvard "Lectures on Pragmatism," Peirce described the "perceptual judgment" as "the *first* judgment of a person as to what is before his senses" (CP 5.115, my emphasis). This is as clear a rejection of his earlier view – that there is no first cognition but that every cognition interprets a preceding cognition – as one could wish. But it does not follow that such judgments are intuitions in the sense of being entirely determined by their objects and, thus, infallible; for the union of concept with index is fallible because conjectural. One can mistakenly take something to be an index when it is not, and one can mistakenly take an index to be of an object of a type other than the type of that object to which it is dyadically connected. In these same lectures of 1903 (and elsewhere) Peirce likened perceptual judgments to hypotheses, from which they differ only in not being inferential (CP 5.181). Peirce's fallibilism, his anti-Cartesian denial of intuitive knowledge, was preserved even while the doctrine of an infinite regress of judgments, on which it was originally based, was jettisoned.

4. CONSEQUENT GENERALIZATION AND DEEPENING OF SIGN THEORY

The discovery of the indexical sign had two further implications for the development of Peirce's semeiotic. First, semeiotic was extended beyond the study of thought and language. For although the index was discovered as playing an essential rôle within cognition, it is by its nature – as being causal or otherwise nonconceptual – not limited to cognition. Natural signs, as smoke is of fire, thunder of lightning, fever of disease, must also be admitted to semeiotic's purview.

Furthermore, indices are of course interpretable by thought, but more essentially by that component of thought which consists in an act of attention. The rôle of an index is to set us in a certain direction when applying an associated idea. An interpretant, then, need not always be another sign of the same object. But this was not made explicit until 1904, when Peirce allowed interpretants to be actions or feelings as well as thought-signs (CP 8.332). That tripartite classification was based on Peirce's list of three categories as revised in the 1880s and 1890s on the basis of the logic of relations, on which he had begun work in the 1870s. Feelings are monadic, actions are dyadic, and signs, as we have seen, are triadic. In 1907, these types of interpretant were named the emotional, the energetic, and the logical (CP 5.475–6), though at that time a logical interpretant was no longer regarded as being invariably a thought-sign (see Section 6).

But if semeiotic's purview is extended to nonconceptual interpretants, then why not to nonhuman interpreters? A person poked turns to look, but so also a browsing deer, startled by a noise, raises its head to look; the seasoned driver, seeing a stop sign, stops without thinking, but so also a bloodhound, nose to ground, follows without thinking the spoor of its quarry. Semeiotic thereby became a study not only of natural signs but also of natural processes of interpretation. And that suggests a way in which the human mind may be located within nature, namely, as a development of more primitive semeiotic capacities.

The second implication of the discovery of indices is that it compels us to recognize a relation of sign to object that is distinct from signification. As we noted earlier, Peirce conceived of significance as a triadic relation in which an interpretant mediates between the sign and the object signified. But indices are also related to their objects dyadically. It follows that the two relations are not the same. Peirce drew that conclusion in 1885 (W 5,162–3) but did not at that time say how the two relations are related. It is obvious that the sign relation must in some way be based on a prior relation of that which is a sign to that which is that sign's object; but the nature of that dependency could not have been formulated before the development of the mature semeiotic, in 1907.

Still, Peirce's most famous division of signs, into icons, indices, and symbols (in different periods variously designated), turns on the different kinds of prior relation a sign has to its object. Even in 1866–7, when this division was differently conceived (W 1, 475, 2:56), the examples Peirce cited anticipated his later view, in writings of 1885, 1893, and 1902–3 (CP 2.274–308) and c.1903 (CP 2.247–9). Here again, the basis of classification is the logic of relations. Briefly, the prior relation of an icon to its object is monadic, that of an index is dyadic, and that of a symbol is triadic.

An icon is related to its object monadically, either by resemblance, wherein sign and object both have the same property, or by exemplification, wherein its object is a property it possesses. Like indices, icons normally function in a context of other signs which direct attention to one or another of a thing's iconic aspects. The index we have discussed. The symbol alone is based on a triadic and intrinsically semeiotic relation, viz., a rule by which it is to be interpreted. Notice, however, that this is distinct from the sign's being interpreted in conformity to that rule; thus, the distinction of the sign-relation from the prior relation on which it is based is maintained.

Most commentators have assumed that a rule of interpretation must be conventional, even though Peirce, as early as 1885, said only that symbols (then named "tokens") are conventional "for the most part" (W 5,162). Later, he specifically said that the interpreting habit may be either "natural or conventional" (CP 2.307, 1902) or that the rule of interpretation may be either a convention, a habit, or a natural disposition (CP 8.335, 1904). Thus, a peacock's mating display does not obey a convention, and yet it means what it does only because of a corresponding instinct, on the part of peahens, so to interpret it.

Two other tripartite classifications of signs, ca. 1902–3, may here be briefly mentioned. A sign in itself is either monadic – a quality of feeling, hence, a qualisign – dyadic – a singular object or event, hence, a sinsign – or triadic – a type defined by a law for forming its replicas, hence, a legisign (CP 2.243–6). A qualisign in itself is a mere possibility and, so, must be embodied in a sinsign actually to function as a sign. Hence, some sinsigns are such because of the qualisigns they embody: they signify not, or not only, in virtue of the particularities of their occurrence, as indices, but in virtue of their qualities, as icons. So also, a legisign signifies only through its replicas, which are sinsigns of a special kind. Legisigns and their replicas are better known as types and tokens, terminology which Peirce also introduced (CP 4.537, 544).

Legisigns alone among signs exist to be used, i.e., replicated; and nothing replicates a legisign that is not formed for that purpose, i.e., to signify according to a rule of interpretation. Peirce sometimes maintained that symbols can only be legisigns and that their replicas are indices that direct attention to the symbol replicated (CP 2.249). But not all legisigns are symbolic. Pronouns are indexical legisigns, since the rules for interpreting their replicas direct one to the circumstances in which they occur (CP 2.259). And geometrical diagrams are iconic legisigns, since the rule for their interpretation directs one to attend to the spatial relations they exemplify (CP 2.258). By contrast, the object of a symbol's replicas is given by the rule of interpretation itself.

A final trichotomy of signs formulated in 1903 was at first based on the category of the sign's object, as a possibility, fact, or reason (CP 2.243), but was reformulated in 1908 as "the Nature of the Influence of the Sign," as being either monadic, dyadic, or triadic (CP 8.373). In 1903, these signs are, respectively, rhemes, dicent signs or dicisigns, and arguments, but in 1906 (CP 4.538) and 1908 (CP 8.373), they are semes, phemes, and delomes. In any case, they are generalizations of the familiar term/proposition/argument trichotomy – a generalization required by the fact that signs are no longer to be limited to human cognition. The idea of the 1908 reformulation is this: a seme merely presents its object; a pheme, such as an assertion, is forceful; while a delome, such as an argument, appeals to the interpreter's own reason. In the case of language, syntax is a guide to the nature of a sign's influence, but a guide only; for in certain contexts, a mere word – "Yes!" – can convey an assertion or an argument.[5]

5. THE SECOND FLAW CORRECTED (1896–1909)

Since interpretation is based on a distinct relation of sign to object – one that obtains whether or not an interpretant is actually formed – it becomes possible to distinguish interpretability from interpretation. From the solution to the third of the three problems we have surveyed, we can thus derive a solution to the second. But it is a solution that Peirce could not have embraced before he developed a realist conception of potentiality (or, as he sometimes said, real possibility). This he did in his later years, when he construed the reality of a law in the strongest possible terms, as a "would-be" that is irreducible to any quantity of actual instances (e.g., at CP 5.467, 6.327, 8.216–7, 225), beginning in 1896 (CP 1.420).[6] But if a law in this sense is real, then so are dispositional properties (which are laws about how one or another individual thing would behave under certain conditions) and so are potentialities. In 1905, Peirce explicitly corrected his 1878 remark on hardness and announced that "it is the reality of some possibilities that pragmaticism is most concerned to insist upon" (CP 5.453).

Thus Peirce was able, after 1896, to identify significance not with actual but with potential interpretation, or interpretability, as he did emphatically and repeatedly beginning in 1902 (e.g., at CP 1.542, 2.242, 274–5). To be sure, he continued to insist that every sign must have an interpretant, but *that* interpretant is a potentiality. This point is embodied in his late distinction between a sign's "immediate" interpretant and its actual, or "dynamic" interpretants (see Section 9).

It is, then, its being interpretable, and not its being interpreted, that makes something a sign. It follows that an infinite *progressus* of actual thought-signs, each interpreting the preceding, is unnecessary.[7] Just as a particular act of thinking can begin with a bang, so also it can end that way: in it, there can be a last as well as a first thought. That is not to deny that every thought remains interpretable by further thought; in principle, there is no end to thinking. But, when in fact it does end, thinking's reality is not thereby cancelled.

6. THE REVOLUTION OF 1907: ULTIMATE LOGICAL INTERPRETANTS

The third and second of our three problems were solved in consequence of developments of 1885 and 1896, respectively, but the first not until 1907, when Peirce suggested, though he did not fully formulate, a new account of how signs signify – one that was entirely different from his earlier identification of significance with an endless process of signs interpreting signs. The first step in this new account was to relinquish the view that every interpretant of a thought-sign must be another thought-sign. If the interpretant of a sign can be something other than a sign, and if this holds for signs of every class, then significance never depends on an infinite series of interpretants, even if only *in posse*.

In 1902, Peirce still claimed that a sign must be so related to its object "as to be capable of determining a Third, called its *Interpretant*, to assume the same triadic relation" to that same object (CP 2.274). Notice the word "capable": a sign need not actually be interpreted. Yet an interpretant, when formed, must have the "same triadic relation" to the object as has the sign it interprets: ergo, the interpretant must be another sign of that object. In 1904, the thesis that interpretants are signs was reiterated (CP 8.191, 226 n10), but also in that year its first modification may be found, where, in a letter to Lady Welby, Peirce suggested that "Taking a sign in its broadest sense, its interpretant is not necessarily a sign," since it might be an action or feeling (CP 8.332).[8] This, as we have seen, became the emotional/energetic/logical trichotomy of interpretants. But in 1904–6, Peirce continued to affirm the 1868–9 view that all *thoughts* must be interpreted in further thought-signs. The reason is that the meaning of a thought cannot be exhausted by any number of feelings and/or actions, and thus a thought's interpretant must fall into the third category of interpretant.

In 1907, Peirce reversed himself by drawing a distinction within the category of logical interpretants between those that are signs and those that are not. The latter he named "ultimate logical interpretants":

> ...far from holding that a sign can be the "naked", that is, the ultimate meaning of a sign, I was just about to insist that it cannot be so; and the great enigma that leads up to pragmatism, – at least to my form of the doctrine, – is, "What can this naked or ultimate meaning be?"
>
> I do not deny that a concept, or general mental sign, may be a logical interpretant; only, it cannot be the ultimate logical interpretant, precisely because, being a sign, it has itself a logical interpretant.[9]

Thus, the meaning of a thought must be something more, or something other, than its translation into further thoughts. While a thought *may* always be interpreted in further thoughts, there *must* also be another form of interpretation, at least potentially.

The ultimate logical interpretant, as the reference to pragmatism indicates, is the habit:

> To say that I hold that the import, or adequate ultimate interpretation, of a concept is contained, not in any deed or deeds that will ever be done, but in a habit of conduct, or general moral determination of whatever procedure there *may come to be*, is no more than to say that I am a pragmaticist. (CP 5.504, Peirce's emphasis)[10]

The habit of conduct in which the meaning of a concept is to be found is that which one would form in adopting the concept or in applying it to specific subjects. If I believe that the stove is hot, then I am disposed to act toward the stove accordingly, avoiding it for some purposes, approaching it for others. And to possess the concept of heat is to be ready to form such dispositions; it is to expect that, upon the observation of certain effects, certain others will occur or can be made to occur if certain conditions are met. Notoriously, it is not possible to specify all of the dispositions that one who adopts a concept might form; but whether that is a problem for Peirce's view or, alternatively, correctly indicates the openness of concepts to growth in light of experience, is another matter.

7. PRAGMATISM AND SEMEIOTIC

Since Peirce's pragmatic theory of meaning was published, albeit not under that rubric, in his 1878 paper, "How to Make Our Ideas Clear," it may be wondered why it took 29 more years for that doctrine to link hands with his semeiotic. Could Peirce have failed for so long to discern the contradiction between his 1878 account of meaning, not forsworn but reaffirmed in later years, and his 1868–9 doctrine of thought-signs? It is true that Peirce did no work on the theory of signs from the spring of 1873 to the writing of his aforementioned paper of 1885; but that does not explain his reiterated assertions, from 1902 to 1906, that interpretants, at least those of thoughts, must be signs.

The answer lies in the way in which the pragmatic maxim of 1878 was formulated: "Consider what effects, which might conceivably have practical bearings, we conceive the object of our conception to have. Then our conception of these effects is the whole of our conception of the object" (W 3, 266). As Peirce himself pointed out in 1906, the emphasis throughout is on conception, in order, he said, "to avoid all danger of being understood as attempting to explain a concept by percepts, images, schemata, or anything but concepts" (CP 5.402n3). Thus, while the rôle of habit in interpreting words or concepts is implicit, the interpretant is taken to be the *concept of* a habit.

The fundamental revolution in doctrine that occurred in 1907 was to have recognized that it is the habit itself, and not a concept of it, that is the interpretant (more precisely, the ultimate logical interpretant) of a concept. Verbal interpretants and verbal definitions, Peirce then said, are "very inferior to the living definition that grows up in the habit."[11] Again,

The real and living logical conclusion *is* that habit; the verbal formulation merely expresses it.... The concept which is a logical interpretant is only imperfectly so. It partakes somewhat of the nature of a verbal definition, and is very inferior to the living definition that grows up in the habit. (CP 5.491)

The revolution of 1907 is, then, a revolution in Peirce's pragmatism as well as in his semeiotic. In both, it is a step away from a too extreme intellectualism. 1907 is also the year when Peirce first drew his pragmatism and his semeiotic together into one formulation.

Unlike actions and feelings, a habit has that character of being general, of being inexhaustible in concrete instances, that a concept itself has. It is, as Peirce said, a "conditional general resolution to act" (CP 5.402 n3). Therefore, pragmatism – which may now be seen, reformulated, as the doctrine of the ultimate logical interpretant – is not reductive: it does not reduce the general to some congeries of particulars. By the same token, pragmatism is not a narrowly practical doctrine. It does not imply that we think only in order to act. To the contrary, in experimental science, we act in order to test our theories, thus, to arrive at true thoughts.

And yet, by this revolution of 1907, we break out of the circle of words, of words interpreting words and thoughts interpreting thoughts. The pragmatic distinction between meaningfulness and meaninglessness becomes this: meaningful speech and thought have ultimate logical interpretants, while nonsensical speech and thought, though they may always be translated into further thoughts and words, lack ultimate logical interpretants. Being interpretable by habits of action, meaningful speech engages with the nonverbal world: for example, assertions may be acted upon and tested against the consequences of those actions.

It should be noted that pragmatism pertains, Peirce said, only to "intellectual" meaning (CP 5.467, 482). Peirce identified meaning in general with interpretants in general (CP 4.536, 5.475). Therefore, emotional and energetic interpretants comprise other dimensions of meaning, e.g., emotive and imperative, respectively. To feel anger when wrongly chastised, shame when rightly chastised, correctly interprets chastisement; one devoid of such feelings may be said not to understand what is being said to him (whether due to linguistic incompetence or to being a sociopath). The action of one who obeys a legitimate command correctly interprets that command, even if the action follows the command automatically, without a mediating thought. Pragmatism thus became but one part of a broader theory of linguistic meaning. And that, in turn, was part of a broader theory of signs: e.g., natural signs (a prey's spoor, for example) are interpreted energetically by the lower animals, and the meaning of a work of art may be grasped partly or wholly in an emotional interpretant.

8. THE REVOLUTION OF 1907: INTERPRETATION
AS END-DIRECTED

A criterion for distinguishing significant speech from insignificant uses of words does not, by itself, tell us what signifying is. Merely to issue in a feeling, an action, or a habit of action does not make something a sign; such results have many causes, few of which we would identify as signs. A second, and final, step Peirce took in 1907 was to describe the process of sign-interpretation, or, as he called it, semeiosis, as being end-directed (CP 5.472–3, 484).[12] That interpretation can only occur for the sake of some end was perhaps implicit before, but now it is made explicit. I shall argue that the end-directedness of semeiosis accounts for significance's essential features. As in Peirce's early theory, process is key; but the process that matters is one in which even a single interpretant is formed.

If semeiosis is end-directed, and if we are to use the idea of semeiosis to explain conscious thought, then end-directedness cannot as a general rule presuppose consciousness. For this reason, Peirce's mature semeiotic rests on the theory of final causation that he formulated primarily in the year 1902 (CP 1.203–31, 250, 267–9, 2.149, 8.272), on the basis of analyses of physical law and theories of evolution made from 1891 to 1898 (CP 6.12–3, 33, 71–81, 296–305, 7.468–83, 518–23) or earlier (see such hints as those at W 6, 63 and W 3, 244). For that theory makes final causation, or directedness to an end, to be independent of conscious direction. It is teleological in an Aristotelian sense, as Peirce's references to Aristotle indicate (CP 1.211). But it is also based on and framed in terms of developments in nineteenth-century natural science, specifically, statistical mechanics and Darwin's theory. This rather heterodox interpretation of Darwinism appears to have been shared by Darwin himself (see Lennox 1993 and Short 2002), who also adopted the language of final causes (introduced in the Latin translation of Aristotle).

There is no room here for a full exegesis, much less defense, of Peirce's idea of final causation (see Short 1981b, 1983, 1999:111–38). But the gist of it is arguably this: when mechanical events, fortuitously varied, result in a tendency that is practically irreversible, that tendency is to be explained statistically as due to variations of one type being favored over those of other types. In the case of Darwinian natural selection, differential retention of genetic variants over many generations is explained by their different types of effect – some increasing chances of successful procreation more than others. This kind of explanation is not mechanistic, even if the particular steps of the process are perfectly mechanical, because the tendency of the process is explained not by mechanical forces, which are always particular, but by selection for general types of outcome (as I argue in detail in Short 2002).[13] Types of outcome as explanatory are what Aristotle, translated, called "final causes."

Peirce's mature semeiotic, as earlier noted, must be constructed from fragments. In the remainder of this section, I fill in some of the blanks Peirce left. First, let us note that when an organic feature, X, is explained as having been selectively retained because of a type of effect, E, that it normally has, then X may be said to exist for the sake of E (following Wimsatt 1972, Wright 1976). In a word, E is X's purpose. A purpose is a type for which there has been or continues to be selection; it makes no difference whether the selection is conscious.[14] If the heart's several features are the result of variations having been retained because they facilitate the pumping of blood, then the heart exists because it pumps blood; ergo, pumping blood is its purpose.

Second, we should distinguish existing for a purpose from acting for a purpose: the heart fulfills its purpose mechanically, not purposefully. When action is purposeful, variation and selection are internal to the action itself, at least potentially: purposeful action is subject to variation when it fails, the successful variants, if any, being then selected. The type selected for is the action's purpose, with reference to which we define success and failure. Selection may consist in repetition of the successful variant, or in making that variant habitual ("learning from experience"), or in cessation of activity. Thus, an animal that moves about randomly until it locates food is acting purposefully; but so also, rigidly repetitive behavior, though it appears mechanical, is purposeful if it would be varied were it unsuccessful.

Third, nothing purposeful is wholly arbitrary. It must have some warrant or basis, however fallible, or even mistaken, that relates it to its purpose or, if mistaken, that seems to relate it to its purpose. Let us take a primitive example. A black bear scratches about among rotting logs in search, we say, of grubs; finding grubs is its action's purpose. Its disposition so to act is based on a past correlation (whether in the bear's experience or in the course of ursine evolution) between the odor of rotting wood and the presence of succulent, protein-rich grubs. And its scratching about in this particular log is based, in addition, on the presence of a particular odor of that type. The correlation on the basis of which an animal acts may be weak; if food is hard to come by, even a 1% correlation would justify this expenditure of the bear's energy. Hence fallibility: the bear's behavior may fail even though it is justified. Mistaken justification is something else. A mistake occurs, for example, if the past correlation of odor to grubs no longer obtains (perhaps all species of insect whose larval forms inhabit rotting wood have become extinct), or if the bear's olfactory organs are defective, so that it responds to one odor as if it were another. This talk – of success and failure, of justification, of reality versus appearance – is neither fanciful nor anthropomorphic. End-directedness grounds our use of evaluative language in describing organic features and animal behavior.

These three points yield this, perhaps surprising, corollary, that animal behavior cannot be fully described and explained without our using general terms that may, in the individual instance, refer to nothing. The bear, we say, is searching for grubs in this log whether or not any grubs are in fact there. Normally (putting aside negative, modal, imperative, and some other contexts), a reference to what does not exist results in false statement. "Sitting on a log" cannot truly describe the bear if the log does not exist. But "Looking for grubs" can truly describe even those unhappy bears that are fated to remain forever grubless. Let us name this a "nonreferential use" of a general term: it is a use made in a positive, nonmodal description of something – something that *does* exist and to which reference *is* made – that in some manner implicates an object that might not exist. The preceding account of purposeful behavior shows how nonreferential usage can be meaningful. The behavior has to be described in terms of types that are involved in selection and in bases of selection, regardless of whether those types are instantiated in the individual case.

But nonreferential usage is essential, also, to any attempt to say what a sign signifies. The object of a sign may be not otherwise manifest (the function of a sign is rooted in that fact), and, in the case of many kinds of sign, the object of a sign might not exist at all.[15] To account for significance is to account for this peculiar sense of "having an object," wherein the object must be specified nonreferentially.

And that is what our theory of purposeful behavior does. Indeed, that purposeful behavior is not wholly arbitrary is but another way of saying that it interprets signs. To act purposefully is to interpret something as a sign of that which, if it obtains, will make that action appropriate to its goal. The bear's actions interpret a certain odor as a sign of grubs.

Our overworked bear should not mislead you: the theory is not restricted to the primitive. Peirce's pragmatism stated "an inseparable connection between rational cognition and rational purpose" (CP 5.412, cf. 402 n3, 428). His mature semeiotic relates significance in general to purpose in general. It is, in that respect, a generalization of pragmatism. And neither doctrine assumes that human purposes are narrowly practical.

For historical reasons, the peculiar property, "having an object," is named "intentionality." When Franz Brentano retrieved the concept and the word from the medieval Scholastics, he maintained that intentionality is fundamentally a feature of mind and that it is what distinguishes the mental from the physical (1814 [1973]: 88–9). By the physical, he meant the world studied in the natural sciences, and by the mental, he meant primarily human consciousness as it is known through a unique form of "inner" perception (4 and *passim*). Much later, Roderick Chisholm pointed out that significance is a form of intentionality and that there are signs outside of anyone's consciousness; but, adopting Brentano's view, he argued that the intentionality of such signs derives from that of the conscious thought in which they may be interpreted (1952). That is in one way close to Peirce's view, since it identifies significance with interpretability. Yet Peirce reversed the dependence of intentionality on consciousness. His mature semeiotic, because it is teleological, accounts for the intentionality of semeiosis *sans* consciousness; and thus it is able to explain thought's intentionality as due to thought's being a special form of semeiosis.

In recent years, some philosophers of mind have developed, independently of Peirce, a similar "teleosemantics" (Millikan 1984, Papineau 1984, 1987). Their theory has been subjected to a strong critique (see, e.g., Fodor 1990: chap. 3) which Peirce's semeiotic evades. The charge is that an animal's goal can be identified at different levels of abstraction, and, thus, that the object of the alleged sign is ambiguous ("the disjunction problem"). The bear's goal, for example, is to find grubs, but more generally it is to locate protein, and more generally still, it is to survive. Is the object which the odor signifies grubs, or is it protein, or is it a means to survival? It would seem that the object can be unambiguously identified only if there is a conscious thought of it. Our solution to this problem is found in the correlation, or seeming correlation, that justifies, or would justify, the bear's response. That correlation, if real, is an instance of what we earlier referred to as the prior relation of a sign to its object. Thus, the object, or supposed object, is exactly as specific as that relation, or seeming relation, makes it to be. The odor is correlated, really or apparently, only with grubs of various wood-infesting species, and not with fish or other sources of protein, and therefore the bear's behavior interprets the odor as a sign of grubs, nothing more and nothing less.

Let us conclude this necessarily hasty sketch by hazarding a somewhat more formal statement of Peirce's mature semeiotic. It is essential that we begin with "interprets... as being a sign" and only then define "sign":

Something (whether feeling, action, thought, etc.), R, interprets something else, X, as being a sign, S, of O if and only if (a) R is formed in response to X, (b) R is goal-directed, (c) R will not contribute to its goal unless O obtains, and (d) R's goal-directed response to X has some basis in a relation or apparent relation of X to O or of things of X's type or apparent type to things of O's type.

In this formula, our symbol "O" stands in the place of expressions used nonreferentially. "Contribute" covers a wide range of cases. At one extreme, O's obtaining makes R itself to be its goal's fulfillment. At the opposite extreme, R is an act of desperation which, if O obtains, lowers the probability of failure minutely. In between, O makes R fulfill a condition of success, but only to some degree of probability whether great or small; and the condition may be necessary and sufficient, or one of these only, or neither.

Next, we can define "sign" in terms of there being an unmistaken basis for interpretation:

X is a sign, S, of O if and only if there is a basis on which a possible creature, having a purpose for doing so, could unmistakenly interpret it as being a sign, however fallible, of O.

Significance is relative to purpose, but possible purpose suffices. This point tends to missed, since human curiosity issues in purposes to which every possible kind of sign is relevant. Notice, also, that one and the same thing, X, may be many different signs, S, S', ..., relative to different bases of interpretation and relative to different possible purposes. A foxy odor is a sign of danger to the rabbit but of dinner to the cougar; "$E = mc^2$" is a statement of physical law to the physicist but to the general public it is an icon of braininess; to those who worshiped it, an ancient religious artifact was an icon, even *qua* embodiment, of suprahuman powers, but to the anthropologist it is an index of social organization and cultural development.

9. RAMIFICATIONS

The preceding might be faulted for filling in the blanks too boldly. In its defense: it makes sense out of what little Peirce said in 1907; it corrects a deficiency in his early theory of signs; and, now to be shown, it is borne out by some further distinctions, of considerable importance, that Peirce developed from 1906 to 1909. For those distinctions are required by, and would make no sense apart from, a teleological account of semeiosis.

In 1904 and 1906, when Peirce first hinted at what would become the emotional/energetic/logical trichotomy of interpretants, he proceeded, in the next paragraph (CP 8.333) or in the same paragraph (CP 4.536), to claim, as a separate matter, that every sign has three interpretants, which, in 1906 and again in 1909 (SS. 110–11), he named the immediate, dynamic, and final. Clearly, then, the two trichotomies are intended to be distinct.[16] In fact, they are not classifications in the same sense. Rather than being an ontological typing of interpretants, the immediate/dynamic/final trichotomy refers to stages of semeiosis. At any one of those stages, an interpretant may be of various ontological types, hence, either emotional or energetic or logical.

"My Immediate Interpretant," Peirce wrote in 1909, "is implied in the fact that each sign must have its peculiar Interpretability before it gets any Interpreter"; again, "The Immediate Interpretant is an abstraction, consisting in a Possibility" (SS.111). In the same passage (cf. CP 8.314–5), he described the dynamic interpretant as an actual effect on an interpreter, and the final interpretant as "the one

Interpretative result to which every Interpreter is destined to come if the Sign is sufficiently considered," or as "that toward which the actual tends." A dynamic interpretant, if it is an interpretant of a sign, S, actualizes S's immediate interpretant; the one is a possible feeling, action, or thought or habit, while the other makes that possibility actual. As the same possibility can be actualized in different ways, most signs can have any number of dynamic interpretants. A dynamic interpretant might refine or supplement the immediate interpretant it actualizes, or even negate it, as when one thinks that a claim (therein understood) is mistaken or dishonest. A series of dynamic interpretants, informed by other observations, may approach the final interpretant, i.e., the one that would be ideally adequate to its purpose.[17] Like the immediate interpretant, the final interpretant may remain an unactualized possibility.

But a sign can be corrected only in respect to some reality that it purports to represent. Even if the object signified fails to exist, there must be an implicit reference to something that does exist – the grubless log, the monsterless loch, the ideal realm devoid of four-sided triangles – in relation to which the failed reference occurs. Hence, Peirce distinguished between a sign's immediate and dynamic objects, the latter being a reality and the former what the sign represents that reality to be. For some signs, e.g., a purely qualitative icon, there would seem to be no distinction between dynamic and immediate objects. Where such a distinction does apply, a sign must somehow indicate its object in a manner that enables one to identify it with the objects of other signs; it is through the agreement or disagreement of diverse signs of the same thing ("collateral observation," in Peirce's phrase) that a discrepancy of an immediate from a dynamic object may be discerned (CP 4.536, 8.314, 333, 343, EP 2:404–9). A sign's immediate object and immediate interpretant are two sides of one coin; so also its dynamic object and final interpretant.

Peirce wrote, " ... my three grades of interpretant were worked out by reasoning from the definition of a sign" (SS.111). But there could be no final interpretant if interpretation were not end-directed. Ergo, these grades presuppose a teleological account of semeiosis.[18] Furthermore, there could not be just one final interpretant per sign, if significance were not correlative with interpretative purpose, making the same thing different signs relative to different purposes. Ergo, the ideas of a final interpretant and a dynamic object presuppose an analysis of signhood like the one I have suggested. I do not see another way to make good sense of Peirce's writings on signs.

Many writers have adopted a version of Peirce's early theory as if it were his only theory of signs, from which they have derived ideas of "unlimited semiosis" (Eco 1976: 68–72) and "the indefiniteness of reference" (Derrida 1974: 49). Even if those doctrines were not combined with an unPeircean insistence that all significance, even of icons and indices, depends on purely conventional "codes," they would entail a relativism and irrealism that are utterly opposed to Peirce's own view. In his mature semeiotic, the ideas of a final interpretant and dynamic object – evidently a generalization of his early identification of truth as a final fixation of belief and of reality as truth's object – extend the structure of objectivity far beyond natural science, factual assertion, and "intellectual meaning," to interpretants that are emotional or energetic and to signs thus interpretable. In some cases, the final interpretant will not be a true theory but, rather, an appropriate action or a just appreciation. The implications of this for ethical theory and aesthetic theory have yet to be exploited.

NOTES

1. Why did Peirce speak of interpretants and not of interpretation? He never says. I suggest that an interpretation is a class of interpretants that are, in some sense yet to be defined, equivalent. An interpretant is thus one particular bearer of an interpretation.   •

2. A nonstandard or Leibnizian conception of continuity is entailed; it is no surprise, then, that Peirce sometimes entertained such a conception. But this is of little importance for Peirce's theory of signs, since, as we shall see, he eventually abandoned the doctrine of an infinite *progressus* and *regressus* of thought-signs.

3. This problem had been noticed by George Gentry, 1952, and William Alston, 1956. See also Short 1981a.

4. I say "thing," meaning individual person, horse, tree, because Peirce sometimes used the term "individual" in an extreme sense that excludes all spatiotemporal continuity and, hence, lawfulness in its make-up. In the terms of his later metaphysics, individuals in this extreme sense are

actual but not real; however, such actualities are comprised within realities, and that distinguishes Peirce's later from his earlier view, wherein
individuality is ideal and neither actual nor real.

5. More remains to be said about these three divisions of sign and their
   intersection (CP 2.254–64), but not in this space (see Short 1982).

6. The change in doctrine is advertised by Peirce himself in a *Monist* article
   of 1897 (CP 3.527) referring to his nominalistic view of possibility only
   one year earlier (in a related *Monist* article, at CP 3.442). Max Fisch
   therefore gives 1897 as the date of the change (Fisch, 1986:193–5, 199
   n24). But the unpublished manuscript, "The Logic of Mathematics,"
   c.1896, anticipates that change (CP 1.420), and, as the second *Monist*
   article was published in January, it must have been written in 1896. So
   1896 seems the more accurate date.

7. This is contradicted by a much-quoted passage of 1902, Peirce's definition of 'Sign' for Baldwin's *Dictionary*: "Anything which determines
   something else (its *interpretant*) to refer to an object to which itself
   refers (its *object*) in the same way, the interpretant becoming in turn
   a sign, and so on *ad infinitum*.... If the series of successive interpretants comes to an end, the sign is thereby rendered imperfect, at least"
   (CP 2.303). 1902 is, however, the date of publication; the passage was
   probably written before the passages in Peirce's unpublished "Syllabus,"
   c.1902, that emphasize, rather, the mere *capacity* of a sign (representamen) to determine an interpretant: " ... while no Representamen actually functions as such until it actually determines an Interpretant, yet
   it becomes a Representamen as soon as it is fully capable of doing this;
   and its Representative Quality is not necessarily dependent upon its
   ever actually determining an Interpretant... " (CP 2.275). This is not
   the only instance in which Peirce's most clear and definite statement of
   an extreme position heralds its rejection or drastic qualification shortly
   after.

8. Possibly, the first mention of this modification is earlier, in the passage
   dated in the *Collected Papers* c.1903, where the term "representamen"
   is used for the broadest sense of "sign" and Peirce wrote, "A *Sign* is a
   representamen of which some interpretant is a cognition of a mind" (CP
   2.242).

9. Both of these passages are from MS318, as numbered in Robin 1967. This
   MS was published in part in CP 5.11–13, 464–96, where the date given is
   c.1906; but it is now known to be of 1907 (see Robin, 1967:36). MS318,
   consisting of labyrinthine multiple drafts of an unfinished article, has
   never been published in its entirety, despite its richness and importance
   (the largest portion published so far is EP 2: 398–433). The first of the

two passages quoted is still unpublished; the second may be found in NE 3/1:493–4. A similar passage, from a variant draft, is in CP 5.491; in it, Peirce substituted "final" for "ultimate," which has engendered some confusion, since, as we shall see, Peirce sometimes used the term "final interpretant" in a quite different way.

10. This passage is dated in the *Collected Papers* as c.1905. However, if my account of Peirce's development is correct, it must be later than the last possible date at which Peirce could have altered his 1906 *Monist* article, "Prolegomena to an Apology for Pragmaticism," from which the quotation from CP 4.536 is taken. And since it is so much akin in wording and thought to MS318, its writing is probably nearer to 1907 than it is to 1905. Richard Robin dates it as c.1905–8 (1967:30).

11. This passage follows the second of the two from MS318 quoted earlier (see n.9).

12. The passage has to be read carefully; see Short 1981a: 204–7.

13. Peirce, as is well known, also posited objective chance, i.e., the occurrence of events not conforming to mechanistic laws ("tychism"). I believe he did this only in order to account for the evolution of law itself, and not to account for irreversible tendencies toward ends in the systems statistical mechanics studies and in biological evolution. However, if I am wrong about that, then tychism only strengthens the present point, that end-directedness is irreducible to mechanistic law.

14. Peirce wrote that "A purpose is merely that form of final cause which is most familiar to our experience" (CP 1.211), implying that in ordinary usage a purpose must be something of which one is conscious. Wright and Wimsatt would agree, but I find nothing in ordinary usage that justifies that view. We ordinarily speak of the purpose of an organ or other organic feature or instinct, etc., and we do so without making any assumption of its having been created consciously. What does seem to be implied is that the item has been selected *somehow* for a type of effect. Hence I adopt the more convenient and familiar term "purpose" in lieu of "final cause." Yet the point is Peirce's: that what matters is selection for type, regardless of how that selection is made.

15. But if its object does not exist, or even if it need not, then is the sign really one of a triad? Peirce's conception of the dynamic object resolves this problem: see Section 9.

16. Yet other commentators, from Buchler 1939 to Lalor 1997, have thought otherwise; for discussion of the issue, see Fitzgerald 1966: 78 n9, Short 1981a: 212–19, Liszka 1990, 1996:120–3. Short 1996a is a full defense of the view presented here.

17. When our purpose is to know the truth, the final interpretant will be symbolic; hence, it will have, but it will not be, an ultimate interpretant.

18. In 1906, Peirce confessed that his conception of the final interpretant was "not yet quite free from mist" (CP 4.536). Nor should it have been at that date, if his semeiotic was not made explicitly teleological before 1907. In fact, his conceptions of the immediate and the final interpretants varied a good deal, as did his terminology (cf. CP 8.333 of 1904 and 8.343 of 1908).

10 Peirce's Semeiotic Model of the Mind

I. INTRODUCTION

In this chapter, I show how Peirce's model of mind is grounded in his semeiotic, or general doctrine òf signs, a grounding made possible by the logical priority, in Peirce's thought, of the concept of sign over the concept of mind. I then compare this model of mind with some more recent doctrines and theories, and conclude with some comments on Peirce's relevance for cognitive science, including both artificial intelligence and human–computer interaction.

2. PEIRCE'S DOCTRINE OF SIGNS

Peirce's doctrine of thought signs was first introduced in his justly famous 1868 articles in *The Journal of Speculative Philosophy* and later developed in greater detail from 1895 until Peirce's death in 1914. In his 1868 papers Peirce specifically targeted Descartes and Cartesianism, and argued that we have no ability to think without signs. This argument presupposes a prior argument that all self-knowledge can be accounted for as inferences from external facts and that there is thus no reason to posit any power of introspection (CP 5.247–9). We need, therefore, to look to external facts for evidence of our own thoughts, and it is then a near-tautology to conclude that the only thoughts so evidenced are in the form of signs: "If we seek the light of external facts, the only cases of thought which we can find are of thought in signs" (CP 5.251). This doctrine is repeated in 1909 in the following words, which recall Socrates and Aristotle: "All thinking is dialogic in form.... Consequently, all thinking is conducted in signs that are mainly of the same general structure as words; ... " (CP 6.338).

By saying that all thinking is dialogic Peirce is here plainly implying what he made explicit on numerous other occasions, to wit, that all thinking is inherently communicational and thus inherently social. Even my solitary ruminations presuppose a communicational structure enabled by my membership in a society. We will note, however, that Peirce is *not* saying that all thinking in conducted in words, only that it is conducted in signs that are of the same "general structure" as words; that is, he is not taking the "Orwellian" position attacked in recent years by, e.g., Steven Pinker, which equates language and thought. Thoughts are not simply words, and Peirce never supposed that they are. In fact, Peirce – like any mathematician – thought natural language inadequate for the special purpose of exact reasoning, which requires a special symbolism, either an algebraic or a diagrammatic one. In keeping with this view, he devoted a great part of his life to the development of algebraic and diagrammatic notations for logic, conceiving of the universal and existential quantifiers independently of Frege, and designing logic diagrams which have lately found fertile applications in artificial intelligence research. The special symbols comprising these and other notations are, however, of the same "general structure" as words, and we turn next to an overview of what Peirce took to be the general structure of signhood.

In 1868 Peirce introduces the concept of "sign" as follows:

Now a sign has, as such, three references: first, it is a sign *to* some thought which interprets it; second, it is a sign *for* some object to which in that thought it is equivalent; third, it is a sign, *in* some respect or quality, which brings it into connection with its object. (CP 5.283)

The sign, then, constructs or imposes an irreducibly triadic relation on the object of the sign, the respect or quality through which the sign signifies, and the thought that connects the sign with its object, a thought which Peirce later was to dub the "interpretant" of the sign. This irreducibility of triadic relations is one of the central themes in Peirce's thought – a theme also later developed by the novelist and essayist Walker Percy, who described himself in this respect as "a thief of Peirce" (Samway, 1995: 130; Percy, 1975: 3–45). A simple example of a triadic relation is 'John gave the book to Jim.' This relation contains as its components the two dyadic relations 'John gave the book' and 'Jim received the book,' but these two dyadic relations do not together exhaust the triadic relation 'John gave the book to Jim,' since the same two dyadic relations would also be present in the case where John gave the book to Jane, who in turn gave it to Jim. Similarly, when a red light signifies to me that I should stop, it may be the case both that I see the red light and that I stop, but these conditions may hold without the red light signifying anything. For instance, I may see the red light, not register its significance, but stop because a pedestrian is crossing the street in front of me or for some other reason. So the two dyadic relations do not together constitute a sign relation. Generally, Peirce held, the physical world can be completely described in terms of dyadic relations and compounds of dyadic relations, whereas mental phenomena can only be described in terms of triadic relations.

This conception of sign needs to be distinguished from Charles Morris's (1946: 7) later, behaviorist definition, which owes a great deal to Peirce, but which Morris also took pains to distinguish from Peirce's definition:

If anything, A, controls behavior towards a goal in a way similar to (but not necessarily identical with) the way something else, B, would control behavior with respect to that goal in a situation in which it were observed, then A is a sign.

As has been noted, e.g., by Gérard Deledalle (2000: 116–18), and before that by Morris himself (1946: 288–9), this is a psychologistic and behavioristic definition, which on both counts diverges from Peirce's communicational definition. Deledalle (2000: 116–118) also correctly notes that Morris adopted Peirce's terminology, but gave Peirce's terms his own new meanings. For instance, Peirce's "interpretant" (of which more anon) is defined by Morris (1946: 17) not as a sign, but as a disposition to respond. What may be open to debate is whether Deledalle is also right in accusing Morris of dissolving Peirce's triadic relations into pairs of dyads. Morris (1946: 288) considered the question and concluded that the introduction of reinforcement into stimulus–response psychology made psychology itself triadic in the Peircean sense, a conclusion rejected by Deledalle (2000: 118). I suspect Deledalle is right, since any irreducibly triadic concept of reinforcement would need to be intensional in nature; any causal conception of reinforcement, such as would be required by any version of behaviorism familiar to me, would be readily reducible to sequences of dyads.

Let us return to the interpretant. It is essential to note that the interpretant of the sign is not identical to the interpreter; i.e., the individual mind interpreting the sign is *not* one of the three references that constitute signhood. The interpretant may, and perhaps normally does, arise in the consciousness of an individual subject, but the sign-character of the sign is not affected by whether or not it does, and an effect on an individual's consciousness is no part of the definition of a "sign." Peirce's semeiotic triad is thus quite different from Walker Percy's triad token–object–mind, exemplified by Helen Keller's mind-opening recognition that the tokens w–a–t–e–r being written into her one hand by her teacher stood for the water running over her other hand, thus constituting a triad among the tokens, the water, and Helen's mind which took one to stand for the other. Percy himself certainly expressed his awareness of this difference in his correspondence with Kenneth Ketner (Samway, 1995: 48). Without sharing Morris's behaviorism, Percy does seem to share his psychologistic conception of signhood. It is true that Peirce sometimes includes a reference to the individual subject, the sign-interpreter, as in this passage from 1897:

A sign, or representamen, is something which stands to somebody for something in some respect or capacity. It addresses somebody, that is, creates in the mind of that person an equivalent sign, or perhaps a more developed sign. That sign which it creates I call the *interpretant* of the first sign. (CP 2.228–9)

Here Peirce may appear to define "sign" in terms of the triad "something–somebody–some respect," i.e., object–interpreter–ground. But this is only an appearance; Peirce goes on, in the very next paragraph, to state that the representamen is "connected with three things, the ground, the object, and the interpretant," not the interpreter. And in his third Lowell Lecture of 1903, Peirce defines "representamen" without any reference to an interpreter:

A REPRESENTAMEN is a subject of a triadic relation TO a second, called its OBJECT, FOR a third, called its INTERPRETANT, this triadic relation being such that the REPRESENTAMEN determines its interpretant to stand in the same triadic relation to the same object for some interpretant. (CP 1.541)

Signs, it may be said, are of particular interest to us human beings because we do, after all, engage in the interpretation of signs, and because this interpretive activity is what constitutes our thinking. But our interpretive activity is in no way constitutive of the sign as a sign, and this is why Peirce can without circularity define thinking, and hence mind, in terms of semeiosis, or sign-action, as signs are in the first instance defined without reference to the interpreting mind. In other words, a potential interpretive activity is presupposed by the concept of signhood, but the subject of that activity is left undefined, *except* in so far as it is precisely the subject of an interpretive activity. This is, as, e.g., Deledalle (2000: 59–61, and *passim*) has noted, a mentalistic, not a materialistic, conception of signhood, but not a psychologistic one. The interpreter might, but need not, be an individual, and Deledalle (2000: 33) approvingly quotes this passage, one of many in which Peirce appears to locate the interpretive activity in the community, rather than in individual minds:

Meantime, we know that man is not whole as long as he is single, that he is essentially a possible member of society. Especially, one man's experience is nothing, if it stands alone. If he sees what others cannot, we call it hallucination. It is not "my" experience, but "our" experience that has to be thought of; and this "us" has indefinite possibilities. (CP 5.402)

Communication, it might be said, is not something we do with thoughts antecedently formed inside our heads. Communication, to Peirce, is the context in which thoughts are formed, and is logically prior to thinking processes taking place in individual minds.

What brings the sign into connection with its object is some material quality it possesses, which enables it to represent its object in a particular way. A picture signifies by means of an association that connects it, in the interpreter's brain, with its object. A weathervane or a tally signifies simply by being physically connected with its object by a chain of causation. Words, finally, can function as signs only because they are capable of being connected into sentences by means of a copula (CP 5.286). Later, Peirce was to classify all signs as *icons*, which signify by virtue of resemblance, *indices*, which signify by virtue of a physical connection with the object, and *symbols*, which signify by virtue of the existence of a rule governing their interpretation (CP 2.276–92). Now, the exact physical embodiment of symbols is of course largely, but not entirely, a matter of convention. The choice of Roman versus Old English lettering may be purely conventional, but that is certainly not the case with one's preference for Arabic over Roman numerals for the purpose of performing long division – a point also made by Peirce; cf. Eisele (1979: 11–34). The important point Peirce made in 1868, and was later to develop in depth, is that the existence of symbols depends crucially on the existence of a notation that is capable of symbolic interpretation, and moreover that our thinking is facilitated or impeded by the specific physical features of our notation.

In "On a New List of Categories," published in 1867, Peirce introduced his famous trichotomy among the three chief types of signs, or *representations*, as Peirce called them at this stage:

> First. Those whose relation to their objects is a mere community in some quality, and these representations may be called *likenesses* [later, *icons*].
>
> Second. Those whose relation to their objects consists in a correspondence in fact, and these may be termed *indices* or *signs*. [The term 'signs' was soon to be extended to cover all representations.]
>
> Third. Those the ground of whose relation to their objects is an imputed character, which are the same as *general signs*, and these may be termed *symbols*. (CP 1.558)

For instance, a weather vane, measles spots, temperature readings, billowing smoke, and exclamations of pain are indices, a painted portrait, an historical novel, or a theatrical performance is an icon, while a photograph or a televised news broadcast is both an icon and an index. The weather vane indicates the direction of the wind by virtue of having a causal connection of a certain kind to its object, the wind. A painted portrait signifies a person by resembling that person. A photograph signifies by means of both relations. An example of a symbol, finally, would be a word, in so far as it signifies by means of a purely conventional relation to its object – unlike, e.g., an onomatopoeia. The three types of sign, finally, stand in a hierarchical relationship: symbols presuppose icons for their own existence, while icons in turn presuppose indices.

The trichotomy of icon, index, and symbol, where signs are classified with specific reference to their relation to their object, is only one – albeit arguably the most basic one – of Peirce's various schemes for classifying signs. Another trichotomy divides signs into terms (later *rhemes*, corresponding to predicates), propositions (later *dicisigns*), and arguments (later *legisigns*); arguments are in turn deductive, abductive, or inductive, and so forth. Peirce's most famous three-dimensional classification of signs recognizes ten classes of signs. We have here only attempted an overview of the general structure shared by words, numerals, pictures, and other signs. Finally, in Peirce's view as in John Locke's before him, thoughts are signs and, as we shall see next, semeiotic thus implies a complete philosophy of mind, in which cognition is thematized as the development of signs, and not as a succession of conscious states of mind.

3. THE SEMEIOTIC MODEL OF THE MIND

Writers as diverse as the philosopher James Fetzer (1990: 31–50) and the novelist Walker Percy (1975: 3–45) have credited Peirce with developing a semeiotic model of the mind, i.e., a model in which sign interpretation and, with it, intentionality are essential attributes of the mind. We now take a closer look at what it means for the mind to be essentially a sign interpreter.

By claiming that all thinking is signification, i.e., the production and interpretation of signs, Peirce was not denying the psychological fact that thoughts can be subjectively experienced as internal states of mind; what he was claiming is that such experiences are *merely* psychological facts: "[Every] thought, in so far as it is a feeling of a peculiar sort, is simply an ultimate, inexplicable fact" (CP 5.289). The meaning or intellectual value of a thought lies in its potential for further interpretation, whether by my mind or by some other mind; that is, it lies in its signhood. Knowledge, in Peirce's semeiotic doctrine, consists less in states of mind ("ultimate, inexplicable facts") than in the potentiality of external objects to induce certain states of mind, and this potentiality depends on the specific physical characteristics of said external objects. Consciousness, Peirce held, is not an *essential* attribute of mind. Thus, in a discussion of the nature of psychology from 1902, Peirce wrote, "I hold that purpose, or rather, final causation, of which purpose is the conscious modification, is the essential subject of psychologists' own studies; and that consciousness is a special, and not a universal, accompaniment of mind" (CP 7.366). In an especially topical passage Peirce goes on to emphasize the dependence of our language faculty on external tools for linguistic expression:

A psychologist cuts out a lobe of my brain *(nihil animale a me alienum puto)* and then, when I find I cannot express myself, he says, 'You see, your faculty of language was localized in that lobe.' No doubt it was; and so, if he had filched my inkstand, I should not have been able to continue my discussion until I had got another. *Yea, the very thoughts would not come to me* [emphasis added]. So my faculty of discussion is equally localized in my inkstand. (CP 7.366)

Having discussed this passage in detail elsewhere (Skagestad 1999a), I will restrict my comments on this occasion. The context makes clear that one thing Peirce is doing in the passage quoted is to ridicule the idea that the faculty of discussion, or any other mental faculty, is localized in the brain or anywhere else. He is not saying, nor does he mean, that the faculty of discussion is localized in the inkstand. That it is not, becomes clear when he goes on to say, in the very next sentence, "It is localization in the sense in which a thing may be in two places at once" (CP 7.366). We might now be tempted to dismiss the reference to the inkstand as *only* a joke: localization in the sense in which a thing can be in two places at once is, of course, the same thing as no localization at all. So, it might be argued, what Peirce is doing is using the very ludicrousness of the idea of the mind being localized in an inkstand as a way of highlighting the equal ludicrousness of supposing the mind to be localized in the brain, or anywhere else.

This, however, will not quite do. The inkstand example is a joke on contemporary psychologists; no doubt about it. But those who would argue that the inkstand example is *only* a joke need to explain precisely how the ludicrousness of the inkstand-localization highlights the ludicrousness of the brain-localization. And when Peirce goes on to say, "On the theory that the distinction between psychical and physical phenomena is the distinction between final and efficient causation, it is plain enough that the inkstand and the brain-lobe have the same general relation to the functions of the mind" (CP 7.366), the answer plainly is that the inkstand and the frontal lobe stand either in identical or in some respect *equivalent* relations to the faculty of discussion. This relation is not literal localization, but rather something that may be called "virtual" localization. This concept, far from being an anachronism, would be quite congenial to Peirce, who traced the concept of virtuality to his intellectual hero

Duns Scotus, and who himself penned the definition of "virtual" in Baldwin's *Dictionary of Philosophy and Psychology*, to wit: "A virtual X (where X is a common noun) is something, not an X, which has the efficiency (virtus) of an X" (Baldwin, 1902: vol. 2, 763, CP 6.372). Similarly, the "localization" of the mind in the inkstand or the brain is not localization, but something which has the efficiency of localization, in the precise sense that this is where you look for the mind. In Peirce's view you do not find the mind inside the brain, any more than you find electricity inside copper wires – an analogy explicitly cited by Peirce. You find the mind where there are inkstands or other means of expressing thoughts, paper or other vehicles for preserving and conveying thoughts, and of course brains capable, through the intermediary of eyes and hands or the equivalent, of interacting with external tools and media. Again, in Peirce's words from 1902:

In my opinion it is much more true that the thoughts of a living writer are in any printed copy of his book than they are in his brain. (CP 6.364)

Underlying these utterances is a fully articulated and well documented semeiotic model of the mind, in which cognition is construed as the development of internal or external signs, and not as a succession of conscious states of mind. Like John Locke before him, and with explicit indebtedness to Locke, Peirce affirmed that thoughts are signs. Thought processes may and often do take place entirely tacitly, but what makes them thought processes is the sign character of the thoughts, and this character consists largely in their potentiality for being expressed and so being susceptible to interpretation. Peirce never denied the existence of consciousness, and he did not deny that we may have introspective knowledge of our conscious mental states, but he simply did not regard cognition as consisting of such conscious states. Cognition consists in the manipulation of signs which may be externally embodied; as each sign is what it is by virtue of its possible later interpretations – i.e., virtually – so the mind itself is virtual. In 1902 Peirce was explicitly arguing for the claim that the essence of mind is not consciousness, but purpose, or final causation. This view of the mind had already been articulated in some of Peirce's early writings, such as his classic 1868 articles which, as we saw earlier, also introduced Peirce's doctrine of signs:

Finally, no present actual thought (which is a mere feeling) has any meaning, any intellectual value; for this lies not in what is actually thought, but
in what this thought may be connected with in representation by subsequent thoughts; so that the meaning of a thought is altogether something
virtual.... At no instant in my state of mind is there cognition or representation, but in the relation of my states of mind at different instants there is.
(CP 5.289)

In a letter to the editor, William T. Harris, Peirce elaborated:

I do not say that we are ignorant of our states of mind. What I say is that the
mind is virtual, not in a series of moments, not capable of existing except
in a space of time – nothing in so far as it is at any one moment. (CP 8.284)

Students of recent philosophy have no doubt by this point found
themselves reminded of Ludwig Wittgenstein. Without wishing to
venture deeply into the very tricky question of the relation of Peirce's
thought to that of the later Wittgenstein, I cannot forbear to note
that Peirce is making a point similar to one which Wittgenstein
(1958: 152e) was later to make as follows in the *Philosophical
Investigations*:

We say "I am expecting him", when we believe that he will come, though
his coming does not *occupy our thoughts*. (Here "I am expecting him" would
mean "I should be surprised if he didn't come" and that will not be called
the description of a state of mind.)

As I understand Peirce, he would agree with Wittgenstein's paren-
thetical comment, but perhaps not with the sentence that precedes it.
Even when NN's expected arrival does occupy my thoughts, Peirce's
view is that what it means for his arrival to occupy my thoughts *is* my
later surprise should NN not show up, and *not* the conscious state
("a mere feeling") experienced while expecting NN; in other words,
what occupies my thoughts is not a state of mind. In Peirce's view,
that is, thoughts are inherently dispositional, a view echoing that of
Duns Scotus (whom Peirce greatly admired) and in turn later echoed
by Karl Popper, who held knowledge to reside exosomatically, in
books, articles, and the like, rather than in the conscious experience
of the authors or readers of said books, etc. That conscious experience – in Popper's view as in Peirce's – was rendered dispensable for
the analysis of knowledge or of mind by that inherently dispositional
nature of knowledge which allows knowledge to be exosomatically

embodied. In Popper's words, which strikingly recall Peirce's definition of 'sign' as something which is capable of being interpreted:

It is its possibility or potentiality of being understood, its dispositional character of being understood or interpreted, or misunderstood or misinterpreted, which makes a thing a book. And this potentiality or disposition may exist without ever being actualized or realized. (1972: 116)

A book, then, regarded specifically as a book, is neither a physical nor a mental object, but resides in a third realm which Popper (1972: 156) refers to as the world of "objective thought contents" and which is distinct from both the physical and the mental worlds. Similarly, when Peirce refused to locate the mind within the realm of consciousness, he was not being a materialist; he was not placing the mind within the physical world. In the inkstand example, to recall, the contrast is not drawn between consciousness and material objects, but between the brain and the inkstand – two *physical* locations – as the location of the faculty of discussion. And just as, to Popper, a book was not a purely physical object, so to Peirce the inkstand was not a purely physical object, but what, in his 1901 review of Karl Pearson's *The Grammar of Science*, he termed a "generalized percept" (CP 8.144).

While Popper does not, to my knowledge, comment on the specific material qualities that may characterize different books, Peirce's awareness of the importance of these material qualities is revealed, for instance, in his praising Charles Babbage (in an obituary in 1871) for publishing a volume of tables of logarithms where he tried fifty different colors of paper, and ten of ink, before settling on the combination that was easiest to read, and that thus maximized the cognitive value of the tables (W 2, 459). Peirce's praise of Babbage in this respect could of course be just a casual observation, of no philosophical significance; however, along the same lines he also credits Babbage with inventing a new notation for keeping track of the intricate workings of his "analytical engine." Later, in his article on "Logical Machines," Peirce (1887: 169) refers to algebra as "the best of all instruments of thought," and he goes on to credit its power, above all, to a purely notational feature, namely the parenthesis. The parenthesis, Peirce observes, could in principle be dispensed with through the use of placeholders to represent the results of intermediate operations – $(a + b) c = d$ could be written $a + b = t$, $ct = d$ – but at the expense of a notational clumsiness that would make algebra a less powerful instrument. And these are just a couple of examples of Peirce's numerous references to concrete instances where the specific material quality of a sign enables it to function as the precise kind of sign it is, thus in turn enabling the precise kind of reasoning it makes possible.

Peirce's observations in the previous paragraph recall the Sapir–Whorf hypothesis and its later offspring, the orality–literacy thesis. I want to make two comments on the relation of Peirce's semeiotic doctrine of mind to these later hypotheses.

In the first place, while Peirce is clearly embracing the view, later articulated by Sapir, Whorf, and others, that language is *a* medium of thought (although not the only one, and not necessarily the most important one), the pronouncements quoted above are quite neutral with respect to the Sapir–Whorf hypothesis proper. That is, the view that thinking with a pen is cognitively different from thinking without one, does not imply (or preclude) that thinking in one natural language is cognitively different from thinking in any other natural language. Nor, as far as I know, has Peirce ever commented on this question one way or another, or shown much interest in natural language – as opposed to specialized artificial languages – as a medium of thought. (I must, however, admit to not having read everything Peirce ever wrote.) On the other hand, what Peirce is saying clearly is at odds with the "mentalese" model which Steven Pinker (1994: 73–82) advocates as an explicit alternative to the Whorfian hypothesis: if thinking were simply and solely mental processing carried out by an internal Turing Machine, whose results are then translated into English, or whatever, then it would seem that the presence or absence of writing implements can make no difference to the thinking process.

In the second place, I do take Peirce to be embracing some version of the orality–literacy thesis later made famous by Eric Havelock, Walter Ong, Marshall McLuhan, and others, but it is important to specify precisely what *kind* of thesis is entailed or suggested by the inkstand example. If all thinking is sign action, then thinking is at least in part an exosomatic process (although not pure behavior), and our thinking processes – and to some extent perforce the content of our thinking – will vary with the sign vehicles available to us. While Peirce, as we have seen, is not denying the existence of consciousness, something else seems here to be either denied or relegated to an insignificant status, namely the occurrence of *unconscious* thought. Peirce, for the record, held that unconscious thought, while differing from conscious thought only by its lesser degree of susceptibility to being controlled, constitutes far and away most of our thinking (CP 6.569; 7.554, both cited in Brent, 1998). However, he clearly distinguished such thinking from reasoning, properly so-called (CP 7.458–9).

4. MINDS AND MACHINES

The relevance of Peirce's semeiotic to cognitive science has not gone unnoticed. For instance, in recent years James Fetzer (1990: 34–50) has contrasted Peirce's semeiotic model of the mind with the currently influential computational model of the mind. As has been pointed out by Fetzer (1990: 31–5), the Newell–Simon concept of the mind as an "abstract and physical symbol system," so fundamental to most if not all versions of the computational model, lacks the triadicity central to Peirce's concept of a sign. Specifically, it lacks the recognition that a sign is inherently a sign to someone. In the Newell–Simon model, symbols are symbols by virtue of certain formal features they display, irrespective of whether or not any organism (or machine) actually takes them to stand for anything. Fetzer has contrasted this model with Peirce's semeiotic model of the mind, in which the mind is essentially a sign user, and in which the recognition of something as a symbol (or any other sign) implies that it is a symbol to some sign-using organism (or machine). The thesis that a sign system cannot first be defined as a purely abstract, formal system, and then afterwards be given an interpretation – and so an interpreter – has of course been most famously argued by Hilary Putnam (1980: 464–82), in what George Lakoff (1987: 229–38) has called "Putnam's Theorem."

It has been pointed out by Eugene Freeman that Peirce's doctrine of signs implies that all reasoning is diagrammatic, a corollary repeatedly made explicit by Peirce himself, e.g., in this passage quoted by Freeman (Freeman & Skolimowski, 1974: 477, CP 3.393): "For reasoning consists in the observation that where certain relations subsist certain others are found, and it accordingly requires the exhibition of the relations reasoned within an icon." To avoid misunderstanding it must be stressed that Peirce is not saying, here or anywhere else, that all *thinking* is diagrammatic; by the word *reasoning* Peirce always means specifically the process of drawing inferences. The value of the iconic representation, Peirce repeatedly insisted, lay in the possibility it afforded of performing experiments on our thoughts, by changing some elements in the diagram and literally seeing new relations appear.

In keeping with this view, Peirce developed his system of "existential" graphs as a new notation for logic. (It is also not coincidental that Peirce wrote extensively on topology and cartography.) It has been claimed by Martin Gardner (1982: 54–8) that the graphs were not intended as a practical improvement over existing algebraic notations, but as a means of laying bare the diagrammatic essence of thought and laying before the reader, in Peirce's words, "a moving picture of thought." But this may be a false dichotomy, and Gardner certainly exaggerates when he postulates the need for "a gigantic effort of practice and study to master Peirce's intricate technique to the point of usefulness...." It has been brilliantly shown by Kenneth L. Ketner (1981: 47–83) that Peirce's graphical notation for propositional logic is not significantly more intricate or difficult to learn than the algebraic notation normally used in introductory logic courses. And John Sowa (1984: 149), working in the field of artificial intelligence, has gone further and argued that Peirce's graphs for first-order logic are easier to read and learn, make possible shorter and simpler proofs, and are thus of *greater* practical value to linguistics and artificial intelligence than the standard algebraic notation. Finally, Jay David Bolter (1991: 85–106) has recognized and documented the fruitfulness of Peirce's semeiotic for interpreting human–computer interaction in general, and hypertext in particular.

Be that as it may, a moving picture of thought can also be exhibited by a machine, as Peirce made clear in his 1887 article on the logic machines constructed by William Stanley Jevons and Allan Marquand:

The secret of all reasoning machines is very simple. It is that whatever relation among the objects reasoned about is destined to be the hinge of a ratiocination, that same general relation must be capable of being introduced between certain parts of the machine. (1887: 168)

To illustrate, the syllogism, 'If A then B; if B then C; therefore, if A then C,' can be embodied in a machine where pushing the lever A activates the piston B, which in turn rotates the wheel C, so that pushing A in effect activates C. Machines, then, are capable of reasoning, in the sense of drawing inferences, but in Peirce's view this is not a peculiarity of logic machines but a general characteristic of machines, including here a wide variety of apparatus not generally thought of as machines: "Accordingly, it is no figure of speech to say that the alembics and cucurbits of the chemist are instruments of thought, or logical machines" (1887: 168). Without here venturing into speculations about what Peirce *might* have said about modern digital computers, we shall observe that he pointed to two differences between people and the logic machines of his day.

First, machines are "destitute of all originality, of all initiative." In a machine, Peirce stresses, this is a good thing; it is precisely the machine's lack of originality that makes it predictable and hence useful; a balloon, for instance, has limited usefulness because it has too much initiative: "We no more want an original machine than a house-builder would want an original journeyman, or an American board of college trustees would hire an original professor" (1887: 169). This is precisely the view of machines later echoed by Popper, who referred to the computer as a "glorified pencil," as well as by computer pioneer J. C. R. Licklider. It was also expressed more than thirty years before Peirce wrote the above, by Charles Babbage's associate Lady Ada, Countess Lovelace, reputedly history's first computer programmer: "The Analytical Engine has no pretensions whatever to *originate* anything. It can do whatever we *know how to order it* to perform" (Bernstein, 1981: 57).

Second, Peirce observes, a logic machine is limited by its design: "it has been contrived to do a certain thing, and it can do nothing else" (1887: 189). Now, Peirce is not denying, but explicitly admitting, that there could be nondeterministic machines constructed like Jacquard looms, incorporating if–then loops, and capable of handling a great variety of problems (1887: 170). A propos of this, Ketner (1988: 50–1) has speculated that Peirce's pioneering distinction between corollarial and theorematic reasoning constitutes proof of the existence of a nondeterministic reasoning machine – which Ketner calls a "Peirce Machine" to distinguish it from the deterministic Turing machine. Peirce's insight was that mathematics itself makes use of – and has to make use of – reasoning which is not purely mechanical, but which essentially involves the formation and trying out of hypotheses. To what extent this reasoning can be represented in a machine, and to what extent Peirce thought it could, are how-ever questions beyond the scope of this paper. What we have seen is that, in Peirce's view machines, hard and soft, ranging from pens and inkstands to mathematical notations and logic diagrams, play a decisive and indispensable role in our thinking. And this recogni-tion, we have seen, is firmly rooted in Peirce's basic conception of thinking as sign action, which essentially involves physical sign ve-hicles, whose specific material qualities contribute to making them the particular types of sign they are, thus enabling us to think the types of thoughts we do think.

In the latter respect, as I have argued elsewhere (1993), Peirce's se-meiotic model of mind is relevant not only to artificial intelligence, but also to the socioculturally far more influential research program known as "intelligence augmentation," the program which brought us word processing, the personal computer, and the Internet. In the manifesto-like "Conceptual Framework" paper from 1962, which spelled out the goals and assumptions of the program, Douglas En-gelbart (1962: 9–11) argued that intelligence should not be regarded as located in the individual human mind, but rather in a *system* com-prising the human being, his/her language, artifacts for thinking – pencils, slide rules, computers, etc. – methods of thought, and finally training in the said methods and the use of the artifacts. He referred to this system as the HLAM-T system, short for "Human using Lan-guage, Artifacts, and Method, in which he is Trained." Within this framework we augment human intellect not by making individual human beings smarter, but by providing them with augmentation means – symbol systems, tools, and methods – so that the result-ing system will be smarter than the unaided human being. Engelbart was strongly influenced by Whorf, but not at all by Peirce. Yet in Engelbart's "Framework" paper we hear a distinct echo of Peirce's comparison and contrast between the human mind and Babbage's Analytical Engine. Like the engine, the human being is also limited by its design (1887: 169):

The unaided mind is also limited in this as in other respects; but the mind working with a pencil and plenty of paper has no such limitation.

No limitation, because the mind, considered as a sign user, does not reside inside our heads, but in the external field of sign-action, which is capable of indefinite augmentation through human inventiveness.

11 Beware of Syllogism: Statistical Reasoning and Conjecturing According to Peirce

I. PROBABLE DEDUCTION

Peirce wrote extensively on deduction, induction, and hypothesis beginning with the Harvard Lectures of 1865 and Lowell Lectures of 1866. The ideas that he examined in those early discussions were re-worked over nearly two decades until the comprehensive statement of his view contained in "A Theory of Probable Inference" of 1883 that was included in the *Studies in Logic, by the Members of the Johns Hopkins University* and is reprinted in W 4, 408–450. This remarkable paper developed a version of the Neyman–Pearson account of confidence interval estimation that incorporated the main elements of the rationale offered for its adoption in the early 1930s and presented it as an account of inductive inference.

In his retrospective reflection on the question of induction in 1902 (CP 2.102), Peirce revealed satisfaction with the views on induction advanced in 1883 and this attitude is confirmed in other remarks from that period. However, Peirce did express dissatisfaction concerning his notion of "Hypothetic Inference." Although Peirce called it Hypothetic Inference or Hypothesis from 1865 to 1883 and later, in 1902, Peirce replaced the term "Hypothesis" with "Abduction."

In what I said about "Hypothetic Inference" I was an explorer upon untrodden ground. I committed, though I half corrected, a slight positive error, which is easily set right without essentially altering my position. But my capital error was a negative one, in not perceiving that, according to my own principles, the reasoning with which I was there dealing could not be the reasoning by which we are led to adopt a hypothesis, although I all but stated as much. But I was too much taken up in considering syllogistic forms and the doctrine logical extension and comprehension, both of which I made more fundamental than they really are. As long as I held that opinion, my conceptions of Abduction necessarily confused two different kinds of reasoning. (CP 2.102)

Peirce's description of the situation seems reasonably accurate, as I hope to show.

Peirce's writings on logic in the period from 1865 to 1870 propose an account of a formal "unpsychologistic logic" that, unlike Frege's later discussion, applies to inductive and hypothetic inferences as well as to deductive inferences.[1] The account of deduction, induction, and hypothesis Peirce offered in these three series of lectures starts with Aristotle's theory of the categorical syllogism as improved by Peirce.

Following Aristotle, Peirce understood induction to exhibit the formal structure of a transposition of one of the premises and conclusion of a valid categorical syllogism (the "explaining syllogism"). In the case considered by Aristotle where the explaining syllogism is figure 1, mood AAA in Barbara, the conclusion of the induction is the major premiss (the "rule") of the "explaining" syllogism and the conclusion (the "result") of that syllogism replaces the major premiss. The minor premise (the "case") of the explaining syllogism remains a premise of the induction. Peirce claimed that this form of argument characterizes induction by "simple enumeration." A favorite example of Peirce's is the inference from information that a selection of cloven-hoofed animals that turn out to be neat, swine, sheep, and deer are also herbivorous to the conclusion that all cloven-hoofed animals are herbivorous. The explaining syllogism is: All cloven-hoofed animals are herbivorous (Rule); a sample of neat, swine, sheep, and deer is selected from the cloven-hoofed. (Case). Hence, the neat, swine, sheep, and deer selected are herbivorous. (Result).

Peirce clearly understood, of course, that the minor premise of a syllogism in Barbara could be a universal affirmative (A) proposition such as "All neat, swine, sheep, and deer are cloven-hoofed" rather than singular statements such as "this neat, this sheep, etc., are cloven-hoofed." But the minor premise of the "explaining syllogism" is retained as a premise of the induction when Rule and Result of the syllogism are transposed to yield the form of an inductive argument. And this minor premise or Case is intended to convey the information that a sample S of individuals have been selected from the population characterized by the middle term M.

According to Peirce's reading, however, the Case or minor premise of the explaining syllogism in Barbara reports more than that each of a given set of individuals is a member of the class characterized by the middle term M. A sample is taken from the class represented by the middle term (in our example, the cloven-hoofed). The report describes the specimens taken from the population characterized by the middle term by the minor term. In our example, it is reported that the specimens selected from the cloven-hoofed are particular specimens of neat, swine, sheep, and deer.

Moreover, in the syllogisms in Barbara eligible to be explaining syllogisms for inductions, the method of selection from the middle term M must be such that the specimens are consciously selected only on the basis of whether they exhibit the characteristics represented by the middle term (W 1, 264–5). In the example, the neat, the swine, the sheep, and the deer are not selected because they belong to one of these four species but solely on the basis of whether they are cloven-hoofed. This is the way Peirce characterized the method of selection in 1865. He used essentially the same characterization in the Lowell Lectures of 1866 but called the method of selection "random." In the 1869 "Grounds of Validity of the Laws of Logic," Peirce was assuming that the long-run relative frequency or statistical probability with which a member of a set will be selected given that it is selected at random is the same for all members of the set (W 2, 268).[2]

Peirce explicitly acknowledged that a psychological or epistemic constraint should be satisfied by the method of sampling.

When we say that neat swine sheep and deer are a sample taken at random of cloven-hoofed animals, we do not mean to say that the choice depended upon no other condition than that all should be cloven-hoofed; we can not know *that* and the presumption is the other way since there is a certain limitation of that class indicated by our having taken so few instances. What we mean, then, in saying that neat swine sheep and deer are taken at random from among the cloven-hoofed animals, is that being cloven-hoofed was the only condition that consciously guided us in the selection of these animals. (W 1, 433).

Peirce admitted throughout that he could not give a purely formal and, hence, logical (in the sense of unpsychological logic) characterization of the strength of inductive arguments. In this respect, they differed fundamentally from deductive arguments. There is no

notion of inductive consequence to correspond to deductive consequence that belongs properly to formal logic. But inferences, can
be classified as inductive on the basis of formal considerations
alone. In the late 1860s, his idea was to appeal to the transpositions of premises and conclusions of categorical syllogisms to provide the characterization.[3] This formal classification constituted
the basis for Peirce's claim that induction and hypothesis could
be objects of study under the rubric of an unpsychologistic formal
logic.

Peirce abhored vacuums in logical space. There is obviously another kind of transposition of the explaining syllogism in Barbara
where the minor premise or case and conclusion or result of that syllogism replace each other. Peirce proposed to think of the resulting
argument as instantiating hypothetic inference.

Hypothetic inferences, like inductive inferences, can be classified by purely formal and, hence "unpsychological" criteria. But the
strength of such inferences, like the strength of inductive inferences,
takes into account considerations that are not purely formal.

One of the problems internal to Peirce's approach is that at least
from the time of the Lowell Lectures of 1866, he wished to regard inference from sample frequencies to population frequencies or, more
generally, to statistical hypotheses as paradigmatic of inductive inference. The difficulty is that statistical claims such as "Most cloven-
hoofed animals are herbivorous" or "90% of cloven-hoofed animals
are herbivorous" are not categorical propositions and are difficult
to construe as categorical propositions for the purpose of integra-
tion into syllogistic argument. But if they could not be so integrated,
the forms of inductive inferences whose conclusions are statistical
claims could not be obtained by transposing the major premises and
conclusions of *categorical* syllogisms.

In 1883, Peirce clearly and explicitly recognized that statistical
claims that he took often to be major premises of the explaining syllogisms for induction in the earlier papers are not categorical propositions. He emphasized that the analogy between syllogisms of the
form "All M are P, S is M, therefore S is P" and probable deductions
of the form "The proportion ρ of the Ms are Ps; S is an M; therefore it
follows, with probability ρ, that S is P" and probable deduction is certainly genuine and important, there are four significant differences
between these modes of inference (W 4, 409–12)[4]:

(1) Probable deduction is related to syllogism as the quantitative branch is to the qualitative branch.

(2) All that is requisite for ordinary syllogism is that the three terms of the syllogism stand in some transitive relation such as inclusion, better than, etc. Probable deduction presupposes quantitative ratios. "For that there must be counting and consequently units must exist, preserving their identity and variously grouped together."

(3) In syllogism, the conclusion follows from the premises according to a formal relation of logical consequence. In probable deduction where the rule or surrogate major premise asserts that the proportion ρ of the Ms are Ps, the information that S is an M does not render the conclusion that S is P even probable. It is necessary that S be selected at random from the Ms. According to Peirce, the requirement of randomness takes into account various subjective circumstances such as the manner in which the premise has been obtained, the absence of countervailing considerations; "in short, good faith and honesty are essential to good logic in probable reasoning." "In choosing the instance S, the general intention should be to select an M, but beyond that there should be no preference; and the act of choice should be such that if it were repeated many times with the same intention, the result would be that among the totality of selections the different sorts of Ms would occur with the same relative frequencies as in experiences in which volition does not intermeddle at all." In other words, random selection is (a) selection without *deliberate* or conscious bias and (b) selection from the Ms that yields Ps with probability (according to the frequency interpretation favored by Peirce) equal to the proportion ρ in the Ms. Random selection, however, is not enough. "A card being drawn at random from a picquet pack, the chance is one-eighth that it is an ace, if we have no other knowledge of it. But after we have looked at the card, we can no longer reason that way."

(4) The conclusion of a syllogism is a necessary consequence. The conclusion of a probable deduction is only probable. That is to say, the rule or major premise of syllogism is such that the inference from Case (minor premise) to Result

(conclusion) is truth-preserving in all applications. In probable deduction, the inference preserves truth with a relative
frequency ρ. Peirce then asserts it is "useful" that we should
have a stronger feeling of confidence the higher the value
of ρ. Although Peirce would never call this degree of confidence a subjective or belief probability, it is clear in all
his writing that it has all the earmarks of what many con-
temporaries would call a subjective probability including the
disposition to take risks. For this reason, I am inclined to re-
construe Peirce's view as one that admits that inquirers may
assign subjective degrees of probabilistic belief to hypotheses
provided those degrees of belief can be grounded or justified
by knowledge of objective, statistical, or frequency probability. His objection is to taking numerically determinate judgments of subjective probability seriously in scientific inquiry
when they lack such grounding.

Peirce extended his account of probable deduction to inferences
from samples of n Ms to the proportions of Ps among the n Ms. He
first invoked the binomial distribution to determine the probability
(long-run relative frequency) of n-fold samples exhibiting any given
relative frequency of Ps among n Ms.

The Weak Law of Large Numbers implies that as n increases, the
probability of obtaining a relative frequency whose absolute difference from ρ is less than some specific value d converges to 1. Peirce
then used the normal approximation of the binomial distribution
(supported by the Central Limit Theorem) to sustain the following
argument he called "Statistical Deduction": The proportion r of the
Ms are Ps (Rule). S', S'', S''', etc. are a numerous set, taken at random from among the Ms. Hence, probably and approximately, the
proportion r of the Ss are Ps.

In keeping with his account of probable deduction, the "subjective" condition that the sample is taken at random should not be
part of the form of this argument. Peirce's concern to distill out
an unpsychologistic component of the reasoning involved precluded
this. Similarly "probably" qualifies the "mode" of the conclusion
and is not part of its content. "Approximately" here is intended to
suggest that the conclusion is not that the relative frequency is exactly r but that it falls in some more or less vaguely specified interval around r. Peirce used the normal approximation to the binomial

distribution to illustrate how bounds can be roughly specified for the interval depending on the sample size n.

The Harvard Lectures of 1865 do not explicitly mention direct inference from statistical hypotheses to the outcome of sampling exemplified by probable and by statistical deduction or the inverse inductive inference from the outcome of sampling to a statistical hypotheses. The Lowell Lectures introduce induction (in Lecture III) as inference of just this kind. However, in discussion of induction and hypothesis as transpositions of Premise and Conclusion of Syllogisms there is no discussion of how induction to statistical hypothesis is to be represented as such a transposition. Yet Peirce did recognize the main points of difference between syllogism and statistical deduction mentioned above in the 1866 Lectures. Apparently Peirce was thinking in 1866 of extending his 1865 account of induction (and hypothesis) to statistical cases but did not have answers of the sort he offers later on concerning the relations between propositions of the form "$r\%$ of Ms are Ps" and "All Ms are Ps" and gradually thought these matters through in the next decade.[5] Thus, the lectures and papers starting in 1866 seem to be attempts to adjust Peirce's engagement with the idea that induction and hypothesis are, formally speaking, transpositions of premises and conclusions of categorical syllogisms to transpositions of probable and statistical deductions. The 1878 and 1883 papers represent the culmination of this effort.[6]

2. TRANSPOSING PREMISES AND CONCLUSIONS OF EXPLAINING SYLLOGISMS AND APOGOGIC INVERSION

In the *Prior* Analytics, Aristotle characterized induction as the product of transposing the major premise and conclusion of a categorical syllogism in Barbara. The minor premise is retained and is spelled out as asserting that the individuals covered by the minor term S are members of the set characterized by the middle term M. But Aristotle also insisted on premising the converse of the minor premise, positing that the Ss are the only Ms. Like most commentators, Peirce took this to mean that Aristotle's induction is induction by complete enumeration and is thus, strictly speaking, a species of necessary or deductive inference (W 1, 263).

Peirce rejected this attempt to reduce induction to deduction. Neither induction nor hypothesis is reducible to necessary inference.

One could not come to know that the sample exhausts the population without some sort of induction. The information conveyed by the sample of Ms observed – to wit, the Ss – cannot warrant such a judgment.

This much Peirce explicitly stated in 1865. Yet Peirce did construe inductions to be transpositions of the major premise and conclusion of a categorical syllogism. In 1883, he explicitly abandoned the notion that an inductive inference is a transposition of the major premise and conclusion of a categorical syllogism. It is rather the transposition of the major premise or Rule of a statistical deduction and the conclusion or Result.

The statistical deduction has the following form: Statistical Deduction

Rule: The proportion r of the M's are P's.

Case: $s_1, s_2, \ldots, s_n$ belong to a numerous set S of objects taken at random from among the M's.

Result: The proportion r of the S's are P's (probably and approximately).

Induction is obtained by transposing the Rule and Result.

Induction

Result: The proportion r of the S's are P's.

Case: $s_1, s_2, \ldots, s_n$ belong to a numerous set S of objects taken at random from among the M's.

Rule: The proportion r of the M's are P's (probably and approximately).

Peirce justified the transposition that yields Induction from Statistical Deduction by arguing that the principle of statistical deduction is that two proportions, that of the Ps among the Ms and that of the Ps among the Ss, are approximately equal. That is to say, as long as the methods of sampling and the available evidence warrant the applicability of the calculus of probability, the weak law of large numbers and the central limit theorem insure that this probable and approximate equality holds. Peirce then wrote:

If then, this principle [of statistical induction] justifies our inferring the value of the second proportion from the known value of the first, it equally justifies our inferring the first from that of the second, if the first is unknown but the second has been observed (W 4, 416)

The phrase "equally justifies" calls for closer scrutiny, as Peirce well understood. In the passage cited from 1883, he claimed that he could specify conditions under which this claim could be made good. In the Harvard Lectures of 1865 and Lowell Lectures of 1866, he adopted a different rationale for claiming that there is equal justification for inferring population frequency from sample frequency as there is for inferring sample frequency from population frequency. He then became silent on the issue until 1878 when he came out with the new rationalization – one he expressed with great clarity in 1883. But in spite of an important change in his views of induction between the late 1860s and the late 1870s, throughout the entire period Peirce thought he could achieve legitimately what Aristotle attempted to achieve illegitimately by the illicit conversion of the minor premise of a categorical syllogism.

I believe that Peirce already endorsed many elements of his view in 1878 and 1883 in Lecture IV of the 1866 Lowell Lectures when criticizing J. S. Mill's contention that inductive inference is "grounded" on a Principle of the Uniformity of Nature (W 1, 420–1). Construing him this way provides a way to understand the argument of the Lowell Lectures even though those lectures often fail to be explicit about the various transitions in the argument.[7]

By using contraposition and conversion, one can transform valid first figure syllogisms into valid second and third figure syllogisms. To obtain the second figure the negation of the Case of a syllogism in Barbara becomes the conclusion and the negation of the Result a premise. To obtain a third figure, the negation of the Rule becomes the conclusion and the negation of the Result a premise. Peirce seemed to have been interested in these "apogogic inversions" because they look similar in form to hypothetic and inductive inference. But if the syllogisms are proper categorical syllogisms this is not strictly speaking so. In 1883, Peirce suggested that if the rule says that the proportion of Ps among the Ms is ρ, the negation of the rule is that the set of Ps among the Ms is one of the real values between 0 and 1 other than ρ. Using this and relying upon the weak law of large numbers, Peirce showed that the apogogic inversion of a statistical deduction is an induction. However, the statistical deduction of which it is an apogogic inversion is not the "explaining" statistical deduction whose rule and result are transposed to obtain the induction. And in the course of making the case for this view, Peirce wrote that it is necessary if an induction is to have any validity at all that the explanatory syllogism should be a valid statistical deduction.

"Its conclusion must not merely follow from the premises but follow from them upon the principle of probability. The inversion of *ordinary* syllogism does not give rise to an induction or hypothesis." That is because the inversion of an ordinary syllogism relies on an illegitimate conversion (W 4, 424–7).

Peirce expressed a similar view in "Deduction, Induction and Hypothesis" in the famous 1878 series published *Popular Scientific Monthly* (W 3, 328).

In "On the Natural Classification of Arguments" of 1867 (W 2, 48) Peirce pointed to "a resemblance between the transposition of propositions by which the forms of probable inference are derived and the contraposition by which the indirect figures are derived." Peirce does not, however, elaborate the point. Still this remark does appear to be an allusion to the idea contained in the 1878 and 1883 papers. Confidence in this interpretation is rendered insecure by the fact that nowhere in the 1867 essay did Peirce require explicitly that the explaining syllogism for an induction have a statistical premise as the Rule. That requirement is present in both 1878 and 1883. Nonetheless, the 1867 essay does suggest the possibility that induction (and hypothesis) could be construed as "apogogic inversions" of statistical deductions.

The Lowell Lecture Series of 1866 does not even recognize the analogy between transposing the Rule and the Conclusion of a syllogism in Barbara and obtaining a third figure syllogism by contraposition from the same syllogism. Yet the 1866 lectures do recognize inverse inference from sample to population frequencies as paradigmatic of induction and recognize the importance of the probable and approximate similarity between sample and population in this respect. Thus, there is a progression from the virtual absence of statistical considerations in Peirce's account of induction (and hypothesis) in 1865 to the irreducibly statistical account of induction offered in 1878 and 1883.

3. FREQUENTISM AND INSUFFICIENT REASON

Even in 1865, Peirce insisted that the Case or minor premise of an explaining syllogism reports that the *S*s (minor term of the explaining syllogism) are a selection from the class characterized by the middle term according to a method that took into account as a principle of selection whether the item is an M or not without regard to other considerations. This method of selection is called random selection in 1866 and thereafter. Again Peirce is more explicit in the later papers that selecting an item at random from a population licenses the assumption that the statistical probability of selecting one item from the population is the same as selecting any other item. This method of random selection is the guarantor of the validity of the probable deduction to the outcome of a single selection and of the statistical deduction to the probable and approximate equality of the sample frequency with the population frequency in a statistical deduction.

I have suggested that Peirce held that there are occasions when one may legitimately judge degrees of belief construed as dispositions to take risks of certain kinds. When the inquirer can justify the result of a statistical deduction by appeal to the statistical rule and the premise that the method of selection is a random one, then *ceteris paribus*, according a degree of belief that the result will be the true equal to the statistical probability of such a result happening due to such selection is legitimate. The problem that Peirce sought to address is how to show that the inverse inference obtained by transposing Rule and Result that is an induction entitles us equally to infer that approximately $r\%$ of the population of Ms are Ps from the data that in a large random sample of Ms, $r\%$ are Ps. Success in this required that no degree of belief be assigned to the conclusion unless it could be derived via equation with a statistical probability deduced according to a proper statistical deduction.

Peirce stood opposed to one approach that many students of induction including Bayes, Laplace, and DeMorgan had favored. Peirce enthusiastically endorsed George Boole's criticism of the use of insufficient reason arguments to form priors in order to obtain posteriors as early as 1865 and even more explicitly in 1866. If the proportion of red balls in the bag is unknown, it is still the case that by statistical deduction based on the weak law of large numbers and the central limit theorem one could claim that no matter what the percentage ρ of red balls in the urn is the true one, the relative frequency of red balls selected at random is with great probability (is almost certainly) approximately equal to ρ. If via the principle of insufficient reason, one assigns equal prior probability to each conjecture regarding the true value of the population frequency as Bayes, Laplace, and De Morgan recommended, then, according to Bayes' Theorem, the posterior probability conditional on evidence that the proportion of red balls in the large sample selected from the urn is r is going to be as high as approximately r of the balls in the urn from which the sample is taken are going to be red.

According to Peirce, the probability of a hypothesis conditional on evidence is the long-run relative frequency of obtaining a true conclusion from true data in inferences of that kind. The inverse inference appealing to insufficient reason would be acceptable to Peirce if the equal prior probability distribution over hypotheses concerning the proportion of red balls in the bag could be obtained on the ground that the bag from which the ball was selected was in turn selected at random from a bag of bags in which all possible proportions were present in equal proportions. Without some such assumption, the appeal to uniform prior probability and to Bayes' Theorem cannot yield a posterior construed in frequentist terms. In 1865 and 1866, Peirce expressed admiration for Boole's algebraic way of expressing the indeterminacy of the posterior probability derived from Bayes' Theorem when no prior is given (W 1, 238-9, 404-5). He also sharply criticized the principle of insufficient reason as a means for relieving the indeterminacy (W 1, 401-3). From the very beginning of his career, Peirce registered unwavering opposition to using insufficient reason and Bayes' Theorem to rationalize induction as Laplace had done.[8] In 1878, Peirce famously wrote:

The relative probability of this or that arrangement of Nature is something which we should have a right to talk about if universes were as plenty as blackberries, if we could put a quantity of them in a bag, shake them up, draw out a sample and examine them to see what proportion of them had one arrangement and what proportion another. But even in that case, a higher universe would contain us, in regard to whose arrangements the conception of probability could have no applicability (W 3, 300-01).

Peirce reinforced this objection to the use of numerically determinate prior credal or belief probabilities without grounding in knowledge of statistical probability with a more specific objection to insufficient reason. In 1866, he complained that if one is ignorant with respect to the truth of h and $\sim h$, insufficient reason assigns h a probability of $\frac{1}{2}$. However, one may be thus ignorant and also ignorant concerning the truth of h, h^*, and h^{**}, where $h^* \vee h^{**} = \sim h$. Insufficient reason recommends assigning h a prior probability of $1/3$. This verdict is inconsistent with the other one. But there is no principled way to resolve the conflict (W 1, 402).

4. UNIFORMITY OF NATURE

Peirce thought judgments of numerically determinate credal probability ought to be grounded in full belief that some statistical probability is true. Mill maintained that inductions ought to be grounded somehow in appeal to a major premise that, if true, would convert the induction into a categorical syllogism. Ultimately there would be a hierarchy of syllogisms where the fundamental major premise would be some principle of uniformity of nature. In 1865, Peirce complained that this demand for converting an induction into a syllogism threatens to yield an infinite regress of uniformity principles.

In 1866, Peirce added an additional more interesting cluster of complaints. The notion of uniformity is unclear. According to one of Mill's formulations, the universe "is so constituted, that whatever is true in one case, is true in all cases of a certain description" (*System of Logic*, v.1, Bk.3, Ch.3, §1). Peirce forcefully called into question the empirical warrant of this claim.

Every student of physics knows that a law which is exactly conformed to in nature without interference from other laws is almost if not quite unknown. Every law that is discovered therefore is found after a few years not to be exact. What do we say? Why that it is true in all cases of a certain description; but we haven't found of what description. . . .

There is still another sense in which we might speak of the uniformity of nature. If we select a good many objects on the principle that they shall belong to a certain class and then find that they all have some common character, pretty much the whole class will generally be found to have that character. Or if we take a good many of the characters of a thing at random and afterwards find a thing which has all these characters, we shall generally find that the second thing is pretty near the same as the first.

It seems to me that it is this pair of facts rather than any others which are properly expressed by saying that nature is uniform. We shall see that it is they which are the leading principles of scientific inference. (W 1, 420.)

Peirce distinguished between formal laws that would hold no matter what the "state of things" might be and material laws that do not.

He argued that the uniformity principle he endorsed will hold as long as there are any laws whatsoever. Since the existence of some laws is a precondition of knowledge, the uniformity he favors is a formal condition of all knowledge.

Peirce then went on to state that the prediction of the approximate equality of the proportion of Ps in the total population of Ms and the proportion found in a random sample of Ms corresponds to a special uniformity in the world. "It is the type of all uniformity and all induction. *Statistics;* that is induction" (W 1, 423).

Peirce clearly thought that adopting this notion of Uniformity of Nature did not adequately account for inductive – i.e., statistical – inference, but merely rebaptised the challenge to do so.

The crucial point is that by the end of this discussion, Peirce had explicitly acknowledged even in 1866 that the conclusion of an induction did not have to be universal or approximately universal. Any proposition stating that the proportion of Ms that are Ps is approximately r can be the conclusion of an induction. In cases like estimation of a statistical parameter such as the proportion of red balls in the bag, all that is required is that the proportion be one of the possible relative frequencies.[9] This is an important departure from Mill's understanding of uniformity.

5. NUISANCE INFORMATION

The progression in the emphasis Peirce placed on statistical considerations in his discussion of induction in 1878 and 1883 pivots on his appeal to the Weak Law of Large Numbers and the Central Limit Theorem in the calculus of probabilities to derive the validity of statistical deductions. Given the rule that states that the proportion r of Ms are Ps and the information that $s_1, s_2, \ldots, s_n$ are a numerous random sample from the Ms, statistical deduction warrants the conclusion that probably and approximately the proportion r of Ss are Ps. That is to say, probably the sample will be representative of the population when the proportion r of Ss are Ps. Moreover, for large n, this claim will hold for all proportions between 0 and 1 inclusive. Consequently, the inquirer who knows nothing about the outcome of the random sample to be taken other, perhaps, than that it will be taken can use statistical deduction and the calculus of probabilities to conclude that the outcome of random sampling will be representative with very high probability concerning the proportion of Ps among the Ms. Hence, the inquirer is entitled before sampling to be nearly certain that he or she will obtain such a representative sample.

Once the sample is taken and the proportion of Ps among the Ss ascertained, the inquirer must reassess his subjective probabilities in the light of the new information available.

Suppose, for example, that an inquirer X intends to sample at random from cloven-hoofed animals, take note of the percentage of herbivorous animals among them, and then estimate that the percentage of cloven-hoofed animals that are herbivorous is approximately equal to the percentage in the sample. Prior to sampling, statistical deduction will warrant almost certainly that the approximate estimate of the population frequency will be true. The inquirer engages in the sampling and obtains the following information:

(1) S is the random sample of Ms. Specimens of neat, swine, sheep, deer have been selected.
(2) The percentage of Ps among the Ss is r.

Can the inquirer conclude via statistical deduction that it is almost certain that the proportion of Ms that are Ps is approximately r as he or she could prior to obtaining the information specified under (1) and (2)? I believe that Peirce gave one answer to this question in 1865 and 1866 and another answer in 1878 and 1883.

Peirce clearly recognized, as is evident from his review of John Venn's *The Logic of Chance* in 1867, that the desired inductive conclusion cannot be derived via statistical deduction from the information contained in (1) and (2). He had already rejected using Bayes' Theorem to secure high probability for that conclusion. So he insisted that no grade of probability grounded in frequencies could be assigned to the conclusion.

What is the problem with continuing to judge it highly probable that the sample is representative? Take first the information about the sample frequency contained in (2). Given the information that the sample frequency is r, the probability that the sample is representative is 1 given a population frequency near r and is 0 otherwise. We can no longer argue that it is almost certain that the sample is representative no matter what the proportion of Ps in the population of Ms is.

Consider now the information given in (1). Even if the information about the sample frequency were unknown to X, knowing that the random sample contained specimens of neat, sheep, swine, deer *might*, as far as X knew, be relevant to being herbivorous in the sense that the frequency of being herbivorous among these kinds of animals is not typical of the entire cloven-hoofed population. To do a proper statistical deduction, X would need to have established that the information that the specimens are of neat, sheep, swine, and deer is irrelevant on the basis of information about frequencies. (This is the burden of the criticism of Venn in Peirce's 1867 review.) Typically this could not be done either.

6. INDUCTION AND SEMEIOTIC

Peirce's initial proposal for addressing these difficulties called for an appeal to a theory of signs. The 1865 and 1866 papers, as well as the series of papers given to the American Academy of Arts and Sciences in 1867, presented the first versions of what later became Peirce's semeiotic. He introduced these ideas into these papers, I contend, in order to provide a basis for confronting the problem of nuisance information in the reference class that faced his account of induction.

Space does not permit an extended discussion of Peirce's early theory of representations. But a brief summary is in order. There are three types of representations: signs (later indices), copies (later icons), and symbols. Neither signs nor copies convey information. Signs have denotation, extension, or breadth but no connotation, comprehension, or depth. Copies have depth but no breadth. Symbols have depth and breadth and carry information. More important, however, is Peirce's insistence that the depth and breadth of a symbol are determined by the information or belief state of the inquirer. According to an inquirer X, the "informed breadth" of a term S is the set of objects of which S might be true as far as X knows. The informed depth of S is the set of traits attributable in the light of what X knows to an object of which S is predicated. If the inquirer's state of information is held constant, term M has more informed breadth than term S if and only if it has less informed depth than S. Both informed breadth and informed depth can increase, however, if the inquirer's state of information increases.

Observe that the claim that S is a random sample from M is the minor premise of the "explaining syllogism." That is the information conveyed by (2). That the proportion of Ps among the Ss is r conveyed by (1) is the conclusion of the explaining syllogism or, more accurately according to the later work, the probable deduction.

The inductive conclusion is obtained by substituting M for S in premise (1). To come to believe that approximately $r\%$ of Ms are Ps involves an increase in information. Peirce characterizes this situation in the following manner.

The extension or breadth of M is at least as great as that of S both relative to the information before and after the shift (typically it is known to be greater). The substitution, as a consequence, incurs a risk of error that may act as a deterrent to the inquirer X. To overcome this risk, the inquirer needs an incentive. That is provided by the fact that the replacement of S by M in (1) increases the informed depth of M due to the addition of the predicate P to its informed depth. And this increase yields an increase in information by adopting the conclusion of the induction. Whether the increase is sufficient to justify the induction depends on the "preferences" of the inquirer. It reflects the extent to which he or she is prepared to risk error to obtain new information.

There is one setting in which the trade-off automatically favors making the substitution of M for S. That is in the case where S is a list of the specimens (the neat, swine, sheep, and deer) selected at random from the Ms. According to Peirce, even if the descriptions of the individuals selected are symbols, the disjunctive term S (is a neat or a swine or a sheep or a deer) is not, according to Peirce, a symbol because it does not characterize any common feature of the alternative species and, hence, carries no information. Peirce then argued that there is an "absolute" preference for "$r\%$ of Ms are Ps" (where M is a symbol) over "$r\%$ of Ss are Ps."

According to Peirce's view, an inquirer is not entitled to assess risk in terms of degrees of belief unless the degrees of belief can be grounded in knowledge of probabilities as frequency in the long run. Peirce denied that this was feasible even in the 1865 Harvard Lectures. Hence, the acknowledged tension between risk of error and value of information gained is not representable as a weighted average of probability of error and the value of information. In the absence of a quantitative representation, Peirce understood the matter to be one of a comparative "preference." And it is possible for one inquirer to refuse to draw the inductive inference whereas the other endorses it.

In the case of induction by simple enumeration, however, the pressure is much stronger – or so insisted Peirce. The nuisance information contained in (1) is no information at all. The disjunctive symbol S has no informed depth. The claim that S is a sample selected at random from the Ms is as informative as the claim that a random sample was selected from the Ms. Hence, the claim that S is P is no more informative than the addendum that the sample randomly selected is included in the Ps. Peirce seemed to think that as long as the term M had more informed depth than S (according to the state of information before reaching the inductive conclusion), the inquirer ought to have a marked preference for "All M are P" then for "All S are P" and, hence, should take the inductive leap. In effect, the inquirer is entitled to ignore the nuisance information contained in S because there is none.

Even if one endorses the distinction between real properties and mere predicates that so many authors advocate these days and denies that disjunctions of real properties are real properties, the strong claims Peirce makes about absolute preference do not appear to follow from the concession. Peirce abandoned this proposal silently, but I believe fairly quickly, in the late 1860s and early 1870s. He explicitly rejected it at the turn of the twentieth century. And by 1878 he had offered an alternative approach to replace this method of finessing the nuisance information.

In spite of its brief duration as Peirce's method of dissolving the problem of nuisance information, this idea is important to the understanding of Peirce's thought for two reasons: (a) it establishes that Peirce's semeiotic was initially used as a means of dissolving some difficulties in Peirce's account of induction and hypothesis and (b) it contributes to our understanding of the reasons why Peirce eventually abandoned the notion of hypothetic inference as distinct from induction and replaced it by a rather different idea at the beginning of the twentieth century.

In addition, it is worth noticing that in 1865 and 1866, Peirce toyed with the idea of rationalizing ampliative reasoning as a quest to seek truth while shunning error in a context where seeking truth and avoiding error means seeking more information while avoiding error and where this objective is seen as a characterization of common features of proximate goals of specific inquiries.

Before turning to the reasons that led to replacing hypothetic with abductive inference, it is time to explain how Peirce came to think of induction in 1878 and 1883.

7. PREDESIGNATION AND SELF-CORRECTION

An inquirer X intends to sample at random from cloven-hoofed animals, take note of the percentage of herbivorous animals among them, and then estimate that the percentage of cloven-hoofed animals that are herbivorous is approximately equal to the percentage in the sample.

Prior to sampling, statistical deduction will warrant almost certainly that the policy the inquirer intends to adopt for making estimates of the population frequency will be true. At that stage, for example, the inquirer will not know what the specimens selected at random from the cloven-hoofed animals are. *Retrospectively*, however, the statistical deduction is undermined by the information that the sample selected is a sample of Ss and that the proportion of Ps in the sample is r.

Moreover, those who seek to use Bayes' Theorem to derive a posterior probability on the data for a statistical conjecture or who seek to use Peirce's early approach to exploit the information obtained retrospectively from the data to make a judgment seem to be in some difficulty.

In 1878 and 1883, Peirce proposed to think of the inquirer as adopting a program *prospectively* for using the data to make statistical estimates. The inquirer chooses a program suited to his or her objectives and then subsequently implements it. Implementation will require collecting data; but the inquirer is committed to using the data as input into the program adopted beforehand.

Before implementing the program, the inquirer can use statistical deduction to argue that the policy of estimating the population frequency to be approximately equal to the sample frequency is almost certainly true. The inquirer at that point lacks the sort of nuisance information that could interfere with statistical deduction.

If in sampling any class, say the M's, we first decide what the character P is for which we propose to sample that class, and also how many instances we propose to draw, our inference is really made before these latter are drawn, that the proportion of P's in the whole class is probably about the same as among the instances that are to be drawn, and the only thing we have to do is to drawn them and observe the ratio. But suppose we were to draw our inferences without predesignation of the character P; then we might in every case find some recondite character in which these instances would agree. (W 4, 434)

The approach expressed here is a clear formulation of the approach advocated nearly 50 years later by J. Neyman and E. S. Pearson and elaborated by A. Wald. Indeed, Peirce, like these authors, required not only that the "characters" whose frequency in the population is to be estimated be specified in advance but also that the size of the sample (as the passage clearly indicates) be stipulated beforehand. The injunction against "optional stopping" is a key methodological marker distinguishing advocates of the Neyman–Pearson–Wald approach to statistics from advocates of the Bayesian approach and their cousins, advocates of the likelihood view.

The innovation is not merely that calculations of probability are relative to the information available to the inquirer before the experiment is instituted but that a plan for implementing a program for taking decisions or reaching conclusions is adopted relative to the pre-experiment information. Moreover, steps are taken to somehow "bind" the experimenter to following that program even after collecting the data necessary to implementing the program.

Peirce did not entirely appreciate the force of his own invention. He continued to think of induction as "inference" from data taken to be premises to an inductive conclusion even in 1878 and 1883. Inference calls for using the data reports as premises judged true, on the basis of which the conclusion is added to the body of beliefs. The data are not used as premises, according to the Peirce–Neyman–Pearson–Wald account. Using data as premises is precisely the source of the difficulties Peirce, Neyman, and Pearson all sought to circumvent. Data are used as "input" into a program that determines what is to be added to an inquirer's beliefs.

In my judgment there is a form of inference from premises recognizable as inductive; but implementation of the kind of preplanned program for adding new information envisaged by Peirce does not fill the bill. Indeed, Peirce's view of induction after 1878 and 1883 and in all subsequent writing stands opposed to any evaluation of hypotheses on the basis of data after the data are collected that may be called inference from premises to conclusion.[10]

Nonetheless, Peirce did worry about retrospective assessment of hypotheses. In 1878, Peirce commented on an inference from a sample of Cretans all of whom are liars to "pretty much" all Cretans are liars: "whether there may be any special probability in that, I do not know" (W 3, 303). On the other hand, in cases where samples of Ms are all Ps, the long-run frequency of claims of the type "Nearly all Ms are P" is very close to 1.

Peirce's remark in 1883 on statistical deduction and induction is both revealing and more interesting:

These two forms of inference, statistical deduction and induction, plainly depend upon the same principle of equality of ratios, so that their validity is the same. Yet, the nature of the probability in the two cases is very different. In the statistical deduction, we know that among the whole body of M's the proportion of P's is ρ; we say, then, that the S's being random drawings of M's are probably P's in about the same proportion, – and though this may happen not to be so, yet at any rate, on continuing the drawing sufficiently, our prediction of the ratio will be vindicated at last. On the other hand, in induction we say that the proportion ρ of the sample being P's, probably here is about the same proportion in the whole lot; or at least, if this happens not to be so, then on continuing the drawings the inference will be not *vindicated* as in the other case, but *modified* so as to become true. The deduction, then, is probable in this sense, that though its conclusion may in a particular case be falsified, yet similar conclusions (with the same ratio ρ) would generally prove approximately true; while the induction is probable in this sense, that though it may happen to give a false conclusion, yet in most cases in which the same precept of inference was followed, a different and approximately true inference (with the right value of ρ) would be drawn. (W 4, 416–7)

As I understand this passage, in making the estimate that the proportion of Ms that are Ps is ρ, the inquirer may fail to add the estimate to his or her stock of full beliefs. In that case, the inquirer might declare that obtaining more data and making a fresh estimate (using the new data as input) would either "vindicate" the first estimate or "correct" it. Alternatively the inquirer might actually come to full belief that the first estimate is true. The inquirer might then think that there is little point in an additional test because given the truth of the first estimate the probability of vindication by repeat performance would be very high indeed. Nonetheless, the inquirer should still admit that if counter to fact the first estimate were false, the new estimate would uncover the mistake.

As the passage just quoted indicates, Peirce thought that claiming that the "conclusion" is probable meant something different than it did in the case of probable deduction. Thus, he stood in disagreement with Bayesians and with advocates of Fisher's fiducial argument. What the claim that the conclusion is probable means is that the conclusion was reached by a highly reliable procedure that if reapplied would uncover any mistake in the estimate. Induction is in this sense *self-correcting*.

Peirce did not offer this account of induction as his contribution to solving Hume's problem of induction. He did think that his account avoids presupposing any principle of uniformity of nature or universal causation. Even so, the inquirer needs to assume beforehand not only the truth of the statistical model (or, at least, of some alternative very similar to that model) but also that the method of sampling implements the requirements of randomness necessary for the acquisition of the kind of data demanded by the model. So induction relies on "matters of fact" that go well beyond the testimony of the senses and the records of our memory. Since Peirce did not demand a justification of current beliefs not subject to serious doubt, this circumstance did not appear a problem to him. For the same reason, Peirce did not seek to avoid Hume's problem by pressing for vindication rather than validation in the sense of Reichenbach, Feigl, and Salmon. He did not think that induction is "self-correcting" in the rather laughable sense promoted by Reichenbach according to which the inquirer interested in positing a limit of relative frequency keeps "correcting" his or her estimates with the acquisition of new data *ad infinitum*.

There is one serious problem with the account of Peirce's view of induction I have just presented. If data are used as input and not as premises, then induction can no longer be considered as inference from premises to conclusion. To be sure, we sometimes speak of drawing inferences from suppositions taken as true for the sake of the argument, but the premises of an inference are otherwise claims judged to be true and used as evidence in justifying the addition of the conclusion to the stock of beliefs. When data are used as input, they are neither suppositions nor premises judged to be true. Since Peirce continued in 1883 to think of inductive inference as an argument from premises to conclusion exhibiting the form of a transposition of the major premise of a statistical deduction and its conclusion, his views seem to contain elements in some tension.

I doubt very much that Peirce succeeded in completely removing this tension in his ideas. But he took a large step in that direction when at the turn of the century he explicitly abandoned two key elements of his earlier account of induction:

(a) The appeal to semeiotic considerations of informed breadth, depth, and information.
(b) The emphasis on taking induction as a transposition of premises and conclusion of a syllogism.

Feature (a) had already been abandoned silently by 1878. Feature (b) had been explicitly modified in 1878 and 1883. At the turn of the century, Peirce realized he had to retrench still more. His reasons had to do with his misclassification of the types of inference he called "hypothetic" as distinct from inductive inference.

8. INDUCTION, HYPOTHESIS, AND ABDUCTION

When Peirce introduced hypothetic inference in 1865 and 1866, he characterized it in terms of its form and contrasted this form with the form of its explaining syllogism and the inductive inference that shared the same explaining syllogism. Peirce attached some importance to this point. Logic is unpsychologistic because it investigates forms. In the case of deductive logic, validity is itself a purely formal matter. By way of contrast, inductive and hypothetic validity are not characterizable entirely in terms of formal considerations. But the forms of inference eligible for evaluation with respect to their strength as inductive or hypothetic arguments can be identified.

By 1883, Peirce had broken with the idea that induction and hypothesis are transpositions of *categorical* explaining syllogisms. Inductive inferences are obtained by transposing the major premise of a statistical deduction with the conclusion after the fashion already explained. Hypothetic inference is also obtained by transpositions of premises and conclusions of statistical deductions. And they differ from inductions in that the transposition is of the minor premise with the conclusion. But the statistical deduction whose premise and conclusion are transposed has a different structure from the explaining statistical deduction for induction. It is a "statistical deduction in depth." The idea seems to be this.

The major premise of the statistical deduction in depth asserts that all Ms are P_1s, P_2s, ..., P_ns. S has an r-likeness to the Ms. Hence, probably and approximately, S resembles an M in r out of the n respects P_i.

There are several unexplained features of this mode of inference. One concerns the interpretation of "r-likeness." Peirce couched matters this way to guarantee that the explaining deduction is transformed into a hypothetic inference by transposing the minor premise and the conclusion. Immediately after presenting his idea, Peirce conceded that in the "extended sense" he had given to the term induction, the argument "is simply an induction respecting qualities instead of respecting things." The P_is are "a random sample of the characters of M and the ratio r of them being found to belong to S, the same ratio of all the characters are concluded to belong to S" (W 4, 419). This suggests an alternative explaining statistical deduction for the so-called hypothetic inference. The major premise asserts that object S has proportion r of the (relevant) characters of Ms. A random sample has been taken of the characters of Ms. Hence, probably and approximately, S has the proportion r of the characters thus selected. By transposing the major premise and conclusion of this probable deduction, the same inference initially classified as hypothetic is exhibited in the form of an induction.

Peirce preferred presenting the inference as hypothetic because of the impossibility of "simply counting qualities as individual things are counted. Characters have to be weighed rather than counted" (W 4, 419). But he clearly had appreciated that the inference could be classified one way or the other. And, in any case, both induction and hypothesis were recognized by Peirce to be ampliative rather than explicative.

Apparently the awkwardness of his system of classification eventually led Peirce to abandon the basic template for classifying scientific inferences that he had used from 1865 to 1883 when he made his most important contribution to the foundations of statistics. By the beginning of the twentieth century Peirce acknowledged not only that his use of his semeiotic to assess the acceptability of inductive and hypothetic inference was overblown but also that so was his use of permutations of syllogisms to classify ampliative inferences into inductive and hypothetic inferences.

Peirce replaced his earlier classification with a new, more ramified account. A division between deduction, induction, and abduction (or retroduction) replaced the trichotomy between deduction, induction, and hypothesis. The change was more than terminological and cosmetic. As already noted, deduction included not only categorical syllogism, propositional logic, the logic of relations, and quantification but also probable and statistical deduction. Both probable (and statistical) deduction are used in scientific inquiry to explicate the consequences (more crucially the testable consequences) of conjectures proposed as answers to a question or problem under investigation. Abduction yields the conjectures. Induction invokes the data obtained by observation or test on the basis of which conjectured answers to the given question are eliminated.

Although Peirce insisted throughout that this classification is of different types of inference, it seems to me better to think of it as focused on different *tasks* that are undertaken in problem-solving inquiry. One needs to identify potential answers to the question under investigation. That is the task of abduction. Deduction focuses on deriving (either apodictically or probabilistically) consequences of conjectures that were obtained via abduction. Induction evaluates the status of conjectures as a result of testing.

The model is neither the hypotheticodeductive model nor a falsificationist model. According to Peirce, the "deductive" component concerns deduction broadly conceived to include statistical deduction. And Peirce appreciated (as Braithwaite later did but Popper apparently did not) that the rejection of a statistical conjecture because the predictions derived via statistical deduction are observed to be false is an ampliative inductive inference.

In his later years, Peirce could understand induction in this way because induction included all ampliative reasoning. In a draft of a letter to Paul Carus from 1910, published as CP 8.214–239, induction so conceived included (a) quantitative induction, induction from a sample whose representativeness of the population from which it is sampled is secured by random sampling; (b) qualitative induction, which Peirce admitted he classified as hypothetic reasoning in 1883; and (c) crude induction, which appears to be induction by simple enumeration.[11]

Throughout this discussion the appeal to transpositions of syllogisms is completely forgotten, as is the semeiotic. There is no effort to offer an account of the difference between deduction, induction, and abduction as a distinction between inferences of different forms. Peirce's early attempts to understand some aspects of scientific reasoning other than deductive logic as part of formal logic are abandoned. The distinction between deduction, induction, and abduction focuses on the differences between the *tasks* that an inquirer will have to address in problem-solving inquiry.

Consider, for example, the task of identifying potential solutions or answers to a given question or problem. That is the task of abductive reasoning. Abductive inference is from the puzzling phenomenon to a conjectured potential answer. Once a potential answer has been proposed, one might bring general critical principles to bear in ascertaining whether the putative potential answer is one that is relevant to the question under study. Peirce thought that there are general principles for evaluating such abductive claims.

The pragmatic or pragmaticist principle is the fundamental principle of abduction. It is not a general principle for distinguishing truth-value-bearing judgments from other kinds of judgments. It distinguishes between propositions that qualify as potential answers to the problem under investigation and propositions that do not by reference to their testable consequences. Here the consequences are consequences of the potential answers given the initial settled body of background knowledge already taken for granted as perfectly free from doubt (though vulnerable to further scrutiny if the results of subsequent inquiry warrant raising new doubts). Since the background knowledge can change, the conditions for being a potential answer can change. Peirce's pragmatic principle is not a verificationist surrogate for truth.

Deduction (which includes both necessary and probable deduction) is used to elaborate the testable consequences of the conjectures formed via abduction. Induction (whether quantitative, qualitative, or crude) contributes to confirming or disconfirming these conjectures. Disconfirming a conjecture, like confirming it, is, in general, an ampliative induction because, for Peirce, conjectures will typically involve some sort of statistical element.

Thus, Peirce's mature view was (a) strongly opposed to the sort of probabilism so widely endorsed by philosophers who endorse Bayesianism, (b) supportive of the importance of forming testable conjectures, as Popper insisted, but (c) in opposition to both the probabilists and the Popperians, strongly in favor of ampliative induction.

It is also clear that by the end of his career, Peirce had jettisoned the narrow antipsychologistic view of the logic of scientific inference with which he had begun. Unlike Carnap and Popper, who sought to keep logic free of context-sensitive normative components, Peirce came to acknowledge the centrality of normativity and context to logic. This must be so once the distinction between the three kinds of "inference" is based on the difference in the tasks and, hence, the aims of these kinds of reasoning. I believe that this heightened sensitivity to context derived from the lessons he learned while attempting to address statistical reasoning – a topic that remained at the core of his philosophical interest from the beginning of his career to its end.

Early on (W I, Lecture VI), Peirce warned of the dangers of too much reliance on syllogistic reasoning. But Peirce himself actually sought to build his account of induction and hypothesis on the formal relations between these kinds of reasoning and deduction – especially syllogism. He came to appreciate fully the dangers of such reliance only in the last decade of his career.

Peirce should not be faulted for his slowness to see the dangers of flirting with transpositions of the syllogism. Much twentieth century and contemporary thought on induction and probability remains too closely tied to paradigms characteristic of deductive reasoning. To Peirce's credit, he appreciated the serious difficulties confronting those who embrace some form or other of probabilism and those who have been bewitched by the deductivism and falsificationism of Popper. He had an understanding of the distinctive issues that the "nonmonotonicity" of inductive reasoning generates. And he did propose an account of "inductive behavior" that anticipated the ideas of Neyman and Pearson a half century before they presented them. His pragmatic principle, taken as the fundamental principle of abduction, is a sophisticated version of Popper's demarcation criterion. But unlike Popper, who seemed mysteriously to think that producing testable conjectures via abduction might have a point without the inductive reasoning needed to decide between them, Peirce understood that the testing of conjectures called for more than deductive reasoning. Peirce learned to be wary of syllogisms in a way that neither Carnap, Popper, nor their epigones ever managed to do.

NOTES

1. The documents to which I refer include the Harvard Lectures of 1865 and Lowell Lectures of 1866 (W 1); "The Classification of Arguments" and "Upon Logical Comprehension and Extension" of 1867, the review of Venn's *Logic of Chance* of 1867, and "Grounds of Validity of the Laws of Logic; Further Consequences of Four Incapacities" of 1869 (W 2).

2. I have no doubt that he assumed this in 1865 as well although there is no textual evidence to support this claim. It seems that Peirce at the very outset of his career thought of inductive inference in a statistical setting where probability is understood in terms of long-run or limiting relative frequency. However, his appreciation of the significance of statistical considerations for his view of induction and hypothesis as transpositions of syllogisms seems to have undergone important changes from that time through 1883, as I shall try to explain.

3. Peirce contended (W 1, 265–6) that other forms of inductive argument can be obtained by transposing syllogistic forms in the second and third figure legitimated by contraposition. (Such transformations are "apogogic inversions." Baconian induction combines a transposition of the major premise and conclusion of a syllogism in Barbara, such as the inference to "All cloven-hoofed are herbivorous," with another induction obtained from a syllogism in Camestres (AEE Figure 2), where the A proposition is the Rule in the syllogism in Barbara, E is the negation of the Result of the syllogism in Barbara, and the conclusion is the denial of the Case of the syllogism in Barbara: All Cloven-hoofed are herbivorous. A sample is taken from nonherbivorous animals). Specimens of rats, dogs, and apes. So we have that rats, dogs, and apes are not herbivorous. And it is discovered that these specimens are not cloven-hoofed. This explains the data in an induction whose premises are the denials of the Case and Result in Barbara and whose conclusion is the Rule. Peirce then explored Figure 3 AII, explaining syllogisms in Datisi. He claimed their inversions can give "indirect" support for the conclusions of the inductions whose explaining syllogisms are in Barbara and Camestres.

   In the final paragraph of "On the Natural Classification of Arguments" of 1867 and more explicitly in "A Theory of Probable Inference"

of 1883, Peirce argued that in the case of probable deduction, where the
Rule or Major Premise is a statistical assumption rather than a categor-
ical one, there is little use for the transpositions in the figure 3 case.
They all are virtually reducible to the statistical analogue of figure 1.

4. "Deduction, Induction and Hypothesis" of 1878 distinguishes between
   "necessary" deductions in Barbara and "probable" deductions "of similar form" (W 3, 329). This may have been Peirce's attitude in the 1866
   Lowell Lectures and the discussion in the paper "The Classification of
   Arguments" of 1867. It is very explicitly the attitude in "Grounds of
   The Validity of the Laws of Logic" of 1869 (W 2, p. 267). In 1883, Peirce
   retained the idea that statistical premises are rules but distinguished between statistical rules and categorical propositions as rules. Syllogisms
   are necessary deductions. Probable deductions are not. So probable and
   statistical deductions are not syllogisms. Peirce retained an analogy between syllogism in Barbara and statistical deduction; but as noted above,
   there are some marked and important differences – many of which he
   recognized in the earlier work but whose significance was more difficult
   to articulate within the framework of his earlier typology.

5. Peirce may have been stimulated by his involvement with his father,
   Benjamin Peirce, in compiling and analyzing statistical data pertaining
   to the authenticity of the signature of Sylvia Ann Howland to an addendum to her will in the Howland Will Case. Benjamin and Charles
   Peirce gave testimony in 1867. He also wrote a review of Venn's *Logic
   of Chance* in 1867 that, as we shall see, raised a question about probable
   deduction that posed issues for induction. I shall argue that he managed
   to finesse these difficulties only in the 1878 and 1883 essays. Consideration of Venn's ideas may also have contributed to the development of
   his ideas on induction.

6. See footnote 4.

7. Peirce expressed a common, mistaken prejudice among probabilists
   when he insisted that probable deduction is the quantitative branch
   of deduction whereas syllogism is the qualitative branch. By implication, this implied a similar relation between inductive transpositions of
   statistical deductions and transpositions of syllogisms. In 1883, Peirce
   explicitly stated that when $r = 1$ or o, the induction is an "ordinary induction," by which he meant an inference to a universal generalization.
   In the earlier discussions, this observation was not made but I think
   Peirce took it for granted. In 1866, Peirce shifted from discussion of induction, illustrated by inference from data obtained from sampling balls
   from a bag to conclusions about the proportions of balls of a given color
   in the bag, to examples of induction by transposing categorical syllogisms. There is only the slimmest of hints as to what the connection

between the two ways of understanding inductive inference might be. Yet Peirce did consider a version of the sampling example where seven balls are selected at random from the bag and all are found to be black and the inference is to "Almost all balls in the bag are black." And it is clear that he thought the difference between "All" and "Almost all" to be important even though he did not explain why he thought so in 1866 as he did in 1883. All of this makes sense if we interpret him as endorsing in 1866 the view of the quantitative and qualitative branches of deduction. In the early years of the twentieth century, Peirce became aware of Borel's work and began to acknowledge that although to say "All balls in the bag are black" warrants claiming that the statistical probability of obtaining a black ball on random selection from the bag is 1, the converse does not hold. How fully he appreciated the ramifications of this point for his views I cannot say.

8. This suggests that even in 1865 Peirce hoped to use his account of induction as transposition of premises and conclusions of an explaining syllogism in order to address statistical inference from sample to population. In that case, the progression in the introduction of statistical issues I have noted in Peirce's papers may indicate the extent to which he was able to address various problems with relating categorical syllogisms to what he later called statistical deductions and, hence, to providing an account of induction and hypothesis as transpositions of premises and conclusions of deductive inferences.

9. If there are n balls in the bag, the number of possible proportions is $n + 1$. Peirce did not address the issue of infinitely many values well; but for countably and even continuumly many values it is possible to address the matter in a coherent fashion. Peirce clearly maintained in 1866 that induction does not presuppose that nature is uniform but that it may instead exhibit statistical regularities.

10. He opposed arguments for balancing arguments essentially rationalized in Bayesian terms both early and late.

11. Peirce was identifying species of induction that are variants of the classification in the draft letter to Carus in 1901 in "The Logic of Drawing History from Ancient Documents." By then Peirce was using the term "abduction" exclusively in the sense of forming conjectured answers to questions that then call for testing (EP 2: 96–106). He further refined quantitative induction to mark off variations where the population from which sampling is done is not finite.

12 Peirce's Deductive Logic: Its Development, Influence, and Philosophical Significance

Logic may well be the single most important key to understanding Peirce's thought and influence. It was his deductive logic that brought him an international reputation in his lifetime and led to conspicuous references to his work by figures such as Peano, Schröder, Russell, Venn, Jevons, and Clifford. Peirce's highest, and in fact only, academic position was as lecturer in logic at Johns Hopkins University. He himself said on numerous occasions – when he wasn't emphasizing his role as a working scientist with the Coast Survey, that is – that he was mainly a logician. He called his existential graphs his *chef d'oeuvre*.[1] Logic, especially the logic of relations, played a central role in the development of his philosophy.[2] His three Categories were based on, and shown to be fundamental by, the logic of relations. The logic of relations is central to his analysis of the fundamental triadic notion of his semeiotics, "__ signifies __ to __." He saw his theory of scientific method as just logic, broadly construed. And of pragmatism itself, he often repeated that it was nothing more than the ideal fixation of belief, and this was the very goal of logic.

In this chapter, I will address three aspects of Peirce's logic: a survey of Peirce's major ideas and influence, a sketch of their development from 1868 (the date of his first publication in logic) until his death in 1914, and finally, several philosophical and logical ideas of enduring value in his work. I will restrict myself here to what both we and he understood as deductive logic. Although his deductive logic is self-contained, and developed for the most part independent of his theory of scientific method, which included also induction and abduction, it is sometimes difficult to separate deductive logic from this method (and from his antilogicist conception of mathematics).

287

I will pay special attention to three themes: to his definitions and conceptions of the purpose of logic, to what he regarded as the core principles and concepts of deductive logic, and to the role that his theory of signs (especially diagrams and iconicity) plays in the development of his logical systems. I will argue that there are several significant changes in what Peirce regarded as the key principles of logic. At first, he regarded the Aristotelian first figure mood, Barbara, as the center and even the whole of logic. In a brief period between 1865 and 1867, he became convinced that Boole's "algebraic" approach to logic was basically correct. By 1870, and under the influence of De Morgan, he moved from Boole's own equation-format to formulas using a subsumption operator (—<) that had the important formal-algebraic characteristics of transitivity and anti-symmetry and discovered an ingenious extension of Boolean logic to relations. Part of this new conception involves the autonomous use of a single logical notion for the calculi of subsumption in the theory of classes, for the material conditional in propositional logic, and for what Peirce termed "illation" ("therefore") – and thereby a theory of deduction in the manner of Gentzen. Peirce's earlier conception implicitly places emphasis on what we would regard as the universal quantifier, with the existential quantifier defined either separately or derivatively (and often, unsatisfactorily). A number of shifts occur in the late 1880s and especially in the 1890s with the first attempts at a diagrammatic logic. The basic logical constant and resulting calculus became unequivocally propositional, and the transitive logical relation is abandoned in favor of disjunction (together with negation). The existential quantifier is treated as coequal and interdefinable with the universal quantifier. The last step was to shift to conjunction (together with negation), a completely diagrammatic notation, and the primacy of the existential quantifier over the universal quantifier. I will argue that this shift actually was to give up some of what was advantageous in his earlier conception of the basic principles of logic; I propose extensions and modifications to the existential graphs so that they might fully function as Peirce himself intended.

His numerous and seemingly vacillating definitions of 'logic,' in broader senses (that embrace all idealized thought and thought processes) and narrower senses (that indicate primarily deductive inference), present a more formidable difficulty to understanding Peirce.

This is likely why early secondary literature has not focused on what is an embarrassment of riches and, at first blush, confusions. I will nevertheless maintain that his mature, and I think very fine, definition of logic is:

Logic in the narrower sense is that science which concerns itself primarily with distinguishing reasonings into good and bad, and with distinguishing probable reasonings into strong and weak reasonings. Secondarily, logic concerns itself with all that it must study in order to make those distinctions about reasoning, and with nothing else. (RLT: 143)

Since "good and bad" are here formal, qualitative aspects that, applied strictly to deductive reasoning, amount to what we would term "validity," Peirce's definition of deductive logic is roughly: "Logic is the science of distinguishing[3] valid from invalid arguments, and the development of all and only those concepts and tools that are necessary to do so." In spite of numerous, and apparently quite different, statements about both the broad and narrow senses of logic, I will argue that Peirce is actually perfectly consistent throughout his life.

MAJOR IDEAS AND INFLUENCE

With Putnam (1982) and Dipert (1989),[4] as well as introductions and notes to the volumes of the *Writings* that have so far appeared, we are *almost* in possession of a clear and complete overview of Peirce's logic and its place in the history of logic. Especially clear now is the influence of his published works, which is far greater than was recognized as recently as 1980. However, a full evaluation of his work in deductive logic must await the assembly and publication in the *Writings* of what remains of the manuscripts for the proposed book, *The Grand Logic* of 1893–4, *The Minute Logic* of 1901–2, and the many fragments and partial manuscripts using the system of the "existential graphs" in the period from 1897 until his death in 1914. Another remaining lacuna in Peirce scholarship is an appreciation and careful portrayal of the work of Ernst Schröder, the differences between Peirce and Schröder on key points, and a careful assessment of Schröder's (and thus Peirce's) influence on developments in the twentieth century.[5]

In a nutshell, Peirce's first contributions were, first, minor improvements to Boole's logic (1867–1868), together with a sophisticated

understanding of Aristotelian syllogism on its own terms and as reflected through this algebra, then the important and original development of a broadly Boolean logic applied to the logic of relations
(1870–1894) and transformed from a system of pure equations, and
finally a burst of activity in the late 1890s that intermingled normative components from his theories of signs (his semeiotic), namely,
iconicity, with his earlier, more traditionally notated logical system, which came to constitute the existential graphs. This later,
diagrammatic approach to logic yielded sophisticated, complete logical theories that lacks the Boolean, algebraic flavor of his previous
work. In fact, they are conspicuously and advantageously unlike anything else in the history of logic. Unlike all earlier diagrammatic logics, Peirce's technique could express multiply quantified relational
expressions. Unlike his earlier, symbolic work in logic, which we
would see as somewhat casual with regard to rules of formation,
axiomatization, and even semantic interpretation, his approach to
diagrams was much more exacting.

An account of the existential graphs unfortunately remained in
unpublished manuscripts until the publication of Volume IV ("The
Simple Mathematics") of the *Collected Papers* in 1933. So their influence on the crucial first decades of the development of modern
logical concepts and notation was nil. Careful descriptions and evaluations of their importance did not occur until the work of J. J. Zeman
and Don Roberts in the late 1960s and early 1970s,[6] and with the publication of more of Peirce's work on the graphs and on mathematics
in *The New Elements of Mathematics* in 1976 (NE).

With De Morgan in his own century and until Alonzo Church
and Benson Mates in the twentieth century, Peirce was one of very
few logicians in recent centuries to view logic as connected to ideas
from previous centuries, especially to Aristotle's own and other ancient logics, and to medieval logic. His encyclopedic, historicist, and
unmodernly broad conception of logic, as well as the complicated
currents of late nineteenth century philosophy and mathematics,
contributes to making his motivations and thinking in logic difficult for modern readers to appraise.

C. S. Peirce was the first person in the history of logic to use
quantifier-like variable-binding operators (briefly in 1870, W 2, 392f,
pre-dating Frege's *Begriffsschrift* of 1879); these "quantifiers" were
still more extensively used in published works of 1880 and especially

1885. In 1885, without any knowledge of Frege's publication of six years earlier, Peirce declares the introduction of quantifiers to be the resolution of a longstanding problem in Boolean logic, namely, the proper expression of existential statements, such as the particular categoricals of Aristotelian logic, "Some F's are (not) G's." He expressed the I-categorical as "$\Sigma_i\ F_iG_i$," using subscripted "indices" (here, i) for variables, and the symbols 'Σ' and 'Π' for what we write, using Peano's notation, as '$\exists$' and '$\forall$.'[7] He was (again in 1870) the first major figure in the Boolean tradition to use a special symbol for class inclusion or subsumption ($-<$) as opposed to using only equations.[8] Schröder followed him in this, but substituting his symbol $\subseteq$. In Peirce's early interpretation, this symbol also stood, autonomously, for what he termed "illation" (the "therefore": '$\vdash$') and derivatively (until 1885) for the material conditional.

Peirce recognized that a property observed by De Morgan (invalidity of the Syllogism of Transposed Quantity in infinite domains) was a logically adequate characterization of the distinction between finite and infinite classes, and he thus gave a definition of an infinite class that is independent of, and distinct from, the better known definitions of Dedekind and Cantor. Interested in what we would now term "computational" aspects of logic, he was the first person in history to suggest an electrical logical circuit and he had some grasp, starting in the 1880s, of the notion of effective computation. He speculated about what became Hilbert's *Entscheidungsproblem* (decidability, 1900) and was later solved by Church's Theorem (1939)[9] – that in first order predicate logic, with quantifiers and relations, there can exist no algorithm for distinguishing valid from invalid arguments (Dipert 1984). Jaakko Hintikka has argued that Peirce was one of the most important figures in a model-theoretic tradition that first arose with Boole, and allowed the universe of discourse to be altered, and that this allowed the modern theory of semantics for logic that we see developed in works by Tarski and Gödel (Hintikka 1988, Hintikka 1997, and Dipert 1989).

Peirce can be credited with the renewal of interest in the Liar Paradox in the twentieth century.[10] Whether part of logic or not, Peirce also made important contributions to the philosophy of collective entities, including sets, and to the theory of numbers, continua, and infinities. With Dedekind, he discovered at almost the same time as Peano a minimal and apparently complete set of postulates for the natural numbers, now known as the Peano Postulates.[11] He anticipated, in an unpublished but finished paper, "the" Sheffer stroke function: the discovery of two propositional connectives such that either one, alone, is sufficient for the expression of the whole of propositional logic. He discovered various techniques for putting quantified expressions into a canonical form, such as a prenex normal form that separates an uninterrupted string of quantifiers from a strictly logical formula that contains no quantifiers (W 5, 178–183, 1885). He understood, proved, and utilized, especially in his existential graphs, the fact that one can define the universal quantifier in terms of the existential, or *vice versa*.

Peirce did not advance the rigorous axiomatization of logic in any ways that were not simply common standards of rigor in nineteenth century mathematics and part of the inheritance from Euclid and early abstract algebraists – although by this severe criterion, Frege made no contributions either, and progress in this dimension of logic was first propelled by the publication of David Hilbert's enormously influential axiomatization of geometry in 1898, and thence the American postulate theorists (Scanlon, 1991).

The great majority of Peirce's earlier, original logical work, in what I will term his Algebraic Period, was published in his lifetime. This period extends from his first published work in logic of 1868 through to his published "On the Algebra of Logic: A Contribution to the Philosophy of Notation" of 1885. In this period, there are already indications of a "semeiotic turn" within logic that eventually developed into his Diagrammatic Period. The unpublished but extensively developed Grand Logic of 1893–4 remains within the Algebraic Period. The *terms* of logic in the first part of the Algebraic Period until 1885 denote classes or operations in the manner of Boolean logic (even when they involve relations), and the symbolism is predominantly nondiagrammatic and linear. That is, notation consists of linear sequences (strings) of symbols.[12] Definitions and inferential rules are algebraic in style, informally mathematical in practice. In the early part of this period, 1868–1885, propositional logic is taken to be just a form of a general calculus. In the language of the time, hypothetical logic is an interpretation of categorical logic, in which propositions denote the classes of occasions or times when they are true (Dipert 1981a). Expanding on De Morgan's insight and the centrality of Barbara in traditional logic, Peirce holds throughout this period that inference – all inference – depends on one algebraic property of logical connectives above all others, namely, transitivity.[13]

In my interpretation, his published article "The Logic of Relatives" (1897) is a transitional work between the Algebraic and the Diagrammatic Periods. Already in 1896 there was the germ of what eventually constituted the system of the Existential Graphs that he used constantly from 1900 until his death in 1914, namely, his "entitative graphs." It is now usual to think of this later work as merely being an "iconic" treatment of his earlier discoveries in the algebra of logic. It is also common to think of the graphs as intended merely as a tool for the visual representation or manipulation of logical propositions, still understood mentally as linearly notated. However, I will argue that it instead represents almost a complete break with most central motifs in his earlier work in the Algebraic Period and is based upon a philosophy of logic that even Peirce himself did not have the opportunity fully to develop.

The greatest tragedy in Peirce's life as a logician was his failure to find a publisher for any book-length work on logic, especially his proposed work, the "Grand Logic" of 1892–3, with the proposed title of *How to Reason: A Critick of Arguments*. The source of the title "*Grand Logic*" is not known (see de Waal 2000 for this and other information), but especially since there is a later book-length project by Peirce from 1902–3 entitled the *Minute Logic*, we may guess that Peirce is possibly alluding to the *Logica magna* and *Logica parva* of Paul of Venice, an author he knew well.[14] Large sections of the *Grand Logic* were complete, but only partly published in CP; any portrayal of his large-scale conception of logic must await a reasonable organization of these manuscripts and their publication – promised to occupy all of Volume 10 of the *Writings*. Peirce's logical work undoubtedly also suffered from his lack of a stable academic position, from the lack of sophistication and following for contemporary developments in logic in America, including in mathematics, and from the paucity of influential students he had from his brief period of teaching at Johns Hopkins (O. H. Mitchell, who died at an early age, and Christine Ladd-Franklin; John Dewey did not devote himself to deductive or symbolic logic). One must also cite the scattered nature of Peirce's efforts and interests, across all manner of philosophical, mathematical, scientific, historical, linguistic, and even literary disciplines, while at the time he was mainly employed as a data gatherer by the Coast and Geodetic Survey and later, after his retirement to Milford in 1890 at age 51, engaged in a variety of money-making schemes, and especially in the last decade of life, combating his poverty when these schemes failed.

THE DEVELOPMENT OF PEIRCE'S LOGIC

In this section, I go rather deeply into selected works, but do not attempt to survey all of his essays and manuscripts with the same degree of scrutiny.

Early Works

The basic idea that there were similarities between some features of algebra and logic, understood in terms of the Aristotelian syllogistic, was observed as early as the late seventeenth century, and independently developed by Leibniz and Lambert, to name just two. Boole's basic idea was roughly that categorical statements, such as "All Xs are Ys," could be treated as an equation, $xy = y$, interpreted roughly as "The class of Xs is identical to the class of things that are both x and y." (In other words, $x = x \cap y$.) This "Boolean" logic had operations of multiplication (roughly, class intersection) and addition (class union, but with qualifications) and multiplicative and additive identity elements 1 (the universal class) and 0 (the empty class). One deviation in particular from standard numerical algebra made it one of the first of the "abstract" algebras, namely $xx = x$.

Peirce's earliest work was part of a Boolean reform movement in the period from 1868 (Peirce, Jevons) to 1878 (Schröder's *Operationskreis*) that interpreted Boolean addition (class union) in a different and more well-behaved way. Namely, for Boole himself, if classes x and y had any members in common, '$x + y$' was undefined; the expression '$x + y$' was only meaningful if x and y were mutually exclusive classes. Peirce had read Boole's 1854 *Laws of Thought* no later than 1865 (age 26). A logic notebook from 1867 survives, and in it we can see some of the developments leading up to the publications of 1868 and 1870. In 1867, Peirce presented five papers to the American Academy of Arts and Sciences, and they were published a year later, 1868, in its *Proceedings*. In the first, "On an Improvement in Boole's Calculus of Logic," Peirce is metaphysically acute enough from the outset to distinguish symbolically the "logical" relationships and operations, performed on classes, from their usual arithmetical interpretations, performed on numbers. Thus he writes '$a =, b$' as a *logical identity* holding between classes, not numerical equality; $a +, b$ is logical addition, and a, b is logical multiplication. This addresses one of the complaints in Frege (1880/1881: 10) and Frege (1882), namely the ambiguous use in Boolean logics of mathematical and logical symbols. Logical addition and multiplication are associative and commutative; logical addition and multiplication are jointly distributive, all as Boolean logic is now understood. The inverse operation is less satisfactorily defined, namely as , $-a = 1 -, a$ or as the maximal class such that $a, -a =, 0$. In fact, 1 and 0 are used before 0 is "defined" as

$$0 =, x-, x = x - x.$$

Peirce apparently intends to say with this double equation both the logical $0 =, x-, x$ and the numerical $0 = x - x$. This is odd, however, since '0' here does double duty as the null class and as a minimal numerical quantity.[15] The remaining part of the article deals with a calculus of probabilities, with the connecting thread being that (27) if $a =, b$ then $a = b$. In Cantorian terms, if a and b are identical classes, then a and b are equinumerous (have the same cardinality). The converse does not hold. Observe that 'a' is problematically ambiguous, referring to a class in the first equation and to the numerical size or cardinality of that class in the second. With these two notations, first for classes but with a class-union-like logical addition, and then for ordinary numerical operations, the shift to probabilities requires that $a + b = a +, b -, (a, b)$.[16] As Peirce observes (W 2, 21 2d), Boole had ensured that operations on probabilities symbolically paralleled logical operations by creating logical operations that already excluded overlapping cases.

One notable difficulty in Boole's 1854 system is in properly expressing the I and O propositions of categorical logic: "Some A is B" and "Some A is not B." It would be natural, at least in hindsight, to express the I-categorical: $a, b \neq, 0$ (Peirce) and $ab \neq 0$ (Boole). However, neither Boole nor Peirce was willing to appeal to a propositional negation that would allow this; their systems are strictly equational.[17] (In Boole's 1847 book this is more satisfactorily expressed.)

Peirce's 1870 article, "Description of a Notation for the Logic of Relatives," is undoubtedly one of the most important works in the history of logic. It is here that a general notation for multiply quantified relations, and techniques for manipulating them, first appear. A *"relative"* is a *term*, in the sense in which it is used by Aristotelian logicians. That is, the relationship between a term and a (one-place) property is precisely duplicated by the relationship between a relative and a relation. As we will see, a relative term ('relative' for short) does double duty, semantically representing a certain extension or class, namely the "logical sum" of (ordered) pairs (n-tuples) of individuals. This is precisely the modern semantic understanding of the extension of a relation of n places as a set of n-tuples. But it also serves as an operation on classes. This 1870 paper is not the very first published symbolic treatment of relations: credit for this would go to Lambert, or better known and crucially influential on Peirce, to De Morgan's "On the Syllogism IV."

This said, Peirce's 1870 paper is remarkable for its sheer imaginativeness, but also for its disorderly presentation. In many cases, the development amounts to experimentation with various notations for relations, and to the following out of algebraic analogies (such as with exponentiation and a binomial theorem, something Boole too attempted, though not for relatives). Some of the notational methods and analogies were not even used again by Peirce himself. Nevertheless, it is obvious that the basic techniques allowed Peirce to express quantified relational statements of enormous complexity and, in many cases, to show their equivalence to other statements. For example, whatever is lover of or servant to a woman is the same class as the nonrelational logical addition of the lovers of a woman and the servants of a woman: $(l +, s)w = lw +, sw$. Here, relations are indicated by italicized letters, and simple classes by nonitalicized letters. Observe too that (as Peirce notes) juxtaposition indicates a notion of "application" of the relative to a class, and not any sort of ordinary logical multiplication (intersection of classes).[18] This is the sense in which a relative behaves more like a function or operator than a class or term.[19] However, modern set theory frequently equivocates in the same manner (once extended, this is the key idea of Category Theory), and predicates were also conceived as "propositional functions" by Frege, Russell, and Whitehead.

There is no list of axioms, nor even an ordering of which theorems are more fundamental than others. In the "Conclusion," Peirce says that certain equations can be taken as axioms, then adds: "But these axioms are mere substitutes for definitions of the universal logical relations, and so far as these can be defined, all axioms may be dispensed with. The fundamental principles of formal logic are not properly axioms, but definitions and divisions" (W 2, 429 1870). In other words, Peirce takes as logic's task the conceptual analysis of its ideas, rather than the ordering of its truths. With the exception of his 1885 essay and the working paper leading up to it, and his later exposition of existential graphs, he was never much concerned with axioms for logic, or any ordering of theorems. This causes for the modern reader an appearance of casualness, even sloppiness, that is, however, more due to a difference in the conception and purpose of logic.

As early as 1872–3, Peirce had some plan to write a book on logic. There exists a series of manuscripts, published as Sections 4–39 of Volume III of the *Writings*, that have chapter headings and a comprehensive and organized subject matter, and there exists a short manuscript from the summer of 1873 entitled "Notes on Logic Book."[20] Some of these essays were incorporated into the *Popular Science* series of 1877–8. This last section contains writing on the copula, relative terms, and the simple syllogism. It contains little that was not evident in the published 1870 paper, but is written in a far more approachable style. Of some interest are his discussions of the "breadth" and "depth" of terms, and his view that algebra is a branch of logic and that algebra is not exclusively a mathematical study of quantity. This essay is modified from his 1867 American Academy of Sciences lecture, "Upon Logical Comprehension and Extension" (W 2, 70–86), and was recycled again, with some modifications, in the proposed *Grand Logic* of 1894 (R-421; also R-725), where much from medieval semantics is interjected or quoted. Although usually refracted through the influence of medieval semantics, the *Port-Royal Logic*, Hamilton, and even J. S. Mill, Peirce was always extremely interested in exploring various semantic dimensions of terms that went under expressions such as extension, intension, denotation, connotation, comprehension, breadth, and depth. Modern philosophy of language tends to start with Frege's distinction between reference (*Bedeutung*) and the problematic notion of sense (*Sinn*). Much as with his historically sophisticated investigations of various collective notions, returning to Peirce's works allows us to see a rich array of new possibilities, sometimes brilliantly examined by Peirce, but that were suddenly, and sometimes with little or no reason, abandoned around 1900.

From 1873 through 1878, Peirce was consumed with his work for the Coast Survey, and, later in that period, with his one published book, *Photometric Researches* (1878), as well as with the preparation of the "Illustrations of the Logic of Science," that is, the *Popular Science Monthly* series of 1877–8. This series begins with a rare witty and trenchant remark: "Few persons care to study logic, because everybody conceives himself to be proficient enough in the art of reasoning already" (W 3, 242). Otherwise, however, the period from the "Notation..." of 1870 until 1880 was the only decade in Peirce's adult life when he did not devote himself extensively to logic. (The other lengthy period without publication is from 1885 until 1897, as Peirce himself notes at CP 3.510.) His one strictly logical publication in this period, a note in the important British journal *Mind* in 1876 (W 3, 191–194), is remarkable for its slightness, dealing with contraposition and conversion in Aristotelian syllogisms, when complementation (non-*X*s) of terms is permitted. The derivation of the many valid moods this technique allows does show Peirce to be still in the grips of the conviction that the Barbara mood in the First Figure is of singular importance.

This period ends with his appointment as lecturer in logic at Johns Hopkins University, Baltimore, from 1879 to 1884. Just as reading De Morgan's paper on the logic of relations had immediately inspired his own published work on relatives, it is clear that reading Schröder's short book *Operationskreis des Logikkalküls* (1878) inspired an effort toward a much more systematic exposition of logical principles than was attempted in 1870. This is evident in the unpublished "On the Algebraic Principles of Formal Logic" (Fall, 1879), with many references to Schröder's postulates and deductions; it became the lengthy and refined 1880 article in the *American Journal of Mathematics*, "On the Algebra of Logic" (W 4, 163–209), in which there are scant references to Schröder, and the exposition is unfortunately less systematic than the earlier notes.

The development of an algebra of logic in the published 1880 "On the Algebra of Logic" is far more leisurely and organized than had been the "Notation..." of ten years earlier. The inventiveness with notation is much more constrained than in 1870, with one notable exception. Peirce uses a dash over the subsumption sign to indicate a propositional negation: $'s \mathrel{\overline{\prec}} p'$ indicates that s is not wholly contained within p. However, the dash over a single letter (or over a more complex term standing for a class) indicates the complement of that class: $'\overline{p}'$ stands for the class of things that are not in p, and $\overline{p+q}$ stands for the class of things that are neither in p nor in s.

The I- and O-categorical statements remain problematic, however, and in this article Peirce proposes that $'\breve{a}'$ indicate "that some part of the term denoted by that letter is the subject, and that that is asserted to be in possible existence" (W 4, 171). The A-proposition "Some a is b" becomes $'\breve{a} \prec b'$, while the O proposition becomes $\breve{a} \prec \overline{b}$. Peirce does not comment that this notation is similar to Boole's proposal in 1847 to write $va \prec b$, where $'v'$ is an operator that selects an arbitrary subset.[21] In any case, Peirce does not use this notation in later work. In fact, by 1882 it is used to "convert" relations; that is, if a_{ij} then $\breve{a}_{ji}$ (W 4, 347), a notation which is still in use.

Peirce's 1885 "On the Algebra of Logic: A Contribution to the Philosophy of Notation" was published in the *American Journal of Mathematics*, and thus was widely disseminated in Europe. It is the last logical publication that appears before Peirce's notation influenced Peano, and before the late Boolean nonrelational and relational logic becomes codified in Schröder's *Vorlesungen über die Algebra der Logik*. This article is the most complete and systematic work Peirce wrote on symbolic, nondiagrammatic deductive logic. It has a number of distinctive and interesting features. First, Peirce announces the purpose of the algebra of logic: "it presents formulae which can be manipulated, and that by observing the effects of such manipulation we find properties not to be otherwise discerned" (CP 3.363). He asserts that this algebra is "adequate to the treatment of all problems of deductive logic" (CP 3.364).

Second, the article at least begins as a highly systematic treatment of this algebra, which Peirce had earlier eschewed. Peirce calls his postulate-like statements of this algebra "icons," and proposes to give eight of them that cover the whole of relational and nonrelational logic. "Icons" are later defined to be "exemplars of algebraic proceedings" (CP 3.385). They begin:

$$x \prec x \tag{1}$$

$$\text{From } x \prec (y \prec z) \tag{2}$$

$$\text{we can pass to } y \prec (x \prec z).$$

This can be stated in the [single] formula

$$\{x \prec (y \prec z)\} \prec \{y \prec (x \prec z)\}$$
$$(x \prec y) \prec \{(y \prec z) \prec (x \prec z)\} \tag{3}$$

v is defined by

$$x \prec v, \text{ for all } x \tag{4}$$

[v is true, *verum*, Frege's "The True" – RRD]
f [*falsum* – RRD] is defined by

$$f \prec x, \text{ for all } x.$$

["Peirce's Law"]

$$\{(x \prec y) \prec x\} \prec x \tag{5}$$

Icon (6) is not stated but is said to be "involved" in a theorem of plane geometry dealing with colinearity among nine points. Icons (7) and (8) are not mentioned, but presumably also involve relatives.[22] (1) is an axiom, autonomously indicating

$$\vdash x \subseteq x \quad \text{where '}x\text{' is a term or class} \tag{1a}$$

$$\vdash x \supset x \quad \text{where '}x\text{' is a proposition} \tag{1b}$$

as well as the rule of inference

$$x \vdash x \text{ where '}x\text{' is a proposition} \tag{1c}$$

In fact, since they are icons of *reasoning*, we might take this last, Gentzen-like sequent reading as primary. Icons (2), (3), and (5) are rules of inference,

$$x \prec (y \prec z) \vdash y \prec (x \prec z) \tag{2a}$$

$$(x \prec y) \vdash (y \prec z) \prec (x \prec z) \tag{3a}$$

$$(x \prec y) \prec x \vdash x \tag{5a}$$

or axioms,

$$\{x \supset (y \supset z)\} \supset \{y \supset (x \supset z) \quad\quad\quad (2a)$$

$$(x \supset y) \supset \{(y \supset z) \supset (x \supset z)\} \quad\quad (3a)$$

$$\{(x \supset y) \supset x\} \supset x \quad\quad\quad\quad\quad (5a)$$

(4) is still more problematic. Icons (2) and (5) are not quite what they seem. Peirce usually indicates that the symbol '$-\!\!\prec$' is equivocal among subsumption, the material conditional, and illation itself. However, in any case where we have an expression of the form

$$x -\!\!\prec (y -\!\!\prec z)$$

the first occurrence of '$-\!\!\prec$' is only sensible as $\supset$, since the expression '$y -\!\!\prec z$' does not denote a class, but a proposition that is true or false. Thus an interpretation such as

$$\{x \supset (y \subseteq z)\} \supset \{(y \supset (x \subseteq z)\} \quad\quad (2b)^*$$

would appear to be nonsense, since in the antecedent of (2b)*, namely, $x \supset (y \subseteq z)$, '$x$' seems to refer to a proposition, and 'y' and 'z' to classes; if so, then the consequent of (2b)* has the form

$$y \supset \dots, \quad\quad\quad\quad\quad\quad 2b.2$$

where 'y' peculiarly or impossibly refers to a class.[23] In general, an icon with m occurrences of '$-\!\!\prec$' will have 3^m interpretations, along the lines of (2a) or (2b)*.[24] Some will seem very odd to us, such as

$$\{x \vdash (y \vdash z)\} \vdash \{(y \vdash (x \vdash z)\} \quad\quad (2c)^*$$

These can be made sensible if we take some occurrences of '$\vdash$' to be in the object-language, some to be occurrences in the meta-language, and one in the meta-meta-language.[25]

These interpretational oddities are a very high price to pay for the algebraic–iconic quality of any logical relation that has the strictly formal (relational) attributes of all of $-\!\!\prec$, $\supset$, $\subseteq$, and $\vdash$, namely, reflexivity, antisymmetry $[(Rxy \supset Ryx) \supset x = y]$, and transitivity. When expressed in this forceful and autonomous way as he did in the icons of the 1885 system, I find it unlikely that Peirce himself did not notice the difficulty. In fact, the failure even to state the seventh and eighth icons, to use this system of icons, or refer to them as "icons" in later logical work, and to develop or to revisit a general, symbolic logical theory or system until the *Grand Logic* of 1894 (and then only in a fragmentary way), almost certainly, I believe, indicate a disillusionment and sense of inadequacy over the development of logical theory along the manner of his 1870–1885 work. My suggestion is that Peirce was himself perplexed by the system he produced and realized that this algebraic approach failed to be truly and broadly "iconic," and more generally, that it failed to be a general treatment of deductive formal logic as a branch of the theory of signs.

Still further evidence for this claim lies an experimental notation in a manuscript from 1886 (discussed below) but quickly abandoned, in the convolutions of his published 1896 paper (especially insofar as they involve iconicity and diagrams), the rapid shift to the graphlike methods after 1897, and one last mention of the "algebraic" doctrine of transitivity, after which the thesis is not repeated:

I have maintained since 1867 that there is but one primary and fundamental logical relation, that of illation, expressed by *ergo*. A proposition, for me, is but an argumentation divested of the assertoriness of its premises and conclusion. This makes every proposition a conditional proposition at bottom. In like manner a "term" or class-name, is for me nothing but a proposition with its indices or subjects left blank, or indefinite. (CP 3.440 *The Monist*, 1896)

This is a remarkable and elucidating passage in more ways than one.[26] It renders the material conditional as an implicit statement of inferrablility, as indeed some speech-act logicians have maintained.[27] And rather than making terms or classes basic, in the manner of traditional categorical logic, and then interpreting propositional logic as certain relationships among classes associated with propositions, as had almost all logicians in the algebra of logic tradition from Boole through Schröder, Peirce takes classes to be merely the n-tuples that satisfy various index-less propositions, that is, positions in a predicate. Although there is no strong indication in earlier works that this is how he had intended his logic all along, there is nothing that contradicts it either. Classes simply are "propositional functions." This is a last word in answer to detracters such as Quine, who had maintained that Peirce's was merely a class- or term-logic, and that formulas, even those containing variable-binding operators, were understood by Peirce in the traditional way of categorical logic.

Transitional Works

The *Grand Logic of 1893–4: How to Reason: A Critick of Arguments*[28]

There are several reasons for considering this work – really a series of manuscripts – as Peirce's nearly completed *magnum opus* in logic. Peirce had publishers interested in the project, had drafts of tables of contents (R-399), and had numerous, neatly written out, sample chapters; he wrote and revised an "advertisement" for the volume (R-398). These advertisements are unfortunately so pompous, obscure, and overwritten that one cannot but think of this not as the Grand Logic but as the Grandiose Logic. Peirce was such a poor marketer of his own work, and so willful in his dealings with even positively inclined publishers, that one has sympathies with the editorial judgment that ran against the publication of any logic book by Peirce, even if this was ultimately a tragedy for the history of logic.

One general interpretational difficulty in studying Peirce's work is of course how seriously to take various notes and drafts; many were clearly not intended to be the final word on the subject, and were undoubtedly more like working notes. Consequently, and owing to the overwhelming majority of Peirce's manuscripts that never approached publication, we cannot say clearly that any one of these represents Peirce's settled beliefs or intention to communicate (perhaps, owing to their tentative, experimental quality, they did not even represent transitory belief).[29] However, the *Grand Logic* is otherwise; additionally, despite or perhaps because of a need to earn money at exactly this time – it followed the collapse of financial schemes and coincided with Peirce's disastrous effort to write fiction – many of the sections we have of the *Grand Logic* seem to be, as indicated by their careful handwriting (and some professional typing and formal submission to an editor) nearly finished products; and while they are sweeping in their scope, including many digressive pages of careful historical background (including long quotations in untranslated Latin), they seemed to have been written with intensity *and* leisure.

Many of the chapters are rewrites of earlier work. For example, "The Association of Ideas" in drafts R-401 through R-403 is largely from the 1867 "New List of Categories," and "The Fixation of Belief" is from 1877, though heavily revised. The first chapters deal with the association of ideas, materialism, categories, consciousness, and signs; the last chapters, largely unwritten or unpolished, were to deal with breadth and depth, clarity, the doctrine of chances, probable inference, the law of continuity, and "Induction etc."[30] Very curiously, there is no highlighted place for abduction, and the discussion of scientific method (of which deduction was usually considered only a part) is muted, falling early in the section on the fixation of belief.

The major and central part of the book was, however, on formal, deductive logic. Furthermore, it was conceived as a "critic(k)" of existing arguments, rather than as anything like rules for the production of valid inferences that would be of use in the method of science. In this respect, with an emphasis on what one might call the passive rather than active side logic, it is a great deal more like logic before Boole, and after Peirce and Dodgson. This core of the *Grand Logic* includes chapters on Aristotelian logic and its extensions, Boolean logic, the logic of relatives, graphs and graphical diagrams, and the logic of mathematics.[31] Unfortunately, the chapter on graphs appears never to have been written. It would have been fascinating to examine at this transitional time, but perhaps Peirce did not have firm opinions on the issues until his work in 1896–8. What is intriguing about the *Grand Logic* is that diagrammatic logic was to receive its own chapter, whereas it had previously been mentioned only in passing.[32]

The theory of signs figures more prominently than usual in Peirce's discussion and very definition of logic. Chapter II, "What is a Sign?"(R-404), begins: "This is a most necessary question, since all reasoning is an interpretation of signs of some kind. But it is also a difficult reflection, calling for deep reflection." The last page begins a discussion of how "[i]n all reasoning, we use a mixture of likenesses, indices, and symbols. We cannot dispense with any of them."[33] Unfortunately, the remaining pages are missing and we receive only a hint of what might have been an explanation of the use of icons as they were used in 1885.

One curiosity that is, I shall argue, more than a curiosity is Peirce's replacement of his subsumption-conditional-illation sign, $-\!\!\prec$, that he had used since from 1870 to 1886:[34]

$$x -\!\!\prec y \qquad \textit{becomes:} \qquad x \ \overline{\ \ }| \ y$$

$$(x -\!\!\prec y) -\!\!\prec z \quad \textit{becomes:} \qquad \overline{x \ \ }| \ y \ | \ z$$

This receives (peculiarly) little explanation in the manuscript. However, we have reason to suspect that since crosses, vertical lines, and daggers are frequently used by Peirce as disjunction-like (or union) operators, and lines (particular over terms) for negation or complement, then the first formula is really functioning as '$\sim x$ v y' and the latter as '$\sim(\sim x$ v $y)$ v z).'

This notation is borrowed from an earlier, short paper "Qualitative Logic" and an accompanying paper applying it to relations, neither of which was published in his lifetime and both from 1886. The negation line over the left disjunct is described as a "streamer." In the paper on relations, he also glosses the notation as "either [the antecedent] is false or the [consequent] is true" confirming, I believe, the intended iconicity of the notation as I suggest. Furthermore the two interpretations of this "streamer" notation are given only as a material conditional or illation, dropping subsumption (W 5, 341), a view that first appeared in the published 1885 paper. In an early version of the 1886 manuscript, Peirce relegated the development of a logic using this notation to an appendix; he said that "this algebra is *logically* more perfect than any other... yet it is found to be *mathematically* very bad" (W 5, 462 n. 361.31–2).

I will explain below what I believe the significance of this modification in 1886 and 1894 is in the light of later developments.

LATER WORKS AND DIAGRAMMATIC LOGIC

Although Peirce had always been intrigued by "diagrams" in logic, and indeed – as we see in the 1885 article – always understood the

symbolism of the algebra of logic as diagrammatic or iconic, it became clear to him that any algebraic notation is incompletely diagrammatic, and contains features that are, in fact, quite non- or
anti-iconic. There are three places in the algebra of logic, and indeed,
in modern logical notation as well, where this is evident.

First, consider the propositional connective of conjunction, "and."
It is obvious that if we write a conjunction in any standard way, then
we first write one symbol for one conjunct, followed by a symbol for
the other on the right. That is, we write:

$$A \;\&\; B \text{ or } A \wedge B$$

However, if we attend only to semantics, what such a compound
sentence means and when it is true, then we will surely note that
the order of 'A' and 'B' does not matter. At this point, in the usual
development of logical theory, we solemnly introduce "inferential
rules" into the syntax such as some or all of:

$$A \;\&\; B \;\vdash\; B \;\&\; A$$
$$A \;\&\; B \;\vdash\; A$$
$$A \;\&\; B \;\vdash\; B$$
$$A, B \;\vdash\; A \;\&\; B$$

What we do not notice is that the necessity of introducing such rules
is simply in order to repair an artifact of our (bad) logical notation,
namely, that we must write or think sentences in an order, (at least if
we are thinking in a language written or thought in a *linearly ordered*
way). One might say that this is "psychologism" or "orthographism"
of a particularly noisome sort, and the problem is with our traditional
ordered notation for conjunction. Frege observes something similar
in his remarks on conjunction, although his difficulty is cashed out
more in terms of whether '$\vdash A \;\&\; B$' is just a way of writing '$\vdash A$' and
'$\vdash B$' together. In any case, the symmetric, commutative "spirit" of
conjunction suggests that we should create a notation that captures
this unordered aspect of the pure logical notion of conjunction, in order not to introduce artifacts of order in our notation and then have
to take steps to remove them by introducing "rules of inference"
for the "commutativity" of conjunction. Peirce's first proposed diagrammatic notation for conjunction is:

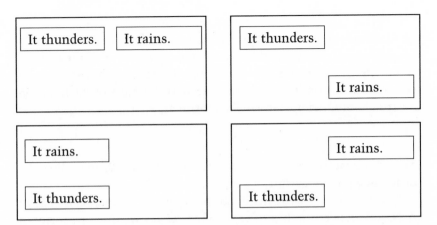

These are all equivalent representations of the conjunctive *idea*, "It thunders and it rains." This manner of order-insensitive representation is in fact often used in logic and mathematics, such as when we say that '{1, 2, 3}' indicates the same set as does '{2, 1, 3}.'

In the above diagram, I have used the outer dark rectangle to represent what Peirce later calls the "sheet" of assertion; Peirce does not use this notation. The lighter squares within it enclose symbolic, which is to say noniconic, representations. (This too is my notation: I enclose noniconic symbols in rectangles.) This technique follows the system of the published "The Logic of Relatives" of 1897 (CP 3.456f) and is used in the existential graphs: assertion of two propositions on a sheet indicates their joint assertion or, equivalently if clumsily, the assertion of their conjunction.

The second, and more interesting, phenomenon where Peirce's earlier logical notation, and contemporary logical notation as well, "bungle" the representation of purely logical phenomena is in the "binding" of identical variables. If 'Fx' represents the one-place predicate 'x is a flower' and 'Bx' represents 'x is blue,' then

$$\exists x (Fx \wedge Bx) \tag{1}$$

represents the proposition that there is (exists) some blue flower: in quasi-English, there exists at least one thing, x, such that x is a flower and x is blue. Here we describe the quantifying expression (a quantifier plus a variable) as *binding* the later occurrences of that variable 'x' that are within the "scope" of the quantifying expression. In this formula, the choice of 'x' as the variable is essentially arbitrary; what is important is not that it is in any sense an x-sort-of-thing, but that the same entity (here an individual) is being referred to at each predicate argument position where there is an occurrence of the symbol 'x' within the quantifier's scope. In other words, the choice of 'x' and its triple repetition in the formula are both artifacts of the notation of variable-binding operators. This formula,

$$\exists y(Fy \wedge By), \tag{2}$$

expresses exactly the same proposition as (1) in all, including the most fine-grained, definitions of 'proposition.'[35]

Contemporary quantificational theory has of course been alert to this equivalence, and has rules, and inferences we must perform, in order to derive (2) from (1) and thereby show the 'logical equivalence' of (1) and (2). However, their logical equivalence is quite evident; it is only notational artifacts of our usual symbolism that require us to *demonstrate* (rather than merely observe) their 'equivalence.'

The ideal notation would not require us arbitrarily to choose and to repeat occurrences of these variables (x, y, ...) in a linear string of symbols, but instead would simply indicate in a manner immediately open to observation, that whatever individual is involved, it is the same individual as elsewhere. Using an idea similar to Quine's (Quine 1955: 70, see also Roberts 1973: 125–6) and perhaps even inspiring Quine through his reading about the existential graphs in 1931, it would look something like

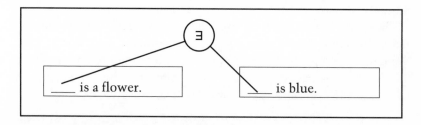

This still differs from Peirce's own notation, since he connects the empty predicate position in "__ is a flower" to the empty position in "__ is blue" as I have, but does not explicitly indicate the quantifier that is binding them. Instead, a line connecting such positions always is tacitly existential (sometimes with an inserted dark node along this line).

Using both quantifiers and relations, the following diagram asserts that some man who loves himself kills a flower:

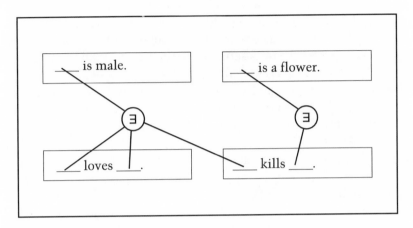

At one point (1896), just before the development of the existential graphs, Peirce used a different notation for the universal quantifier, namely enclosing predicates (or predicate positions) by circles. This is unsatisfactory, for reasons that we need not go into here and that Peirce soon realized; for one thing, there is no represented logical or diagrammatic relationship between the existential and universal quantifiers. Peirce called this first more fully diagrammatic system the "entitative graphs" and realized even while their debut was in proofs for the article that this was a flawed system.[36] One might suggest that an iconic representation of the diagrammatic *rule* for the reasoning in the Aristotelian mode Barbara should look something like:

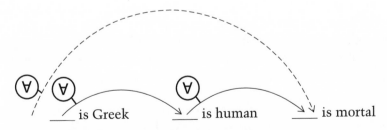

That is, "All Greeks are human" (left solid arrow), "All humans are mortal" (right solid arrow), therefore "All Greeks are mortal" (overarching arrow with dashes).

The third and last issue is a subtle one, involved in the phenomenon of branched quantifiers (first observed by Leon Henkin in 1961 and best known through Quine 1970/1986; see Sher 1997 for details). As is well known, and usually a first exercise in logic, $\exists y \forall x\, Lxy$ ("There is someone whom everyone loves") is distinct from $\forall x \exists y\, Lxy$ ("Everyone loves someone"); the first logically implies the second, but not *vice versa*. This little lesson teaches that the order of quantifiers matters, at least sometimes. But it does not matter in other cases, for example in $\forall x \forall y\, Lxy$, and in general, order is unimportant within an unbroken string of universal quantifiers.[37] Consequently, an ideal notation would not represent an order when that order was insignificant: perhaps we should properly write something like: $\{\forall x, \forall y\}\, Lxy$. This is analogous, and conceptually connected, to the unimportant order of conjuncts.

In cases with two or more occurrences of existential quantifers (in the scope of the first occurrence), or with mixed quantifiers, sometimes it matters and sometimes it does not. That is, the substitution values for one quantified variable that make an expression true may depend on, or not depend on, the substitution value of an earlier quantified variable.[38] Essentially, what is properly necessary for quantifiers is not linear ordering, which is the only one possible in traditional symbolisms and which is guilty of unnecessary and distracting exactitude, but a partial ordering of quantifiers, that is, a tree-like arrangement, showing when quantifiers depend on others and when they don't. Diagrammatic notations are ideally suited for portraying this relationship (although, as it happens, Peirce's graphs do not).[39]

Peirce's mature diagrammatic system was called the "existential graphs" and was not substantially altered in later years. It is in fact composed of three related systems: the Alpha Graphs for propositional logic, the Beta Graphs for quantified predicate logic, and the Gamma Graphs for modal logic. I will here discuss only the quantificational Beta Graphs, since their notation is so strikingly successful and in fact embodies the notation for the propositional Alpha Graphs. The diagrammatic system of the Beta Graphs for first-order predicate logic is extremely elegant, and has not, to my knowledge, been superseded or improved upon (at least for simplicity). Its notational devices are only three: juxtaposition on a "sheet of assertion," indicating propositional conjunction; a heavy dash connecting

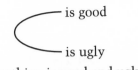

Something is good and ugly.

It's not the case that something is good and ugly.

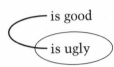

Something is good but not ugly.

It's not the case that something is good but not ugly.
(All things that are good are ugly.)

argument-positions ("hooks"), indicating the existence of a nonspecified individual; and an encircling finer line ("cut") indicating propositional negation.

The cut, a circle which indicated propositional negation, divides the sheet of assertion into an "inside" and an "outside." Peirce intended to capitalize on topological properties such as that if we pass to the inside, and encounter another circle within it (surrounding the same entities) then we have passed back to the outside again. For this reason he speaks of the "odd" and the "even" number of enclosed regions.

This notational system requires several rules for transforming a graph into another, or alternatively, adding the transformed graph to the sheet of assertion as another, jointly asserted proposition. These transformation rules play the role of rules of inference. The system easily handles relational predicates, that is, expressions with two or more argument-positions ("hooks") and complex, embedded quantification. Although it is beyond the scope of this paper, Peirce's choice of these rules of inference is fiendishly clever. The rules of inference, their completeness and independence, are discussed in Roberts (1973), Shin (2002), and Norman (2003).

MAJOR PHILOSOPHICAL ISSUES IN PEIRCE'S LOGIC

Beyond the Existential Graphs

Despite the entrenched positions of their detractors (starting with Quine in 1931), and promoters (J. J. Zeman, D. Roberts, J. Barwise, S.-J. Shin, and especially K. Ketner and J. Sowa), I do not think we yet understand clearly what exactly is iconic in the existential graphs and exactly what advantage this iconicity confers upon diagrams. With the careful and very visible presentation in Shin's *The Iconic Logic of Peirce's Graphs* (2002), Peirce's diagrammatic logic and its motivations are much more likely to receive the attention they have deserved. Nevertheless, Shin is more concerned with certain fine points in translation between the diagrams and standard notation (which inadvertently takes traditional notation as the *de facto* gold standard) and with clarifying the rules of formation and semantics for interpreting them. Few authors have addressed what I regard as fundamental obscurities in Peirce's account of them (especially in their motivation or purpose), and almost no one has attempted to be as critical and experimental as Peirce himself was, such as dealing with branched quantifiers. There is no reason to suppose that any one diagrammatic system is ideal for all purposes, let alone that Peirce's was ideal in all respects – and in fact there are good Peircean reasons always to strain for improvement along multiple dimensions of normativity. Scholarship sometimes borders on premature sanctification, or the sanctification of letter and not spirit.

Other issues in the existential graphs, and diagrammatic logic in general can only be surveyed here:

(1) Peirce stressed that the existential graphs were primarily to be understood as an analysis of reasoning, and not merely as an efficient calculus or proof-discovery method. This was a frequent theme of his explanation about what logic was about, including in his algebraic period.[40] However, to the extent that the existential graphs are iconic, they represent some aspects of the logical form of sentences iconically, but not any reasoning itself. The dashed arrow indicating inferred flow of truth in my proposed diagram for Barbara does represent reasoning.

(2) Quine (1989/1995: 29) notes that we should separate the phenomena of binding (e.g., variables) from quantification *per se*. This is philosophically important, since binding without quantification gives us *free logic* (Lambert 2003). Although Roberts and Shin (2002: 53f) have noted the iconicity of the "line of identity" in the existential graphs, they have failed to note that in its pure identity/binding role this line is iconic, while in its dual role as an existential quantifier, it is merely something of a convenient trick, and not at all iconic.[41] My own notation, with the circled '∃,' separates the role of quantification and makes no pretenses to being iconic; it is generalizable to other quantifiers as well (∃!, etc.) Peirce himself occasionally uses a thickened dot on the line of identity, and thus might have been aware of a separate, existential quantificational role; he is explicit about this dot representing an individual.[42]

(3) The topological features of Peirce's graphs have not been adequately examined.

(4) Peirce's mature existential graphs make the existential quantifier (though conflated with a notation for binding) basic, and the universal quantifier derivative.[43] This flies in the face of the vast Aristotelian tradition that Peirce consistently praised, since valid moods other than Barbara (exclusively universally quantified) were there regarded as derivative or weakened. Contemporary logical theory is studiously neutral on this point, observing only that the two quantifiers are interdefinable. Furthermore, reasoning with a universal quantifiers seems more natural, frequent, and even basic: for example, from a set of purely existentially quantified sentences, nothing of interest follows. Peirce does not make this move purely for notational convenience, or without deliberation. As early as 1884, he called the proposition that "real things exist" the fundamental axiom of logic (W 4, 545); this was in the midst of a period in which he rejected his earlier flirtation with nominalism and became a realist of a very special sort.[44] This philosophical position only has an impact on his notation for logic after 1896. But has Peirce inadvertently confused *existence* with *reality*? These are for Peirce usually strongly contrasting notions. One would think that

logic does not require anything to exist (although Boole and Peirce, against Schröder, did require something to "exist" in the universe of discourse, as does contempory model theory).

(5) Logical notations can have many goals or purposes, and some are at cross purposes. Among these goals are to represent the "smallest" logical inferences, following "naturalness" or ubiquity in human reasoning, simplicity (minimum numbers of connectives or other symbols, axioms, rules of inference; eliminating parentheses, etc.), enhancing the recognizability of correctness of inferences (or sentencehood), representing deductions for oneself or communicating them to others in the available technology, facilitating translations of sentences from (a specific) natural language, and enhancing the ability to construct, or see how to construct, derivations of (i) given premises and conclusions, or (ii) "interesting" conclusions from given premises – not to mention a "conservativeness" to which Peirce was prone, in retaining past historical conventions and techniques if those are otherwise adequate. Even here, the list is incomplete.[45] Merely to declare as Peirce (or Frege) sometimes does that our purpose is "the analysis of reasoning" is unhelpful – it is more likely the ideal representation of ideal reasoning, and even here there will be many dimensions of normativity to which a thoroughgoing pragmatism must always attend.[46]

The Definition and Nature of Logic

What did Peirce think logic was? What was his definition of logic? At first glance (as I'll show below) this is not a pretty picture: it looks as if Peirce gave many, confusingly conflicting, definitions, and that they cannot even be coherently grouped by chronological period. In fact, I want to argue that Peirce's central conception was consistent throughout his life, that it is original and fascinating, and that his other remarks constitute facets or implications of this central conception. I want furthermore to argue that this conception guided his refinements and additions to logic, and, in the last decades, motivated his novel existential graphs. This central proposal is, roughly, that logic is the theory of signs. More precisely, it is the theory of the preconditions for using any "meaningful" signs. It is a proposal that looks backward to the idea of a "speculate grammar" in John

Duns Scotus, and forward to the necessity of, and conditions for, "grammaticality" in Wittgenstein.

While Peirce consciously avoided outright psychologism, and in fact argued strongly against it, his definitions of logic are centered on the *necessary conditions for thought of any sort* (and since thought is "about" something, the necessary conditions for signification). The penultimate goal of thought is to have correct representations of the world, and these are ultimately grounded for the pragmatist in the goal of effective action in the world. Important for logic in the semi-broad sense are the conditions necessary for inference (as opposed to the conditions necessary for any kind of thought) and especially, some kind of "good" inference. Modern formal logic steers much further away from any entanglement with the mind and thought (such as investigating the abstract theory of "logical consequence" between sentences, in Benson Mates' words), but is then left with the formidable question: *why* think logically? In other words, the relation of logic to thought, and especially to norms in thought, becomes something of a mystery, itself requiring extensive analysis and argument.

In Peirce's characterizations of logic, not all of which are definitions, we encounter these four themes. (A) A *formal element*. The necessary treatment in logic of aspects of structure or pattern in concepts, propositions, and inference. (B) A *semeiotic element*. Necessary conditions for the use of any signs, especially signs that are components of true propositions. (C) A *doxastic element*, relating logic to what is believed and doubted: what is *held* to be true. (D) A *mathematical element*. Peirce's views here are likely to startle the modern reader, brought up on a lingering attraction to the failed logicism of Frege and Russell. For Peirce, logic is a branch of mathematics, not *vice versa*. Additionally, and less distinctively Peircean, there is an *antipsychologistic* view of logic, and a conception of logic as essentially *normative*. These latter two features have already been amply demonstrated.[47]

(A) FORMAL ELEMENT

In short, we may state as historical fact that logic has been essentially the science of the structure of arguments whereby we can distinguish good arguments from bad ones, can estimate the value of an argument [?], can determine upon which conditions it is valid, how it needs to be modified, and what can be inferred from a given state of facts. (W 2, 351, 1869–1870)

The chief business of the logician is to classify arguments. (W 3, 323, 1878)

[Logic's] central problem is the classification of arguments, so that all those that are bad are thrown into one division, and those which are good into another, these divisions being defined by marks recognizable even if it be not known whether the arguments are good or bad. Furthermore, logic has to divide good arguments by recognizable marks into those which have different orders of validity, and has to afford means for measuring the strength of arguments. (CP 2.203; Baldwin 1902)

[Logic's] heart lies in the classification and critic of arguments. Now it is peculiar to the art of argument that no argument can exist without being referred to some special class of arguments. The act of inference consists in the thought that the inferred conclusion is true because *in any analogous case* an analogous conclusion *would be true*. (EP 2: 200, 1903, CP 5.120ff)

(B) SEMEIOTIC ELEMENT

Logic in its general sense, is, as I believe I have shown, only another name for semiotic..., the quasi-necessary, or formal, doctrine of signs.... The second [part of semiotic] is logic proper. It is the science of what is quasi-necessarily true of the representamina of any scientific intelligence in order that they may hold good of any *object*, that is, may be true. Or say, logic proper is the formal science of the conditions of the truth of representations. (CP 2.227, 2.229 c. 1897).

Logic is the science of the general necessary laws of Signs and especially Symbols. As such, it has three departments. Obsistent logic, logic in the narrow sense, or Critical Logic, is the theory of the general conditions of the reference of Symbols and other Signs to their professed objects, that is, it is the theory of the conditions of truth, (CP 2.93, *Minute Logic*, 1902)

Logic is the science of thought, not merely of thought as a psychical phenomenon but of thought in general, its general laws and kinds. (EP 2: 36, 1898).

Logic, for me, is the study of the essential conditions to which signs must conform in order to function as such. (EP 2: 309, 1904; NE 4:235ff).

(C) DOXASTIC ELEMENT

The only justification for reasoning is that it settles doubt, and when doubt finally ceases, no matter how, the end of reasoning is attained. (W 2, 15, 1872)

the art of devising research, – the method of methods [< Plantagenet Peter of Spain] (W 4, 378, 1882)

Logic may be defined as the science of the laws of the stable establishment of beliefs. Then, *exact* logic will be that doctrine of the conditions of establishment of stable belief which rests upon perfectly undoubted observations, and upon mathematical, that is, upon *diagrammatical*, or, *iconic*, thought. (CP 3.429, Monist, 1896)

Logic regarded from one instructive, though partial and narrow, point of view, is the theory of deliberate thinking. (EP 2: 376 c. 1906, CP 1.573).

(D) MATHEMATICAL ELEMENT

Indeed, logical algebra conclusively proves that mathematics extends over the whole realm of formal logic. (W 2, 389, 1870)

Logic can be of no avail to mathematics; but mathematics lays the foundation on which logic builds.... (CP 2.197, Minute Logic, 1902) (See Hawkins (1997) for a thorough discussion of and quotations supporting what I call Peirce's "reverse logicism": logic depends on mathematics.)

RESOLUTION

Peirce's conception of the objects of logic is taken from the Renaissance syllabus that was made famous by the Port-Royal syllabus of concept, proposition, and inference – to which the Port-Royal Logic's authors added a fourth of "method," sustained and organized inferences. The goal of all thought, and thought-processes, is belief of propositions that are true – even if logic's narrower interest is on truth-preserving inferences. (Although clarity of concepts, and his famous 1878 paper on this topic, have been sometimes treated as an anomaly, one cannot have true propositions if their component concepts are not clear.)[48] If every proposition that was true could be easily and immediately believed, and no untrue ones, then logic would be frivolous; its purpose then is to *obtain* beliefs that are true. However, beliefs are "about" something, and the relationship between thoughts and what they are about (and hence whether they are true) – that is, what we call the intentionality of such mental states – is for Peirce precisely what he examines in his theory of signs: the necessary conditions for, nature of, and kinds of aboutness. Formal logic, insofar as it succeeds, proceeds by observations about the related structures of propositions without regard to what they may, in fact, refer to: patterns of inference. Mathematics simply is the study of the nature of structure of all sorts, or at least of necessary relationships among all ideal (and often hypothetical) structures. That is why logic depends on mathematics and not *vice versa*.

CONCLUSION

Such, roughly, is the nature of Peirce's greatest contribution to thought: his logic and his ideas about the nature of logic and its relation to the world and to the mental. Even if its details are now relatively clear, do we yet grasp the leading ideas of Peirce's logic and philosophy? Have we thoroughly examined them, and extended them as our own exercise in doing philosophy? I do not think so: at least we don't grasp these ideas very well and even Peirceans have not taken them sufficiently seriously as philosophical proposals, to be seriously debated. I have evidence. First, I think his apparently sprawling definitions of logic, and his "reverse logicism" (that logic depends on mathematics), are regarded as huge embarrassments, not likely to promote his image. Although I have not adequately pursued these ideas here, I think they are in facts gems: some of the very few profound contributions in the history of philosophy to the big picture of what logic is, and of the normative dimensions of all of thought.

Second, it is obviously a truism to say that the theory of relations is one of Peirce's most important contributions to logic. Yet in the Frege–Russell tradition, the distinctively important and complicated contribution of adding relations to logic, is all but lost. The "constructivism" that is associated with Peirce's distinction between corollarial and theorematic reasoning point in this direction; so too would the application of contemporary complexity theory (and combinatorics) that paid special attention to the roles of relations. But perhaps the worst failing in our appraisal of Peirce's philosophy has been a continuing unwillingness to take up relations not as a privileged historical or even logical subject, but as a philosophical and specifically metaphysical topic. Are relations (2- or 3-place or higher) real? What is it for a relation to be real – as opposed to its *relata* existing? Relations and relations alone are the source of the only substantive complications that confound us – not even infinity (which is after all only tractable, insofar as it is, through the study of certain characteristic relations). To the extent that we have not explored the metaphysics and phenomenology of relations, we cannot understand Peirce's unique variety of realism. And we can't understand much else about his philosophy *really well*, either. In the vicinity of taking relations – and Peirce – philosophically seriously, it is fascinating that most Peirce scholars would widely agree that Peirce's "Reduction Thesis" (namely that relations are necessary for an account of the world, but that no higher than three-place ones are necessary) is one of the several most important basic principles of his philosophy. As we approach the century mark after Peirce's death, it is striking how little work we have expended on understanding what this thesis might mean and why Peirce would have held it.[49] I do not think we have progressed much beyond Murphey 1961, after nearly a century of Peirce scholarship. While work by Robert Burch, John Lango, myself, and perhaps a handful of others is suggestive of what we have yet to do, there is some truth to the claim that the most important work on Peirce's logical philosophy remains to be done.

NOTES

1. See Roberts (1973:12) and CP 4.291n 2.
2. Murphey (1961: 2).
3. Classifying already-complete arguments (that is, with premises and conclusion given) as valid or invalid is both the traditional and our own notion of logic. Within Peirce's conception of scientific method, deduction plays the role of *producing* valid and testable conclusions from premises that arise as hypotheses from abduction. (This purpose of deductive logic in the service of abduction is explicit in 1885 at W 5, 181–2.) Since he seems to have been aware of the undecidability of logic with relations and quantifiers (discussed below), and since deduced conclusions within this method should have characteristics other than mere formal validity, this perhaps explains the qualification of what logic "primarily" does. Furthermore, given the unavailability of algorithms to obtain some desired results, it is also sometimes called an "art." On the "art" of logic see W 3, 242, W 4, 378, 400 and the 1903 EP 2: 200 (CP 5.120f).
4. As well as Hintikka (1997) and Brady (2000). A general claim of Peirce's influence in the twentieth century was already clear in Murphey (1961: 152), citing the authority of C. I. Lewis, Morris Cohen, and I. M. Bochenskí.
5. No translation into English is available of all or important parts of Schröder's *Vorlesungen*, nor even a summary. We now have biographies of Schröder (Dipert 1981b and Dipert 1991a) and discussions of Peirce's and Schroder's differences on fine points with respect to sets, the universe of discourse, and individuals (Dipert 1997b and Dipert 1991b) and

on the impact of Schröder on Skolem (Brady 2000). There is careful research on Schröder in a series of publications by Volker Peckhaus (1990/1991, 1993, 1994, 1996a, 1996b, in addition to 1997) – but most of this research is in German.

6. W. V. Quine's review of CP 2–6 in (Quine 1933–35) rejected the existential graphs as cumbersome and uninsightful; Peirce's other logical work was described as mired in the pre-Fregean Boolean tradition. This view was amended slightly, but basically repeated in his last word on the subject (Quine 1989/1995).

7. He did use the symbol '∀' at least once: in a loose page in R-1261 he abbreviates 'American' as 'A,' and 'Unamerican' as '∀.'

8. In the sporadic attempts at a symbolic logic before Boole, there do occur symbols for subsumption or subclass, such as those in works by Leibniz, Lambert, and Drobisch, and there were diagrammatic notations as well.

9. Hookway (1985: 199–200), Dipert (1984).

10. His article on "Insolubilia" in *Baldwin's Dictionary* caught the attention of Bertrand Russell.

11. From a lecture at Johns Hopkins on December 17 of 1879, seven premises based on a "process of increase by 1" (which was later known as the successor function), cited in Fisch, Kloesel, and Houser (1982 –, Introduction: xliv). There is no inductive postulate. These views are developed in another manuscript, Vol. IV, sect. 24 from winter 1880–1881. There are now fifteen "assumptions" and they are based upon a "greater than" relation. Dedekind's four postulates, governing what he called the "simply infinite," were published in 1888; Peano's five postulates appeared in 1889.

12. In Peirce's own vocabulary, some of these "symbols" are actually indices – namely, what we would now term variables. The symbol '—<' is deliberately and iconically asymmetric and thus, in a sense, diagrammatic, as well as resembling the iconic but quantitative '≤.'

13. W 3, 85–6, 97; W 4, 174, 190; W 5, 337–8.

14. Perhaps this is well-known, but the connection was made for me by Paul V. Spade in conversation in 1977. See CP 5.340 n.1 and CP 2.618.

15. Schröder is sympathetic to Peirce's distinctions (*Vorlesungen* I, 1880–1905: 191–2) and suggests something like distinct null classes (each with respect to a considered property), o' and 1' (I: 189–90).

16. Using $C(x)$ for the "cardinality of x" (in the finite case, number of members of x), this is better rendered as $a' + b' = C(a) + C(b) - (a, b)$, where $a' = C(a)$ and $b' = C(b)$. In my copy of W 2, the type is broken but looks more like $a + b = (a+, b) + (a, b)$. It is of course unclear in the first place whether this should be '=' or '=,.'

17. Since propositional logic was conceived as being reducible to categorical logic, there would have been no conceptual progress, or even a vicious regress.

18. The special symbol for the identity of classes used in 1867, '=,' has disappeared.

19. An expression such as 'lsw' is not a proposition, but only (in one interpretation) the name of a class: the class of lovers of servants of some woman or other. A proposition might be stated as $lsw = slw$, which is generally false. The juxtaposition of relatives is more akin to functional application, which applies to sets and generates sets. It is noncommutative.

20. Partly published in CP 7. See Robin (1967: 45–8).

21. Peirce refers to this work in 1880 (W 4, 182 n. 17) and shows an awareness of the work in 1869 when he discusses not times, as was usual, but "cases" in which the components of a hypothetical proposition are true (W 2, 257–8).

22. In an 1884 draft of this paper, Peirce gives an orderly list (if of mixed definitions and axioms) of twelve axioms, the last five of which concern quantifiers. It is difficult, however, to determine which are basic and which follow from definitions or principles involving v and f. He remarks "It seems to me that the principles of formal logic, as it is ordinarily understood, are really exhausted, when it is brought to this point...." (W 5, 113–15). As the editors note, icons 1–5 provide a complete though not minimal propositional logic. W 5, 440 n. 173.10–11.

23. At places earlier than 1885, Peirce flirts with the thesis that the extensions of propositions are indeed classes: classes of times or states-of-affairs in which they are true. This would make 2b.2 sensible, but then '⊃' is *nothing more than* '⊆,' which is contrary to Peirce's remarks about the equivocal or autonomous use of '—<.'

24. Couturat explicitly mixed algebraic equations with equations that were intended to express categorical relationships within propositional (hypothetical) contexts.

25. The editors briefly address this problem (W 5, 440), but only note the double, not the triple, interpretation of '—<.'

26. It is echoed in a slightly later paper, published in 1897: "Moreover it must be acknowledged that the illative relation (that expressed by 'therefore') is the most important of logical relations, the be-all and the end-all of the rest. It can be demonstrated that formal logic needs no other elementary logical relation than this ... no other copula will of itself suffice for all purposes" (CP 3.472). Here, Peirce must be using 'illation' in the broad sense that also includes the material conditional

and class- or term-subsumption, since he identifies it as a "copula." The remark is trivial if he only means deducibility or validity.

27. In (Searle and Vanderveken, 1985) and far more successfully and attractively, in the ongoing work of my colleague John Kearns, described in (Kearns, 1997).

28. An earlier title was the oddly punctuated *How to think? A Critic of Argument*. The spelling of "Critick" is probably an allusion to Locke's divisions. See Max Fisch's comments (W 1: xxxiii) and Peirce's own discussions of Locke in the Harvard Lectures of 1865 (W 1: 169–172), whose "Critic" he finds "wholly inadequate and false." His objections are complicated and interesting, noting that Locke suggests that representation is often illusory (Locke says we "suppose" that they are equally ideas in others' minds and that they refer to reality) and considers the mental symbol (token) in an individual's mind, rather than functioning of symbols in general, and for (but not "in") mind in general.

29. And some of Peirce's published papers, while in some sense "final judgments," are fragmentary, incomplete, and suggestive, owing to Peirce's seeming rush to get large, sweeping papers into print, without careful editing by himself or others. This is especially evident in the published 1870 and 1885 papers in logic.

30. I have merged two separate proposed tables of contents in R-399.

31. In the single large manuscript for Chapter XVII, R-423, "The Logic of Mathematics," "Mathematics" is crossed off and replaced with "Quantity." This may seem an odd correction, given Peirce's frequent assertion that, contrary to Grassmanians and Hamiltonians, mathematics was not just about quantity. Namely, the Boolean calculus itself was mathematics, but did not deal with quantity; it was "algebra without quantity" or "mathematics of quality" (Jevons), W 4, 509 1883. However, since Peirce had already treated nonquantitative mathematics earlier in the work, he perhaps saw this chapter as turning to the remaining, and main, branch within mathematics.

32. There is a diagram in R-410: 12, Bk. II, Introductory Chapter 7. "Analysis of Propositions." It is of the relational "Every mother loves some child of hers" and is duplicated in Roberts (1973: 23). It is ugly and complicated, involving squares, diamonds, solid and empty circles, and over 25 lines that cross each other in complicated ways. He admits the proposition "is somewhat hard to put into a shape in which linkings [bindings of variables] take the place of inherences" (R-410:11). Elsewhere, he says that the diagrams in the chapter on graphs will allow the nonalgebraic mind much more easily to grasp propositions. He must have intended to make progress on diagrammatic representations.

33. Contrasted with his 1867 view that logic has "no immediate application to likenesses or indices" (W 2, 56).

34. R-411, Chapter 8: 189f.

35. Furthermore, and this becomes a syntactic flaw, if we had one line of a deduction $\exists x\,(Fx \wedge Bx)$, and another that was $\exists y\,(Fy \wedge By) \supset P$, we could *not*, by modus ponens, simply infer P.

36. Roberts (1973: 27). Peirce's choice of 'graph' is unfortunate and he should have known better, since Cayley had already employed 'graph' in the way it is now used in mathematics in graph theory.

37. "The order of two Πs or Σs is indifferent" (W 5, 109, 1884).

38. This functional dependence of substitution values can be shown by Skolem functions, and this technique is preferable to the usual notation in requiring us to express functional dependence, or lack thereof, of a variable on an earlier variable's value. Game-theoretic semantics for quantifiers, which Peirce was the first to explore (Hintikka 1997: 19–21, an insight due to Risto Hilpinen) also highlights these phenomena and perhaps was inspired by Peirce's study of *obligationes*. The possible dependence of an existential quantifier on an earlier one is rarely noticed.

39. In the example concerning flowers, one needs to notate that one existential quantifier dominates the other; presumably, as it was expressed in English, the left dominates and determines the value of the right.

40. See W 4, 170 n. 4 1880, W 5, 363, and the distinction between an algebra and a calculus (W 5, 464 n. 369.5).

41. Inside of a cut, Peirce sometimes points out, particularly with the entitative graphs, the line functions as, or "is," a universal quantifier. The line itself thus cannot be iconic for quantity. Shin (2002: 56) discusses this, rejecting the objection that this feature of being inside-vs.-outside a cut is not iconic by arguing that Peirce's choice is not "arbitrary." I do not follow. It is not arbitrary, *given* Peirce's use of cut for negation, but cut is not iconic, and nonarbitrariness does not, in any case, establish iconicity.

42. But then again, the sheet of assertion is not a universe of discourse, with points on it representing individuals as they do in Venn or Euler diagrams, so these dots are also unsatisfactory in their iconicity.

43. A related phenomenon is that the graphs make negation and conjunction primary, diminishing the importance of the conditional that had dominated Peirce's logic since 1885 and of some transitive and antisymmetry logical connective that had dominated his whole adult life (from 1867 through the 1890s); Frege and Schröder retained a basic such notion, and no modern syntactic treatment in logic has proposed banishing from its notation some form of a conditional.

44. Relations (Peirce's "secondness") are real (see Dipert 1997a) and patterns of change (natural laws; Peirce's "thirdness") are also real, not equivalent to mere Humean sets of changes, a position also endorsed by contemporary philosophers D. M. Armstrong and Peter Menzies.

45. Such as conformity to widespread use, even if not historical but otherwise adequate; ability to prove metalogical properties of the system in this notation (such as consistency, completeness, and so on).

46. Elsewhere (R-145 p. 1) Peirce is explicit that he does not think there "is any one ultimate analysis of logical relations which, from a purely logical standpoint, excluding all psychological considerations, can be said to be the *true* analysis . . ."

47. "Logic is the theory of *right* reasoning, of what reasoning ought to be, not of what it is. On that account, it used to be called a *directive* science, but of late years Überweg's adjective *normative* has been generally substituted" (CP 2.7, Minute Logic, 1902).

48. They are true to the *degree* their component concepts are clear. An exploration of this remark would take us into Peirce's theory of (epistemological) vagueness, and a correlative doctrine of the intrinsic vagueness of reality.

49. One need only look at the casual and superficial treatment of the issue in Christopher Hookway's otherwise very fine *Peirce* (1985: 86–101) – and I know of no better discussion.

NOTE ON REFERENCES

References to Peirce's work in this collection are as follows. 'MS' refers to the Peirce manuscripts, which are available on microfilm from Harvard University. 'CP n.m' refers to the *Collected Papers*, where n is volume number and m is paragraph number. 'W n,m' refers to the new, but as yet incomplete, *The Writings of Charles Sanders Peirce*, where n is volume number and m is page number. 'NE n, m' refers to *The New Elements of Mathematics*, where n is volume number and m is page number. RLT refers to *Reason and the Logic of Things*, the Cambridge Lectures of 1898. 'EP n:m' refers to *The Essential Peirce*, where n is volume number and m is page number. 'N n, m' refers to *The Nation*, where n is volume number and m is page number. 'SS.n' refers to *Semiotic and Significs*, where n is page number. R–n refers to the *Annotated Catalogue of the Papers of Charles S. Peirce*, where n is the manuscript number.

Very special thanks go to Danielle Bromwich, who chased down countless references, compiled the bibliography and the index, and generally was an enormous help in putting together this volume.

(CP) 1931–58. *The Collected Papers of Charles Sanders Peirce*. 8 vols. Edited by C. Hartshorne and P. Weiss (Vols. 1–6) and A. Burks (Vols. 7–8). Cambridge, Mass.: Harvard University Press.

(EP) 1992–8. *The Essential Peirce*. 2 vols. The Peirce Edition Project, edited by N. Houser and C. Kloesel. Bloomington and Indianapolis: Indiana University Press.

(MS) 1963–6. *The Charles S. Peirce Papers*. The Houghton Library. Cambridge, Mass: Harvard University Library Microreproduction service. 30 reels of microfilm.

(N) 1975–87. *Contributions to The Nation*. 4 vols. Edited by K. L. Ketner and J. E. Cook. Lubbock: Texas Tech University.

(NE) 1976. *The New Elements of Mathematics*. 4 vols. Edited by C. Eisele. The Hague and Paris: Mouton; Atlantic Highlands, N.J.: Humanities Press.

(R) 1967. *Annotated Catalogue of the Papers of Charles S. Peirce*. R. S. Robin. Worcester: University of Massachusetts Press.

(RLT) 1992. *Reasoning and the Logic of Things: The Cambridge Conferences Lectures of 1898*. Edited by K. L. Ketner. Cambridge, Mass. and London: Harvard University Press.

(SS) 1977. *Semiotic and Significs: The Correspondence Between Charles S. Peirce and Victoria Lady Welby*. Edited by Charles S. Hardwick. Bloomington: Indiana University Press.

(W) 1982–. *Writings of Charles S. Peirce: A Chronological Edition*. 6 vols. The Peirce Edition Project, edited by M. Fisch, C. Kloesel, and N. Houser. Bloomington: Indiana University Press.

Peirce, C. S. 1887. Logical Machines. *American Journal of Psychology* 1(1):165–70.

Peirce, C. S. 1929. Guessing. *Hound and Horn* 2:269–83.

BIBLIOGRAPHY

Adams, M. 1987.*Ockham*. 2 vols. Notre Dame, Ind.: University of Notre Dame Press.

Almeder, R. 1975a. Fallibilism and the Ultimate Irreversible Opinion. *American Philosophical Quarterly Monograph* 9:33–54.

Almeder, R. 1975b. The Epistemological Realism of Charles Peirce. *Transactions of the Charles S. Peirce Society* 11:3–17.

Almeder, R. 1980. *The Philosophy of Charles S. Peirce*. Oxford: Basil Blackwell.

Almeder, R. 1985. Peirce's Thirteen Theories of Truth. *Transactions of the Charles S. Peirce Society* 21:77–94.

Alston, W. 1956. Pragmatism and the Theory of Signs in Peirce. *Philosophy and Phenomenological Research* 17:79–88.

Altshuler, B. 1982. Peirce's Theory of Truth and Revolt Against Realism. *Transactions of the Charles S. Peirce Society* 18:34–56.

Anderson, D., and Goff, P. S. 1998. Peirce on Berkeley's Nominalistic Platonism. *American Catholic Philosophical Quarterly* 72:165–78.

Apel, K.-O. 1981. *Charles S. Peirce: From Pragmatism to Pragmaticism.* Translated by J. M. Krois. Amherst: University of Massachusetts Press.

Aristotle. 2002. *Nicomachean Ethics*. Translated by J. Sachs. Newburyport, Mass.: Focus Publishing/R. Pullins.

Ayer, A. J. 1968. *The Origins of Pragmatism*. London: Macmillan.

Baldwin, J. M. 1901–1902. *Dictionary of Philosophy and Psychology*. New York: Macmillan.

Bambrough, R. 1981. Peirce, Wittgenstein, and Systematic Philosophy. *Midwest Studies in Philosophy* 6:263–73.

Bastian, R. 1953. The Scholastic Realism of C.S. Peirce. *Philosophy and Phenomenological Research* 14:246–9.

Bergman, M. 2000. *Meaning and Mediation: Toward a Communicative Interpretation of Peirce's Theory of Signs*. Helsinki: University of Helsinki, Department of Communication.

Bernstein, R. 1964. Peirce's Theory of Perception. In *Studies in the Philosophy of Charles Sanders Peirce*, 2nd ser., edited by E. C. Moore and R. Robin, 105–89. Amherst: University of Massachusetts Press.

Bernstein, J. 1981. *The Analytical Engine*, 2nd ed. New York: William Morrow.

Boler, J. 1963. *Charles Peirce and Scholastic Realism: A Study of Peirce's Relation to John Duns Scotus*. Seattle: University of Washington Press.

Boler, J. 1980. Peirce, Ockham and Scholastic Realism. *The Monist* 63:290–302.

Boler, J. 1985. Ockham's Cleaver. *Franciscan Studies* 45:119–44.

Boler, J. 1996. The Ontological Commitment of Scotus's Account of Potency in His Questions on the Metaphysics, Book IX. In *John Duns Scotus: Metaphysics and Ethics*, edited by L. Honnefelder, R. Wood, and M. Dreyer, 145–60. Leiden: E. J. Brill.

Bolter, J. D. 1991. *Writing Space: The Computer, Hypertext, and the History of Writing*. Hillsdale, NJ: Lawrence Erlbaum Associates.

Brady, G. 2000. *From Peirce to Skolem*. Amsterdam: North Holland Publishing.

Brent, J. 1993. *Charles Sanders Peirce: A Life*. Bloomington, Ind.: Indiana University Press.

Brent, J. 1998. Freud and Peirce on the Unconscious Mind. Paper delivered at the annual meeting of the American Philosophical Association in Washington, DC, December 29, 1998.

Brentano, F. 1874. *Psychology from an Empirical Standpoint*. Edited by L. McAllister. New York: Humanities Press, 1973.

Buchler, J. 1939. *Charles Peirce's Empiricism*. New York: Octagon Books.

Burch, R. W. 1991. *A Peircean Reduction Thesis: The Foundations of Topological Logic*. Lubbock: Texas Tech University Press.

Burks, A. W. 1949. Icon, Index, Symbol. *Philosophy and Phenomenological Research* 9:673–89.

Bursill-Hall, G. L. 1971. *Speculative Grammars of the Middle Ages*. The Hague: Mouton.

Chisholm, R. M. 1952. Intentionality and the Theory of Signs. *Philosophical Studies* 3(4):56–63.

Christensen, C. B. 1994. Peirce's Transformation of Kant. *The Review of Metaphysics* 48:91–120.

Conant, J. 1997. The James/Royce Dispute and the Development of James's "Solution." In *The Cambridge Companion to William James*, edited by R. A. Putnam, 186–213. Cambridge: Cambridge University Press.

Cousin, V. 1836. *Ouvrage inedit d'Abelard*. Paris: Imprimerie Royale.

Crocker, T. P. 1998. Wittgenstein's Practices and Peirce's Habits: Agreement in Human Activity. *History of Philosophy Quarterly* 15:475–93.

Dauben, J. W. 1982. Peirce's Place in Mathematics. *Historia Mathematica* 9:311–25.

de Waal, C. 1996. The Real Issue between Nominalism and Realism: Peirce and Berkeley Reconsidered. *Transactions of the C. S. Peirce Society* 32:425–42.

de Waal. C. 1998. Peirce's Nominalist–Realist Distinction, an Untenable Dualism. *Transactions of the C. S. Peirce Society* 34:183–202.

de Waal, C. 2000. The History of Peirce's 1894 Logic Book. *Peirce Project Newsletter* 3 (2):4–5.

Deledalle, G. 2000. *Charles Peirce's Philosophy of Signs: Essays in Comparative Semiotics*. Bloomington: Indiana University Press.

Derrida, J. 1974. *Of Grammatology*. Translated by G. C. Spivak. Baltimore: Johns Hopkins University Press.

Dewey, J. 1922. The Development of American Pragmatism. In *Philosophy and Civilization*, 13–35. New York: Minton, Balch and Co., 1931.

Dewey, J. 1923. The Pragmatism of Peirce. In *Chance, Love, and Logic: Philosophical Essays*, by C. S. Peirce, edited by M. R. Cohen, 301–08. Bison Books Edition. Lincoln and London: University of Nebraska Press, 1998.

Dewey, J. 1929. *The Quest for Certainty: A Study on the Relation between Knowledge and Action*. New York: G. P. Putnam's Sons, 1960.

Dewey, J. 1936. What Are Universals? *The Journal of Philosophy* 33:253–61.

Dewey, J. 1938. *Logic: The Theory of Inquiry*. Boston: Holt, Rinehart, and Winston.

Dewey, J. 1946. *The Problems of Men*. New York: Philosophical Library.

DiLeo, J. 1991. Peirce's Haecceitism. *Transactions of the C. S. Peirce Society* 27:79–107.

Dipert, R. 1981a. Peirce's Propositional Logic. *Review of Metaphysics* 34:569–95.

Dipert, R. 1981b. Ernst Schröders Beitrag zur Logik und den Grundlagen der Mathematik. In *Fredericiana*, 23–44. Karlsruhe, West Germany.

Dipert, R. 1984. Peirce, Frege, Church's Theorem and the Logic of Relations. *History and Philosophy of Logic* 5:49–66.

Dipert, R. 1989. Peirce's Underestimated Place in the History of Logic: A Response to Quine. In *Peirce and Contemporary Thought*, edited by K. L. Ketner, 32–58. New York: Fordham University Press.

Dipert, R. 1991a. The Life and Work of Ernst Schröder. *Modern Logic* 1 (2/3):1–21.

Dipert, R. 1991b. Individuals and Extensional Logic in Schröder's *Vorlesungen über die Algebra der Logik*. *Modern Logic* 1 (2/3):22–42.

Dipert, R. 1994. The Life and Logical Contributions of O. H. Mitchell, Peirce's Gifted Student. *Transactions of the C. S. Peirce Society* 30:515–42.

Dipert, R. 1997a. The Mathematical Structure of the World: The World as Graph. *Journal of Philosophy* 94:329–58.

Dipert, R. 1997b. Peirce's Philosophical Conception of Sets. In *Studies in the Logic of Charles Sanders Peirce*, edited by N. Houser, D. D. Roberts, and J. Van Evra, 53–76. Bloomington: Indiana University Press.

Dummett, M. 1959. Truth. *Proceedings of the Aristotelian Society* 59:141–62.

Duns Scotus, J. 1950. *Opera Omnia*. Vatican City: Typis Polyglottis Vaticanae.

Duns Scotus, J. 1997. *Quaestiones Super Libros Metaphysicorum Aristotelis*. St. Bonaventure: The Franciscan Institute.

Eco, U. 1976. *A Theory of Semeiotics*. Bloomington: Indiana University Press.

Eisele, C. 1979. *Studies in the Scientific and Mathematical Philosophy of Charles S. Peirce*. The Hague: Mouton.

Engelbart, D. 1962. Augmenting Human Intellect: A Conceptual Framework. Summary Report, SRI Project No. 3578, AFOSR-3223, Contract AF49(638)-1024.

Engel-Tiercelin, C. 1992. Vagueness and the Unity of C. S. Peirce's Realism. *Transactions of the Charles S. Peirce Society* 28:51–82.

Esposito, J. 1980. *Evolutionary Metaphysics: The Development of Peirce's Theory of Categories*. Athens: Ohio University Press.

Fetzer, J. H. 1990. *Artificial Intelligence: Its Scope and Limits*. Dordrecht: Kluwer Academic Publishers.

Fisch, M. 1986. *Peirce, Semiotic, and Pragmatism: Essays by Max Fisch*. Edited by K. Ketner and C. Kloesel. Bloomington: Indiana University Press.

Fisch, M., Kloesel, C., and Houser, N., eds. 1982–. Introduction. In *Writings of Charles. S. Peirce: A Chronological Edition*. Bloomington: Indiana University Press.

Fitzgerald, J. 1966. *Peirce's Theory of Signs as Foundation for Pragmatism*. The Hague: Mouton.

Fodor, J. 1990. *A Theory of Content and Other Essays*. Cambridge, Mass.: MIT Press.

Forster, P. 1992. Peirce and the Threat of Nominalism. *Transactions of the C. S. Peirce Society* 28:691–724.

Freeman, E. & Skolimowski, H. 1974. The Search for Objectivity in Peirce and Popper. In *The Philosophy of Karl Popper*, edited by P. A. Schilpp, 464–519. LaSalle, Ill.: Open Court.

Frege, G. 1880/1881. Boole's Logical Calculus and the Concept-Script [*Begriffsschrift*]. In *Posthumous Writings*, edited by H. Hermes, F. Kambartel, and F. Kaulbach, translated by P. Long and R. White, 9–46. Chicago: University of Chicago Press, 1979.

Frege, G. 1882. Boole's Logical Formula–Language and the Concept-Script [*Begriffsschrift*]. In *Posthumous Writings*, edited by H. Hermes, F. Kambartel, and F. Kaulbach, translated by P. Long and R. White, 47–52. Chicago: University of Chicago Press, 1979.

Frege, G. 1884. The Foundations of Arithmetic: A logico-mathematical enquiry into the concept of number. Translated by J. L. Austin, 2nd revised edition. Evanston Ill.: Northwestern University Press, 1980.

Gardner, M. 1982. *Logic Machines and Diagrams*, 2nd ed. Chicago: University of Chicago Press.

Gavin, W. J. 1980. Peirce and "The Will to Believe." *The Monist* 63:342–50.

Gentry, G. 1952. Habit and the Logical Interpretant. In *Studies in the Philosophy of Charles Sanders Peirce*, edited by Wiener and Young, 75–92. Cambridge, Mass.: Harvard University Press.

George, R. 1982. Vorstellung and Erkenntniss in Kant. In *Interpreting Kant*, edited by M. S. Gram, 31–19. University of Iowa Press.

Goldstein, L. 1988. Logic and Reasoning. *Erkenntnis* 28:297–320.

Goodwin, R. 1961. Charles S. Peirce: A Modern Scotist? *New Scholasticism* 35:478–509.

Goudge, T. 1950. *The Thought of C. S. Peirce*. Toronto: University of Toronto Press.

Grajewski, M. 1944. *The Formal Distinction of Duns Scotus*. Washington, DC: Catholic University Press.

Gruender, D. 1983. Pragmatism, Science, and Metaphysics. In *The Relevance of Charles Peirce*, edited by E. Freeman, 271–92. La Salle, Ill.: The Hegeler Institute.

Gullvåg, I. 1981.Wittgenstein and Peirce. In *Wittgenstein – Aesthetics and Transcendental Philosophy*, edited by K. S. Johannesen and T. Nordenstam, 70–85. Vienna: Hölder-Pichler-Tempsky.

Haack, S. 1976. The Pragmatist Theory of Truth. *The British Journal for the Philosophy of Science* 27:231–49.

Haack, S. 1977. Pragmatism and Ontology: Peirce and James. *Revue Internationale de Philosophie* 31:377–400.

Haack, S. 1992. Extreme Scholastic Realism: Its Relevance to Philosophy of Science Today. *Transactions of the C. S. Peirce Society* 28:19–50.

Haack, S. 1993. Philosophy/philosophy, an Untenable Dualism. *Transactions of the Charles S. Peirce Society* 29:411–26.

Haack, S. 1997. "We Pragmatists..."; Peirce and Rorty in Conversation. *Partisan Review* 64:91–107.

Haack, S. 1998. *Manifesto of a Passionate Moderate: Unfashionable Essays*. Chicago and London: University of Chicago Press.

Hacking, I. 1980. The Theory of Probable Inference: Neyman, Peirce, and Braithwaite. In *Science, Belief and Behavior: Essays in Honour of R. B.*

Braithwaite, edited by D. H. Mellor, 141–60. Cambridge: Cambridge University Press.

Hausman, C. 1990. In and Out of Percepts. *Transactions of the Charles S. Peirce Society* 26:271–308.

Hausman, C. 1991. Peirce's Evolutionary Realism. *Transactions of the Charles S. Peirce Society* 27:475–500.

Hausman, C. 1993. *The Evolutionary Philosophy of Charles S. Peirce*. Cambridge: Cambridge University Press.

Hawkins, B. 1997. Peirce and Russell: The History of a Neglected Controversy. In *Studies in the Philosophy of Charles Sanders Peirce*, edited by N. Houser, D. Roberts, and J. Van Evra. Bloomington: Indiana University Press.

Hempel, C. G. 1945. Studies in Logic and Confirmation. *Mind* 54:1–26.

Hingst, K-M. 2000. James' Transformation der Pragmatischen Maxime von Peirce. In *William James, Pragmatismus*, edited by K. Oehler, 33–68. Berlin: Akademie Verlag.

Hintikka, J. 1988. On the Development of the Model-Theoretic Viewpoint in Logical Theory. *Synthese* 77:1–36.

Hintikka, J. 1997. The Place of C. S. Peirce in the History of Logical Theory. In *The Rule of Reason*, edited by J. Brunning and P. Forster, 13–33. Toronto: The University of Toronto Press.

Honnefelder, L & Wood, R. 1996. *John Duns Scotus: Metaphysics and Ethics*. Leiden: E. J. Brill.

Hookway, C. J. 1985. *Peirce*. London: Routledge and Kegan Paul.

Hookway, C. J. 1997. Logical Principles and Philosophical Attitudes: Peirce's Response to James's Pragmatism. In *The Cambridge Companion to William James*, edited by R. A. Putnam, 145–65. Cambridge: Cambridge University Press.

Hookway, C. J. 1998. Peirce, Charles Sanders (1839–1914). In *Routledge Encyclopaedia of Philosophy*, London and New York: Routledge. Vol. vii; 269–84.

Hookway, C. J. 2000. *Truth, Rationality, and Pragmatism: Themes from Peirce*. Oxford: Clarendon Press.

Hookway, C. J. 2002. Wahrheit und Realität: Putnam und die pragmatische Auffassung der Wahrheit. In *Hilary Putnam und die Tradition des Pragmatismus*, edited by M.-L. Raters and M. Willaschek, 93–116. Frankfurt: Suhrkamp.

Houser, N. 1992. Introduction. In *The Essential Peirce*, Vol. 1. The Peirce Edition Project, edited by N. Houser and C. Kloesel, xix–xli. Bloomington and Indianapolis: Indiana University Press.

Houser, N. 1998. Introduction. In *The Essential Peirce*, Vol. 2. The Peirce Edition Project, edited by N. Houser and C. Kloesel, xvii–xxxviii. Bloomington and Indianapolis: Indiana University Press.

James, W. 1890. *The Principles of Psychology*. In *The Works of William James*, edited by F. H. Burkhardt, F. Bowers, and I. K. Skrupskelis, 8–10. Cambridge, Mass. and London: Harvard University Press, 1981.

James, W. 1897a. The Moral Philosopher and the Moral Life. In *The Will To Believe and Other Essays in Popular Philosophy*, 141–62. Cambridge, Mass.: Harvard University Press, 1979.

James, W. 1897b. *The Will to Believe and Other Essays in Popular Philosophy*. In *The Works of William James*. Vol. 6, edited by F. H. Burkhardt, F. Bowers, and I. K. Skrupskelis. Cambridge, Mass. and London: Harvard University Press, 1979.

James, W. 1898. *Essays in Philosophy* in *The Works of William James.* Vol. 5, edited by F. H. Burkhardt, F. Bowers, and I. K. Skrupskelis. Cambridge, Mass. and London: Harvard University Press, 1978.

James, W. 1902. *The Varieties of Religious Experience: A Study in Human Nature*. In *The works of William James*. Vol. 15, edited by F. H. Burkhardt, F. Bowers, and I. K. Skrupskelis. Cambridge, Mass. and London: Harvard University Press, 1985.

James, W. 1907. *Pragmatism: A New Name for Some Old Ways of Thinking*. In *The Works of William James*. Vol. 1, edited by F. H. Burkhardt, F. Bowers, and I. K. Skrupskelis. Cambridge, Mass. and London: Harvard University Press, 1975.

James, W. 1909a. *The Meaning of Truth: A Sequel to Pragmatism*. In *The Works of William James*. Vol. 2, edited by F. H. Burkhardt, F. Bowers, and I. K. Skrupskelis. Cambridge, Mass. and London: Harvard University Press, 1978.

James, W. 1909b. *A Pluralistic Universe*. In *The Works of William James*. Vol. 4, edited by F. H. Burkhardt, F. Bowers, and I. K. Skrupskelis. Cambridge, Mass. and London: Harvard University Press, 1977.

James, W. 1912. *Essays in Radical Empiricism*. In *The Works of William James*, Vol. 3, edited by F. H. Burkhardt, F. Bowers, and I. K. Skrupskelis. Cambridge, Mass. and London: Harvard University Press, 1976.

James, W. 1988. *Manuscript Lectures*. In *The Works of William James*, Vol. 19, edited by F. H. Burkhardt, F. Bowers, and I. K. Skrupskelis. Cambridge, Mass. and London: Harvard University Press.

Kant, I. 1781–1787. *Kritik der reinen Vernunft*. Edited by R. Schmidt. Hamburg: Felix Meiner, 1990.

Kearns, J. 1997. Propositional Logic of Supposition and Assertion. *Notre Dame Journal of Formal Logic* 38:325–49.

Ketner, K. L. 1981. The Best Example of Semiosis and its Use in Teaching Semiotics. *American Journal of Semiotics* 1 (1–2):47–83.

Ketner, K. L. 1988. Peirce and Turing: Comparisons and Conjectures. *Semiotica* 68 (1–2):33–61.

Kilpinen, E. 2000. *The Enormous Fly-Wheel of Society: Pragmatism's Habitual Conception of Action and Social Theory*, Research Report 235. Helsinki: Department of Sociology, University of Helsinki.

King, P. 1992. Duns Scotus on the Common Nature and the Individual Differentia. *Philosophical Topics* 20:51–76.

King, P. 2001. Scotus on Metaphysics. In *Cambridge Companion to Duns Scotus*, edited by T. Williams, 15–68. Cambridge: Cambridge University Press.

Kloesel, C. 1981. Speculative Grammar: From Duns Scotus to Charles Peirce. In *Proceedings of the C. S. Peirce Bicentennial International Congress*, edited by K. Ketner, 127–34. Lubbock: Texas Tech University Press.

Lakoff, G. 1987. *Women, Fire, and Dangerous Things: What Categories Reveal about the Mind*. Chicago: University of Chicago Press.

Lalor, B. J. 1997. The Classification of Peirce's Interpretants. *Semiotica* 114 (1–2):31–40.

Lambert, K. 2003.The Philosophical Foundations of Free Logic. In *Selected Essays*, 122–75. Cambridge: Cambridge University Press.

Lee, H. 1982. Peirce, Boler and Idealism. *Southern Journal of Philosophy*. 20:433–40.

Lee, R. J. 1998. Peirce's Retrieval of Scotistic Realism. *American Catholic Philosophical Quarterly* 72:179–96.

Lennox, J. G. 1993. Darwin Was a Teleologist. *Biology and Philosophy* 8:409–21.

Lenz, J. 1964. Induction as Self-Corrective. In *Studies in the Philosophy of Charles Sanders Peirce*. 2nd series, edited by E. C. Moore and R. Robin, 151–62. Amherst: University of Massachusetts Press.

Levi, I. 1980. Induction as Self-Correcting According to Peirce. In *Science, Belief and Behavior: Essays in Honour of R. B. Braithwaite*, edited by D. H. Mellor, 127–40. Cambridge: Cambridge University Press.

Levi, I. 1983. *The Enterprise of Knowledge*. Cambridge, Mass.: The MIT Press.

Levi, I. 1984. Messianic vs. Myopic Realism. In *Proceedings of the 1984 Biennial Meeting of the Philosophy of Science Association*. Vol. ii, edited by P. D. Asquith and P. Kitcher, 402–07. East Lansing, Mich. Philosophy of Science Association.

Levi, I. 1991. *The Fixation of Belief and Its Undoing*. Cambridge: Cambridge University Press.

Lewis, C. I. 1929. *Mind and the World Order*. New York: Dover Publications.

Liszka, J. J. 1990. Peirce's Interpretant. *Transactions of the Charles S. Peirce Society* 26:17–62.

Liszka, J. J. 1996. *A General Introduction to the Semeiotic of Charles Sanders Peirce*. Bloomington: Indiana University Press.

Locke, J. 1690. *An Essay Concerning Human Understanding*. Revised ed., edited by J. W. Yolton. London: Dent, 1965.

Mackie, J. 1977. *Ethics: Inventing Right and Wrong*. Harmonsworth: Penguin.

Margolis, J. 1993. The Passing of Peirce's Realism. *Transactions of the Charles S. Peirce Society* 29:293–330.

McCarthy, J. 1990. Peirce's Proof of Pragmatism. *Transactions of the Charles S. Peirce Society* 26:63–113.

McKeon, C. 1952. Peirce's Scotistic Realism. In *Studies in the Philosophy of Charles Sanders Peirce*, edited by P. Wiener and F. Young, 238–50. Cambridge, Mass.: Harvard University Press.

Menand, L. 2001. *The Metaphysical Club: A Story of Ideas in America*. New York: Farrar, Straus and Giroux.

Michael, E. 1976. Peirce's Earliest Contact with Scholastic Logic. *Transactions of the Charles S. Peirce Society* 12:46–55.

Michael, E. 1977. A Note on the Roots of Peirce's Division of Logic into Three Branches. *Notre Dame Journal of Formal Logic* 18:639–40.

Michael, E., and Michael, F. 1979. Peirce on the Nature of Logic. *Notre Dame Journal of Formal Logic* 20:84–8.

Michael, F. 1980. The Deduction of the Categories in Peirce's "New List." *Transactions of the Charles S. Peirce Society* 16:179–211.

Michael, F. 1988. Two Forms of Scholastic Realism in Peirce. *Transactions of the Charles S. Peirce Society* 24:317–48.

Migotti, M. 1999. Peirce's Double Aspect Theory of Truth. In *Pragmatism, Canadian Journal of Philosophy*, edited by C. Misak. Supp. Vol. 24:75–108.

Millikan, R. G. 1984. *Language, Thought, and Other Biological Categories*. Cambridge, Mass.: MIT Press.

Misak, C. J. 1991. *Truth and the End of Inquiry: A Peircean Account of Truth*. Oxford: Clarendon Press.

Misak, C. J. 1994. Pragmatism and the Transcendental Turn in Truth and Ethics. *Transactions of the Charles S. Peirce Society* 30:739–75.

Misak, C. J. 1995. *Verificationism: Its History and Prospect*. London: Routledge.

Misak, C. J. 2000. *Truth, Politics, Morality: Pragmatism and Deliberation*. London and New York: Routledge.

Moody, E. A. 1953. *Truth and Consequence in Medieval Logic*. Amsterdam, North Holland Publishing.

Moore, A. W. 1910. *Pragmatism and Its Critics*. Chicago: The University of Chicago Press.

Moore, E. C. 1952. The Scholastic Realism of C. S. Peirce. *Philosophy and Phenomenological Research* 12:406–17.

Moore, E. C. 1953. Professor Bastian's Comments on Peirce's Scholasticism. *Philosophy and Phenomenological Research* 14:250–51.

Moore, E. C. 1964. The Influence of Duns Scotus on Peirce. In *Studies in the Philosophy of Charles Sanders Peirce*. 2nd ser., edited by E. C. Moore and R. Robin, 401–13. Amherst: University of Massachusetts Press.

Morris, C. 1946. *Signs, Language, and Behavior*. New York: Prentice–Hall.

Mounce, H. O. 1997. *The Two Pragmatisms: From Peirce to Rorty*. London and New York: Routledge.

Murphey, M. G. 1961. *The Development of Peirce's Philosophy*. Cambridge, Mass.: Harvard University Press.

Murphey, M. 1965. On Peirce's Metaphysics. *Transactions of the Charles S. Peirce Society* 1:12–25.

Nesher, D. 1981. Peirce on Realism, Reality and Existence. In *Proceedings of the C. S. Peirce Bicentennial International Congress*, edited by K. L. Ketner, 247–50. Lubbock: Texas Tech University Press.

Niiniluoto. I. 1999. *Critical Scientific Realism*. Oxford and New York: Oxford University Press.

Norman, J. 2003. Provability in Peirce's Graphs. *Transactions of the Charles S. Peirce Society*.

Nubiola, J. 1996. Scholarship on the Relations between Ludwig Wittgenstein and Charles S. Peirce. In *Studies on the History of Logic: Proceedings of the III Symposium on History of Logic*, edited by I. Angelelli and M. Cerezo, 281–94. Berlin: Gruyter.

Ockham, W. 1990.*Ockham: Philosophical Writings*. Indianapolis: Hackett.

O'Connor. D. D. 1964. Peirce's Debt to F. E. Abbot. *Journal of the History of Ideas* 25:543–64.

Olshewsky, T. M.1981. Realism and Semiosis. In *Proceedings of the C. S. Peirce Bicentennial International Congress*, edited by K. L. Ketner, 87–92. Lubbock: Texas Tech University Press.

Panofsky, E. 1957. *Gothic Architecture and Scholasticism*. New York: Meridian Books.

Pape, H. 2000. Zur Begründungslogik des Pragmatismus: Die Wahrheit des Gedankens und die Erfahrung der Bedeutung: Über die Grundlegung der Jamesschen Wahrheitstheorie durch seine Psychologie der Symbolerfahrung. In K. Oehler (ed.) *William James, Pragmatismus*, edited by K. Oehler, 235–62. Berlin: Akademie Verlag.

Papineau, D. 1984. Representation and Explanation. *Philosophy of Science* 51:550–72.

Papineau, D. 1987. *Reality and Representation*. Oxford: Basil Blackwell.

Parker, K. 1990. C. S. Peirce and the Philosophy of Religion. *Southern Journal of Philosophy* 28 (2):193–212.

Parker, K. 1998. *The Continuity of Peirce's Thought*. Nashville: Vanderbilt University Press.

Peckhaus, V. 1990/1991. Ernst Schröder und die pasigraphischen Systeme von Peano und Peirce. *Modern Logic* 1 (2/3):174–205.

Peckhaus, V. 1993. Ernst Schröder und der Logizismus. In *Philosophie und Logik. Frege-Kolloquien Jena 1989/1991*, edited by W. Stelzner and W. de Gruyter, 108–19. Berlin: Berlin/New York.

Peckhaus, V. 1994. Wozu Algebra der Logik? Ernst Schröders Suche nach einer universalen Theorie der Verknüpfungen. *Modern Logic* 4:357–81.

Peckhaus, V. 1996a. The Influence of Hermann Günther Grassmann and Robert Grassmann on Ernst Schröder's Algebra of Logic. In *Hermann Günther Grassmann (1809–1877): Visionary Mathematician, Scientist and Neohumanist Scholar*. Boston Studies in the Philosophy of Science, Vol. 187, edited by G. Schubring, 217–27. Dordrecht; and Boston: Kluwer Academic Publishers.

Peckhaus, V. 1996b. The Axiomatic Method and Ernst Schröder's Algebraic Approach to Logic. *Philosophia Scientiae* (Nancy, France) 1 (3):1–15.

Peckhaus, V. 1997. *Logik, Mathesis universalis und allgemeine Wissenschaft. Leibniz und die Wiederentdeckung der formalen Logik im 19. Jahrhundert*. Berlin: Akademie-Verlag.

Percy, W. 1975. *The Message in the Bottle*. New York: Farrar, Straus, and Giroux.

Perriah, A. R. 1989. Peirce's Semiotic and Scholastic Logic. *Transactions of the Charles S. Peirce Society* 25:41–9.

Perry, R. B. 1935/1936. *The Thought and Character of William James*, 2 vols. London: Humphrey Milford and Oxford University Press.

Pihlström, S. 1996. *Structuring the World: The Issue of Realism and the Nature of Ontological Problems in Classical and Contemporary Pragmatism*. Acta Philosophica Fennica 59. Helsinki: The Philosophical Society of Finland.

Pihlström, S. 1998a. *Pragmatism and Philosophical Anthropology: Understanding Our Human Life in a Human World*. New York: Peter Lang.

Pihlström, S. 1998b. Peircean Scholastic Realism and Transcendental Arguments. *Transactions of the Charles S. Peirce Society* 34:382–413.

Pihlström, S. 1998c. Peirce vs. James: Susan Haack on Old and New Pragmatism. *The Philosophical Forum* 29:66–85.

Pihlström, S. 2003. *Naturalizing the Transcendental: A Pragmatic View*. Amherst. N.Y: Prometheus/Humanity Books.

Pinker, S. 1994. *The Language Instinct: How the Mind Creates Language.* New York: William Morrow and Company.

Plato. 1976. *Phaedo.* Translated by D. Gallop. Oxford: Clarendon Press.

Popkin, R., and Meyers, R. 1993. Early Influences on Peirce. *Journal of the History of Philosophy* 31:607–21.

Popper, K. R. 1972. *Objective Knowledge: An Evolutionary Approach.* Oxford: Oxford University Press.

Potter, V. 1967. *Charles Peirce on Norms and Ideals.* Amherst: University of Massachusetts Press.

Potter, V. 1972. Vaguely Like a Man: The Theism of Charles S. Peirce. In *God, Knowable and Unknowable,* edited by R. Roth, 241–54. New York: Fordham University Press.

Potter, V. 1976. C. S. Peirce's Argument for God's Reality: A Pragmatist's View. In *The Papin Festschrift,* edited by J. Armenti, 224–44. Villanova: Villanova University Press.

Potts, T. 1965. Review of Boler (1963). *Philosophical Quarterly* 15:361–2.

Prantl, C. 1955. *Geschichte der Logik im Abendlaende.* Graz Akademische Druck u. Verlagsanstalt.

Putnam, H. 1980. Models and Reality. *Journal of Symbolic Logic* 45:464–82.

Putnam, H. 1981. *Reason, Truth and History.* Cambridge: Cambridge University Press.

Putnam, Hilary 1982. Peirce as Logician. *Historia Mathematica* 9:290–301.

Putnam, H. 1990. *Realism with a Human Face.* Edited by J. Conant. Cambridge, Mass. and London: Harvard University Press.

Putnam, H. 1992a. Comments on the Lectures. In *Reasoning and the Logic of Things: The Cambridge Conferences Lectures of 1898,* edited by K. L. Ketner, 55–102. Cambridge, Mass. and London: Harvard University Press.

Putnam, H. 1992b. *Renewing Philosophy.* Cambridge, Mass.: Harvard University Press.

Putnam, H. 1994. *Words and Life,* edited by J. Conant. Cambridge, Mass. and London: Harvard University Press.

Putnam, H. 1995a. *Pragmatism: An Open Question.* Oxford and Cambridge, Mass.: Blackwell.

Putnam, H. 1995b. Pragmatism. *Proceedings of the Aristotelian Society* 95:271–306.

Putnam, H. 1997. James's Theory of Truth. In *The Cambridge Companion to William James,* edited by R. A. Putnam, 166–85. Cambridge: Cambridge University Press.

Putnam, H. 1999. *The Threefold Cord: Mind, Body, and World.* New York: Columbia University Press.

Quine, W. V. O. 1933. Review of *Charles Sanders Peirce. Collected Papers Vol. II: Elements of Logic.* Isis 19(55):220–29.

Quine, W. V. O. 1934–35a. Review of *Charles Sanders Peirce. Collected Papers Vol. III: Exact Logic*. Isis 22(63):285–97.

Quine, W. V. O. 1934–35b. Review of *Charles Sanders Peirce. Collected Papers Vol. IV: The Simplest Mathematics*. Isis 22(64):551–53.

Quine, W. V. O. 1955. *Mathematical Logic*. Cambridge, Mass.: Harvard University Press.

Quine, W. V. O. 1986. *The Philosophy of Logic*. 2nd ed. Cambridge, Mass.: Harvard University Press.

Quine, W. V. O. 1989/1995. Peirce's Logic. In *Peirce and Contemporary Thought*, edited by K. L. Ketner, 23–31. New York: Fordham University Press.

Raposa, M. 1984. Habits and Essences. *Transactions of the C. S. Peirce Society* 20:147–68.

Raposa, M. 1989. *Peirce's Philosophy of Religion*. Bloomington: Indiana University Press.

Rescher, N. 2000. *Realistic Pragmatism: An Introduction to Pragmatic Philosophy*. Albany, N.Y.: SUNY Press.

Roberts, D. D. 1970. On Peirce's Realism. *Transactions of the C. S. Peirce Society* 6: 67–83.

Roberts, D. D. 1973. *The Existential Graphs of Charles S. Peirce*. The Hague: Mouton.

Rohatyn, D. 1983. Peirce and the Defense of Realism: The Unfolding of Pragmatic Logic. *Transactions of the C. S. Peirce Society* 19:45–61.

Rorty, R. 1982. *Consequences of Pragmatism*. Brighton: The Harvester Press.

Rorty, R. 1998. *Truth and Progress*. Cambridge: Cambridge University Press.

Rosenthal, S. B. 1968. The would-be Present of C. S. Peirce. *Transactions of the C. S. Peirce Society* 4:155–62.

Rosenthal, S. B. 1969. Peirce's Theory of the Perceptual Judgment: An Ambiguity. *Journal of the History of Philosophy* 7:303–14.

Rosenthal, S. B. 2000. William James on the One and the Many. In *William James, Pragmatismus*, edited by K. Oehler, 93–108. Berlin: Akademie Verlag.

Roth, R. J. 1965. Is Peirce's Pragmatism Anti-Jamesian? *International Philosophical Quarterly* 5:541–63.

Royce, J. 1885. *The Religious Aspect of Philosophy*. Gloucester, Mass.: Peter Smith, 1965.

Rumfitt, I. forthcoming. Asserting and Excluding: Steps towards an Anti-realist Account of Classical Consequence. In *The Philosophy of Michael Dummett*. The Library of Living Philosophy, edited by R. Auxier. Chicago and La Salle, Ill.: Open Court Press.

Samway, P. H., ed. 1995. *A Thief of Peirce: The Letters of Kenneth Laine Ketner and Walker Percy*. Jackson, Miss.: University Press of Mississippi.

Savan, D. 1965. Decision and Knowledge in Peirce. *Transactions of the C. S. Peirce Society* 1:38–49.

Scanlon, M. 1991. Who Were the American Postulate Theorists? *The Journal of Symbolic Logic* 56 (3):981–1002.

Schiller, F. C. S. 1903. *Humanism: Philosophical Essays.* London: Macmillan.

Schiller, F. C. S. 1907. *Studies in Humanism.* London: Macmillan.

Schröder, E. 1880–1905. *Vorlesungen über die Algebra der Logik.* Vols. I, II.1, III, II.2. Leipzig: Teubner. Reprinted The Bronx: Chelsea, 1966.

Searle, J. R., and Vanderveken, D.1985. *Foundations of Illocutionary Logic.* Cambridge: Cambridge University Press.

Seigfried, C. H.1990. *William James's Radical Reconstruction of Philosophy.* Albany, N.Y.: SUNY Press.

Sher, G. 1997. Partially Ordered (Branching) Generalized Quantifiers: A General Definition. *Journal of Philosophical Logic* 26:1–43.

Shin, S-J. 2002. *The Iconic Logic of Peirce's Graphs.* Cambridge, Mass.: MIT Press.

Shook, J. R. 1998. *Pragmatism: An Annotated Bibliography 1898–1940.* Amsterdam and Atlanta: Rodopi.

Shook, J. R. 2000. *Dewey's Empirical Theory of Knowledge and Reality.* Albany, N.Y.: SUNY Press.

Short, T. L. 1981a. Semeiosis and Intentionality. *Transactions of the Charles S. Peirce Society* 17:197–223.

Short, T. L. 1981b. Peirce's Concept of Final Causation. *Transactions of the Charles S. Peirce Society* 17:369–82.

Short, T. L. 1982. Life Among the Legisigns. *Transactions of the Charles S. Peirce Society* 18:285–310.

Short, T. L. 1983. Teleology in Nature. *American Philosophical Quarterly* 20:311–20.

Short, T. L. 1996a. Review Article. *Synthese.* 106:409–30.

Short, T. L. 1996b. Interpreting Peirce's Interpretant: A Response to Lalor, Liszka, and Meyers. *Transactions of the Charles S. Peirce Society* 488–541. Vol. 32 no. 4.

Short, T. L. 1999. Teleology and Linguistic Change. In *The Peirce Seminar Papers.* Vol. 4, edited by M. Shapiro and M. Haley, 111–58. New York: Berghahn Books.

Short, T. L. 2000. Peirce on the Aim of Inquiry: Another Reading of "Fixation." *Transactions of the Charles S. Peirce Society* 35 (1):1–23.

Short, T. L. "Darwin's Concept of Final Cause: Neither New Nor Trivial," *Biology and Philosophy,* Vol. 17, No. 3, June 2002.

Short T. L. forthcoming. Robin on Perception and Sentiment in Peirce. *Transactions of Charles S. Peirce Society.*

Skagestad, P. 1981. *The Road of Inquiry: Charles Peirce's Pragmatic Realism*. New York: Columbia University Press.

Skagestad, P. 1993. Thinking with Machines: Intelligence Augmentation, Evolutionary Epistemology, and Semiotic. *Journal of Social and Evolutionary Systems* 16(2):157–80.

Skagestad, P. 1999a. Peirce's Inkstand as an External Embodiment of Mind. *Transactions of the Charles S. Peirce Society* 35:551–61.

Skagestad, P. 1999b. Review of Samway (1995). *Minds and Machines* 9(2):273–6.

Smith, J. E. 1978. *Purpose and Thought: The Meaning of Pragmatism*. New Haven: Yale University Press.

Sowa, J. 1984. *Conceptual Structures: Information Processing in Mind and Machine*. Reading, Mass.: Addison–Wesley.

Sowa, J., ed. 2000. *Knowledge Representation: Logical, Philosophical, Computational Foundations*. Belmont, Calif.: Brooks/Cole.

Strawson, P. F. 1965. "Truth, A Reconsideration of Austin's Views," *Philosophical Quarterly*, Vol. 15.

Sturt, Henry ed. 1902. *Personal Idealism*. London and New York: Macmillian.

Thayer, H. S. 1968. *Meaning and Action: A Critical History of Pragmatism*. Indianapolis and New York: The Bobbs-Merrill Co.

Thayer, H. S. 1996. Peirce and Truth: Some Reflections. *Transactions of the Charles S. Peirce Society* 32:1–10.

Thompson, M. 1952. The Paradox of Peirce's Realism. In *Studies in the Philosophy of Charles Sanders Peirce*, edited by P. P. Wiener and F. H. Young, 133–42. Cambridge, Mass.: Harvard University Press.

Thompson, M. 1953. *The Pragmatic Philosophy of Charles S. Peirce*. Chicago: University of Chicago Press.

Tiles, J. E. 1988. *Dewey*. London and New York: Routledge.

Trammell, R. 1972. Religion, Instinct, and Reason in the Thought of Charles. S. Peirce. *Transactions of the Charles S. Peirce Society* 8:3–23.

Turrisi, P. A. 1997a. Introduction to *Pragmatism as a Principle and as a Method of Right Thinking: The 1903 Harvard Lectures on Pragmatism*, by C. S. Peirce, edited by P. A. Turrisi, 1–20. Albany: SUNY Press.

Turrisi, P. A. 1997b. Commentary on *Pragmatism as a Principle and as a Method of Right Thinking: The 1903 Harvard Lectures on Pragmatism*, by C. S. Peirce, edited by P. A. Turrisi, 21–105. Albany: SUNY Press.

Vilkko, R. 2000. *A Hundred Years of Logic and Philosophy: Reform Efforts of Logic in 19th Century Germany*. Academic dissertation. Department of Philosophy, University of Helsinki.

Wiggins, D. 1996. Sufficient Reason: A Principle in Diverse Guises, both Ancient and Modern. *Acta Philosophica Fennica* 61:117–32.

Wiggins, D. 1999. C. S. Peirce: Belief, Truth, and Going from the Known to the Unknown. In *Pragmatism*, edited by C. Misak. *Canadian Journal of Philosophy* Supp. Vol. 24:9–29.

Wiggins, D. 2002. An indefinibilist cum normative view of truth and the marks of truth. In *What is Truth?* edited by R. Schantz W. de Gruyter, 316–32. Berlin and New York.

Williams, B. 1978. *Descartes: The Project of Pure Inquiry*. Harmondsworth: Penguin.

Williams, B. 1985. *Ethics and the Limits of Philosophy*. Cambridge, Mass.: Harvard University Press.

Wimsatt, W. C. 1972. Teleology and the Logical Structure of Function Statements. *Studies in the History and Philosophy of Science* 3:1–80.

Wittgenstein, L. 1921. *Tractatus Logico-Philosophicus*. Translated by D. F. Pears and B. F. McGuinness. London: Kegan Paul, 1961.

Wittgenstein, L. 1958. *Philosophical Investigations*. 3rd ed. New York: Macmillan.

Wright, L. 1976. *Teleological Explanations*. Berkeley: University of California Press.

INDEX

Abduction, 16–19, 25, 65, 88, 102–104,
    113, 123–124, 159, 163, 172,
    193–196, 283, 284, 287, 304
  Abductive hypothesis, 122, 123,
    318–319
  Abductive inference, 25
  Ampliative, 18–19
  Cannot believe abductive inferences,
    163
  Conjecture, 281
  See retroduction and hypothesis
Abelard, 63
Absolute, 56
Act, 121, 229, 231
  Act purposefully, 233
Action, 7, 10, 11, 15, 21, 30, 32–35, 38,
    49, 143, 153, 163, 169, 171, 179,
    180, 197, 226, 229–230, 236, 315
  Diagrammatic, 11–12
  Dyadic action, 222
  Habits of action, 43, 52, 156, 229
  Intersubjective action of scientific
    community, 52
  Paralysis of action, 11
  Thought-experiments, 11–12
Actuality, 21–23
Aesthetics, 127, 145
  Aesthetic theory, 237
  As a normative science, 39, 170
  Limited to matters of taste, 170
Agape, 180, 186–187, 191
  Basis of religious of attitude, 182
  Employing agapasm, 192
  Used to overcome self-interest, 186
  Used to overcome self-love, 186
Agnosticism, 11

Agreement, 166–167
Albert the Great, 63
Alexander of Hales, 63
Algebra, 290, 294, 299–302, 305,
    317–323
  Algebraic Period, 292–293, 312
Almeder, R., 207–209
American, 42, 320
  American postulate theorists, 292
  American transcendentalists, 188
  Un-American, 320
'Analysis of Propositions', 322
Ancient Philosophy, 62
Anderson, D., 2
Angell, J. R., 56
Anselm, 63
Anti-Cartesianism, 62, 74, 215
  Anti-Cartesian denial of intuitive
    knowledge, 222
Apogogical Inversion, 263–266, 284
  Of a statistical deduction, 265–266
Appearance, 197–200, 207
Aquinas, T., 63, 66, 67, 73, 77, 78, 84
Architectonic system, 2
Argument, 7, 9, 12, 15, 150, 152, 154,
    158, 169, 171, 258–274, 291, 315,
    316, 318–319
Arisbe, 63
Aristotle, 19, 24, 59, 63, 66, 77, 78, 121,
    230, 241, 258, 263–266, 290
  Aristotelian account of signs, 216–217
  Aristotelian syllogistic, 294
  Aristotelian syllogism, 290, 298
  Aristotelian/Scholastic method, 20
  Aristotelian logic, 291, 296, 304
Barbara, 288, 309

343

Aristotle (*cont.*)
  Categorical syllogism in Barbara, 6–7,
    265, 266, 284, 285
  Causality, 78
  Final cause, 231
  Induction, 263
  Teleological, 230
  Theory of categorical syllogism,
    258–263
Artifacts, 118, 136–137
Artificial intelligence, 241, 254, 256
Assertion, 7–9, 15, 22, 109, 115–116,
    126, 146, 147, 229, 307
  Commitments of assertion, 7
  Practice of assertion, 7
  Sheet of assertion, 310–311, 323
'Association of Ideas (the)', 304
Augustine, 63, 124
Authority, 60–61, 78
Averroes, 63
Avicenna, 63
Axioms, 26, 290, 292, 297, 313, 321
Ayer, A. J., 101

Babbage, C., 251, 255
Bacon, R., 58, 63, 77
  Baconian induction, 284
Bain, A., 10
Baldwin's *Dictionary of Philosophy and
    Psychology*, 63, 139, 249, 320
Bayes, T., 267
  Bayes' Theorem, 268, 271, 275
  Bayesianism, 276, 278, 283, 286
Behaviour, 232–233
Belief, 5–8, 10, 12–15, 18–19, 31, 48,
    50–51, 55, 87, 88, 95, 97, 101–102,
    105–106, 109–113, 119, 127, 141,
    145, 148, 152, 154, 157, 160, 168,
    172, 267, 276, 278, 282, 304, 315,
    317–319
  Answerable to reality, 96, 109
  Background beliefs, 13, 123, 139, 153,
    160–162, 164, 167
  Belief and action, 10, 36, 151, 156,
    162, 164, 172
  Belief and assertion, 109
  Belief out of place in science, 151–152,
    160–162, 165
  Belief-habit, 11
  Cannot be improved upon, 150, 171

Coherent system of beliefs, 128, 153
Collective belief fixation, 52
Commitments of believing, 7, 146
Common sense belief, 153, 177,
    179–192
Concern for truth, 91
Dissatisfaction of not knowing what
    to believe, 95
Distinction between hope and belief,
    40–41
Doubt-resistant belief, 11–12, 15, 98,
    150
Ethical belief, 150, 151
Fallible beliefs, 15, 48, 152, 153
False belief, 144
Fated to believe, 130, 136, 146
Final belief, 16, 51
Indefeasible belief, 7, 12, 14
Infallible beliefs, 14, 161
Instinctive beliefs, 160, 177–178, 180,
    187, 219
Mathematical belief, 150
Methods of fixing belief, 11–12,
    87–126, 193
Natural belief in God, 129
Not extraneous to the facts, 94–95, 98,
    105–110, 114, 119
Object of belief, 51
Perceptual belief, 5, 101
Permanently settled belief, 14, 171
Practical belief, 156–157
Psychological aspect of belief, 11, 91
Rational belief, 119
Religious belief, 49, 128, 177–178,
    180–181
Responsive to experience, 153, 154,
    168
Scientific belief, 42, 57, 109, 139, 150,
    169
Seek state of belief, 90, 92–93,
    98–99
Sensitive to reality, 109
Settled belief, 7, 10–14, 87, 92
Stable belief, 24, 130, 142, 152, 153,
    317
Subjective degrees of probabilistic
    belief, 262
Theoretical belief, 156–157
True belief, 12, 15, 150, 152, 154, 168,
    171, 211

Vague belief, 178, 202
Vital belief, 173
Bergson, J., 54
Bergsonian conception of philosophy,
    32
Berkeley, G., 2
Berkeley review, 54, 68, 71, 73, 74
Bernstein, R., 201
Binomial, 262–263
Bivalence, 16, 115–116, 126, 147, 166,
    168
    Fails more in moral inquiry, 166, 169
    Regulative assumption of inquiry,
    165
Boethius, 63
Boler, J., 2
Bolter, J. D., 254
Boole, G., 267, 294, 299, 302, 304, 314,
    320
    Boolean algebraic logic, 288, 290
    Boolean calculus, 322
    Boolean logic, 289–292, 294–296,
    304
    Boolean, 25, 320
    Difficulty with expressing I and O
    propositions in categorical logic,
    295, 299
Borel, 286
Braithwaite, R. B., 281
Brandom, R., 148
Brentano, F., 233
British Empiricists, 2, 216
Buried secrets, 127, 130
    See lost facts

Calculus, 288, 292, 312, 317–323
    Calculus of probabilities, 295
Calderoni, M., 32
Cambridge Conference Lectures, 33,
    163–165
Cantor, G., 16, 291
Carnap, R., 283, 284
Carnegie Institute, 162
Cartography, 254
Carus, P., 18, 135, 281
Cassiodorus, 63
Categories, 19–23, 27, 33, 39, 64–65, 71,
    75, 80, 82, 83, 145, 304
    Abstract characterization of
    categories, 65

Dyadic, 21–23, 65, 80
    Kantian derivation, 20
    Logic of relations, 21
    Monadic, 21–23, 65, 80
    Phenomenology, 20–21
    Three methods for arriving at
    categories, 20
    Triadic, 21–23, 65, 80
Causality, 106
Causation, 142
Cause
    Causal determination, 106
    Cause/effect, 21
Central limit theorem, 264, 267, 270
Certainty, 13, 14
    Absolute certainty, 14, 200
    Intuitively certain, 123
    Pragmatic certainty, 200, 202
Chance, 56
    Absolute chance, 23
    Doctrine of chances, 304
    Objective chance, 239
    Pure chance, 23
Chance, Love and Logic, 28, 42
Chisholm, R., 233
Church, 78, 186–188
    Agapastic church, 186
    Commitment to vague instinctive
    beliefs, 188
    Dewey's concern, 187
    Inclusive, 187–188
    James's concern, 187
    Nontheological church, 185, 188
    Universal church of love, 187,
    263
Church, A., 290
    Church's Theorem, 291
Clarity, 304
    First grade of clarity, 117–123
    Grades of clarity, 22, 118
    Second grade of clarity, 117
    Third grade of clarity, 117–118
Classification, 137
'Classification of Arguments (the)', 284,
    285
Clifford, W., 287
Cognition, 41, 82, 215, 218, 220–222,
    249–250
    Immediate cognition, 193
    Object of cognition, 218

Cognitive
    Cognitive science, 241, 253–256
    Cognitive states, 147
Cognitivism, 159, 165, 168–169, 171
    Anticognitivist, 165
    Cognitivist pragmatist, 168, 169
Collected Papers, 28, 58–60, 77, 290
Collective, 33
Colours, 128, 131, 136, 141
    External, 136
    Place in the absolute conception of
        reality, 136
    Reality of colours, 128, 131
    Response dependent, 131, 140
Common sense, 56, 119, 159–162, 176,
        189, 202, 203, 210
    Authority of common sense, 145
    Common sense beliefs and instincts,
        172
    Common sense beliefs and vital
        matters, 172
    Common sense view of morality,
        172
    Faith in common sense, 180
    Truth of common sense beliefs, 179
    Vagueness of common sense beliefs,
        178
Communication, 245
    Communication studies, 49, 57
Community, 30, 38, 46–53, 78, 94, 152
Conant, J., 39
Concepts, 227, 229, 317–323
    Relative to human perspective, 137
Conceptual, 67
Conceptualism, 83
Conditionals, 3
    Indicative conditionals, 3
    Subjunctive conditionals, 3, 14
Conduct, 36, 161, 178, 191
    Compare conduct to a standard, 171
    Conduct criticized, 171
    Conduct of life, 33, 176, 178–180
    Controlled by ethical reason, 171
    Habits of conduct, 171
Confidence, 146, 147, 262
Conjecture, 257–286
    Statistical element, 283
Conjunction, 288, 306–307, 310, 323
Connotation, 4, 8
    'Internal' meaning, 9

Consciousness, 247, 249, 253, 304
    Conscious awareness, 211
    Conscious experience, 250–251
    Conscious state, 250
Conservativism, 152, 176, 180
Constitutive principle, 135
Content, 203
Continuity, 21, 84
    Doctrine of continuity, 35
    Spatio-temporal, 237
Continuum, 216
Contraction, 72–73
Convergence, 122, 127–132, 134, 136,
        137, 139, 141, 143, 146, 147, 208,
        210–211
    Fated convergence, 134, 135, 144, 148
Convergence thesis, 133–135, 137, 138
    Tension with law of bivalence,
        138–139
Convention, 221
Copula, 297, 322
Countess Lovelace, 255
Cousins, V., 79
Couturat, L., 321
Critical commonsensism, 13–14, 17, 56,
        145, 162, 164, 178, 181, 184, 186
    Instinct, 172
    Reconciled with fallibilism, 14
Custom, 221

Darwin
    Theory of natural selection, 230–231
De Morgan, A., 267, 288, 290–292, 296,
        298
de Waal, 78
Dedekind, 16, 291, 320
Deduction, 16–19, 65, 123, 159, 172,
        257–259, 281–283, 285, 288, 304,
        317–319, 323
    Deductive inference, 286
    Deductive reasoning, 156, 283–284
    Deductive, 122
    Probable deduction, 257–263, 267,
        273, 281
    Qualitative branch of deduction, 285,
        286
    Quantitative branch of deduction, 286
    See explicative
'Deduction, Induction and Hypothesis',
        265, 285

Deledalle, G., 243–245
Deliberation, 5, 7–8, 153, 158, 171
Denotation, 4, 9, 297
 'External' meaning, 9
Descartes, R., 13, 97, 178, 193, 202, 215, 241
'Description of a Notation of the Logic of Relatives', 296
Desire, 137
'Detached Ideas on Vitally Important Topics', 162
Dewey, J., 1, 24, 27, 29, 31–32, 40, 41, 44, 45, 47–50, 53–57, 127, 175, 180, 188, 293
 A Common Faith, 175
 Differences with Peirce, 42–44
 Experimentalism, 42
 Inquiry, 43–44
 Instrumentalism, 42, 44
 'Pragmatism of Peirce (the)', 42
 Rejection of religion, 185
 Rejection of supernaturalism, 175
 Rejection of credalism, 185
 Rejection of the church, 175, 185, 190
 Rejection of vicious conservatism, 185
 Religious experience, 189–190
 Science, 43
 Social theory, 49
 Supernaturalism, 185
 The method of procedure, 42
 Warranted assertibility, 31
Diagrammatic, 288, 309, 317
 Diagrammatic Period, 292
Diagrams, 288, 302, 306, 312
 Graphical diagrams, 304
Dipert, R., 16, 289
Dispositions, 3, 9, 10, 23, 30, 227, 231
Doubt, 6, 10, 12–15, 18, 55, 95, 97, 119, 153, 160, 172, 194, 200, 278, 315, 316
 Cartesian doubt, 152–153
 Irritation of doubt, 12, 93–94, 98
 Motive for inquiry, 15
 Object of doubt, 94, 95, 98
 Paper doubt, 13, 153
 Proper response to doubt, 95
 Psychological aspect of doubt, 11, 91

Real and living doubt, 94, 97
 Seek to end the state of doubt, 90, 92–93, 98
Drobisch, M., 320
Duhem, P., 164
Dummett, M., 115–116, 126
Duty, 143
 Truth about what duty is, 169
 Objective matter, 169
Dyadic relation, 21–23, 71, 222, 224

Elementarlehre, 64
Emerson, 188
Empirical, 101, 146, 156
 Empirical adequacy, 153
 Empirical consequences, 143
 Empirical generalization, 122
 Empirical judgements, 99
Empiricism, 11, 35, 36, 76, 193
 Radical empiricism, 28, 191
End-directedness, 230, 232, 236
Engelbart, D., 256
 'Conceptual Framework', 256
Epistemology, 1, 31, 44, 126, 152–154, 158, 171
 Epistemological difficulties, 50
 Epistemological practices, 5
Erfurt, T., 64–79
Erkenntnislehre, 64, 65, 80
Error, 148, 198, 200, 275
Ethics, 151–152, 160–162, 165–169, 171
 As a normative science, 39, 170
 Based on aesthetics, 170
 Ethical deliberator, 161, 162
 Ethical issues/matters, 41, 162
 Ethical theory, 237
 In between domain of taste and domain of physical sciences, 169
 Positive science, 151
 Truth, 161
Evidence, 150, 169, 171, 203
Evolutionary cosmology, 23
'Evolutionary Love', 192
Evolutionary metaphysics, 36, 49
Exemplification, 223
Existence, 68, 71
Expectation, 11, 52, 156, 157, 167, 195, 197, 203
 Habit of expectation, 11

Experience, 1, 2, 6, 7, 11, 15, 17–22, 30, 35–37, 40, 43, 51, 87, 96, 101–102, 114, 117, 143, 151–155, 158–165, 170–172, 193, 195, 197, 204, 207, 209, 211, 212, 220, 227, 231
 A matter of thirdness, 21
 Broad sense of experience, 11, 143, 154, 156, 171
 Direct experience, 178
 Experimental, 17–18, 155, 156, 203, 229
 Force of experience, 154–155, 169
 Future experience, 117, 126, 196–199, 201–202
 Ideal experience, 155
 Inner experience, 156–157
 Logical experience, 5, 169
 Mathematical experience, 5, 154–158
 Metaphysical experience, 154–158
 Moral experience, 5, 154–158, 161, 169
 Outer experience, 156–157
 Psychological fact, 247
 Real experience, 155
 Recalcitrant experience, 7, 11, 15, 150, 153–154, 165
 Religious experience, 49
 Scientific experience, 169
 Sensory experience, 5, 10–11
 Surprising experience, 10, 13, 15, 18, 153, 157, 159, 167–169
Explicative, 18–19
 See deduction
Extension, 9, 297, 299
External, 129, 137, 142–146
 External facts, 206, 241–242
 'External' meaning, 9
 External object, 218
 External permanency, 110
Euclid, 292
European grammar, 80

Fact, 112, 224
Faith, 32, 121, 184
Fallible, 123, 159, 161, 221, 231
Fallibilism, 13–14, 17, 48, 101, 152, 162, 202, 222
 Contrite fallibilist, 14
 Reconciled with critical common-sensism, 14

Falsification, 116, 281
Feeling, 177, 226, 229, 230, 236, 250
 Monadic, 222
Feigl, H., 278
Fetzer, J., 247, 253
Final causation, 229–230, 239, 247, 249
 Distinction between final and efficient causation, 248
Firstness, 19–24, 71, 73, 76, 82, 84
Fisch, M., 63, 74–76, 78, 238
Fixation of Belief (the), 1, 10, 12, 88–102, 105, 110–113, 118, 124, 132, 148, 152, 219, 287, 304
Frazer's *Berkeley*, 63, 67, 83, 85
Freedom of the will, 139–141
Frege, G., 16, 25, 104, 114, 219, 242, 290–292, 295–296, 306, 314, 315, 318–320, 323
Frequency, 262, 266, 267, 271
 Frequentism, 266–269
 Long run relative frequency, 259, 262–263, 268, 284
 Population frequencies, 260, 265, 267, 271, 275, 276
 Sample frequencies, 260, 265, 267, 269–272, 275
Fundamental hypothesis, 122–123

Galileo, 177
Gardner, M., 254
Generalisation, 123, 222–225
Generality, 21, 22, 24, 30, 37, 43, 45, 84, 145, 220
 Realism of generality, 43, 72
Generals, 23, 42, 69, 73, 104, 212, 213, 220, 221, 229, 316
 General types, 81
 Nonpsychological, 35
 Reality of generals, 23, 35, 39, 69
 Non-referential use of a general term, 232
Gentzen, 288, 300
God, 45, 54, 56, 66, 157, 177–179, 191
 God is vague, 178–184
 God's reality, 157, 172
 Humble argument for reality of God, 177, 179
 Living belief in God, 185
 Love, 182–183, 191
Godel, 291

Goodman, N., 104
Goudge, T., 2, 190
Grand Logic, 75, 88, 289, 292–294, 297,
    302–305
Graphs, 302, 304, 317–323
  Alpha graphs, 310
  Beta graphs, 310–311
  Entitative graphs, 293, 309, 317–323
  Existential graphs, 119, 287–290, 292,
    293, 297, 304, 307–314
  Gamma graphs, 310
'Ground of Validity of the Law of Logic',
    259, 284, 285
Gruender, D., 194, 212

Haack, S., 28, 30–31, 34, 47–49
Habits, 3, 10, 11, 23–24, 30, 33, 34, 37,
    43, 84, 120, 121, 157, 160, 162,
    179–188, 192, 196, 197, 203, 224,
    228–229, 231, 236
  Good/bad, 120
  Habit of action, 43, 117, 230
  Habit of conduct, 227
  Habit of expectation, 11, 18
  Habit of reasoning, 159
  Habit of response, 196
  Habitual cognitive skills, 160
  Reasonableness, 120
  Role of habit, 228–229
Haecceity, 66–67, 71, 75, 83, 84
Harris, W. T., 250
Harvard, 63, 144, 257
Harvard Lectures, 1, 79, 263, 265, 284,
    322
Hausman, C., 51, 194
Havelock, E., 252
Hegel, G. W. F., 44, 70
Hempel, C. G., 104
Henry of Ghent, 63
Hilbert, D., 291, 292
Hintikka, J., 291
History of Philosophy, 62, 75
Hookway, C. J., 8, 29–31, 35, 40, 48, 51,
    56, 62, 65, 78, 91, 144, 146, 160,
    167, 172, 190, 194, 324
Hope, 15, 19, 40, 114, 116, 118, 119,
    134–138, 141, 146, 147, 159, 166,
    171, 211
  Distinction between hope and belief,
    40–41

Hope for convergence of opinion, 135
  Regulative hope, 15–16
  See Regulative assumptions
Houser, N., 148
'How to Make Our Ideas Clear', 1, 3, 36,
    60, 89, 113, 132–134, 218, 219, 228
Howland Will Case, 285
Human
  Human Nature, 168
  Human-computer interaction, 241,
    254
Humanists, 58–60, 77
Hume, D., 88, 119–123, 126, 324
  Problem of induction, 16–17, 119–123,
    278
  The response Peirce can make to the
    problem of induction, 120–123
Hypertext, 254
Hypothesis, 16–19, 65, 88, 102–104, 114,
    123, 219, 257, 263, 274, 277–284,
    286
  Ampliative, 280–281
  Explanatory hypothesis, 177
  Formal unpsychological logic applied
    to hypothesis, 258, 260
  Transposition of premises and
    conclusion of a categorical
    syllogism, 263, 279
  See abduction and retroduction
Hypothetic
  Hypothetic inference, 212, 257, 260,
    265, 275, 279–280
  Hypothetic validity, 279
Hypothetico-deductive model, 281

Icons, 8–9, 65, 155, 223–224, 236,
    245–247, 272, 299–302, 305
Iconicity, 288, 290, 293, 312–313, 317,
    323
  Anti-iconic, 306
Ideal, 142, 156, 171, 318
  Ideal world, 205
Idealism, 24, 51, 57, 74–76, 204, 208–209
  Absolute idealism, 83, 84
  Epistemological idealism, 213
  Idealism vs. materialism, 24
  Metaphysical idealism, 213
  Objective idealism, 76, 85
  Realism vs. idealism, 29, 49, 57, 68,
    85, 86, 208

Idealist, 51, 69, 71, 76, 141, 208–209
Ideas, 216
'Illustrations of the Logic of Science', 1,
    298
Indexical, 144, 222
Indices, 8–9, 220, 223–224, 245, 246,
    272–273, 304, 308, 317–323
    See signs
Individual, 68, 69, 71, 73, 74, 219–220,
    232, 237–238, 311, 319
    Individuality, 42, 220
    Relationship with universals, 43
Indubitable, 178, 193, 202
Induction, 16–19, 65, 102, 104, 123, 126,
    156, 159, 163, 172–173, 219, 247,
    257–260, 263–264, 267, 270–287,
    320
    Ampliative, 18–19, 280–281, 283
    Crude induction, 17, 282
    Inductive argument, 284
    Inductive inference, 257–260, 263,
        265, 266, 270, 276
    Qualitative induction, 17, 259, 282
    Quantitative induction, 281, 282
    Self-correcting, 278
    Transposition of premises and
        conclusion of a categorical
        syllogism, 258, 260, 263, 279, 285,
        286
Infallible, 123, 221
Inference, 43–44, 102, 283, 293, 300,
    304, 306, 308, 315–323
    Deductive, 102
    Inference to the best explanation, 16
    Inferential, 222
    Probable inference, 304
    Reasonable inference, 123
    Rules of inference, 306, 311
    Theory of inference, 39, 43, 102
    Three types of inference, 65, 283
Information, 273
    Nuisance information, 270–272,
        274–275
Inquirer, 10–15, 25, 40, 43, 69, 96, 97,
    102, 113, 128, 130, 131, 134, 138,
    148, 153, 155, 272–278, 282
    Cognitive failure of inquirers, 133,
        146, 271
    Community of inquirers, 48, 78, 85,
        91, 128, 173, 184, 186, 188

Information, 146
    Inquirers with different interests, 137
    Role of inquirer, 95–96
    Scientific inquirer, 52
Inquiry, 5–7, 10–18, 25, 30–31, 33, 40,
    43–44, 47, 49–52, 55, 78, 87–91, 94,
    102, 104–108, 113–115, 117–119,
    122, 126–128, 130, 133–136, 140,
    143, 145, 147, 148, 150–156,
    159–163, 168, 171–172, 186, 208,
    214
    A priori method, 12, 56, 90, 93, 98, 113
    Aim of inquiry, 13, 98–99, 127, 168
    Block path of inquiry, 13, 30, 154
    Community driven inquiry, 44, 74, 90
    Deductive inquiry, 155
    Different kinds of inquiry, 167
    Different methods of inquiry, 148
    Experimental inquiry, 41, 172
    Fated end of inquiry, 141, 150
    Fundamental hypothesis, 88, 96
    Gathers rational strength, 90
    Mathematical inquiry, 155
    Method of authority, 12, 60, 90,
        93–94, 148
    Method of tenacity, 12, 42, 90, 93–94,
        113
    Presupposition of inquiry, 16, 40, 134
    Psychology kept out of inquiry, 11, 51,
        91
    Regulative assumption of inquiry,
        122, 160, 166
    Scientific inquiry, 40, 44, 128, 129,
        159, 165
    Scientific method/method of
        experience, 17–18, 40, 45, 55, 56, 90,
        93, 95, 98, 99, 102–105, 109, 111,
        113, 114, 119, 124, 148, 153, 154,
        159, 193, 287, 304, 318–319
    Well conducted inquiry, 129–131,
        134–136, 138, 140, 146, 150
'Insolubilia', 320
Instinct, 40, 55, 94, 137, 151, 152,
    159–162, 164, 173, 176–177, 180,
    189, 191, 221, 239
    Acritical instinctive beliefs, 180
    Vague instincts, 178, 184, 190–191
Insufficient Reason, 266–269
Intellectual augmentation, 256
Intension, 297

Intention, 21, 171
Intentionality, 8, 233
Interpretants, 10, 214–218, 221–222,
    225–230, 235–238, 244
  Dynamical interpretant, 10, 225, 235
  Emotional interpretant, 222, 235, 237
  Emotional/energetic/logical
    trichotomy of interpretants, 226,
    235
  Energetic interpretant, 222, 235, 237
  Final interpretant, 10, 235–237, 239,
    240
  Immediate interpretant, 10, 225,
    235–236, 240
  Immediate/dynamic/final trichotomy,
    235
  Logical interpretant, 222, 227–229,
    235
  Three types of interpretants, 10
  Ultimate interpretant, 240
  Ultimate logical interpretant, 34
Interpretation, 8, 196, 203, 204, 211,
    217–218, 223, 225, 227, 230–235,
    237, 245, 249, 254, 280
  Rule of interpretation, 215, 223–224
Interpreter, 8–10, 222
Irrationality, 120, 121
  Practical irrationality, 123

James, H., 54
James, W., 1, 24, 25, 27–33, 35–44,
    46–50, 52–57, 116, 127, 161–163,
    175, 177, 178, 180, 184, 185, 188,
    191
  A Pluralistic Universe, 32, 34, 40,
    44–46
  Abstractions, 35, 37
  Action, 30, 41
  Applied pragmatism to itself, 39, 45
  Constructivistic pragmatism, 30, 49
  Differences with Peirce, 29–42
  Ethical science, 161
  Faith ladder, 40
  Function of Cognition (the), 36
  Generalities, 35, 39
  Harvard Crimson, 55
  Humanism and Truth, 37
  Humanist, 42, 49
  Individualism, 38
  Meaning of Truth (the), 36

Moral Philosopher and the Moral Life
    (the), 161
  No distinction between hope and
    belief, 40–41
  Nominalist, 30, 34, 35, 38
  Nonmathematical/logical mind, 27,
    38–39, 42, 164
  Particulars, 30, 37
  Pluralism, 46, 127
  Pragmatic consequences, 39
  Pragmatism, 36, 37
  Pragmatism as a Principle and
    Method of Right thinking, 55
  Principles of Psychology (the), 32
  Psychology, 32, 35, 38
  Radical empiricism, 28, 148
  Radical pragmatist, 40
  Reality, 35, 41, 137
  Rejection of credalism, 185
  Rejection of organized religion, 185
  Rejection of the church, 185
  Rejection of vicious conservatism, 185
  Religious experience, 175, 189–190
  Science vs. ethics dichotomy, 41
  The Varieties of Religious Experience,
    36, 54, 56, 175
  Truth, 30–31, 41
  Will to believe, 54
  'Will to Believe' (the), 32, 33, 36, 40,
    42, 45
Jevons, W. S., 254, 287, 294
John of Salisbury, 63
Johns Hopkins University, 62–73, 79,
    287, 293, 298, 320
Journal of Speculative Philosophy (the),
    54, 215, 241
Judgment, 137, 138

Kant, I., 1, 19–20, 30, 55, 62, 64, 69, 83,
    107, 212, 213, 215–216
  Categories, 79
  Distinction between praktisch and
    pragmatisch, 41
  Empirical realism, 50
  Kantian concept of cognition, 219
  Kantian idealism, 49
  Kantian problem of knowledge, 215
  Transcendental idealism, 50
  Truth, 111
  Vorstellungen, 216

Kantian, 52, 53, 69, 169
Keller, H., 244
Ketner, K., 244, 254–255
Kilpinen, E., 28
Knowledge, 15–16, 19, 35, 43, 51, 55, 78,
    82, 150, 151, 167, 179, 193–194,
    200, 207, 209, 210, 212, 215–224,
    241, 247, 249–251, 265
  Antifoundationalist, 194, 204
  Background knowledge, 135, 221, 282
  Foundationalist, 194, 201, 202, 204,
    207, 212
  Growth of knowledge, 128
  Objective knowledge, 67, 70
  Scientific knowledge, 42
  Spectator theory of knowledge, 51,
    204
Kuhn, T., 164

Ladd-Franklin, C., 293
Lady Ada, 255
Lady Welby, 226
Lakoff, G., 253
Lambert, K., 294, 296, 320
Language, 197, 212, 222, 242, 254, 306
Laplace, P. S., 8, 267, 268
Law of continuity, 291
Law of double negation elimination,
    115–116, 119
Law of excluded middle, 116, 204, 205,
    212, 213
Law of non-contradiction, 115, 204, 205,
    212, 213
Laws, 21, 23–24, 30, 71, 81, 136, 142,
    145, 239
  Formal law, 269
  Laws of nature, 23, 143, 145, 324
  Material law, 269
  Physical law, 23, 230
  Reality of laws, 23, 225
'Lectures on British Logicians', 79
Lectures on Pragmatism, 221
Leibniz, G., 59, 77, 96–123, 126, 237,
    294, 320
  Sufficient Reason, 117–124, 126
Levi, I., 17
Lewis, C. I., 44, 53
Liar paradox, 291
Licklider, J. C. R., 255
Locke, J., 216, 247, 249, 322

Logic, 1, 19, 25, 31, 34, 38–39, 43, 47, 53,
    55, 57, 58, 62–64, 74, 77, 78, 84,
    90–91, 102, 120, 123, 129, 133, 140,
    145, 156, 163, 164, 168, 171, 190,
    195, 208, 220, 256, 258–284,
    287–324
  Algebraic, 220, 242, 293, 297, 299,
    302, 306
  Ancient logic, 290
  Antipsychological, 11, 91, 283, 306,
    315–316
  Art of logic, 318–319
  As a normative science, 39, 43, 170
  Barbara, 292, 298, 312, 313
  Based on ethics, 170, 173–174
  Binding, 307, 308
  Bungle, 307
  Categorical logic, 292, 302, 303, 321
  Computational aspects of logic, 291
  Conceptual analysis of ideas, 297
  Deduction, 90, 287–324
  Deductive logic, 90, 279, 282, 304
  Definition of logic, 288–289, 314–315
  Development of Peirce's logic, 35
  Diagrammatic, 242, 288, 290, 304–312
  Doxastic element, 315–317
  Epicurean logic, 63
  Existential graphs, 254
  First order predicate logic, 219, 291
  Formal element, 315–323
  History of logic, 62, 79, 290–294, 296,
    303
  Humanistic logic, 44
  Hypothetical logic, 292
  Illation, 288, 291, 301, 302, 305, 321
  Imperative logic, 124
  Induction, 90
  Logic is theory of signs, 305–311,
    314–315
  Logic of relations, 21, 75, 83, 222, 223,
    281, 287, 290
  Logic of relatives, 39, 80, 84, 304
  Logical addition, 295
  Logical equivalence, 308
  Logical identity, 295
  Logical method, 29, 59–60
  Logical multiplication, 295–296
  Logical notation, 306, 307, 314
  Logical principles, 298
  Logical relation, 288, 301, 321, 324

Logical theory, 66, 306
Logical theory of universals, 43
Material conditional, 301, 302, 305
Mathematical element, 315
Medieval logic, 65–79, 290
Modal logic, 310
Normative, 64, 170, 283, 290, 312,
    314, 316–317
Normative science, 98
Propositional logic, 281, 288, 292, 302,
    310, 321
Quantification theory, 308
Quantification, 281, 311, 313
Quantifier, 307, 309–310, 312
Relative term, 296–297
Reverse logicism, 317–319
Scholastic logic, 58–60
Semiotic element, 315–316
Stoic logic, 63
Subsumption, 301, 305
Symbolic logic, 290, 302, 320
Vacuums in logical space, 260
'Logic of Drawing History from Ancient
    Document (the)', 286
'Logic of Mathematics (the)', 238
'Logic of Relatives (the)', 293, 307
Logica utens, 160
'Logical Machines', 251
Logical Positivists, 4, 154, 157
    See Verificationists
Lost facts, 127
    See buried secrets
Love, 178, 186
Lowell Lectures, 1, 79, 177, 244–245,
    257, 259, 260, 263, 265–266, 284,
    285

Machines
    Logic machines, 255–256
    Turing Machine, 252
    Peirce machine, 255
Mackie, J. L., 152
Marquand, A., 254
Mates, B., 290, 315
Mathematics, 16, 27, 55, 58, 115, 141,
    154, 156–158, 166–168, 220, 255,
    256, 287, 290, 292, 305, 307,
    317–323
    Mathematician, 155, 167, 242
    Nonphysical reality, 168

Reality of mathematical objects/
    propositions, 167
    Truth, 167–168
Manuscript Lectures, 36
McCarthy, J., 194, 201
McLuhan, M., 252
Mead, G. H., 29, 43, 44, 53
Meaning, 9, 34, 116, 117, 157, 216–217,
    227–229, 237
    Pragmatic meaning, 9–10, 113, 228
Mediation, 145
Medieval Philosophy, 1, 58–77, 233
    Aristotelian/Scholastic method, 20
    Influence on Peirce, 63–65
    Medieval realists, 72
    Medieval texts, 62–63
Memory, 99–102, 104–105, 195, 197, 199
    Casual theory of memory, 99, 105
Metaphysics, 1, 4, 6–7, 23–24, 30, 36, 43,
    59, 61, 71, 72, 74, 78, 111, 129, 150,
    154, 157, 158, 168, 237, 318–319
    Evolutionary metaphysics, 36
    Mature metaphysics, 82
    Scientific metaphysics, 141
    Transcendental metaphysics, 12
Metaphysical, 62, 66, 140, 145–147, 154,
    210
    Metaphysical Club, 28, 53, 55
    Metaphysically neutral, 142
    Open metaphysical question, 140,
    142
Metaphysicians, 160, 167
Mill, J. S., 206, 265, 269–270, 297
Mind, 241, 247–249, 251, 256, 322
    Computational model of the mind,
    253
    Mentalese model, 252
    Newell–Simon concept of the mind,
    253
    Semiotic model of mind, 241–256
    Synechistic account of mind, 214
Mind-dependent, 67, 142, 204, 206, 208
    In anima, 68
Mind-independent, 40, 45, 67, 68, 129,
    141, 142, 173
    Extra animam, 68
    Mind-independent laws, 142
Minute Logic, 136, 289, 293, 316
Misak, C. J., 2, 5, 33, 40, 54, 123, 124
Mitchell, O. H., 219, 220, 293

Modalities, 37
Modes, 104–105
  Mode of grasping, 211
  Mode of inference, 260, 280
  Mode of reality, 70
  Modes of being, 64, 68, 69, 71, 74,
    82–84, 111, 129, 139–142, 145
  Modes of propositions, 64
  Three modes of being, 68, 71, 75, 80,
    82, 85
Monadic, 21–23, 72, 224
Monist, 46, 238
Moral, 151, 152, 154, 158, 165, 191, 210
  Moral action, 180
  Moral cognitivism, 150–152
  Moral decision, 158
  Moral deliberation, 154, 158, 169
  Moral facts, 141
  Moral inquiry aims at truth, 173
  Moral judgments, 141, 150, 151, 157,
    161, 169–170
  Moral laws, 41
  Moral nature, 140
  Moral realism, 33, 54
  Moral truth, 150–152
  Nonphysical reality, 169
  Responsive to experience, 158
Morality, 41, 140, 142, 161, 162,
    168–169, 180
  Distinct from matters of taste, 165
  Influence of science, 184
  Objective, 168–169
  Subjective, 168–169
Morris, C., 243–244
Murphey, M., 135, 220

Natural
  Natural classes defined by human
    needs/purposes, 137–138
  Natural classes, 67, 136–137
  Natural kinds, 66, 142
  Natural science, 230
'Nature of the Influence of the Sign
  (the)', 224
Nature, 37, 73, 205, 209
  Common nature, 66, 72
  Theory of nature, 79
  Uniformity of Nature, 269–270
Nation (the), 32
Necessity, 21, 145

Neglected Argument for the Reality of
  God (a), 157, 176–180, 185
Neopragmatism, 28, 46–53
Neurath's boat, 15
Neyman–Pearson, 16, 257, 276, 283
Nicod, 104
Nominalism, 2, 3, 22, 30, 35, 45, 68–70,
    72–77, 80, 82–86, 113
  Nominalistic idealism, 69
  Nominalistic Platonism, 68, 69, 73
  Realism vs. nominalism, 30, 34, 42,
    53, 58, 64, 67, 71
Noncognitivism, 151
Normative sciences, 39, 43, 91, 169–170
  Aesthetics, 39, 170
  Beauty, 170
  Ethics, 39
  Logic, 39, 42, 43
  Right, 170
  Theoretical science, 170
  Truth, 170
Norms, 156, 315
'Notes on Logic Book', 297
Numbers, 75, 142

Object, 8, 21, 112, 144, 147, 214–217,
    221–222, 238
  Hypothetical objects, 142
  Mathematical objects, 141, 142
  Object of a true proposition, 112, 142
  Object of perception, 145
Objective, 70, 198
Objectivity, 52, 128, 197–198, 237
Observation, 156, 158, 194, 212, 308,
    317–323
Obligationes, 317–323
Ockham, W., 63, 67–69, 77, 81
  Great logician, 59
  Nominalist, 59, 67
  Ockham's Razor, 6
  Priority of first substance, 67
'On a New List of Categories', 20, 64,
    246
'On an Improvement of Boole's Calculus
  of Logic', 294–295
'On the Algebra of Logic: A
  Contribution to the Philosophy of
  Notation', 292, 298–299
'On the Algebraic Principles of Formal
  Logic', 298

'On the Natural Classification of
Arguments', 266, 284
Ong, W., 252
Ontology, 43, 66, 69, 71
Ontological, 205, 206
Opinion, 12, 47, 50–52, 59, 69, 74, 91,
93–94, 138, 141, 164
Convergence of opinion, 31, 51, 128,
132, 138, 139, 143, 144, 148, 208,
210
Destined opinion, 133
Eventual opinion, 89
Fallible opinion, 48
Fated convergence of opinion, 133,
143, 145
Final opinion, 30, 69, 76, 197, 208, 209
Settled opinion, 14, 87, 98, 109, 124,
133
True opinion, 69, 89, 97, 133, 211
Orality literary thesis, 252
Organic features, 231, 239

Panofsky, E., 77
Pape, H., 35
Papini, 56
Parenthesis, 251
Parker, K., 161, 182
Particulars, 34, 35, 42, 229
Patterns, 145
Paul of Venice, 63, 293
Pearson, K., 251
Peano, G., 287, 291, 292, 299, 320
Peirce, B., 62, 79, 285
Peirce Papers, 162
Percept, 101, 144, 194–199
Distinguished from perceptual
judgment, 199
Generalized percept, 207, 251
Infallible, 198
Wide and narrow sense, 195
Perception, 88, 96, 99–102, 106, 129,
143, 154–155, 177–178, 186,
193–203, 213
Casual theory of perception, 99, 105
Immediate Perception, 71–77, 194,
245–246
Laws of perception, 99
Object of perception, 145
Perceptual awareness, 143, 194–195,
201–204

Perceptual claims, 207
Perceptual disappointment, 6
Perceptual facts, 205, 207
Perceptual judgments, 101, 144,
194–198, 200–202, 207, 212, 221,
222
Wide and narrow sense of perceptual
judgments, 195
Percipuum, 194–196, 199, 203
Wide and narrow sense, 195
Percy, W., 242, 244, 247
Perry, R., 34–35
Peter of Spain, 63
Phenomenology, 20–21, 39, 65, 83, 145,
318
Phenomenalism, 204
Ontological phenomenalism, 213
Phenomenalist, 208–209
Photometric Researches, 298
Philström, S., 1, 30, 39
Pinker, S., 242–254
Plato, 66, 81, 121
Political issues, 41
Popper, K., 250–251, 255, 281, 283, 284
Demarcation criterion, 283
Falsification, 283
Non monotonicity of inductive
reasoning, 283
Objective thought contents, 251
Port-Royal Logic, 297
Possibility, 21–24, 72, 205–206, 224,
236, 238
Real possibility, 225
Potentialities, 218, 225
Practical
Practical concerns, 127, 178
Practical matters, 33–34, 41
Practice, 1, 15, 31–37, 39–40, 48, 123,
157, 158, 163, 176, 179, 180, 184,
188
Theory and practice, 49
Pragmatic Maxim, 2–5, 10, 36–42, 53,
55, 75, 154, 157, 228, 283
Abduction, 282
Applied to the nature of truth and
reality, 5
Applied to truth, 131
Methodological principle, 3
Not verificationist, 282
Pragmatic consequences, 39

Pragmatic Maxim (*cont.*)
  Pragmatic elucidation, 4–5, 146
  Standard for determining empty
    expressions, 2
  Standard for determining
    metaphysical gibberish, 4
Pragmatic meaning, 9–10
  Pragmaticist meaning, 157
'Pragmatic method (the)', 53
Pragmatic method, 32, 42
Pragmatism, 144
Pragmatism, 1–3, 27–39, 42–43, 55–57,
    75, 228–229, 287
  Absolute pragmatism, 44
  Applied to itself, 39
  Conceptualistic pragmatism, 44
  Constructivistic pragmatism, 30
  James's definition, 36
  Kantian influence, 57
  Origin of the term, 27–29
  Pluralistic pragmatism, 46
  Pragmaticism, 28–29, 32, 45, 51, 54,
    72, 75, 115–116, 180
  Spirit of pragmatism, 2
  Truth of pragmatism, 39
Prantl, C., 64–79
Predesignation, 275–279
Presupposition, 13, 16, 39, 40
Probable deduction, 285
Probabilism, 283, 285
Probability, 17–18, 64, 173–174,
    258–264, 267–272, 274–279, 283,
    284
  Subjective probability, 262, 271
  Theory of probability, 39
'Prolegomena to an apology for
    pragmatism', 239
'Prope-positivism', 89
Psychology, 11, 32, 35, 39, 44, 247
  Antipsychologism, 35, 38
  Psychological hypothesis, 12
Purpose, 231–232, 239, 247, 249
  Difference between existing for a
    purpose and acting for a purpose,
    231
  Interpretive purpose, 237
  Purposeful action, 231
Putnam, H., 25, 29, 47–48, 50–52, 56, 57,
    113, 128, 132, 143, 147, 148, 253,
    289

Natural realism, 56, 148
On William James's theory of truth,
    149
Putnam's theorem, 253
Truth as idealized warranted
    assertion, 47

'Qualitative Logic', 305
Quality, 64, 71
Quantity, 322
Quine, W.V.O., 25, 164, 302, 308,
    312–313, 320

Ramsey, F., 47, 56
Raposa, M., 185
Rational, 120, 233
  Rational conduct, 9
Rationality, 23–24, 38, 43, 49, 119, 211
Real, 22, 23, 30, 40, 44, 50, 55, 67–69,
    72, 76, 81, 83, 96, 104–105, 107,
    109, 110, 112, 129, 136, 141–145,
    205, 207, 211, 219
  Real continuity, 75
  Real dispositions, 3
  Real effects, 147
  Real events, 147
  Real generals, 30, 39, 43
  Real habits, 3
  Real kinds, 128
  Real object, 69, 206
  Real things, 52, 68, 70, 145, 313
  Real world, 204–205
  Real would-bes, 3, 72
  Relative to human purposes, 137
Realism, 29–31, 42, 45, 50–52, 65–76,
    81, 83–86, 133, 142, 143, 145, 146,
    186, 192, 204, 208–209, 318–319
  Antirealism, 86
  Basic realism, 142
  Causal realism, 96
  Direct Realism, 76, 145
  Discursive realism, 57
  Epistemological realism, 86, 208–209
  Extreme realism, 30, 72, 74, 81, 85
  Metaphysical realism, 50
  Moderate realism, 81
  Moral realism, 33
  Ontological realism, 86
  Realism about laws, 143
  Realism vs. antirealism, 207

Realism vs. idealism, 29, 49, 57, 68, 85, 86, 208
Realism vs. nominalism, 30, 34, 42, 53, 58, 64, 67, 71
Realism vs. relativism, 207
Scholastic realism, 1, 3, 22–23, 30–31, 37–39, 42, 45, 54, 81, 83–85
Scotistic realism, 65, 191
Realist, 22, 34, 51, 57, 69, 82, 85, 86, 141, 173, 208–209, 313
Antirealist, 115–116, 119
Empirical realist, 52
Evolutionary realist, 51
Metaphysical realist, 51, 128
Reality, 5–8, 19, 35, 45, 46, 48, 50–52, 56, 57, 67–69, 71, 73, 78, 82, 83, 87, 95–96, 99, 104–107, 110–112, 116, 122, 127–131, 136–138, 141, 143, 147, 168, 194, 204, 206, 208, 209, 212, 236, 237, 313
Absolute conception of reality, 56, 128–132, 146
Comes apart from truth, 143
Definition of reality, 129
Different kinds of reality, 166–167, 173
Different metaphysical accounts for what reality consists in, 141
Fated object of opinion, 135, 138
Independent of opinion, 51, 138
Independent of the human mode of grasping, 205
Independent of thought, 138–139, 141
Nonphysical reality, 167–169
Not independent of thought in general, 51
Realistic view of reality, 69, 71
Reality of universals, 34
Reality without truth, 139–140
Relative to human capacities, 137, 140
Relative to human desires, 137
Relative to human interests, 137, 145
Relative to thought, 56, 137, 140
Three grades of reality, 22
Transcendental reality, 52
Truth's object, 237
Two views of reality, 68
Reason, 150, 151, 158, 160, 170, 171, 224
Growth of reason, 170
First rule of reason, 48

Reason Rules, 156
Reasonable, 123
'Concrete Reasonableness', 170
Reasoning, 64, 90, 99, 156, 170, 173, 220, 253, 255, 274, 283, 304, 309, 312, 316
Abductive reasoning, 99
Algebraic reasoning, 242
Deductive reasoning, 155
Diagrammatic reasoning, 242, 253
Distinction between corollarial and theorematic reasoning, 255
Logic of right reasoning, 289, 324
Methods of reasoning, 59
Scientific reasoning, 282
Statistical reasoning, 283
Syllogistic reasoning, 283
Reduction Thesis, 319
Reference, 144, 232
Referent, 215
Regulative
Regulative assumptions, 40
Regulative ideal, 134, 180
Regulative principle, 24, 135, 136, 211, 213
See hope
Reichenbach, H., 278
Relation, 64, 305, 309, 318–319, 323
Dyadic, 21–23, 65, 243
Monadic, 21–23, 65
Triadic, 21–23, 65
Religion, 54, 169, 176–177, 181, 185, 187, 189
Antifundamentalist, 183
Community of religious believers, 190
Conduct, 184, 186, 187
Conservative, 176
Golden Rule, 186
Jamesian philosophy of religion, 180
Living religion, 189
Open to growth, 184, 187–188, 191
Origins, 177–181
Principle of love, 187, 191
Reciprocal dependence on science, 185, 189
Religious belief, 178, 184, 185
Religious belief is felt, 178
Religious belief is practically indubitable, 177

Religion (*cont.*)
　Religious experience, 176–179, 185,
　　189
　Religious life, 177
　Religious practice, 179, 184
　Religious sentiment, 179
　Respect for truth, 184, 188–189
　Science, 175–176, 184, 189, 191,
　　192
　Social, 186–187
　Spirit of religion, 176, 179, 181, 189
　Theorizing religious belief, 181–185
　Vague religious belief, 178
'Religion and Politics', 188
Replicas, 224
Representamen, 238, 244
Representation, 8, 21, 64, 76, 86, 111,
　214, 250, 274
　Iconic representation, 309
　Symbolic representation, 307
　Theory of representation, 272
　Triadic representation, 8
　Trichotomy of representations,
　　246
Rescher, N., 47
Resemblance, 223
Retroactive legislation, 48
Retroduction, 16–19, 87, 101, 102, 117,
　281
　See abduction and hypothesis
Roberts, D., 290, 313
Rorty, R., 25, 29, 47–48, 52, 57
　Antirealist, 48
　Antirepresentationalism, 47
　'Cautionary' use of true, 47
　Ethnocentrist, 48
　Regulative 'absolute' truth, 47
Rosenthal, S., 35
Royce, J., 27, 29, 32, 44, 52, 53, 144,
　175
　Absolute pragmatism, 44, 175
　Church as 'beloved community', 175,
　　185
　Critic of James, 44–46
　The Problem of Christianity, 175
　The Religious Aspect of Philosophy,
　　143, 148
Rumfitt, I., 126
Russell, B., 287, 296, 315–316, 318,
　320

Salmon, 278
Sampling, 259, 262–264, 285, 286
　Random sample, 270–273, 275, 280,
　　281, 286
Sapir–Whorf hypothesis, 252, 256
Savan, D., 202
Scepticism, 138, 151, 207
Schiller, F. C. S., 27–29, 32, 44–46, 49,
　53, 56, 175
　Applied pragmatism (or humanism) to
　　itself, 45
　Distinct from Peirce's pragmatism,
　　45–46
　Definition of pragmatism, 175
　Humanism, 45–46
　Humanistic logic, 44
　Mutability of truth, 45
　Nominalism, 46
　Personal Idealism, 45
　Pragmatic maxim, 46
　Psychologism, 46
　Radical subjectivist, 44
Scholasticism, 58–61, 65–71, 73, 74, 78,
　79, 81, 82, 84, 85
　Criticism of scholasticism, 77
　'Dunses', 58–59, 77
　Respect for authority, 60–61
Schroeder, E., 25, 134, 287, 289, 294,
　298–299, 302, 314, 319–320,
　323
Science, 14, 30, 34, 43, 45, 48, 52,
　55, 59, 72, 110, 120, 128,
　132, 137, 151–152, 154,
　162–163, 165–169, 176, 184, 189,
　237
　Dispassionate, 91
　Double position of the scientist,
　　162
　Final opinion of scientific
　　community, 47
　Living and growing body of truth, 176,
　　189
　Objectivity of scientific laws, 68
　Observational science, 158
　Physical sciences, 157
　Physics, 23, 113
　Progress of science, 15, 151
　Religion, 175–176, 191, 192
　Selflessness, 186
　Special sciences, 158

Spirit of science, 176, 180, 181, 184, 187–189, 192
Three types of inferences of the scientific method, 17–18
Scientific, 119, 210
  Scientific community, 30, 33
  Scientific discovery, 185
  Scientific experience, 177
  Scientific inference, 280
  Scientific inquiry, 158, 193, 281
  Scientific knowledge, 42
  Scientific methodology, 41
  Scientific outlook, 76
  Scientific philosophy, 30, 41
  Scientific realism, 47, 49
  Scientific theory, 164
Scotus, D., 58–59, 61, 63–73, 77, 79–81, 83, 249, 250, 314
  Abstract entities, 66
  Common natures, 66, 67, 70
  Essences, 66
  Formal distinction, 70
  Formalitates, 70–77
  Haecceity, 70, 75, 83, 84
  Halting realism, 84
  Individual substances, 66, 72
  Individuation, 66
  Metaphysics, 60
  Mode of the individual, 67–72
  Nominalist, 72
  Ontological priority of first substance, 72
  Questions of Metaphysics, 63
  Real generals, 72
  Realitates, 70, 71
  Reality of common natures, 66
  Science, 66
  Substance, 67, 73
  Universals, 63, 72
Scotus Eriugena, 63
'Search for a method (the)', 88
Secondary qualities, 128, 131, 136–138
  Reality of secondary qualities, 128, 145
  Response dependent, 136
Secondness, 19–24, 33, 71–73, 75, 76, 82–84, 96, 100, 104–106, 109, 112, 114, 142, 143
  Real secondness, 142, 324
Seigfried, C., 35

Selection, 231–232
  Method of random selection, 267
  Method of selection, 231, 259, 261, 266–269
  Random selection, 267, 274
Self-control, 170, 180
  Manifest in ethics, 171
Self-correction, 275–279
Semantics, 66, 154, 290, 291, 306, 312, 317–319
  Semantic operationalism, 118
  Medieval semantics, 297
Semeiosis, 230, 233, 235
Semeiotics, 1, 8, 25, 39, 44, 47, 49, 57, 118, 190, 214, 216, 222–223, 225, 228–229, 254, 272–275, 279, 282, 287, 290
  Mature semeiotic, 86, 230–235, 237
  Semeiotic thought, 215, 216
  Teleological, 233, 235, 236, 240
  Used to dissolve difficulties in hypothesis, 274
  Used to dissolve difficulties in induction, 274, 281
Sensation, 219
Sense-data, 194
Sensory content, 196
Sentiment, 40, 160, 161, 163, 173
  Sentimental dispositions, 140
  Sentimentalism, 152
Sheffer Stroke, 16, 292
Shin, S.-J., 312, 313
Shook, R., 43
Short, T., 8
Significance, 117, 218, 223, 225–226, 230, 233, 235, 236
  Signification, 89
Signs, 8–10, 21, 64, 66, 86, 111, 119, 146, 214–216, 218–219, 221–227, 230, 232, 234–238, 242–247, 272–273, 304, 314–316
  Definition, 234, 238, 251
  Delomes, 224–225
  Dicent signs, 224
  Dicisigns, 215–224, 247
  Different signs relative to different purposes, 236–237
  Distinction between immediate and dynamic signs, 236

Signs (cont.)
  Divisions of signs, 8, 223
  Doctrine of signs, 241–247, 249, 253
  Early theory of signs, 214–217, 230,
    237
  Flaws in the early theory of signs,
    217–219
  Function of a sign, 232
  General sign, 246
  Hierarchical relationship of the
    different types of sign, 246
  Indexical sign, 221
  Interpretant of signs, 9, 242
  Legisign, 224, 247
  Logical interpretant, 227
  Mature theory of signs, 214
  Meaning of a sign, 79, 227
  Monadic, 224
  Natural signs, 222, 223, 229
  Object of sign, 223, 232–234, 245
  Phemes, 224–225
  Qualisign is dyadic, 224
  Representamen, 214
  Representation, 214
  Rhemes, 224, 246
  Semes, 224
  Sign relation, 223
  Signs of exclusion, 119
  Sinsign, 224
  Subsumption-conditional-illation
    sign, 305
  Theory of signs, 8, 10, 89, 214–225,
    240, 272, 288, 290, 302, 304,
    317–323
  Three dimensions of a sign, 238
  Tradic, 222, 224
  Triad of signs, 65, 224, 242–243
  Trichotomy of signs, 224, 246
'Simple Mathematics (the)', 290
Sinn/sense/signification, 117
  Pragmaticist conception of Sinn/
    significance, 116
  Significance of a declarative sentence,
    116
  Sinn of a declarative sentence, 116,
    118
Skagestad, P., 8
'Sketch of Logical Critic (a)', 172
Skolem, 317–320, 323
Smith, J. E., 208

Social, 42–43, 49
Socrates, 241
'Some Consequences of Four
  Incapacities', 74, 129
Sowa, J., 254
Speculative grammar, 64–67, 79, 80, 314
Statistics, 7, 23, 230, 260, 263, 270, 280,
  284, 285
  Distinction between statistical rules
    and categorical propositions, 285
  Statistical conjecture, 275, 281
  Statistical deduction, 14, 262–272,
    275, 277, 279, 281, 285, 286
  Statistical estimates, 275
  Statistical hypothesis, 16, 260, 263
  Statistical inference, 1, 25, 270, 286
  Statistical mechanics, 230
  Statistical model, 278
  Statistical probability, 259, 262,
    267–269
  Statistical ratios, 17
  Statistical reasoning, 257–286
  Statistical regularities, 286
Studies in Logic, by the members of the
  Johns Hopkins University, 257
Substance, 65, 66
Summum bonum, 140, 170, 178, 189
"Syllabus," 238
Syllogism, 254, 257–266, 283–286, 297
  Categorical syllogism, 260, 265–266,
    269, 281, 286
  Syllogism in Barbara, 258
Symbol, 8–9, 65, 117, 223–224, 242,
  245–247, 253, 272–274, 285, 304,
  316, 320
  Symbolism, 306
  Tradic, 223
Synechism, 35, 207
Syntax, 225, 306

Tarski, A.
Taste, 94, 168
Teleosemantics, 233–234
Tertium non datur, 115–116
Theologians, 181, 183
  Obstruct the scientific spirit, 182
  Politicize religious life, 183
Theology, 181–185
  Absence of growth, 182
  Antagonistic to religion, 182

Antagonistic to the spirit of science, 182, 185
Closure of inquiry, 182, 183
Dogmatic, 181
Exclusionary, 182–183
Insulated from criticism, 181
Method of authority, 181–182
Method of tenacity, 181–182
Opposes the principle of love, 182
Rejects religious perception/ sentiment, 182–185
Unscientific, 181–182
Vicious conservatism, 183
Theorem, 215, 297
Lowenheim's theorem, 26
Theoretical, 64, 164
Speculativa, 64
Theory, 31–36, 39–40, 48, 59, 128, 157, 194, 212
Accepted theories, 153
Background theories, 165
Liberal, 188
Test theory, 229
Theory and practice, 49, 54, 173
'Theory of Probable Inference (a)', 257, 285
Thing in itself, 6, 52, 69, 86, 111, 138–142, 144, 219
Thinking, 244–245, 247, 252–253, 256, 306, 317
Communication, 242
Reasonable thinker, 107
Social, 242
Thirdness, 19–24, 71–73, 76, 82, 84, 142, 143, 145, 191, 203, 226
Reality of thirdness, 73, 324
Thompson, M., 78
Thoreau, 188
Thought, 10, 22, 33, 36, 40, 43, 56, 59, 69, 73, 106–107, 113, 137, 155, 170, 197, 202, 215–218, 222, 226–227, 229, 236, 241–242, 245, 247, 250, 252, 254, 315, 317–323
Algebra, 251
As action, 170
Conceptual, 216
Ethical thought, 158
Independent of thought, 70, 78, 111, 137, 141, 143–146 (See mind independent)

Interpretant, 215
Meaning of thought, 226–227
Object of thought is real, 219
Semiotic, 216
Sign, 214, 226
Thought experiments, 11–12, 155, 158
True thoughts, 229
Unconscious thought, 253
Thought signs, 214–215, 217, 222, 224, 226, 228, 249–250
Individual thought signs, 216, 237
Infinite progressus, 218, 231–232
Infinite regressus, 218, 237
Topology, 254, 311, 313
Trammel, R., 173, 185
Transcendental idealism, 30, 52, 57
Transcendental metaphysics, 12
Triadic, 224
Triadic relation, 21–23, 214, 226
True, 6, 11, 12, 14, 15, 40, 114, 130, 136, 138, 141, 147–148, 165, 195, 317–319, 323
'Cautionary' use of true, 47
Commitments of taking a proposition to be true, 147
Truth, 1, 5–6, 8–10, 14, 15, 17, 19, 24–25, 29–31, 33, 42–44, 46–49, 51–53, 87–89, 92, 99, 109–114, 116, 118, 119, 125–127, 129–130, 132–133, 138–148, 150–154, 157, 171, 173, 191, 203, 207–211, 213, 240, 268–269, 271, 275
Absolute truth, 31, 48
Approximation of the truth, 118
Coherence theory of truth, 31, 51, 146, 208–209, 213
Constitutive account of truth, 146, 148
Convergence of opinion/theory of truth, 47, 127, 129, 146
Correspondence theory of truth, 6–7, 31, 51, 111–112, 146, 208–209
'Cosmopolitan' theory of truth, 31
Definition of truth, 110
Different kinds of truth, 141, 166–167
Distinction between truth and belief, 111–117
Distinction between truth and reality, 113, 166

Truth (*cont.*)
  Epistemic concept of truth, 52
  Established truth, 14, 153, 163, 164
  Getting closer to truth, 15–16
  James's theory of truth, 30, 41
  Mathematical truth, 125, 141
  Metaphysical truth, 6, 25
  Minimalist accounts of truth, 7–8
  Moral truth, 141, 158
  Pragmatic elucidation of truth, 6, 91,
    114, 127, 173
  Realist notion of truth, 115, 116, 127,
    173
  Regulative 'absolute' truth, 47
  Regulative status of truth, 135
  Transcendental truth, 6–7, 40
  Truth as a logical concept, 114, 141,
    142
  Truth as idealized warranted
    assertion, 47
  Truth without reality, 140, 167
'Truth, Reality and Error', 166–168
Tychism, 23, 239
Types, 232
Type/token distinction, 8
  Replicas are types and tokens, 224
Turrisi, P., 39

Understanding, 4
Universality, 66
Universals, 23, 30, 43, 66, 81
  Universal generalization, 17, 285
  Logical theory of universals, 43
  Problem of universals, 66
  Reality of universals, 34, 68
  Relationship with individuals, 43–44
'Universe of discourse', 144, 319
'Upon Logical Comprehension and
    Extension', 284, 297

U.S. Coast Survey, 1, 294, 298
Utilitarianism, 169

Vagueness, 137, 139, 146, 324
Vailati, 56
Values, 128, 142
Variation, 231
Venn, J., 285, 287, 323
  The Logic of Chance, 271, 284, 285
Verification, 115, 116, 118
Verificationism, 89
Verficationist, 5, 154
  See Logical Positivists
Virtual, 249, 250
  Definition of virtual, 249
Vital Matters, 34, 39, 54, 55, 150–174
  Instinct, 172
  Knowledge, 165
  Reason out of place, 163, 173
  Tension with science, 158
  Truth, 165
  Vital questions, 49

Weak Law of Large Numbers, 262, 264,
    265, 270
'What is Christian Faith?', 183
'What Pragmatism is', 28, 133, 135
Whitehead, A., 296
Wiggins, D., 5, 13
William of Auvergne, 63
Williams, B., 128, 158
Wimsatt, W., 239
Wittgenstein, L., 47, 56, 154, 250, 315
Would-bes, 3, 22–23, 73–75, 84, 218,
    225
Wright, L., 239
Writings of C. S. Peirce (the), 1, 289

Zeman, J. J., 290